Religion in Culture and Society

Religion in Culture and Society

Edited by John R. Bowen
Washington University

Allyn and Bacon
Boston • London • Toronto • Sydney • Tokyo • Singapore

Series Editor: Sarah L. Kelbaugh
Editor-in-Chief, Social Science: Karen Hanson
Consulting Editor: Sylvia Shepard
Executive Marketing Manager: Suzy Spivey
Composition and Prepress Buyer: Linda Cox
Manufacturing Buyer: David Suspanic
Cover Administrator: Jenny Hart
Editorial-Production Service: York Production Service

A Viacom Company
Needham Heights, MA 02194

Internet: www.abacon.com
America Online: key word:College Online

Library of Congress Cataloging-in-Publication Data was not available at the time of printing.

ISBN: 0-205-20010-9

Copyright acknowledgments continue on page 248, which constitutes an extension of the copyright page.

Printed in the United States of America.

10 9 8 7 6 5 4 3 2 1 02 01 00 99 98 97

Contents

Religion in Culture and Society

Introduction

This volume includes articles from leading journals of anthropological research, providing a sampler of current concerns and findings regarding religion and ritual throughout the world. Today's ethnographers of religion and ritual study the ways that religious practices shape and are shaped by broader social and cultural contexts, from gender asymmetries, to political movements, to the activities of missionaries. The articles presented here thus deal with what one might call fundamental religious events—rituals of initiation, worship, or burial, for instance—but they also examine the processes by which those events are shaped through time in contexts of colonial domination, the rise of nationalist movements, or processes of urbanization.

A Threefold Shift in Cultural Anthropology

This emphasis on religion in society and culture is part of a general shift within the discipline of cultural anthropology, a shift that can be characterized as movements toward three kinds of analyses: the macro-analysis of institutions and categories; the micro-analysis of actors' experiences and understandings; and the incorporation of multiple perspectives into anthropological work.

The first movement involves changes in the spatial and temporal scope of anthropology, from small-scale societies studied at one point in time to large-scale and changing contexts of movement, contact, and revolution. Marshall Sahlins (1985), for example, enlarged the framework of his studies of Hawaii and Fiji from traditional investigations of social structure to the history of long-distance trade, colonial encounters, and the collapse of the taboo system. Eric Wolf (1982) moved from the study of peasant societies and revolutionary movements to the study of the effects of world capitalist developments on native societies in Asia, Africa, and the Americas. Despite their differences, both anthropologists underscore the ways in which world historical changes take on local accents, and both argue that people appropriate and transform the ideas, objects, and institutions offered by international commerce and colonialism. In the works of other anthropologists (Comaroff & Comaroff

1991; Hefner 1993), religious conversion has increasingly figured prominently as an additional mode of world impingement on small-scale societies.

At the same time, ethnographers have also focused on the concrete, often everyday practices through which people live, reproduce, and create culture. Recent works retain earlier insights into the symbolic and structural properties of culture, the discovery by Boas, Lévi-Strauss, and others that knowledge is preshaped by the interconnections and oppositions among concepts. But they add to those insights the further discovery—one building on the work of Marcel Mauss—that cultures are lived, experienced, and changed in real time. People engaged in religious or other cultural activities perceive a complex sequence of sights, smells, bodily positions, symbols, and ideas, all the while taking cognizance of the social norms that govern their activities. The work of Pierre Bourdieu (1977) has provided one theoretical framework for these developments in analysis; a return to the work of Max Weber (1978) on action has provided another.

Finally anthropologists in the 1990s have developed a greater awareness of the multiple points of view, including their own, from which social reality is understood. This awareness has had important consequences for ethnography. Anthropologists now are more likely to include as part of their ethnographic writing the multiple, often conflicting positions held within a society, and they are more likely to write about their own cultural history, from the analytical categories they use to understand society, to the tastes and prejudices that shaped the selection of topics and friends. Far from being an indulgence in self-regard, this reflexivity is intended to bring to the ethnographer's interactions with others the same intellectual rigor usually brought to interactions among the people studied. It also encompasses studies of the genealogies of analytic categories, including those of "religion" and "ritual."

Religion and the Politics of Categories

These three shifts in ethnographic perspective have opened anthropology out toward large-scale processes, focused it inward on everyday practices, and turned it back on its own analytical categories. The discipline is thereby less easily divided into traditional topics (kinship, history, or religion), as the topics themselves come to be seen as offering partial and often misleading perspectives on complex social phenomena. As the studies collected in this volume indicate, to study "religion and ritual" is also to study the structure of race and class, the history of colonialism and nationalism, and the differentiation of knowledge by gender and age.

Built into many current studies are examinations of differences in categories of "religion" across societies and periods. Of late, anthropologists have taken up Michel Foucault's (1984) call for the study of the genealogy of social categories. Foucault's studies have shown how what we may take to be fundamental social categories—even natural ones, such as sexuality, life, and speech—are the product of simultaneous historical developments in the science of classification and the social organization of power. So, too, with ritual (Asad 1993) and religion. The scholar of comparative religion Wilfred Cantwell Smith (1978) demonstrated that the modern European idea of "religions" as distinct systems of beliefs arose from

17th-century Enlightenment desires to classify things in the world. The model for identifying other religions was taken from Judaism and Christianity. Europeans assumed that all religions have as their fundamental features a key text, read and subscribed to by all adherents; exclusivity, such that one could adhere to one and only one religion at any one time; and the separation of religion from other domains of social life.

Smith showed that this model fundamentally distorted the field of religious ideas and practices found in most of the rest of the world, where one might follow a teacher, study certain works, and yet not conceive of oneself as a member of an exclusive religious group. Ethnographers have not only confirmed Smith's claims about different societies and different categories of "religion," but they have also traced in detail the consequences of contact between societies with contrasting ideas of proper religion. In some cases, new nation-states have adopted Judaeo-Christian-Islamic definitions of religion and enforced them on other peoples. The Indonesian state, for example, requires that all its citizens profess one of five large-scale religions, not recognizing small-scale societies' practices of possession and healing as being properly "religion" (Kipp & Rodgers 1987).

In this volume, Cornelia Kammerer examines the attitudes and responses of the Akha people of highland Burma and Thailand to Christian missionaries, showing how categories of religion shape these interreligious encounters, and that the categories themselves may change as a result of these encounters. She begins with a double puzzle: why did the Akha resist conversion to Christianity when their culturally similar neighbors were converting in droves, and then why, all of a sudden, did the Akha begin to convert? Kammerer starts her investigation of this puzzle with the Akha cultural logic about events and actions. The Akha word *zah* is the closest word to English *religion,* but it has a far different range of meanings, encompassing the rules for planting, funerals, healing, and marriage. Akha see their zah as defining who they are. Other peoples have their own zah, and one should not mix zahs. Akha are more insistent on the exclusivity of customs than are their neighbors.

When asked to convert to Christianity, Akha were being asked to give up activities that both constituted their entire way of practical life and distinguished them from their neighbors. Understandably they refused, but at a certain point the situation "tipped" into massive conversions. Why? Again, the answer is to be found in their cultural logic. Precisely because their customs are many and intricate, some Akha in the new, school-attending generation found the Akha zah too difficult to learn and, as an alternative, decided to convert. After all, the concept of zah was already highly relativistic, in that each people was held to have their own zah, none superior to another.

Akha conversion involves a replacement of one religion by another and very little blending or "syncretism," because of the Akha view of religion as exclusive—a view in accord with Christian notions of religion. But the Akha view religion as mainly about practice, and not about faith, and thus conversion is understood more as a matter of choice than of change of heart—a difference from Christianity that may give rise to controversy in the future.

Other critiques of the idea of "syncretism" are provided in this volume by Watanabe, Sallnow, and Shapiro, all for societies in the Americas. In each case, the distinct categories of religion in play, and the specific power relations they invoke, shape what happens when diverse religious ideas and practices are brought together. Religions do not blend—indeed "religions" do not do anything on their own—rather, people negotiate among different ideas of religion and different practical consequences of engaging in one rather than another religious tradition.

Jennifer Anderson, in her analysis of the Japanese ritual of Tea, presents us with another case in which religion is approached primarily as a set of practices, but without the idea of exclusivity held by the Akha (and in Judaeo-Christian-Islamic faiths). Anderson addresses squarely the question of what pouring tea has to do with religion, and she takes on the hardest possible case by analyzing not tea poured before shrines or temples, but private ceremonies held in a person's home. She finds religion in Japan to be at base a way of recovering a "condition of original wholeness" in our lifetimes, what Max Weber called a "this-worldly" focus. The order created in these elaborate rituals seeks to purify the world and cure it of its chaos—aims derived from both a long-standing Japanese emphasis on purification and an inherited Chinese emphasis on social order. Seen in the light of her general idea of religion and in the light of Japanese views of order and purity, the complex of practices that include Tea but also aesthetically oriented spatial arrangements and geomancy appear more understandably religious.

The articles by Jean and John Comaroff and by Mary Hancock explore the significance of specific categories of "religion" and "politics" in two quite different contexts of colonial and postcolonial change. The Comaroffs examine how 19th-century Methodist missionaries to southern Africa threatened the established complexes of religion and politics. Samuel Broadbent tried to keep African rulers in power but also endeavored to create a separate sphere of "religion," and his efforts undermined the authority of chiefs whose roles depended on their monopoly of sacred as well as secular powers. Two other missionaries, Joseph Ludorf and John Mackenzie, tried to promote new political arrangements for South Africa, but despite their personal powers and social connections found their efforts undermined by the prevailing British ideology of separate political and religious spheres.

Mary Hancock investigates a Hindu nationalist movement in southern India, where such movements are often assumed to be weak because of the sharp cultural differences between the Hindi-speaking north and the Tamil-speaking south. Hancock shows how southern Brahman groups were able to exploit colonial categories of religion and politics to object to affirmative action policies, by contending that such policies discriminated against them, a religiously defined group. And yet these same Brahman groups also skillfully created new forms of public religious practice in which women were at the fore, thereby drawing on cross-caste associations of domesticity, women's spiritual power, and national identity. The India example thus evinces a high degree awareness of the categories and how they might be transgressed advantageously (see also van der Veer 1994).

The Interrelations of Structure and Practice

Anthropology in the 1990s has retained the insights of the symbolic and interpretive studies developed in preceding decades but also has emphasized agency and process. The papers by Anderson on Tea, Dolores Shapiro on Afro-Brazilian ritual symbolism, and John Watanabe on Mayan religion all have at the center of their analyses of religion a synoptic view of symbolic structure, but they accompany this structural analysis with a study of practice and historical process. Anderson explores structure in two ways. The spatial organization of the ritual, its patterns of seating and moving, draws on geomancy—the science of how space confers auspicious qualities. The ritual as a whole combines Confucian, Taoist, Buddhist, and Shinto traditions. Taken together, these several traditions highlight values of purity, harmony, respect, and tranquility, each of which has its specific realization in individual religious practice. Anderson equally stresses the ways that temporal movement through the ritual changes its significance for practitioners: at distinct moments of the sequence, for example, social rank ordering or social equality may be emphasized, as both have their positive values. Smells, tastes, postures all give immediate, bodily sense to the religious values evoked by the ritual, but conversely it is only because the practitioners share this set of meanings and values that the experiences are religious to the actors. Structure and practice require each other to imbue, embody, and teach—a perspective instantiated in the idea of religion as a specific discipline (Asad 1993), and in such other Japanese institutions as the healing sects or New Religions (Davis 1980).

Shapiro's paper also highlights systems of symbols and shows how distinct spirit possession groups in Brazil give divergent public interpretations to those symbols. Brazilian society is organized as a hierarchy of whiteness and class, along which people negotiate identity in many ways, including through their choice of possession groups (each of which is identified with a particular race-class position) and through their efforts to produce lighter-skinned children. Central to these processes of identity negotiation is the set of four ritual substances used in possession groups: blood, oil, honey, and water. All possession groups draw on this single set of symbols to discriminate among themselves; blood, for instance, stands for the animal sacrifices practiced by members of the Candomble sect. But practitioners may use several of these substances in their sessions, highlighting or concealing certain of them in keeping with the main tendencies of their own group. Shapiro thus shows that possession practices both maintain a homogeneity of religious ideology and ethnic-class composition within each possession group and also allow for a highly varied repertoire of ritual practices.

John Watanabe also combines analyses of structure and practices, in this case regarding the historical processes by which Mayans negotiated their relationships between older traditions and new religious ideologies, the latter received as part of Spanish conquest. The Mayan religion that emerged from these interactions was neither "mainly" indigenous nor "mainly" Catholic—both positions having been argued by other scholars—but a purposive combining of elements from both. The result is a structured set of tensions among three kinds of figures: ancestors, saints, and "earth lords." Mayans understand saints as local, and as possessing their own creative or protective powers, and have resisted efforts to make worship more universal, more focused on Mary and Christ as generalized images. In this respect their particular negotiated relationship with the Catholic Church can be seen as a further development of the local-universal tension described by William Christian (1989) for Spain.

Watanabe emphasizes the relational, oppositional quality of religious structure. Saints and cave-dwelling earth lords differ not so much in their essential qualities, but in their contrasting social references. The saints, who according to local myths were discovered by village ancestors, symbolize the close ties between the living and the founders of the community. The earth lords, controllers of the rain and the land, have come to symbolize Ladino outsiders, imperious (to villagers) Spanish-speaking landowners, bureaucrats, or shopkeepers.

Both Watanabe and Michael Lambek underscore the oppositional quality of structure, following, at least in spirit, Claude Lévi-Strauss (1963). Lambek points to practices of negation, statements of "things we do not do," as ways of creating social identity. Taboos are the clearest way in which negation creates identity, and Lambek shows how taboos make social proscriptions part of our physiological experience. Central to Lambek's analysis is the argument that taboos are not only part of social structure, but that they are a type of social action: they are imposed or lifted, followed or flouted. Furthermore, they are experienced as temporal processes when one ingests or refuses to ingest certain foods, wears or removes a particular amulet. The sum of these taboo-related actions is the creation of the person and the embodiment of society.

The Context-Sensitivity of Ritual Processes

The interrelationships of structure and practice are further shaped by social context. Whereas an earlier generation of theorists (for example, Clifford Geertz 1968 and Victor Turner 1967) studied religion as a societywide system of symbols, current work, though building on the earlier studies, highlights the ways that features of society inflect and transform religious rituals in specific contexts. Two types of social context analysis are illustrated here: analyses of the limited range of meaning a particular ritual enjoys, and analyses of the variable uses and interpretations of a ritual.

Simon Harrison argues that men's initiation rituals in Papua New Guinea societies, often taken as a general model of gender relations in the society, may provide only a very limited model. Papua New Guinea initiation rituals are well known for two features, both analyzed by Harrison. They emphasize distinctions between men and women, sometimes involving male homosexuality in an effort to construct a subsociety without women, and often involving pain and suffering on the part of initiates. They also characteristically involve secrecy; the older men sometimes reveal to initiates that what they were taught at an earlier stage of initiation was just a ruse (Herdt 1982).

Harrison argues that in Avatip society on the Sepik River (a river of many famous ethnographic studies of ritual and society), these male-dominated, hierarchical rituals provide only one model for social life; another model, featuring gender equality, derives from everyday social life. Although the men's cult teaches that men are absolutely superior to women, Avatip everyday life is characterized by relative equality among individuals, male and female. Men's rituals "do not correspond to the everyday social order but temporarily suspend it." More generally, Harrison argues that societies are not characterized by a single "cultural logic" but of different logics, each with its own social domain (see also Lutkehaus 1995).

David Graeber, working in Merina society, Madagascar, shows how men and women provide quite different interpretations of a major ritual. The *famadihana* ritual involves exhuming ancestral bones and wrapping them in silk shrouds. The ritual is performed for ancestors dead 4 to 10 years, or who died elsewhere, and is supposed to bring their blessings. Although the ritual has been generally treated as creating an ideology of timeless ancestral authority and blessings (for example, in Bloch 1982), Graeber observed that, although older men did indeed speak of the ritual in that way, women stressed the ancestors' savage and violent actions toward the living. For many of them, the supposed "blessings" were merely the ancestor's decision not to harm the living or to remove a taboo. Women hold corpses of fathers or grandfathers in their laps, experiencing the sadness of loss, while men wrap the bones and crush them. Effacing the memory of the ancestor will allow some men to become the eponymous ancestor of the tomb. Having, in a sense, finally killed off their male ancestors, older men wish to deny the violence inflicted by and on the ancestors; an ideology of unchallenged authority and benevolence is now in their interest. For women the significance of the ritual is quite different; for them the cruelty appears more shocking and the violence of reburial more traumatic.

Mary Hancock's analysis of gender and nationalism in southern India discussed earlier traces the political significance of moving a worship ritual from the domestic to the extradomestic context. Advocates of the Hindu nationalist movement among the southern Brahman caste group Smarta sought to portray their practices as identical to those of the Hindu nation as a whole, and thereby to proclaim themselves and the movement of which they were a part as guardians of the nation. One means of so doing was to convert the worship of the goddess usually carried out by women into a more public ritual attended by a diverse audience from differing castes. Why? Part of the answer lies in the universal character of these rituals, their lack of any specific caste or class content and thus potential appeal to a broad Hindu constituency. The other part lies in the symbolic importance of the *cumankali* or "married woman," who by her marriage becomes auspicious; her religious and sexual power, *sakti,* is now channeled. The image of married women conducting worship outside the domestic context combine auspicious domesticity with a religious idea of the Hindu nation. In Hancock's words it creates a public "purdah culture."

My own article similarly examines the effect of social context on the interpretations given to a religious ritual. I compare the Muslim rite of worship, or *salāt,* in three societies of Indonesia, and conclude that the ritual takes on very distinct social meanings in the three cases. Muslim worship takes its primary religious meaning not from its intrinsic symbolism but from its accordance with the example set by the Prophet Muhammad. But additional social meanings are developed in specific historical contexts. The article contrasts three different social contexts for worship in contemporary Indonesia. In lowland Acehnese society, the image of everyone performing the ritual in the same way has become a symbol of provincial political unity. Provincial leaders see deviations in ritual form to be politically and socially subversive—not because of the intrinsic meaning of those deviations, but because of their implicit denial of religious unity. For the highland Gayo, where the correctness of ritual interpretation has been foregrounded, controversies about worship turn on whether one performs it only in ways followed by Muhammad, or takes it as a communicative act with God and adds to it to improve that communication. In the capital, Jakarta, worshiping together in neighborhood prayer-houses has become one of the few events to knit together the urban community, and groups that decide to carry out worship on their own are perceived by many as threatening that community, even when the form of worship looks the same as that performed by everyone else. One group's refusal to admit outsiders was seen as implying that all outsiders were polluted. The national government saw this claim as endangering national unity, and they banned the group.

Several authors draw on the influential model of ritual process proposed by Victor Turner (1969, 1974), who drew on the work of Arnold van Gennep (1960). Turner analyzed social and religious movements in terms of a tension between structure and *communitas*, the latter term referring to the ideal of direct, unmediated relationships among humans. Pilgrimages, he argued, are one form in which the rigidity of structure is attenuated, offering a model of communitas.

Michael Sallnow draws on his studies of Andean pilgrimage to argue that Turner's model of pilgrimage as *communitas* is too general, that it needs to be supplemented by analyses of the forms of sociability specific to particular pilgrimage traditions. Sallnow carried out ethnographic research in southern Peru in the 1970s. As in the Mayan society described by Watanabe, communities are differentiated from each other through the symbolic contrasts among specific saints' shrines. Pilgrimages to regional shrines augment the community-level organization of religion by supplying a broader spatial unity. The pilgrimage shrines are often dedicated to Christ but are known by the name of the location, and each site has mythological associations with a distinct spirit. Worshipers visit specific shrines on the occasion of annual festivals, bringing a small icon with them and leaving it to rest with the shrine image before returning it to the community.

Contingents from several communities encounter each other on the paths to shrines, and on these occasions they engage in fierce competitions. Factions within communities also compete for the privilege of sponsoring the contingent, and shrines themselves are separated into those frequented by Indians and those visited by *mestizos*. Sallnow argues that although an ethic of egalitarianism characterizes each contingent during the pilgrimage, as Turner predicted, this egalitarianism is maintained through competition, not communitas. New forms of reciprocity and competition emerge between groups.

As in other articles here, Sallnow's contribution underlines the importance of inspecting the specific practices and social forms found in particular contexts, and not imputing a general value to a type of activity or institution. Studies of pilgrimages elsewhere (for example, that by Ann Gold [1988] in northern India) make the same point, that the social context of pilgrimage itself may offer differently structured, but not communitas-based models of society.

The Continuing Importance of Social Theory

These studies point to ongoing intellectual processes in the social and humanistic sciences whereby older "grand theory" traditions are being rethought and reworked with newer material in mind. As is often the case, the questions posed by earlier theorists retain their immediacy even as the specific solutions they proposed are modified. In the case of the essays gathered here on religion, it is the continued importance of questions associated with Emile Durkheim and Max Weber that are most in evidence.

Durkheim's major question for religion concerned the relationship between religion and society (Durkheim 1995). His own answer located the birth of religion in the ideas and emotions generated in collective social action. Some of his followers, such as Mary Douglas (1966), operationalized the argument that religion had social origins as a hypothesis that religion has social functions, such as maintaining group solidarity by sacralizing social boundaries.

Others continue to work in the spirit of Durkheim's question, even as they modify his answer, by searching for other religiously sanctioned mechanisms that create or affirm social distinctions. In Brazil these mechanisms include the ways that belonging to a possession group, and thus enjoying a privileged tie to a spirit, bears a message about one's position on the race-class hierarchy. In Japan they include the fine distinctions in rank affirmed at various points in the ritual of Tea. Indonesian Muslims (and Muslims in most other parts of the world) detect messages about social boundaries in the degree of universality or openness of participation in worship ritual. The Andean pilgrimage provides social models other than those experienced in everyday village life, but they, too, involve distinctions, based on reciprocity ranging from strict to negative, and strong opposition between pilgrimage groups and between factions in the community vying to sponsor the pilgrimages.

In some of these cases it is distinctions across social or ethnic groups that are marked by religious practices. The highland Akha studied by Kammerer conceptualize "ethnic groups" as bundles of customs. The category of "custom" makes conversion potentially easy because of its built-in concept of relativity: "other peoples, other customs/religions/identities." Harrison argues for Sepik River societies that the graded initiation rituals and the social hierarchy they create have their social importance in the message they send to other, neighboring societies, that this society is prestigious because of its elaborate and secretive rituals. The ritual hierarchy also may keep men somewhat united, with a military benefit to the society. The Mayan opposition of saints to "earth lords" similarly reinforces a sense of social distinctiveness by loading onto the Mayan/Ladino ethnic boundary an analogous opposition between community and outsider, and between qualities of continuity and exploitation.

The Malagasy case arguably represents a Durkheimian extreme, where the social distinctions articulated through religion are those that identify each person. When an individual determines which foods are tolerated by his or her body, and thus which taboos he or she must observe, these observations indicate which of the many kinship ties that might be activated are the true ones. Lambek therefore sees this society as an instance in which it is the individual body that instantiates society on a religious basis, thus rejecting Durkheim's notion that society always finds its embodiment outside or above the individual. But indeed the bodily absorption of society through religious experience and discipline is a theme running through articles here (Anderson, Bowen, Harrison) and elsewhere (Asad 1993, Comaroff & Comaroff 1993).

Max Weber's question was quite different: What religious understandings are associated with particular status groups in society? Of particular importance are his comparative investigations into ideas of theodicy—Why evil from a God? How salvation? What is the road to Heaven? Kammerer's analysis depends on this kind of analysis for the Akha: What is their orientation toward religion? And what are the ends they hope to achieve by its means? Anderson's analysis similarly draws on the Weberian category of "this worldly" orientation, and the specific Japanese goals of restoring purity and harmony, to validate her defense of Tea as part of a religious system.

Islam, Catholicism, and the several ascetic branches of Protestantism create distinctive maps of salvation and are analyzed here in Weberian "ideal-typical" ways. It is precisely because Muslim views of the righteous path, *shari'a,* highlight correct ritual practice that small deviations from the current ideas about such practice can become highly politically charged. The emphasis within Catholicism of salvation through the body of the Church helps explain both the continued efforts of the church to promote its own cross-culturally generalized ways of worship and the resistance to that notion within Catholicism, exemplified here in the Mayan and Andean focus on local saints.

Jean and John Comaroff make the Methodist message of salvation central to their account of the complex and unintended consequences of conversion for liberation. Methodist ideas of conversion contrast with those practiced by Catholics in New Spain (as described by Watanabe). Both sets of missionaries emphasized forms of devotion, but whereas Catholics underscored the importance of markedly religious acts, a theater of worship, and the dramatization of Christ's passion, the Methodists, valuing ordinary labor and self-fashioning as the road to salvation, concentrated their forces on ways of working the fields. Digging wells and uncovering valuable water was both a way to promote self-improving agricultural work from the Methodist perspective, but also, from the Tswana point of view, it was a sign of the religious power of the missionaries—the power to make rain being a critical element of chiefly authority. The plow, "rational" time management, and nuclear families were additional instruments of "civilization" imparted by the missionaries.

But the missionaries were unable to deliver on the complete self-determination required by their theology and promised by their new tools for material and cultural advancement—precisely because of their own powerlessness in the political world. Those educated in the mission schools took the promise of the Bible, powerful especially for its literal truth, as the text for demanding justice and liberation. As in the U.S. civil rights movement, it was the language and ideals of evangelical Christianity that provided the inspiration for resistance to racism.

In these studies and in others (Geertz 1968, Peacock & Tyson 1989), anthropologists continue to pose these Weberian issues. The more interested anthropologists become in processes of conversion and religious complexity, the more central questions of religious orientation and attitudes toward salvation will become.

Religion and ritual have become recast in ways detailed here because anthropologists have increasingly turned to the study of large-scale religious movements and changes. In part this change comes from realizing the limitations of studying societies as if they could, at least for the purposes of the ethnography, be considered as small-scale, culturally static, spatially well-bounded units. In part the change comes from a general realization among social scientists and other students of society that, contrary to the predictions of religion's demise issued in the 1950s and 1960s, religious commitment is one of the most important forces contributing to new social and political movements throughout the world, in Asia, Africa, Europe, and the Americas.

It is in the intersections of these large-scale movements and forces with the everyday importance of religion that anthropology makes one of its greatest contributions to understanding our contemporary world. For many people religion's importance comes from its potential for improving their lives on many planes, from healing their bodies to answering questions about the sources of their misery and possibilities for their redemption. Religious practices are deeply interwoven with the daily and the not so daily lives of many people in the world, whether they live in agrarian or industrialized societies. The capability of religions to energize social and political movements must be traced back to these roots in social and cultural life.

References

Asad, Talal (1993). *Genealogies of religion: Discipline and reasons of power in Christianity and Islam.* Baltimore: Johns Hopkins University Press.

Bloch, Maurice (1982). Death, women and power. In Maurice Bloch and Jonathan Parry (Eds.). *Death and the regeneration of life* (pp. 211–230). Cambridge: Cambridge University Press.

Bourdieu, Pierre (1977). *Outline of the theory of practice.* Cambridge: Cambridge University Press. (Original work published 1972)

Christian, William A., Jr. (1989). *Person and God in a Spanish valley.* (Rev. ed.). Princeton, NJ: Princeton University Press. (Original work published 1972)

Comaroff, Jean, & Comaroff, John (1991). *Of revelation and revolution.* Chicago: University of Chicago Press.

Comaroff, Jean, & Comaroff, John (Eds.) (1993). *Modernity and its malcontents.* Chicago: University of Chicago Press.

Davis, Winston (1980). *Dojo: Magic and exorcism in modern Japan.* Stanford, CA: Stanford University Press.

Douglas, Mary (1966). The abominations of Leviticus. In Mary Douglas (Ed.), *Purity and danger* (pp. 41–57). London: Routledge & Kegan Paul.

Durkheim, Emile (1995). *The elementary forms of the religious life.* (Karen E. Fields, Trans.). New York: The Free Press. (Original work published 1912)

Foucault, Michel (1984). Nietzsche, genealogy, history. In Paul Rabinow (Ed.). *The Foucault reader* (pp. 76–100). New York: Pantheon Books.

Geertz, Clifford (1968). *Islam observed: Religious developments in Morocco and Indonesia.* New Haven, CT: Yale University Press.

Gold, Ann Grodzins (1988). *Fruitful journeys: The ways of Rajasthani Pilgrims.* Los Angeles: University of California Press.

Hefner, Robert W. (Ed.) (1993). *Conversion to Christianity: Historical and anthropological perspectives on a great transformation.* Los Angeles: University of California Press.

Herdt, Gilbert H. (Ed.) (1982). *Rituals of manhood: Male initiation in Papua New Guinea.* Los Angeles: University of California Press.

Kipp, Rita Smith, & Rodgers, Susan (Eds.) (1987). *Indonesian religions in transition.* Tucson: University of Arizona Press.

Lévi-Strauss, Claude (1963). *Totemism* (Rodney Needham, Trans.). Boston: Beacon Press.

Lutkehaus, Nancy C. (1995). Gender metaphors: Female rituals as cultural models in Manam. In Nancy C. Lutkehaus and Paul B. Roscoe (Eds.). *Gender rituals: Female initiation in Melanesia* (pp. 183–204). New York: Routledge.

Peacock, James L., & Tyson, Ruel W., Jr. (1989). *Pilgrims of paradox: Calvinism and experience among the primitive Baptists of the Blue Ridge.* Washington, DC: Smithsonian Institution Press.

Sahlins, Marshall (1985). *Islands of history.* Chicago: University of Chicago Press.

Smith, Wilfred Cantwell (1978). *The meaning and end of religion.* San Francisco: Harper & Row. (Original work published 1962)

Turner, Victor (1967). *The forest of symbols: Aspects of Ndembu Ritual.* Ithaca, NY: Cornell University Press.

Turner, Victor (1969). *The ritual process: Structure and anti-structure.* Ithaca, NY: Cornell University Press.

Turner, Victor (1974). Pilgrimages as social processes. In Victor Turner (Ed.), *Dramas, fields, and metaphors* (pp. 166–230). Ithaca, NY: Cornell University Press.

van der Veer, Peter (1994). *Religious nationalisms: Hindus and Muslims in India.* Los Angeles: University of California Press.

van Gennep, Arnold (1960). *The rites of passage* (Monika B. Vizedom & Gabrielle L. Caffee, Trans.). Chicago: University of Chicago Press. (Original work published 1908)

Weber, Max (1978). *Economy and society.* 2 vols. Los Angeles: University of California Press. (Original work published 1956)

Wolf, Eric (1982). *Europe and the people without history.* Los Angeles: University of California Press.

Customs and Christian Conversion among Akha Highlanders of Burma and Thailand

CORNELIA ANN KAMMERER

A chronicle of Baptist evangelism in Burma published in the 1960s lamented that "only hundreds of Akha have been won" (Sowards and Sowards 1963:419). This contrasted sharply with the large numbers of converts among members of other ethnic minorities sharing the mountains of eastern Burma with Akha. Karen and Lahu highlanders, for example, eagerly entered the Christian fold. In fact, the Reverend William Young brought so many Lahu souls to Christ in the single year of 1905–06—4419 to be exact—that instead of being elated, his overseers at the Burma Baptist Mission headquarters were suspicious and sent a team to investigate (McCoy 1972:304). Elaine Lewis (1957:229), a Baptist missionary to Akha, complained in 1957 about their unwillingness to accept the "Good News": "For some reason which we do not fully understand, the religion of the Lahus presents fewer serious obstacles to the Gospel than that of the Akhas. . . . [T]he religion of the Akhas has stood as a formidable barrier to the Christian witness among that race." Yet whereas in the 1950s and 1960s missionaries bemoaned their lack of success in converting Akha, by the 1980s some missionaries were anticipating a "mass movement." Although this movement has still neither materialized nor spiritualized, there has nonetheless been rapid growth not only of Protestant churches but also of the Catholic Church among Akha in Thailand. Based upon statements by visitors and recent immigrants to Thailand from Burma, it seems that similar growth is under way across the border.

Intrigued by this growth, I returned to the field, not to gather in a Christian harvest like the missionaries, but to gather information about the nature and consequences of conversion. Why, I wondered, were Akha now accepting Christianity? Why, unlike many of their highland neighbors, were Akha reluctant to convert in the past? Only later did I realize that in addition to examining the differential receptivity to Christianity over time, it is important to ask, "Why convert at all?" In this article I contend that none of these questions can be answered without an understanding of Akha traditional religion, that "formidable barrier" to Christian witness. My argument is that the past rejection of Christianity on the part of Akha, as opposed to other highlanders, is related to the nature of their traditional religion and, furthermore, that the recent increase in conversion has less to do with Christianity itself than with Akha traditional religion.

I approach the cultural change currently taking place among Akha in Thailand largely from the inside out, that is to say, in terms of indigenous cultural forms and categories. In doing so, I do not mean to suggest that these forms and categories are independent of the larger sociopolitical and historical context. Quite the contrary, as I hope to make clear, Akha traditional religion is the religion of a "perennial minority" that has throughout the centuries been surrounded not only by other kinds of highlanders but also by more powerful lowlanders (Alting von Geusau 1983). Yet, as the contrast between Akha and those mountain people who responded more readily and rapidly to the gospel clearly demonstrates, the larger sociopolitical context and historical forces are not in themselves sufficient to explain the speed and direction of cultural change.

Akha responses to Christianity have been shaped by two indigenous equations: a general one between religion and ethnicity and a particular one between Akha traditional religion and Akha identity. In attempting to understand Akha reactions to the Christian call, I therefore confront a subject of long-term fascination to the students of the hill-valley interface in mainland Southeast Asia, namely, ethnic identity. Leach's (1954) famous account of hill-dwelling Kachin becoming valley-dwelling Shan and vice versa brought the phenomenon of shifts in ethnic affiliation to the attention of anthropologists. The Akha case suggests that willingness to change identity is culturally relative and itself subject to change through time. It also demonstrates that indigenous definitions of ethnic identity undergo alteration. This examination of the Akha encounter with Christianity thus engages the issue of ethnic nationalism addressed in previous studies of Christian and Islamic missionization and conversion elsewhere in the Southeast Asian region such as Indonesia (Kipp & Rodgers 1987), and in more distant regions such as the Pacific (Keesing & Tonkinson 1982) and Africa (Burton 1985).

Christian Contact

The earliest contact between a Christian missionary and Akha that I have been able to discover occurred in 1869, when an American Baptist pastor toured eastern Burma in and around the Shan city of Kengtung (Cushing 1870).[1] It was not, however, until 40 years later in 1909 that the Baptists claimed their first converts (Sowards & Sowards 1963:419). An Akha Baptist Church "was organized in 1936 as a result of ten years of persistent effort" (Sowards

& Sowards 1963:318). Except during World War II, American Baptists were active in the Kengtung "field" until the government of Burma evicted foreign missionaries in the mid-1960s. Paul and Elaine Lewis, the last American Baptists to serve in Kengtung, operated a Bible school and a middle school for Lahu and Akha (Maung Shwe Wa 1963:232, 237). Across the border in Thailand, Akha Protestants celebrated their Silver Jubilee in 1987; the first converts had been "won" in 1962—more than 50 years after their counterparts in Burma—by an Akha evangelist from Burma and an Australian couple belonging to the Overseas Missionary Fellowship (OMF, formerly the China Inland Mission). For several years now, the Baptists and OMF Protestants have been united under the banner of the Akha Churches in Thailand.

Catholic evangelists were also active in Kengtung, where they established a mission in 1912. Unfortunately, I cannot precisely date the first Akha conversion to Catholicism, but I met an old woman who had become a Catholic in approximately 1923 when, as a nine-year-old orphan, she had gone to live at the mission in Kengtung. I suspect, however, that the earliest conversions to Catholicism among Akha living in a traditional village context were later. In Thailand the initial convert was "won" in 1971 by a priest belonging to the same order as the Kengtung mission (Urbani 1971).[2]

As is evident from this brief sketch, mission work among Akha in Thailand began long after similar work in Burma. Just as various mountain minorities of mainland Southeast Asia have moved south over time, so too have various missionaries and the organizations they represent. Some foreign missionaries transferred their work to Burma after being expelled from China following the 1949 revolution; a number of foreign missionaries working in Burma, including some who had earlier served in China, moved to Thailand after the Burmese government expelled them in the mid-1960s. Paul Lewis is the only missionary to have worked extensively among Akha in Thailand after first working among them in Burma. (In Thailand Elaine Lewis concentrated on Lahu work.) Yet it seems safe to say that the OMF would not have the concentration of missionaries it currently has among Akha in Thailand were China still an open field. Similarly, the Catholic order that founded the Kengtung mission only began its work in north Thailand after the expulsion of foreign missionaries from Burma.

Since Protestant missionization began among Akha in Thailand in 1955 (Nightingale 1968:263), the OMF has sent four couples and at least three individuals (two of whom subsequently became a couple). From 1986 to 1988 there were six OMF missionaries (three couples) at work among Akha, a number which I believe to be the largest ever. Paul Lewis, who retired from missionary service in June 1989, is the only American Baptist missionary to work among Akha in Thailand, although, unlike the OMF representatives, he dedicated most of his time to medical, educational, and development projects rather than to direct evangelism. Recently a Protestant preacher originally from north Burma has been teaching the gospel to Akha with the help of his Lahu wife and father-in-law, both of whom speak Akha. He and his followers are not affiliated with either the Baptists or the OMF. Besides these foreign missionaries, two Thai couples and a number of Akha Protestant evangelists are also engaged in spreading the "Good News" to non-Christian Akha. Since Catholic missionization began among Akha in Thailand in the 1960s, three Italian priests, several Italian nuns, and one Thai laywoman have been involved.

Roughly one-fifth to one-third of the approximately 200 Akha villages are fully or partially Christian; Protestants outnumber Catholics. According to Akha knowledgeable about the situation in Burma, from the city of Kengtung southward the largest group of Akha is Catholic, the second largest Protestant, and the third largest traditionalist. Unfortunately, it is difficult to obtain accurate data on the size of the Akha Christian population for Thailand and, to an even greater extent, for Burma. Extant census and baptismal information is incomplete and sometimes unreliable. Besides, many Akha who count themselves Christians are unbaptized.

Judging from the number of foreign missionaries and native evangelists calling Akha to Christ in recent years, it would be easy to assume that the growth in conversions reflects an intensification of proselytization. To do so, however, ignores the fact that this intensification is found in Thailand but not in Burma at a time when both Thailand and Burma are experiencing a growth in Akha converts. In addition, it is clear from talking to foreign missionaries and Akha evangelists in Thailand that this intensification is as much a reaction to as a cause of the increasing responsiveness to the Christian message. Thus, it is necessary to look further to understand Christian conversion among Akha. What is it about the traditional religion that originally blocked conversion? And why was this barrier eventually breached?

Akha Zah$^{\vee}$*: Traditional Religion*

In the article cited at the outset, Elaine Lewis (1957:229) speculates that the differential receptivity to the Christian message on the part of Lahu and Akha may be due to the fact that Akha religion is, in her words, "more highly developed." Unfortunately, the phrases "highly complicated" and "highly demanding," also applied by Lewis (1957:228, 230) to Akha religion, are the only indications of what she means by "highly developed." Although she does not provide the Akha term that she is glossing as religion, I assume that it is *zah*$^{\vee}$, the word defined as "customs, religion, way of doing things" in the Akha-English dictionary compiled by her husband (P. Lewis 1968:351), a missionary-anthropologist.[3] What is Akha *zah*$^{\vee}$? At least three dimensions would need to be considered in a full anthropological account: first, the kind of cognitive structure referred to by *zah*$^{\vee}$; second, the pragmatic functions the term *zah*$^{\vee}$ has in social use; and third, the folk model of *zah*$^{\vee}$. In this discussion, the focus is on the third dimension because it is this indigenous understanding of *zah*$^{\vee}$ that has guided Akha reactions to Christian proselytization.

Leo Alting von Geusau (1983:249), an anthropologist who has worked with Akha in Thailand for many years, describes what *zah*$^{\vee}$ is for Akha as "religion, way of life, customs, etiquette, and ceremonies," all of which are "traditions handed down by the father." As he observes, it "meticulously describes proper daily behavior" and "includes the whole of what anthropological literature calls calendric and non-calendric ceremonial and ritual behavior" (1983:249, 250). For Akha, *zah*$^{\vee}$—henceforth glossed as "customs"—is indeed the multitude of rituals that are part of everyday life, such as yearly ancestor offerings, annual and nonannual rice rituals, curing and corrective ceremonies, and life-cycle rites (Kammerer

1986:63–67). Furthermore, it encompasses much that anthropologists label kinship, including principles of lineage segmentation, marriage rules, and norms of affinal responsibilities.

Akha frequently and animatedly discuss customs, in particular at the many feasts that accompany the rituals of *zah*$^{\vee}$. Indeed, customs themselves enjoin such discussions. On these occasions, adults, especially male elders, drinking tea or enjoying pipes of tobacco after a filling meal, list in elaborate detail the various segments of a given rite, describe the correct procedures, identify who properly undertakes each required action, and delineate differences in inherited ritual practices between lineages and subgroups.[4]

In the Akha language a special final particle, *k'm*$_{\vee}$, is used solely to denote that an action is permissible or not permissible according to *zah*$^{\vee}$. The construction "verb + *k'm*$_{\vee}$" means that the stated action is in keeping with customs, whereas the construction "negative + verb + *k'm*$_{\vee}$" means that the stated action is against customs' dictates. Thus, for example, when I was asking about marriage rules, the response "*la*$_{\vee}$ *k'm*$_{\vee}$," in which *la*$_{\vee}$ means "to fetch a bride," indicated that the union in question is allowed, while the response "*ma*$_{\vee}$ *la*$_{\vee}$ *k'm*$_{\vee}$," in which *ma*$_{\vee}$ is the negative, indicated that the union in question is not allowed by *zah*$^{\vee}$.

"From the native's point of view," then, Akha *zah*$^{\vee}$ is behavioral rules, ranging from specifications for proper ritual procedures and appropriate recitations to precepts concerning conduct between kin to more mundane prescriptions for everyday actions. It is therefore not surprising that bilingual Akha translate *zah*$^{\vee}$ into the Thai language as *kòdmaaj*, best rendered into English as "law."

For Akha, their *zah*$^{\vee}$ is not, however, simply rules governing action; it is also action governed by those rules. Thus, the male leader of every village (*dzoe*$_{\vee}$ *ma*) is described in ritual texts and in normal conversations as the one who "does *zah*$^{\vee}$." His job is to cleanse ritually the rice seeds used in the yearly first planting and to enact other rites essential to the maintenance of purity in the village domain. This leader, who must perform *zah*$^{\vee}$ but who need have no textual expertise, is ranked above the reciter (*pi*$^{\vee}$ *ma* or *boe*$^{\vee}$ *maw*$_{\vee}$), the male ritual specialist responsible for chanting the appropriate verses from the vast oral tradition at various ceremonies. The fact that any ritual—even an elaborate funeral at which a buffalo is killed for the deceased—can be performed without the presence of a reciter demonstrates that for Akha the efficacy of ritual is rooted in actions rather than words. This contrasts with traditions as diverse as Vedic and Trobriander in which ritual's efficacy depends upon the spoken word.

According to Akha mythic history, long ago people of every kind—Shan, Thai, Chinese, Lahu, and Akha themselves—were given *zah*$^{\vee}$ by the creator, A$_{\vee}$ poe$_{\vee}$ mi$_{\vee}$ yeh$_{\vee}$. Everyone except the Akha man went to the creator's dwelling carrying a loosely woven basket. Only the Akha man went to fetch *zah*$^{\vee}$ carrying a tightly woven sack. As those carrying loosely woven baskets were returning home, their newly received *zah*$^{\vee}$ fell out through the holes; but the Akha walked home without losing a single piece. For Akha, this story explains why their *zah*$^{\vee}$ is so vast and demanding as compared to that of others: as Akha say, "Akha *zah*$^{\vee}$ is numerous" and "Akha *zah*$^{\vee}$ is difficult."

This story also accounts for the differentiation of ethnic groups. To be Akha is to uphold the prescriptions and proscriptions of Akha *zah*$^{\vee}$. Akha is as Akha does; and what Akha should do is follow the behavioral rules handed down from parent to child through the roughly 60 generations memorialized in the patrilineal genealogies of all Akha. Similarly, to be Lahu, for example—this is from the Akha, not the Lahu point of view—is to follow whatever *zah*$^{\vee}$ has been handed down from one generation to the next since the creator distributed *zah*$^{\vee}$ to Lahu. Akha are cultural relativists: frequently heard expressions are "everyone has their own customs" and "everyone's customs are their own"—in our words, "to each his own."

During my first period of fieldwork I never mentioned my religious background because there was tension between traditionalists and Christians and because, as a Westerner, I was liable to be taken for a missionary. Late in my research, however, my teacher asked me if I followed "*Ye*$_{\vee}$ *su*$^{\vee}$ *zah*$^{\vee}$," that is, "Jesus customs," the Akha term for Christianity. When I answered that my parents are Christians but I do not practice, he was visibly upset. "Didn't you listen to your parents?" he scolded me. Despite the fact that this man was staunchly opposed to conversion to Christianity, he nonetheless thought that I should adhere to the *zah*$^{\vee}$ of my parents and of their parents before them. From the Akha perspective, it is appropriate for people of each sort to adhere to their inherited traditional rules for proper action. This, then, is identity in action.

Why Not Convert in the Past?

Having examined the history of Christian missionization and the Akha folk model of traditional religion, I turn now to the first of the three questions posed at the beginning. Why, when confronted with foreign missionaries preaching the Christian gospel, did Akha fail to adopt the new religion? Proselytizers asked them to abandon their ancestral, agricultural, and local spirits in favor of the religion of the one true God, to leave the "darkness" and enter the "light." To do so would involve giving up their ancestor offerings and other rites regarded by Westerners "bearing witness" among them as misguided at best and demonic at worst (Nightingale 1968:263). What did this call to Christianity mean to Akha? From the Akha perspective, conversion to Christianity entailed more than simply religious change, and to understand why this was the case we must look once again at Akha *zah*$^{\vee}$.

When missionaries demanded that Akha forsake the practices of their forebears and accept Christianity, they were essentially asking them to cease being Akha by Akha criteria for ethnic self-definition. Since missionaries did not recognize that for Akha *zah*$^{\vee}$ is a cultural subsystem equivalent to what anthropologists term ethnic identity, they did not realize the implications of conversion for Akha. At the 1987 Silver Jubilee of Akha Protestantism in Thailand, Jean Nightingale, one half of the first foreign missionary couple to evangelize Akha in Thailand, commented that I probably did not like what the missionaries had done. I answered something to the effect that as an anthropologist I respect the diversity of cultures. This prompted her to point out that she and her husband had encouraged Akha converts to retain their culture by keeping their language and their traditional clothes. For her and her husband, to be Akha is to speak Akha and to wear Akha clothes. But for Akha themselves language and clothing are not central to their ethnic identity; what is central, the core of Akha-ness, is *zah*$^{\vee}$ (Kammerer 1988:268–273). Here we have not just a clash of cultures but also a clash of concepts of culture and identity.

It is not enough, however, to explain the Akha resistance to the Christian call by saying that to become Christian is to stop being Akha, at least as traditionally defined. After all, the anthropological literature on upland Southeast Asia is replete with instances of oscillation in ethnic affiliation. Akha, however, seem to be less willing to shift their identities than many other highlanders. Moreover, there is an unwillingness to absorb others into their group. The ritual texts of the oral tradition admonish an Akha woman not to take a Tai-speaking husband: "Don't marry a Shan. . . . Shan are the people who drown." In other words, if you wed a Shan, your fate will be drowning, which is categorized by Akha as a "bad death." (Those who die by violence or drowning cannot join the ancestors unless elaborate rituals of purification are performed.) The texts also instruct Akha not to turn into A^{v} boe^{v}, Mon-Khmer-speaking highlanders. Thus, allegiance to Akha identity is highly valued in their cultural system.[5] This allegiance to ethnicity as zah^{v} accounts for the missionaries' laments about the lack of Akha converts.

Missionaries in Burma and Thailand note that converts were not allowed to stay in their villages (Nightingale 1968:265). Indeed, the Nightingales themselves were not permitted to live in the traditional Akha community from which the first converts inside Thailand were won (Nightingale 1968:263–264). One of these initial Christians, together with Jean Nightingale, recounted the early history of the Akha church in Thailand as part of the Silver Jubilee. Prominent in their account was how the first converts were forced to move outside the gates of the heathen village where they had been living. In contrast, Christian converts among Karen (Iijima 1979:112) and Hmong (Cooper 1984:68, 82) continue to reside within the confines of their communities. For Akha, zah^{v} is exclusive; one should be either this or that. That mixed Christian and non-Christian (that is, traditional) Akha villages are to be found in Thailand today does not mean that zah^{v} is conceived of as any less exclusive. Rather, mixed villages result from a weakening of the traditional authority structure—a traditional village leader who orders Christians out may well not be heeded—the increasing numerical strength of Christians, the lack of land for new villages, and, perhaps most important, government restrictions on movement.

Although Akha express a pronounced cultural preference for maintaining their own ethnic affiliation and have a culturally countenanced unwillingness to absorb non-Akha into their midst, it is by no means true that shifts either into or away from Akha identity do not occur. In fact, they do. For example, I know several Akha women who have married Lisu. These women live in Lisu villages, wear Lisu clothes, speak the Lisu language, and identify themselves as Lisu. There are also cases of non-Akha men marrying Akha women and becoming Akha. *Zah*^{v} itself specifies the method by which such outsiders can adopt a named Akha lineage.[6] As these examples demonstrate, I am *not* saying that changes in identity do not take place; I *am* saying that Akha culture discourages such shifts and, indeed, they appear to be less frequent among Akha than, for instance, among Lisu.

Another factor contributing to the initial Akha reluctance to embrace Christianity is the absence of a key motivation for conversion found among both Karen and Hmong: the quest for literacy. According to Tapp (1989:77), this quest is linked to the "messianic contours" of indigenous legends invoked to explain conversion. Many highland groups, including not only Karen and Hmong but also Akha, have stories of a lost book or lost writing. To Karen in Burma, missionaries bearing the Bible were their "foreign brothers" bringing back their "golden book" (Keyes 1977:55; see also Marshall 1922 and Stern 1968). Similarly, Hmong in China interpreted the arrival of the famous missionary Samuel Pollard, with his Bibles and other texts (written in a Hmong script devised by him), as the return of their lost book (Tapp

1989). Both Karen and Hmong associate the return of literacy with the appearance of the millennium, which for Hmong is also connected with the reappearance of their king (Tapp 1989:78). The Akha myth about lost literacy, on the other hand, lacks a messianic message. Like Karen and Hmong, Akha say that they had writing in the past, but unlike Karen and Hmong, they say nothing of its anticipated return. Bibles did not, therefore, hold for Akha the millenarian promise that brought masses of Karen and Hmong to Christianity.

During fieldwork I encountered no evidence that the quest for the written word, so critical to early Hmong converts, has motivated Akha converts. Paul Lewis (personal communication, 1989), who served as a missionary to Akha for 40 years, confirms that the "desire for *literacy*," identified by Tapp (1989:75; emphasis in original) as the key to Hmong conversions, is not a primary impetus in Akha conversions. According to the Akha legend about the loss of writing, long ago the creator gave an Akha a book written on buffalo skin, but on the way home the man got hungry and ate the book (P. Lewis 1969–70:787–789). In another variant, the book is written on a rice cake, which, like the buffalo skin, is consumed. Although in the version reported by Lewis the loss of literacy is associated with the loss of "right to rule," no mention is made of the anticipated return of either one. While other highlanders were awaiting the return of their book and sometimes also their king, Akha were content with their excellent memories, said to result from their having ingested the written word. Admittedly, the Akha myth is not alone in attributing cleverness to having eaten the book; the parallel Hmong myth, for instance, does the same (Tapp 1989:77). Yet Akha may well be alone when they conclude their myth with an expression of satisfaction with their present cleverness rather than anticipation of future literacy and future kings. This self-satisfaction is in keeping with their avowed allegiance to their ethnic identity.

Why Convert Now?

In the course of my recent fieldwork, I had occasion to ask many Akha Christians, both Protestant and Catholic, why they had converted to Christianity in the past decade. I was surprised by the uniformity of the answers, almost all of which could be divided into two basic categories: because they did not know *zah*ᵛ or because they could not afford to do it. A young Akha man, for example, said, "I knew nothing," meaning he knew no Akha *zah*ᵛ. He went on to say that all his patrilineal relatives who knew *zah*ᵛ had died, leaving him alone and unable to perform *zah*ᵛ for himself, his wife, and their children. "I had no chickens; I had no pigs," an old woman told me to explain her conversion. During research I heard these phrases, "I knew nothing" and "I had no chickens; I had no pigs," repeated like a litany by many people in far-flung villages. Neither response refers at all to the appeal of the religion brought by foreign missionaries and Akha evangelists. Conversion in these cases is, thus, not explicitly based upon any characteristic of the religion being joined, but rather on characteristics of the religion being discarded.

Lack of either the informational or the financial wherewithal to perform Akha *zah*ᵛ is the stated reason for conversion.[7] In the 1960s Peter Nightingale (1968:263) described Akha as "deeply steeped in their own animistic religion and apparently well satisfied with their own complicated culture, language, and society." This satisfaction is consistent with Akha contentment with their prodigious faculty for memory in place of literacy and with their loyalty to Akha identity. Among converts what is seemingly shaken is not satisfaction with their traditional religion itself but their ability to satisfy its requirements.[8] Since, as Akha attest, their *zah*$^{\vee}$ is both "numerous" and "difficult," intricate knowledge is necessary to follow its dictates properly. In addition, the many calendric and noncalendric ceremonies a single family must perform in a given year require the killing of a great number of animals, not to mention the rice, the other food, and the labor needed for the accompanying feasts.

When Elaine Lewis observes that the traditional religion blocks the spread of Christianity among Akha, she attributes this to the fact that their religion is "highly developed." Her additional descriptions of it as "highly complicated" and "highly demanding" suggest that what she means is exactly what Akha mean when they characterize their religion as numerous and difficult. Akha *zah*$^{\vee}$ from any perspective, whether that of Akha or that of outsiders—be they missionaries or anthropologists—is both extensive and expensive.

Ironically, it is precisely those aspects of traditional religion that missionaries considered a barrier to conversion that are currently cited by Akha as the impetus for conversion. To understand this seemingly paradoxical situation we must turn once again to Akha *zah*$^{\vee}$ itself and to the politico-economic context in which Akha in Thailand and Burma now find themselves. One of the important features of *zah*$^{\vee}$ is its resistance to change. According to the dictates of *zah*$^{\vee}$, Akha should do *zah*$^{\vee}$ exactly as taught to them by their forebears.[9] Moreover, precise ritual performance is a prerequisite for ritual efficacy. Both this cultural opposition to change and this requirement of exact observance encourage Akha to retain their inherited *zah*$^{\vee}$ in its traditional form. But for many Akha today, even these factors are not enough to impel them to continue to follow the customs of their ancestors. Lest it seem that I am claiming that Akha live in some sort of timeless and static "primitive" world, I hasten to emphasize that *zah*$^{\vee}$ has changed in the past and will continue to change in the future. Change does, however, happen slowly, and once it is made, it is masked; an innovation, like a long-standing practice, acquires the stamp of the ancestors by being labeled *zah*$^{\vee}$ (Kammerer 1988:270–271).

As Akha are increasingly incorporated into the Thai nation-state, Akha men who in bygone days would have jovially competed with one another to gain knowledge of their *zah*$^{\vee}$ instead eagerly attempt to attain as much education in the Thai school system as possible. I remember vividly an occasion when I sat alone with a reciter as he chanted a corrective ceremony. Upon completing the chanting, he said sadly that long ago, when he was learning the text to the ritual just performed, he was but one among many young men who surrounded the reciter to watch and listen to the proceedings.

Akha are now facing an unprecedented challenge to their mode of subsistence. As slash-and-burn cultivators of rice, other foods, and cash crops, Akha require sufficient land for either field rotation or migration. The shallow tropical soils of the highlands are rapidly depleted by agricultural use and demand long fallow periods in which to regain their fertility. But it is no longer possible in Thailand to leave a field untilled for years because of the pressure of population and the politics of land distribution. Neither is it possible for Akha and other hill-dwellers to search out unoccupied or unclaimed land as they could in the past. Now, many Akha no longer plant the corn necessary to feed the pigs, chickens, and other animals needed for the rituals of *zah*$^{\vee}$. Since many Akha cannot grow enough rice to last from one harvest to the next, available cash is used not to buy animals for offerings to feed ancestors and other spirits but to buy rice to feed the family. Although it is difficult to get information about the current situation in Burma, it is clear that Akha there are experiencing similar ecological and economic pressures. Their difficulties are compounded by the social disruption and dislocation caused by the war, raging since Burma's independence in 1948, between ethnic troops and the Burmese army.

Among Akha in Thailand, the quest for Thai education is related to the draw of the encroaching dominant culture and to the recognition that alternative modes of livelihood must be sought. Knowledge of the Thai language and Thai ways, rather than knowledge of *zah*ᵛ, can lead to new economic opportunities. Thus, despite its mechanisms for self-preservation, Akha *zah*ᵛ is becoming a casualty in a threatened culture. *Zah*ᵛ's own requirements that it be done completely and correctly are contributing to its demise: those without adequate knowledge or sufficient animals can do it neither completely nor correctly.

Why Convert at All?

Surely Akha could react to the current crisis by altering their customs or by abandoning them without adopting another religion. Indeed, among traditional Akha today, there are those who might be termed conservatives and those who might be labeled innovators (there are more of the former, I should point out, than of the latter).[10] Both recognize that *zah*ᵛ is complex and costly, but the former insist upon meeting rather than changing its exacting requirements; for them, economic impoverishment should not be allowed to result in the impoverishment of *zah*ᵛ. The innovators, on the other hand, are actively trying to transform *zah*ᵛ in order to make it less demanding. They seek to make it cheaper to practice by, for example, replacing a pig with a chicken in a ritual. The conservatives oppose the innovators by quoting *zah*ᵛ's own strictures against internal change. Yet, despite the existence of innovators among traditionalists, conversion to Christianity appears to be a more prevalent response to economic stress than is change in Akha *zah*ᵛ itself. This is not surprising when it is recognized that change in *zah*ᵛ, though possible, is not easy: allegiance to *zah*ᵛ discourages such change.

Converts to Christianity do not respond to economic marginalization by digging in their heels and doggedly observing *zah*ᵛ in all its elaborateness as do conservative traditionalists. And unlike the innovative traditionalists, they do not attempt to effect transformations of Akha customs to make them more readily realizable in practice. Instead, they choose to replace their own *zah*ᵛ with another, to abandon their old religion in favor of a new one. This makes sense, for, in the Akha scheme of things, to be human is to have *zah*ᵛ of some kind.

Despite the equation of *zah*ᵛ with identity, some Akha do respond to their present economic plight by abandoning their traditional religion without adopting a new one. In 1988 one of my teachers, a conservative traditionalist, described with sadness and disapproval the poverty-stricken Akha living on the outskirts of a nearby Chinese settlement who did not practice *zah*ᵛ of any sort.[11] These Akha eke out a meager existence as laborers in tea plantations belonging to Yunnanese Chinese. My teacher described these *zah*ᵛ-less Akha as "bats" because, like bats, they are neither one thing nor another. This characterization is not idiosyncratic; in fact, people with no *zah*ᵛ were described to Paul Lewis (1969–70:24) in identical terms. For Akha, bats are a prototypical example of categoric ambiguity. My teacher is not alone in his disapproval of individuals without *zah*^{v}. In the eyes of this man and of many other Akha traditionalists, being Christian, that is, following Jesus customs, is preferable to having no *zah*^{v} at all. The same is seemingly true in the eyes of those Akha who convert to Christianity.

Conversion and Identity

Why is Christianity selected rather than some other possible *zah*^{v}? A ready explanation is that Christianity is a proselytizing religion. There are, for example, no itinerant Lisu visiting Akha villages to urge Akha to adopt Lisu rituals. There are, however, Buddhist missionary monks, sponsored by Thailand's Department of Public Welfare of the Ministry of Interior, active among Akha and other highlanders (Keyes 1971:562–567; Tambiah 1976:434–448). These Buddhist missionaries, called Thammacarik monks, run a school for male highlander youths at a temple in Chiang Mai, the largest city in the north. Although many traditionalist Akha become novices and even monks while attending this school, they resume their traditional religious practices after leaving. Although both Christianity and Buddhism are proselytizing religions, only Christianity has been embraced by large numbers of Akha. That Akha traditionalists seeking a replacement *zah*^{v} choose Christianity rather than Buddhism seems to support the suggestion made by Lehman (1967:97–98) and Provencher (1975:108) that conversion to Christianity by Southeast Asian mountain minorities is simultaneously a claim to difference from and a claim to equality with valley-dwelling Buddhists (cf. Tapp 1989).

Significantly, Christianity offers a way to continue to be different from the dominant Buddhist majority while retaining some semblance of Akha-ness. Converts are aware that Akha Christians continue to speak the Akha language, to wear Akha clothes, and to retain their patrilineal affiliation. In traditional Akha culture, while humanness is predicated on practicing *zah*^{v} of some kind, particular identity depends upon the kind of *zah*^{v} practiced. Those who practice Akha customs are Akha, those who practice Lahu customs are Lahu, and so on. It follows, then, that those who adopt Jesus customs are "Christ people" (*Ka li za*$_{v}$ in Akha). But they are Christ people who speak the Akha language, wear Akha clothes, and retain their Akha patrilineal affiliation. A convergence is thus evident between the ideas about identity outlined by the missionary Jean Nightingale and the reformulated definitions of Akha-ness among converts.

These converts do not simply become Christians; they become Akha Christians. Despite the proclaimed "universal brotherhood of Christ," both Akha Protestants and Akha Catholics have few ties with non-Akha Christians (either hill-dwelling or valley-dwelling). When I returned to the field, I was interested in discovering whether or not Christianity was contributing to the development of a pan-highlander solidarity or even identity similar to that forged among mountain people (montagnards) in Vietnam by French colonialism and the Vietnam War (Hickey 1982). I found no indication that Akha Christians are joining with other Christian mountain-dwellers. Among Lua and Karen Catholics in Thailand, the existence of a "Catholic 'hill tribe' " identity has been documented by Kunstadter (1983:151). Yet Lua and Karen have long lived in association with one another, whereas Akha have long held themselves apart from others. It is possible that in the future Akha Protestants may merge with other highland Protestants and Akha Catholics with other highland Catholics; however, little evidence points in this direction. For example, Akha studying at Thai schools in the northern city of Chiang Rai reside at an exclusively Akha hostel sponsored by Protestant missionaries. One missionary-run student hostel in Chiang Mai houses children from different hill tribes, but even there I observed voluntary ethnic segregation in socializing; Akha youngsters keep largely to themselves.

As of 1988, both non-Christian and Christian Akha reserved the phrase "*A*$_{\vee}$ *kha*$_{\vee}$ *zah*$^{\vee}$" for traditional religion and "*Ye*$_{\vee}$ *su*$^{\vee}$ *zah*$^{\vee}$" ("Jesus customs") for Christianity. An intriguing possibility is that eventually Christian customs will be considered one kind of Akha customs. In a sense, this potential transformation, the internalization of an entire alien religious system, would represent the ultimate form of indigenization—a totalized syncretism, if you will. There is a traditional cultural pattern to which such a transformation could be assimilated: in the Akha world view, Akha themselves recognize that customs are not uniform among all Akha. As noted above, Akha are wont to outline differences between the inherited practices of various lineages and subgroups. Precisely such a global indigenization of Christianity is already under way among one subgroup of Hmong highlanders in China (Tapp 1989:93).

Christianity is exclusive in the sense that its adherents should belong to it alone and to no other religion. This is compatible with the traditional Akha view of *zah*$^{\vee}$, especially its equation with identity.[12] Christianity is also exclusive in another way: it claims to be the one true religion. Akha religion, on the other hand, makes no such claim. This second form of exclusiveness is a major source of tension between Akha Christians and Akha traditionalists. While traditionalists respect the customs of others, even those of Christian Akha, many Christian Akha, adopting the attitude of missionaries and Akha evangelists, judge other religions to be inferior, if not downright evil. Whereas Akha customs do not prohibit participation in (as opposed to adoption of) the *zah*$^{\vee}$ of others, Protestantism and to a lesser degree Catholicism forbid taking part in the "demon worship" of non-Christian Akha. If the occasion arises, Akha traditionalists join in Christian observances as a sign of respect for the *zah*$^{\vee}$ of their neighbors. But Christian Akha, in particular Protestant Akha, fail to return similar displays of respect for traditional Akha religion. This disparity angers traditionalists, who rightly view it as evidence of disdain. Should Akha adherents actually indigenize Christianity in the manner described above, this tension between traditional and Christian Akha, if still present, might prevent non-Christians from accepting the Christians' claim that their religion is simply a form of Akha customs.

Is It "Conversion"?

The argument presented here about why conversion follows lack of conversion could be interpreted as an example of economic determinism, since the deteriorating economic circumstances of Akha contribute to the movement into Christianity.[13,14] Such an interpretation, however, by ignoring how this economic hardship is culturally experienced by Akha, fails to provide a full account. The argument could also be interpreted as an application of theories of deprivation or relative deprivation, according to which social change, including religious conversion, is a response to a gap between expectation and actuality. Although difficult to prove wrong, such theories, like economic determinism, seek a single explanation for complex phenomena and minimize the importance of cultural factors (cf. Tapp 1989:81–82). What is perceived as deprivation is culturally relative. Finally, the Akha case could be viewed as falling within the stress model of conversion, which identifies cognitive or psychological dissonance as the impetus for change in religious affiliation.[15] Again, complexity and culture are not given their due. Thrupp's (1970:26) comment that the deprivation hypothesis "has never yet dealt satisfactorily with the problem that resort to millennialism is only one of many ways of reacting to deprivation" is true for conversion as well as for millennialism and is applicable not only to deprivation but also to economic hardship and to stress of one form or another. This observation thus effectively underscores the inadequacy of the deprivation hypothesis, economic determinism, and the stress model as explanations of conversion.

Since the issue of economic factors in conversion has been raised, mention should be made of so-called rice Christians. In fact, the phenomenon of conversion to maximize material advantages, whether they be rice, access to education and medical care, or other benefits, is much less prevalent among Akha than I had anticipated. This is in part due to the fact that the activities of most of the foreign missionaries active among Akha do not encourage such conversions. OMF workers, for example, devote more energy to Bible study than to supporting secular schools. With the growing penetration of state-supported education into Thailand's highland villages, the draw of mission-sponsored schools has weakened. While rice Christians are rare, opium—or rather anti-opium—Christians are common, although less so in recent years than in the past. As missionaries have long recognized, one reason Akha convert is to escape addiction by entering the supposedly opium-free environment of a Christian community (E. Lewis 1957:228; Wilson 1981). What this has meant is that some Christian villages are full of addicts who either fail to break their habits or relapse into addiction. Since it is now widely known among traditionalists and Christians alike that Christian villages are frequently not opium-free, the desire to kick an addiction to smoking opium is no longer a major factor in conversion.[16] In Thailand, although not in war-torn Burma, the state now provides access to some of the material advantages earlier available only through missionaries, yet the rate of conversion has increased rather than decreased.

Akha Christianity does not fit the many social science models of religions in contact situations, models such as "coexistence" (Green 1978; Kopytoff 1987), a dual system in which two religions are present but do not intermingle; "compartmentalization" (Dozier 1961), a variant of coexistence in which one religion is hidden from the other; and "syncretism," in which elements from different religions mix or merge. Instead, Akha Christianity is best characterized as replacement: Jesus customs substitute for traditional customs. This replacement should not be understood as total; indeed, given the profound human ability to accommodate, a complete absence of syncretism is probably an impossibility. Nonetheless, Akha Christianity exhibits a striking lack of influence from the indigenous religion. This is not remarkable when it is remembered that the impetus toward syncretism—at least toward piecemeal rather than total syncretism—inherent in Akha traditional religion is weak to nonexistent.[17]

Classic definitions of conversion stipulate a "change of heart," a radical transformation of the soul accompanying the acceptance of a new faith (Heirich 1977). Akha conversion, not normally marked by a dramatic, internal sea change, does not entail "a turning which implies a consciousness that a great change is involved, that the old was wrong and the new is right" (Nock 1933:7). But neither can Akha adherence to Christianity be described as "adhesion," which involves having "one foot on each side of a fence," that is, lacking "any definite crossing of religious frontiers" (Nock 1933:6–7). Akha Christians definitely leave their old religion, explicitly forsaking Akha *zah*ˇ for a new religion. In most cases conversion among Akha involves, quite simply, an avowed change in religious identification and participation. Unlike Bacdayan (1970:120), I see no reason to label this change "affiliation" rather than "conversion" on the grounds that there is no evidence of a transformation of the soul. In essence, classic definitions of conversion are ethnocentric, presupposing a particular and recent correlation between religion and belief (cf. Firth 1970:320–321). What is important in this case is that Akha converts count themselves as Christians and missionaries count Akha Christians as converts.

Although converts and missionaries concur that *zah*ˇ is equivalent to "religion," they have very different conceptions of "religion." From the Akha point of view, it is basically liturgy, that is, the rituals themselves; yet from the Protestant perspective, faith is a crucial component of religion, so ritual actions, such as accepting communion or baptism, are empty forms devoid of meaning and efficacy if undertaken without a proper spiritual attitude. But belief is not a problem in the traditional Akha world; indeed, it is not relevant to *zah*ˇ. Tooker (1987), in the same vein as Needham (1972), correctly points out that Akha never say that they "believe" (*jah-eu*) in their *zah*ˇ. Thus, for an Akha Christian convert to consider communion or baptism solely as ritual action is orthodox from the perspective of traditional religion, even though it is unorthodox from the perspective of Protestantism. Foreign missionaries working among Akha express their pleasure in the growth of their flocks, but they also voice their reservations about or dissatisfaction with the kind of Christians Akha converts are. These missionaries are concerned about the spiritual state of Akha Christians. A recently updated and reissued OMF publication praises the "turnings" to Christ but observes that villagers "desperately need teaching to bring them from their rather nominal faith to a true commitment to Christ" (Kuhn 1984:148–149). In other words, missionaries are skeptical about Akha understanding of and faith in the Christian message.

This discussion is not intended to give the impression that there are no convinced Akha Christians. In fact, there are. Many Akha Christians enthusiastically participate in Bible study sessions, and some gain familiarity with and even belief in the teachings of Christ. But conversions of conviction are rare. Most Akha converts to Christianity are simply seeking a replacement *zah*ˇ that is cheaper and easier than their own.

Notes

Acknowledgments. Financial support for the research (1979–81 and 1986–88) upon which this article is based was provided by the Fulbright-Hays Doctoral Dissertation Abroad Program and by the International Doctoral Research Fellowship Program and the Postdoctoral Fellowship Program of the Social Science Research Council and the American Council of Learned Societies under grants from the Ford Foundation and the National Endowment for the Humanities. The National Research Council of Thailand twice kindly granted permission for fieldwork. As always, to my Akha friends and teachers, my abiding gratitude. Thanks also to Paul Lewis, Father Pensa, and other foreign missionaries working among Akha for answering my queries and accepting my presence at various Christian gatherings. Preliminary versions of this article were presented at colloquia at Northern Illinois University and Brandeis University. I thank members of both audiences for their helpful questions and suggestions, which inspired beneficial reworkings. Richard O'Connor's reactions to a different article aided me in formulating this one. In addition, I extend my appreciation to Donald Joralemon for a clarifying conversation; to Judith Nagata, Deborah Tooker, and Edwin Zehner for comments on a draft; and especially to F. K. Lehman for extensive written criticisms of the manuscript and to Richard J. Parmentier for suggestions on several versions. Lastly, thanks to the four anonymous *American Ethnologist* readers, whose criticisms helped to guide my final revisions.

1. Regrettably, I have not been able to locate the kind of rich archival documentation that is available for the reconstruction of mission history in many parts of Africa, Oceania, and elsewhere. I am, therefore, forced to rely mainly on published sources and on data collected during fieldwork in Thailand.

2. Factors influencing whether a convert becomes Protestant or Catholic are beyond the scope of this article. Most often, however, choice is not involved; many Akha traditionalists, and indeed some long-term Christians, are unaware that Christianity comes in kinds.

3. The orthography for Akha terms is adopted from Paul Lewis's *Akha-English dictionary* (1968).

4. Younger adults are also present at these discussions, more as listeners than contributors, and children are often within earshot. These discussions thus serve to transmit knowledge of *zahˇ* from one generation to another.

5. The rigidity of ethnicity as culturally constituted by Akha parallels discredited "ethnographic conventions" about what Leach disparagingly calls "*a* culture or *a* tribe" (1954:281; emphasis in original). Theoretical advances concerning the fluidity of ethnicity, culture, and society pioneered by Leach and developed by Lehman (for example, 1967), among others, should not blind analysts to the fact that a given cultural system can construe ethnicity in the manner of outmoded structural-functionalism. Restructured ethnographic conventions must not lead observers to restructure ethnographic reality.

6. Both these types of shifts involve Akha women rather than men. In fact, I know of fewer cases of Akhamen marrying non-Akha than I do of Akha women marrying non-Akha. Their society's patrilineal structure and system of affinity contribute to this: the loss of women is less significant than the loss of men, and the natal kin of non-Akha wives cannot meet required affinal responsibilities both because they (or related surrogates) do not reside locally and because they do not know Akha *zahˇ*.

7. Numerous students of conversion have drawn attention to the "restructuring of biography" which is part of the construction of accounts of religious conversion (Jules-Rosette 1976:164). Because such accounts are "socially constructed," drawing upon the "universe of discourse" of the new religion, Snow and Machalek (1984:173, 175–176) argue that they represent an "alignment process" to "group goals, ideology, and rituals." What is particularly interesting about Akha converts' accounts is that their universe of discourse belongs to the old religion rather than the new; the phrases used are not taken from Christian rhetoric. Of course, this does not preclude the possibility that in the future Akha conversion accounts will undergo an alignment process.

8. Following conversion, however, some new Christians adopt the negative view of their traditional religion espoused by missionaries.

9. This aspect of *zahˇ* may be at least a partial explanation for the relative absence of messianic and millenarian movements among Akha as opposed to many other highlanders, such as Lahu, Hmong, and Karen. Such movements center on a charismatic leader proclaiming individual inspiration. Direct revelation, then, replaces repetition of ancestral practices, and inspiration replaces inheritance as the basis of legitimacy. Significantly, Christianity is itself messianic and millenarian.

10. I have found no clear-cut social diacritics that distinguish conservatives from innovators. They are not, for example, differentiated by age, sex, wealth, residence, or lineage or subgroup affiliation. Although many innovators in Thailand participate in the activities of the Mountain People's Culture and Development Education/Research Programmes, founded by the anthropologist Leo Alting von Geusau, this participation signals as much as molds their attitude toward Akha customs.

11. Such Akha are a new phenomenon. Jane Hanks and Lucien Hanks (1975) encountered them in 1974 while surveying hill tribes in Thailand's northernmost province, the home of the vast majority of the nation's Akha. Had such Akha been around in 1964 or 1969 when the Hankses crisscrossed the same mountains conducting two earlier surveys, the Hankses surely would have found them.

12. Christianity's exclusivity has drawn the attention of numerous students of Christian missionization. Hamer (1985:66) notes that among the Sadama of Ethiopia "there is no indication that those who became converts had any initial knowledge of the exclusiveness of rules and values of the Christian fundamentalism" introduced by foreign missionaries. While Akha, like Sadama, may well have lacked such knowledge prior to conversion, the exclusivity of their traditional *zah*$^{\vee}$ and the equation of *zah*$^{\vee}$ with identity would lead Akha to presume that, like their own customs, Jesus customs are exclusive. That Akha traditional religion is exclusive suggests that the common assumption, made by Nock (1933:6) among others, that exclusiveness belongs solely to prophetic or world religions is incorrect.

13. From the data presented it might appear safe to assume that a two-tiered society is developing in which richer Akha are traditionalists and poorer Akha Christians. The situation is, however, not so clear-cut. Although many Akha respond to impoverishment by becoming Christian, many others do not. Moreover, some Christians, like some traditionalists, have enjoyed agricultural success or have found other means of making a decent living.

14. It is worth considering whether or not the sharp contrast between the initial reluctance of Akha to convert to Christianity and the enthusiasm evidenced by their highland neighbors is attributable to differing structural positions in Burma. Kachin, Naga, and Karen, who were willing Christians, are more numerous and more concentrated geographically than Akha. Yet the fact that Lahu, who became proselytes by the thousands, are, like Akha, a relatively small and scattered group suggests that conversion is not caused by structural positioning in the larger national society.

15. This model is prevalent in the literature on cults and other new religious movements, but the intellectualist position advanced by Peel (1968) and Horton (1971, 1975a, 1975b) can be seen as a variant in which the stress identified involves a challenge to the system of rationality: the traditional cosmology proves inadequate to explain a changed world. Although this position is presented as having general applicability, at least in Africa, it is clearly irrelevant to Akha conversion, which does not pivot on the perceived greater explanatory power of the new religion: Akha converts view Christianity as an alternative rather than a superior form of *zah*$^{\vee}$.

16. This is also a less significant factor because there are now other ways of kicking a habit. For example, the Royal Thai Government and some development projects support detoxification programs, and Akha are curing themselves using drugs available in valley pharmacies.

17. Some apparently syncretic features of Akha Christianity—for example, the division of the church into a side for women and a side for men similar to the gendered division of the traditional house—may have been motivated by missionaries rather than by Akha themselves, although historical material to corroborate this is lacking.

References

Alting von Geusau, Leo (1983). Dialectics of Akhazan: The interiorizations of a perennial minority group. In John McKinnon and Wanat Bhruksasri (Eds.), *Highlanders of Thailand* (pp. 241–277). Kuala Lumpur: Oxford University Press.

Bacdayan, Albert S. (1970). Religious conversion and social change: A northern Luzon case. *Practical Anthropology, 17*, 119–127.

Burton, John W. (1985). Christians, colonists, and conversion: A view from the Nilotic Sudan. *Journal of Modern African Studies, 23*, 349–369.

Cooper, Robert (1984). *Resource scarcity and the Hmong response.* Singapore: Singapore University Press.

Cushing, J. S. (1870). Letter (Journal of Journey to Shan Land) to Rev. Dr. Murdock. Ms., American Baptist Historical Society/American Baptist Archives Center, Valley Forge, PA.

Dozier, Edward P. (1961). Rio Grande pueblos. In Edward H. Spicer (Ed.), *Perspectives in American Indian culture change* (pp. 94–186). Chicago: University of Chicago Press.

Firth, Raymond (1970). *Rank and religion in Tikopia: A study of Polynesian paganism and conversion to Christianity.* London: George Allen and Unwin.

Green, Edwin C. (1978). *Winti* and Christianity: A study in religious change. *Ethnohistory, 25*, 251–276.

Hamer, John (1985). Practice and change: An episode of structural disjunction and conjunction among the Sadama of Ethiopia. *Anthropological Quarterly, 58,* 53–74.

Hanks, Jane R., and Hanks, Lucien M. (1975). Reflections on Ban Akha Mae Salong. *Journal of the Siam Society, 63*(1), 72–85.

Heirich, Max (1977). Change of heart: A test of some widely held theories of religious conversion. *American Journal of Sociology, 83,* 653–680.

Hickey, Gerald Cannon (1982). *Free in the forest: Ethnohistory of the Vietnamese Central Highlands, 1954–1976.* New Haven, CT: Yale University Press.

Horton, Robin (1971). African conversion. *Africa, 41,* 85–108.

Horton, Robin (1975a). On the rationality of conversion, part I. *Africa, 45,* 219–235.

Horton, Robin (1975b). On the rationality of conversion, part II. *Africa, 45,* 373–399.

Iijima, Shigeru (1979). Ethnic identity and sociocultural change among Sgaw Karen in northern Thailand. In Charles F. Keyes (Ed.), *Ethnic adaptation and identity: The Karen on the Thai frontier with Burma* (pp. 99–118). Philadelphia Institute for the Study of Human Issues.

Jules-Rosette, Bennetta (1976). The conversion experience: The apostles of John Maranke. *Journal of Religion in Africa, 7,* 132–164.

Kammerer, Cornelia Ann (1986). *Gateway to the Akha world: Kinship, ritual, and community among highlanders of Thailand.* Ph.D. dissertation. University of Chicago.

Kammerer, Cornelia Ann (1988). Territorial imperatives: Akha ethnic identity and Thailand's national integration. In Remo Guidieri, Francesco Pellizzi, & Stanley J. Tambiah (Eds.), *Ethnicities and nations: Processes of interethnic relations in Latin America, Southeast Asia, and the Pacific* (pp. 259–292). Houston: Rothko Chapel (distributed by the University of Texas Press, Austin).

Keesing, Roger M., and Tonkinson, Robert (Eds.) (1982). Reinventing traditional culture: The politics of Kastom in Island Melanesia. *Mankind, 13*(4) (Special Issue).

Keyes, Charles F. (1971). Buddhism and national integration in Thailand. *Journal of Asian Studies, 30,* 551–567.

Keyes, Charles F. (1977). *The golden peninsula: Culture and adaptation in mainland Southeast Asia.* New York: Macmillan.

Kipp, Rita Smith, & Rodgers, Susan (Eds.) (1987). *Indonesia religions in transition.* Tucson: University of Arizona Press.

Kopytoff, Barbara K. (1987). Religious change among the Jamaican Maroons: The ascendance of the Christian God within a traditional cosmology. *Journal of Social History, 20,* 463–484.

Kuhn, Isobel (1984). *Ascent to the tribes: Pioneering in North Thailand.* Singapore: OMF Books.

Kunstadter, Peter (1983). Animism, Buddhism, and Christianity: Religion in the Life of Lua People of Pa Pae, North-Western Thailand. In John McKinnon and Wanat Bhruksasri (Eds.), *Highlanders of Thailand* (pp. 135–154). Kuala Lumpur: Oxford University Press.

Leach, E. R. (1954). Political systems of highland Burma: A study of Kachin social structure. Cambridge, MA: Harvard University Press.

Lehman, F. K. (1967). Ethnic categories in Burma and the theory of social systems. In Peter Kunstadter (Ed.), *Southeast Asian tribes, minorities, and nations* (vol. 1, pp. 93–124). Princeton: Princeton University Press.

Lewis, Elaine T. (1957). The hill peoples of Kengtung State. *Practical Anthropology, 4,* 224–230.

Lewis, Paul (1968). *Akha-English Dictionary.* Data Paper No. 70. Ithaca, NY: Southeast Asia Program, Cornell University.

Lewis, Paul (1969–70). *Ethnographic notes on the Akhas of Burma* (vols. I–IV). New Haven: Human Relations Area Files, Inc.

Marshall, Harry Ignatius (1922). *The Karen people of Burma: A study in anthropology and ethnology.* Columbus: Ohio State University Press.

Maung Shwe Wa (1963). Burma Baptist chronicle, Book 1. Rangoon: Board of Publications, Burma Baptist Convention.

McCoy, Alfred W. (1972). *The politics of heroin in Southeast Asia.* New York: Harper & Row.

Needham, Rodney (1972). *Belief, language, and experience.* Chicago: University of Chicago Press.

Nightingale, Peter (1968). The Akha work. In Isobel Kuhn (Ed.), *Ascent to the tribes: Pioneering in north Thailand* (Appendix 1, pp. 263–267). London: Overseas Missionary Fellowship (agents Lutterworth Press).

Nock, A. D. (1933). *Conversion: The old and the new in religion from Alexander the Great to Augustine of Hippo.* London: Oxford University Press.

Peel, J. D. Y. (1968). Syncretism and religious change. *Comparative Studies in Society and History, 10,* 121–141.

Provencher, Ronald (1975). *Mainland Southeast Asia: An anthropological perspective.* Pacific Palisades, CA: Goodyear.

Snow, David A., & Machalek, Richard (1984). The sociology of conversion. *Annual Review of Sociology, 10,* 167–190.

Sowards, Genevieve, & Sowards, Erville (Eds.) (1963). Burma Baptist chronicle, Book II. Rangoon: Board of Publications, Burma Baptist Convention.

Stern, Theodore (1968). *Ariya* and the Golden Book: A Millenarian Buddhist Sect among the Karen. *Journal of Asian Studies, 27,* 297–328.

Tambiah, S. J. (1976). *World conqueror and world renouncer: A study of Buddhism and polity in Thailand against a historical background.* Cambridge: Cambridge University Press

Tapp, Nicholas (1989). The impact of missionary Christianity upon marginalized ethnic minorities: The case of the Hmong. *Journal of Southeast Asian Studies, 20,* 70–95.

Thrupp, Sylvia L. (1970). Millennial dreams in action: A report on the conference discussion. In Sylvia L. Thrupp (Ed.), *Millennial dreams in action: Studies in revolutionary religious movements* (pp. 11–27). New York: Schocken Books.

Tooker, Deborah E. (1987). *Skepticism and continuity in the Akha world.* Paper presented at the annual meeting of the Association for Asian Studies. Ms., files of the author.

Urbani, Arialdo (1971). Ai-la, le premier baptisé Ikho. *Feuilles missionaires, 64,* 13–14.

Wilson, May (1981). *Smoke away!* Sevenoaks, Kent: OMF Books.

Japanese Tea Ritual: Religion in Practice

JENNIFER L. ANDERSON

Introduction

Despite its centrality to Japanese cultural identity, Japanese Tea ritual or *chanoyu*[1] has been treated superficially in the ethnographic literature (Dore 1958, 1967; Vogel 1968; Hsu 1965; Lebra & Powers 1976; Plath 1980). Dorinne Kondo's article, "The way of tea: A symbolic analysis" (1985), is the only published attempt to consider *chanoyu* in light of anthropological theory.[2]

There are good reasons for the apparent neglect of this vital and widely practiced complex of rituals. A thorough understanding of *chanoyu* presupposes knowledge of a belief system as well as actual practice. As an anthropologist who practices *chado* (the 'way' of Tea) intensively, I am putting forward an analysis of Tea which reconciles a definition of religion based on salvation with the kind of orthodox exegesis standard among Tea adepts of the school with which I practice, Urasenke.

N. J. Girardot has succinctly stated what I consider to be the goal of all religious behavior, including tea ritual. He maintains that the aim of such activity is "periodically recovering in this lifetime a condition of original wholeness, health or holiness" (1983:7). The Urasenke grandmaster Sen Soshitsu XV similarly states the purpose of ritual tea preparation—"to realize tranquillity of mind in communion with one's fellow men within our world" (Sen 1979:9).

While theoretical assertions such as these are easily expressed, the supporting ethnographic data are more elusive. Anyone living in or near a Japanese community may observe the formal preparation of tea but the symbolic language which conveys its meaning cannot be fully interpreted out of the context of disciplined practice and conscientious study. Tea is not meant to be easily understood. *Chado* means the "way" or "road" of Tea.[3] Surmounting obstacles is perceived by its practitioners as an inevitable and desirable aspect of the endeavor. Recognizing that undertaking the journey is not separable from arriving at one's ultimate destination is an inherent aspect of this analogy.

In this context, let me briefly discuss some of the problems of the participant observer as they relate to my own experience with *chado.* Unfortunately, the critical difference between the viewpoint of the "native" observer and that of the trained ritual practitioner (who may not be a "native") blurs when subsumed under the anthropological category of emic interpretation. Specifically, most Japanese do not grow up in an environment where they are socialized to the subtle symbolic language of Tea. In fact, while tea ritual is a cherished symbol of national identity, Japanese who have not formally studied *chado* often feel uncomfortable in the tearoom, as they are not familiar with its specialized etiquette or attuned to the symbolic exchanges which give the experience its true meaning.

Tea ritual is learned behavior. True, no one enters the tearoom empty-handed. All students and observers of Tea begin with culture-specific preconceptions about what they are seeing and doing. But, having studied with both native and non-Japanese, I observed that there was little difference in the amount of time and energy Tea instructors exerted attempting to rid both types of students of inappropriate assumptions related to Tea practice. The ideal student is born into the world of Tea with only a willingness to learn and unquestioning respect for the authority of the teacher.

It has been my experience that, rhetoric to the contrary, students from all cultural backgrounds find submitting to the discipline inherent in Japanese schools of instruction in the traditional arts (*iemoto*) the most difficult part of *chado.* An aspiring practitioner must be prepared to accept the fact that attitudes and goals as well as ritual form are dictated by historic tradition. By custom, all three are authoritatively interpreted only by the grandmaster of one's school (*oiemoto*) and communicated almost exclusively through one's teacher (on *iemoto,* see further, Ortolani 1969).

As an initiate of the intermediate level (those of the "secret" or orally transmitted tea procedures), I accepted an obligation to adhere to orthodox interpretations of meaning in Tea. Like any other student, I entered into a social contract with the grandmaster of my tea school, my teacher, and my fellow students. They put considerable time and effort into sharing *chado* with me and I agreed to respect the tradition and eventually pass it on intact.

I am fully aware that accepting this responsibility as primary will raise questions about my objectivity among my fellow professionals. In response, I should point out, first, that I see no logic in jeopardizing my relationship with informants by expounding on any behavior which might be perceived as deviant when the norm has yet to be established in the professional literature. The Way of Tea is a highly developed and carefully preserved cultural system which has not been comprehensively described in English. In this article, I briefly discuss only one of *chado*'s major aspects, its religious character. The social element, the aspect of formal etiquette and the aesthetic factors must regretfully remain unexplored for lack of space (see Anderson 1985 for an expanded discussion). Thus, while I am fully aware that the behavior of tea people is sometimes at odds with the values they express, with so much groundwork uncompleted I feel no intellectual imperative to discuss "flaws" in the system at this time.

Secondly, I represent my work only as that of an anthropologist who is learning ritual in a uniquely circumscribed and highly structured environment (that of the tearoom). Because I have been functioning under these particular circumstances for many years and have cross-checked my information with other practitioners and the written literature, I feel confident that my training differs little from, that of native participants and that it is comprehensive (for my level of expertise). I know that most fieldwork is not conducted under such controlled conditions and do not claim my experience is typical or exemplary in any way.

Finally, I make no claim either to etic super-objectivity or emic hypersensitivity. My approach to ethnography is best described by Robert Feleppa's (1986) linguistically based research model rather than that of an emic-etic continuum (cf. Boas 1943; Frake 1962; Goodenough 1970; Harris 1976). Feleppa views ethnography as a work of translation, pointing out that "Translation does not *reflect* preexisting structure, it *creates* a structure" (1986:250, the emphasis is Feleppa's). He goes on to explain that while linked to the cognitive framework of both the observer and the subject, the translation itself must be viewed as an independent framework for description rather than a distortion of another reality.

As regards this research, I can only say that as a responsible translator, I have tried to create a model which is scrupulously faithful to the vocabulary and grammar of Tea as it is experienced by my teachers and fellow students. My work can be labeled emically oriented only to the extent that Tea practitioners recognize it as descriptively accurate. I reject a predominantly "etic" approach because I have found the explanations of meaning presented symbolically in the tearoom and in the Tea literature fully adequate and reconcilable with anthropological theory. Kondo's (1985:20) conviction that culturally constructed meaning alone cannot account for tea ritual's symbolic power is not supported by my research.

My experience has been that Tea practitioners are in command of their own symbolic language. They know what they want to communicate and how to do it. They clearly recognize their own ritual goals and effectively communicate them to their fellow adepts—be they Japanese or not. Thus, while every practitioner may not be aware of all aspects of *chado*'s complex explanatory model, the depth and sophistication of the literature on Tea philosophy is such that anthropological theory must be regarded as a necessary gloss rather than a prerequisite for discussions of the meaning of Tea.

Chado and Definitions of Religion and Ritual

The Japanese tradition of ritual tea preparation has been recognized as a very special kind of social event ever since Alessandro Valignano (A.D. 1539–1609) recommended the practice to his fellow Jesuit missionaries in the late sixteenth century (Cooper 1970). Since then westerners have struggled to place it in theoretical contexts which will clarify its meaning.

Making tea according to the principles of *chado* (the "way" of Tea) may be defined as a ritual act in anthropological terms because something is being said "in a formal way, not to be said in ordinary language or informal behavior" (Firth 1973:176). Such ritual also functions, as Nancy Munn suggests, as "a symbolic intercom between the level of cultural thought and complex cultural meanings on one hand, and that of social action and immediate event on the other" (1973:579). Specifically, practitioners of *chanoyu* use the act of preparing tea as a link between daily life and some of the most sophisticated social and philosophical concepts in the oriental tradition.

Sen Soshitsu XV, grandmaster (*iemoto*) of the Urasenke school definitively states the emic interpretation of *chado:* "Tea is the practice or realization of religious faith, no matter what you believe in" (1978). As the grandmaster, Sen Soshitsu XV is the ultimate living authority on Tea belief and practice for the members of his school. Accepting his primacy in matters which relate to *chado* is an inherent aspect of tea school membership. But, setting aside for the moment the grandmaster's role as spiritual leader and spokesman, let us examine his tantalizing statement as it relates to anthropological theory.

The grandmaster suggests that *chado* has something in common with all religious behavior which is not strictly dependent on doctrinal content. If this is the case, identifying the essential religious characteristics of Tea within its broad spectrum of ritual action and relating these traits to various definitions of religion should constitute an interesting line of inquiry.

Let us begin with Clifford Geertz's thought-provoking suggestions. He defines religion as:

> *(1) a system of symbols which acts to (2) establish powerful, pervasive, and long-lasting moods and motivations in men by (3) formulating conceptions of a general order of existence and (4) clothing these conceptions with such an aura of factuality that (5) the moods and motivations seem uniquely realistic. (1973:90)*

Geertz's emphasis is on the way symbols function to create a cognitive environment which allows men to order their perception of reality in a way which relieves anxiety associated with the suspicion "that life is absurd and the attempt to make moral, intellectual, or emotional sense out of experience is bootless" (Geertz 1973:108). By acting out an ideal or postulated relationship based on universal principles of order, ritual participants briefly experience conflict resolution in a way that makes ultimate satisfaction seem possible; human effort, therefore, appears reasonable. This appears to be what happens at a tea gathering, as will be discussed.

A major criticism of Geertz's definition has been that it does not include elements which allow the analyst to distinguish religious from other behavior (Guthrie 1980:183).[4] The factor which seems to be missing from the definition itself—one which would allow religious thought to be distinguished from political ideology—is a development of the process of "formulating a general order of existence" (1973:90). It needs to be made clear that this order includes a cosmological aspect. The believer must be convinced that resolution of man's angst is bound up in his relationship to the Ultimate.

In *Myth and meaning in early Taoism,* N. J. Girardot addresses this problem by suggesting that religion is "a system of symbolic thought and action that is 'focused on salvation' and is interpretively grounded in mythical or cosmological 'formulations of a general order of existence'" (1983:6). Girardot acknowledges his debt to Geertz and drawing further inspiration from the work of Patrick Burke (1979:17–18) he also asserts that religion is "a cultural system of symbols . . . concerned with a means of transforming, temporally or permanently, some 'significant ill' that seems to be part of the cosmological or existential order of human life."

Girardot's approach to the definition of religion is particularly appropriate to this research as he arrived at it in the course of trying to show that the texts of early Taoism, a precursor of Tea philosophy, are "properly 'religious in nature.' " Thus he considers salvation not in the Western sense of being something predominantly concerned with conquering death but in the Eastern sense of "periodically recovering in this lifetime a condition of original wholeness, health or holiness" (1983:7).

With this concept of salvation, Girardot offers the key to the meaning of Tea as well as a potential solution to the problem of religion in anthropological hermeneutics. It accounts for Tea's ability to syncretize diverse philosophical traditions and its internal consistency, and relates well to emic explanations of religious motive. Let us briefly examine the way Tea ritual has developed and the manner in which it is practiced to understand better the effective way *chanoyu* functions to satisfy practitioners that they have discovered a way of "recovering in this lifetime a condition of original wholeness, health, or holiness."

The Origins of Tea Philosophy

To understand the syncretic nature of its religious symbolism and values, the analyst must examine Tea in its historical context. Since the development of *chanoyu* is uniquely well-documented, this also provides a special opportunity to note the importance of individual contributions to the creation of collective ritual.

The use of tea is first mentioned in the Chinese *Book of Songs* (circa fourth century B.C.). Foreshadowing a developing relationship with Taoist practice, the sage Lao Tze is offered a drink by a disciple which is believed to have been tea.[5] The beverage's next major historical association is with the Indian Buddhist missionary Bodhidharma (Williams 1974:388). It is said that he carried tea to China in A.D. 526 as a medicine and aid to meditation.

By the middle of the Tang period (A.D. 618–906), tea drinking was widespread in southern China both among members of religious communities and the secular elite. During this period, the Zen Master Pai Chang (A.D. 720–814) wrote a code governing the communal preparation and consumption of tea in temples (*charei*) (Hayashiya 1971:53). Subsequently, Lu Yu (d. A.D. 804) an eccentric poet (later to be revered as the god of Tea by the Chinese) produced his influential *Classic of Tea.*

Lu Yu is particularly interesting in the context of religious syncretism in *chanoyu* because his adoptive father was the Abbot of the Dragon Cloud Monastery of Ch'an Buddhism, a sect heavily influenced by Taoism and the precursor of Zen thought in Japan (Blofeld 1985:5). The poet's tea treatise includes constant references to the principles of *yin* and *yang,* the trigrams of the *I Ching* and the Taoist five elements of wood, fire, metal, earth and water (Lu Yu 1974). Attempts to integrate these elements physically and symbolically also characterized contemporary Taoist alchemy directed towards the production of an elixir of immortality. Interestingly enough, the suggested formula sometimes included tea as one of its principal ingredients (Young 1970:29). Lu Yu's preoccupation with the proper directional disposition of fire and water in relationship to utensils of wood, metal, and clay remains significant for tea ritual.

Historians are divided as to the identity of the individual who first brought tea to Japan but it is generally agreed that it was either Saicho in A.D. 805 or Eichuin A.D. 815 (Hayashiya 1970:40). Both were Japanese Buddhist priests who had probably encountered tea in Chinese monasteries. In any case, it is clearly recorded in the *Nippon Koko* (a work preserved in the Imperial Repository at Nara) that Eichu presented tea to the Japanese Emperor Saga on the shores of Laka Biwa in A.D. 815.

From that time on, tea ritual experienced cyclical periods of popularity among both the religious and lay communities of Japan. During the early Kamakura period (A.D. 1185–1249), for example, elaborate tea tasting contests (*cha awase*) were a favorite pastime of the aristocracy. Prizes were lavish and the atmosphere ornate. Chinese tea utensils and etiquette dominated. In conjunction with these activities and those of the temples, the tea commentaries of Pai Chang, Lu Yu, and Eisai (A.D. 1141–1215, the priest who introduced Zen to Japan) were circulated and discussed.

The contrast between the materialistic emphasis of court tea ritual and Buddhist asceticism prompted Dogen (A.D. 1200–1253), the founder of Soto Zen, to issue strict regulations governing the preparation of tea in the temples he administered (Hayashiya 1971:53). As time went on members of the ruling elite also began to sense a need for a less sybaritic approach to tea ritual.

The stylistic innovations of Murata Shuko (A.D. 1421?–1502, a priest acquainted with both temple and court tea etiquette) were critical in better integrating tea with Japanese culture and restoring lay interest in its religious character. Shuko advocated a simple, Zen-influenced approach to all tea practice and is considered the founder of today's *wabi* style.[6] It is said that Shuko was the first to hang calligraphy in the decorative alcove of the tearoom (*tokonoma*), to prepare tea in a four and one-half mat room (*yojohan*), to use the native Japanese hearth cut in the floor (*ro*), and to employ Japanese utensils.

Not much later, the powerful *samurai* (warrior) leaders of Japan found both a passion and a useful tool in Tea ritual. They discovered that they could use it to enhance their own status and as a mode of controlling their followers. The Shogun (a kind of military dictator) Oda Nobunaga (A.D. 1534–1582) rewarded loyal followers with fine utensils and restricted the practice of *chanoyu* to those who had his permission. Sen Rikyu (A.D. 1521–1591), member of the newly influential merchant class, became Nobunaga's tea master and upon the warlord's assassination, that of his successor, Toyotomi Hideyoshi (1536–1598).

Rikyu was respected in his day as an enlightened adept of Zen and the finest tea master of all time. Because of the extraordinary range of services he performed for Hideyoshi, he also became nationally known as a political figure (Bodart 1977). In the end, however, Rikyu's efforts as teacher, mediator, messenger, and confidant served him ill. The aging and paranoid Shogun compelled his tea master to commit ritual suicide (*seppuku*) at the age of seventy to atone for an offense never clearly identified (for some discussion of the evidence, see Bodart 1977).

Because of his unwavering courage, high ideals, and dedication to Tea, Sen Rikyu is revered almost as a saint by practitioners of the many tea schools which trace their history to his inspiration. After his death, Rikyu's influence on Tea lived on in his students. For a time his egalitarian philosophy was subverted by Hideyoshi's desire to promote a ritual which emphasized the rank of the *samurai.* Ultimately, however, it was Rikyu's way of Tea, not the Shogun's, which triumphed.

Rikyu's greatest legacy is held to be the emphasis he placed on religious values. Hundreds of anecdotes are handed down which exemplify his sensitivity to artistic and symbolic nuance. Each stresses in some way his conviction that the simple act of preparing a bowl of tea can become a positive step towards achieving enlightenment.

*The Ritual Complex of the "Way" of Tea (*Chado*)*

Though banished from Kyoto at the time of Rikyu's death, his heirs eventually returned and reestablished themselves as prominent tea masters. Rikyu's grandson Sotan divided the family property in Kyoto into three parts in his old age and gave one to each of his sons. They established three schools of Tea, Omotesenke, Urasenke, and Mushanokojisenke. All three continue to practice Tea in Rikyu's spirit but diverge slightly in practice and philosophy.

Today's tea practice consists of a variety of rituals which differ somewhat in form and intent. The most solemn and infrequently performed gatherings are those which are intended as intercessional rituals. The term *okencha* is used for events which involve offering tea to gods (or God) in Shinto shrines or Christian churches. *Okucha* is the name applied to tea ritual performed at Buddhist temples or memorials for the dead. Both involve very advanced techniques of tea preparation, follow forms believed to be Chinese, and are usually conducted by high ranking tea people such as the grandmaster (*oiemoto*). Taoist symbolism and Chinese-style utensils are prominent in these rites. Students practice these procedures at the advanced level but seldom perform them in public. As rituals created to intercede with spiritual beings, *okucha* and *okencha* are members of the class of rituals readily recognized as religious by most analysts.

Although not intended for intercession with spiritual beings and held in private rather than public settings, a more often observed class of tea events, the *chaji*, is as religiously effective as *okencha* or *okucha.* In its most standard form a *chaji* is a gathering of a relatively small number of people (ideally three to five guests) which is conducted over a period of about four hours. It frequently (but not always) includes greetings, a meal, two charcoal preparations, and the presentation of both thick (*koicha*) and thin (*usucha*) tea.

There are seven main types of *chaji* incorporating most of the elements mentioned above in different sequential orders.[7] Variation at these gatherings is mainly based on consideration for the comfort and convenience of the guests. *Chaji* diversify further by seasonal theme and through the specific tea and charcoal procedures (*temae*) performed. The *chaji* is a form of ritual which developed out of the concern for Tea as a vehicle for enlightenment. A Shinto awareness of the integration of natural and social spheres is also highly apparent. Paradoxically, the symbolism which puts a *chaji* in the class of religious events is so subtle that outside observers often mistake this ritual for a secular activity.

In addition to intercessional ritual and the *chaji,* there is yet another class of tea ritual to be considered—the *chakai. Chakai* are usually conducted when the group of guests is larger than can be served at a *chaji.* They tend to be shorter in duration than *chaji.* Frequently only thin tea and sweets are served. The emotional power and intimacy of a *chaji* are difficult to develop at a *chakai*—particularly when the guests are numerous and not well acquainted. Though they are supposed to be approached with the same seriousness of purpose and include much of the same symbolism as the other tea events (*okencha, okucha,* and *chaji*), *chakai* tend to be the most secular of tea rituals. Concern with issues of relative status, group membership, and material display is more likely to be evident at *chakai* than other classes of tea gatherings. *Chakai* are probably the most frequently conducted and publicly visible class of tea rituals.

Since the intercessional practices (*okucha* and *okencha*) include a deistic element which qualifies them as religious ritual even in the most conventional sense and *chakai* are ideally abbreviated *chaji*, I will analyze only the *chaji* in detail. The choice of illustration is further narrowed to the noon *chaji* because it is considered the "standard" *chaji*. Structurally, it includes all the basic units of action necessary to a full tea gathering. For this reason, it has become the central point of reference used by Tea teachers explaining potential variability among *chaji*. This type of ritual also takes place frequently, is appropriate to any time of year and is considered the cautious alternative for the relatively inexperienced host.[8]

The Symbolic Analysis of an Individual Tea Ritual

Planning a *chaji* usually starts many months in advance of the proposed date. The host (*teishu*) first decides on the main guest (*shokyaku*), preferably one experienced in Tea. Familiarity with the ritual is a prerequisite for establishing the kind of delicate verbal and nonverbal intercourse which keeps the event moving smoothly. If the first guest is inexperienced, a second guest who can assist him will be chosen. By selecting guests who understand their roles and will interact smoothly, the host takes the first step towards developing within the tearoom at least the illusion of an ideal social environment.

Once the guests have been agreed upon and it has been orally determined that the proposed date is convenient, formal invitations and acceptances are exchanged. The host also begins to think of the theme of the event, how to express it through the specific procedures (*temae*) chosen and the nature of the symbolism to be included. The date selected narrows the options because many tea procedures and symbols are connected with particular events in Japanese history and on Buddhist and Shinto ritual calendars.

Foods, flowers, artistic motifs on utensils, the message on the hanging scroll, even the choice of procedures are suggested by the season. Thus, a semiformal (*gyo*) procedure using gorgeous utensils reflects the cheerful elegance of the lunar New Year,[9] while the subtle regret felt at the end of the Tea year in October is usually expressed by conducting informal (*so*) procedures with *wabi* implements. In selecting the symbolic motifs to be employed at his *chaji*, the host makes a series of delicate discriminations ritually locating the gathering within geographic, religious and ethnic boundaries as well as establishing cyclical and historic time coordinates.[10]

In the days immediately prior to the *chaji*, the host does many practical tasks which also have symbolic significance. Some relate to shopping and preparing seasonal food items, arranging the ash in the brazier or hearth and removing utensils from storage.[11] Most have to do with purification. For as the host cleans the waiting areas, the garden, the tearoom, preparation area, and even the privies (traditionally there is one for use and one for inspection), he quietly orders his mind. Sweeping the tearoom and the garden path are explicitly recognized as attempts to "clear the dust of the world" (Sen 1979:14).

The day of the *chaji,* the conscientious host's activity starts before dawn when he draws the water to be used at the gathering.[12] The house is bustling with cooking and other last-minute preparations, but when the guests arrive they experience an illusion of tranquillity and find the gate in the wall which surrounds the host's family compound slightly ajar as a sign of welcome. The path to the house has been sprinkled with water in a Shinto gesture of purification which also imparts a sense of coolness and indicates the host is prepared for the guests' arrival. Usually a family member or the host's assistant will indicate a room (*yoritsuki*) for changing from street garb to *kimono.*[13]

From the *yoritsuki,* the newly arrived guests proceed to another room (*machiai*) to wait for their companions. This room serves a transitional function. It is the first in a series of physical spaces which mediate between everyday life and the ritual event. Aesthetically, a Japanese-style room is preferred but, as its structure has no symbolic importance, this is not a ritual requirement.[14] Frequently the Japanese-style parlor (*zashiki*) of the host's family is used.

The decorations of the transitional room (*machiai*) should suggest the theme of the gathering. If the room contains an alcove for hanging the scroll (*tokonoma*), for example, it may be decorated with a subtle painting or an aesthetic object (such as a musical instrument). Also present might be aids to relaxation such as a traditional Japanese smoking set (*tabako bon*), and, perhaps, some heavy felt mats to soften the *tatami* mats. When all are assembled, the host's assistant (*hanto*) or the last guest serves a light beverage. For a *shogo chaji,* either plain hot water (*osayu*) or water lightly flavored with something like salted cherry blossom or seaweed is served.[15]

Finished with their beverages, the guests then walk through the *roji* ("dewy path" or "dewy ground") to the waiting arbor (*koshikake machiai*). Rikyu selected the word *roji* from the Lotus Sutra and applied it to this path to the tearoom. It is an unequivocally soteriological reference to a area where noblemen's children fled to escape a distressing life (Nakane 1970:44): "Escaping from the fire-stricken habitations of the Three Phenomenal Worlds [Desire, Form, and Formlessness] they take their seats on dewy ground" (from the Lotus Sutra quoted in Sadler 1962:19).

Generally speaking, the inner *roji* is less direct than the outer—indicative of the increased difficulty encountered in the final stages of following the path to enlightenment. And the inner *roji* tends to look less showy or contrived because worldly concerns are already supposed to have been left behind. It is often compared to a natural mountain path. Its other characteristics are dictated by physical necessity and express the way the individual host has chosen to deal with the physical circumstances in which he prepares tea.[16]

After a quiet stroll through the garden, led by the main guest, the guests quietly await the host's invitation to enter the inner *roji.* They sit in the *koshikake machiai* which is usually either a covered waiting bench or a section of the veranda which normally surrounds a Japanese-style house. It often appears to be half of a small house and symbolically it is a mediator halfway between an ordinary house and the teahouse.[17] A smoking set and cushions indicate that the guests may relax. A palm leaf broom frequently hangs on the structure as another reminder to "sweep away the dust of the world." If included in the tea garden, the ornamental privy (*setchin*) is located somewhere nearby.

The guests sit in rank order to facilitate their orderly entrance into the tearoom. The main guest may go first and have a higher stone on which to rest his feet (indicative of his honored status) but he still humbly distributes the straw cushions for the other guests. This manifests a Confucian respect for ranked social order mediated by Rikyu's insistence on egalitarianism in *chado*.

Soon the host leaves the tearoom through the small door the guests will soon enter.[18] He goes to a low stone basin (*tsukubai*) in the inner *roji* and crouches, purifying his hands and mouth with water scooped up in a wooden ladle.[19] The remaining water in the basin is scattered around the area. This part of the ritual sequence is almost identical to behavior practiced at Shinto shrines. Finally, the host pours fresh water into the basin from a wooden bucket which he has brought with him. He then goes to the middle gate (*chumon*) to greet his guests. All bow but no words are exchanged.

The host returns to the tearoom and after a brief interval, the guests proceed to the basin where they will also purify themselves. In the course of their journey, they also inspect a symbolic waste pit (*chiriana*) where a few leaves and branches have been discarded. Once again they are wordlessly admonished to leave the dust of the world behind them. Heart-sized stones bound with black twine (*sekimori ishi*) have been placed on paths which do not lead to the tearoom by the host. These indicate his desire to help the guest follow the most direct spiritual path.

The door to the tearoom itself (*nigiriguchi*) is so low and small that a guest can enter only in an awkward crouched position. This arrangement was suggested to Rikyu when he saw fishermen entering their boats through small hatches. Previously, *samurai* warriors had swaggered into the tearoom upright and armed.[20] The crawling-in entrance *nigiriguchi* physically compels humility. The discomfort experienced entering the tearoom also symbolizes rebirth.

The exterior of a *wabi* tea house (*soan*) is supposed to give a humble impression like that of a charcoal burner's hut. As Rikyu said "If one can live in a house whose roof does not leak and can eat enough not to starve, that is sufficient. This is the teaching of Buddha and the spirit of *chanoyu*" (Rikyu, in Ito 1976:9). The size of tearooms themselves (*chashitsu*) vary from tiny one and three-quarters mat areas to large areas (*shoin*) of sixteen mats or more.[21]

Zen tea masters such as Shuko and Rikyu considered a four and one-half mat room (*yojohan*) ideal. The dimensions of this kind of tearoom are frequently identified with those of the dwelling of Vimlakirti, a Buddhist saint who supposedly preached to eighty-four thousand disciples in his ten foot square room. Okakura Kakuzo identifies this as "an allegory based on the theory of non-existence of space to the truly enlightened" (Okakura 1956:60).

Considering the Chinese origin of tea ritual and the fascination with directional divination rampant during the early years of *chado* in Japan, it is not surprising to discover that this ideal room (the *yojohan*) also served as a model of the Taoist cosmos. As indicated in Figure 2.1, a four and one-half mat room can be divided into nine equal segments. Each of the eight peripheral segments is then assigned one of the trigrams originally suggested by Chinese tortoise shell divination. The middle square is the abode of the Tao. Each of the eight trigrams is further associated with a direction, an attribute such as wind, water, fire, etc. and a virtue such as strength, pleasure, etc. (Williams 1974:149).

The relationship between the virtues associated with the eight peripheral segments of the *yojohan* and the tea activities that take place on them is suggestive. Guests enter from the direction associated with flexibility or penetration. The main guest sits on the mat segment

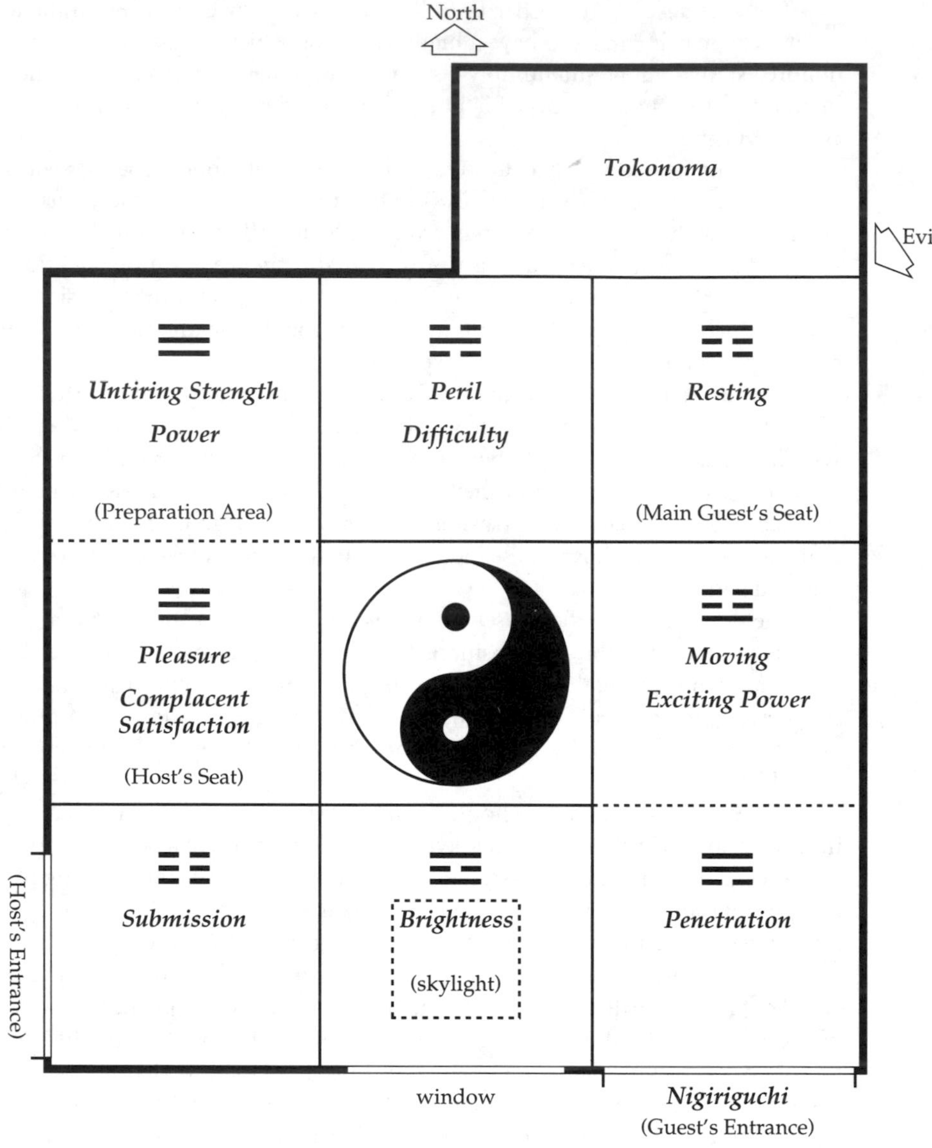

FIGURE 2.1

linked with resting. The host makes his entrance from the direction of submission and sits on the segment related to pleasure. Tea is prepared in the area of the room connected with strength and power and the completed bowl of tea is placed on the middle half mat assigned to the Tao. The segment of peril or difficulty is normally left unused.[22]

Possibly influenced by this system, the one surviving *yojohan* in Rikyu's style (Yuin), has both a window and a skylight (*tsukiage mado*) near the mat segment devoted to brightness.

Significantly there is no opening in the northeast corner, traditionally considered the source of malevolence by the Japanese (on Japanese geomancy see Beardsley et al. 1959:78). It appears most likely that the spatial elements of the Taoist cosmic model are preserved in tea architecture.

The Confucian element of the model is revealed as participants enter the tearoom in rank order and examine the objects displayed there. The guests first individually view the scroll hanging in the alcove. The scroll is the highest ranking object in the tearoom and sets the emotional tone for the gathering. The preferred hanging (*kakemono*) is one written by a Zen priest of great virtue. Its calligraphic style and binding contribute to the feeling it conveys. The words themselves are usually of a didactic or inspirational character. Examples might be: "The direct mind is the training ground"; "Harmony, respect, purity, and tranquillity"; or "One moment, one chance."

After bowing respectfully in front of the alcove, the guests (still in rank order) also examine the assembled tea utensils. Here the material element of the Taoist cosmos is symbolically represented. Most traditionally, the brazier (*furo*) is made of clay. The element of water is present in the water jar (*mizusashi*) and the hidden trigram for water written under the ash in the brazier. The kettle itself is made of metal and is supported by an iron tripod called a *gotoku* (five virtues). Wood and fire are represented by burning charcoal.[23]

After viewing the tea utensils, the guests then return to the places on the *tatami* mat traditionally assigned to them by their relative rank. Once they are seated, the host opens the door between the tearoom and the preparation area and, with the permission of the main guest, enters. Once inside the tearoom he greets the guests and announces (in the case of a summer *shogo chaji*) that he will serve a light meal. Exiting, he closes the host's door (*sadoguchi*) behind him.

The meal the host serves during the next segment of the ritual is called *kaiseki*. It means "breast stones." The term was adopted for use with the tea ceremony meal by Zen tea masters who had noted the common temple practice of placing hot stones next to the belly to warm the stomach and fend off hunger during long hours of meditation. Inspired by the spartan regime of temple life, Rikyu suggested the meal consist of "one soup, three dishes" (*ichiju san sai*). Today, it has become a culinary art form but the ideal of barest sufficiency remains.

This meal is yet another complex vehicle for symbolism. The food is served on a tray with lidded bowls similar to those used in Buddhist monasteries. The care taken in preparation has religious implications because of the Zen belief that enlightenment can be achieved in the performance of even the simplest tasks—such as washing rice. Temple and *kaiseki* cuisine also share the premise that nothing should be wasted. Even the browned rice which is stuck to the bottom of the pot is served.

The Shinto feeling for oneness with nature and a profound respect for the products of land and sea are evident in the careful treatment and aesthetic arrangement of the food. This is most succinctly expressed in a course called *hassun*. The *hassun* is a square, unlacquered cedar tray like those used to present offerings at the Hachiman Shrine. It contains small samples of food from both the mountains and the sea. Rice wine (*sake*) accompanies this course and the host participates in an exchange of cups with each guest. (This bit of ritual within ritual resembles the Shinto *naorai* rituals, on which see Ishikawa 1984:11.) *Sake* is considered the essence of rice, the food of the gods and spirits (*kami*).

The *kaiseki* meal contributes to the "aura of factuality" (Geertz 1973:90) necessary in effective ritual by appealing to senses of taste, sight, smell, and texture. The meal also conveys the message that a small quantity of inexpensive and simply prepared food can fulfill every aesthetic requirement if both preparer and diner take time to appreciate their true nature. Sharing food and *sake* also, of course, promotes good feeling among the guests. And, when the host exchanges *sake* cups with the guests, he too participates in the camaraderie.

The meal is followed (at a brazier [*furo*] season *shogo chaji*) by the first charcoal ceremony (*shozumi*). This is essentially a practical procedure during which the fire is built to boil water for tea. Sandalwood incense is also burned at that time.[24] It is sometimes called "the scent of Buddha's paradise" and it "materializes the atmosphere of a world separated from mundane reality" (Sanjonishi 1977:32). The ephemeral quality of the season is reflected in the shape and decoration of the utensils, particularly the incense container (*kogo*).

After admiring the incense container and appreciating the beauty of the carefully arranged ash and charcoal, the guests return to their places. There they are served a special kind of sweet by the host—*omogashi* (main sweets). These also reflect seasonal themes, although in an abstract manner. A pink and green sweet, for example, might be named "Dew on bush clover" but bear little resemblance to the actual phenomenon.

After eating the sweets, the guests once more pay their respects to the scroll and retire to the transitional area (*konshikake machiai*) to stretch their legs and relax (*nakadachi* or middle break). While they are out, the host cleans and airs the tearoom, arranges flowers to replace the scroll and prepares the room for making thick tea (*koicha*). He also dampens the inner *roji* area again. When everything is fresh and clean, the guests are summoned to the room from the waiting arbor by a gong. They kneel respectfully in the attitude of monks being summoned to prayer until the last sound dies away. They will purify themselves again at the stone basin before reentering the room.

As they did when they first entered, the guests inspect the alcove, this time noting the host's efforts to convey the essence of the natural world through a few thoughtfully placed flowers. They also examine the utensils which have been placed on the preparation mat in readiness for the next procedures and observe the changes which have taken place in the fire.

Koicha, the segment of the ritual which follows, is the most solemn and spiritually intimate part of the *chaji.* Yet, in structure it differs very little from the most basic tea-making procedures. The utensils are purified, tea is scooped, water is added and tea is kneaded (rather than whipped as with thin tea). One cup of tea is shared by the assembled guests, the bowl is returned to the host, and the utensils are cleaned. The major differences between thick (*koicha*) and thin (*usucha*) tea making are the way the silk wiping cloth is examined before use,[25] the concentrated nature of the tea,[26] and the manner in which it is shared.

The high point of the entire ritual takes place as the main guest tastes his initial sip of *koicha* tea. If host and guest are to experience a deep sense of shared tranquillity, it will be now. Ideally, the guest feels deep gratitude for everything that has gone into creating the wonderful experience epitomized by the first sip of tea. And the host senses that he has successfully communicated something deeply important to someone who understands the meaning of his effort. For one moment, both have the opportunity to experience an unfathomable sense of "wholeness, health, and holiness" (cf. Girardot 1983:7). *Chado* exists to make this moment plausible. Symbols which link host and guest to their forebears, to society, to various philosophies, to the phenomenal world, and ultimately to the cosmos are concentrated in this one cup of tea.

After the other guests have shared the remaining *koicha,* the bowl is examined and returned to the host for cleaning. Everyone bows in appreciation for the moment. Then, while the host is cleaning the utensils, the main guest asks about the history of the bowl. Later, he also requests another look at the tea container, its bag, and the tea scoop. The host prepares the items the guests have asked to see and clears the room of various other utensils. When he returns, he answers questions about the origins of the utensils the guests have just inspected. Particularly critical is the name of the tea scoop since this is usually a major symbol of the host's theme. For *koicha,* it is customary to use a tea scoop with a name which has religious connotations.

After the thick tea portion of the *chaji,* the emotional tone of the gathering becomes lighter. The host reenters the room with his charcoal basket and utensils. The second charcoal ceremony (*gozumi*) is quite similar to the first. It is a practical procedure designed to rebuild the dying fire and add incense to it.

Now comes the ritual of thin tea (*usucha*), the most wordly portion of the *chaji.* The host brings in a smoking set as an indication that guests may relax and offers some dry sweets (*higashi*). These are frequently accurate representations of seasonal indicators. They may imitate flowers, butterflies, autumn leaves, mushrooms, etc. Conversation is lighter and shared more freely among the guests. The host prepares a bowl of thin tea for each guest. They are quite free to ask for a second, if they wish. The *usucha* segment of a *chaji* is analogous to the "Downward Training" portion of Zen discipline. It is a tension reducing mechanism which mediates between the ideally enlightened condition in which *koicha* is consumed and everyday life.

After viewing the utensils used for *usucha,*[27] the guests thank the host for his kindness. As they leave the room, they take one last look at the flowers in the alcove and at the glowing embers in the brazier. Standing in the inner *roji,* the guests turn to make one bow to the host. He has reopened the low entrance and bows to see them off. The host watches the guests until they are out of sight.

The Religious Character of Tea Ritual

Observers of *chaji* who note the relatively formal demeanor of participants and the archaism of the tea-making procedure usually identify this behavior as "ritual." However, in the absence of readily identifiable iconography, vestments, liturgy, or sacred objects, they seldom realize that they have witnessed a religious activity. Only knowledge of the manner in which *chado*'s symbolic language contributes to achieving a religious goal reveals a tea gathering as something other than an elaborate manifestation of hospitality.

The interpretive shortcomings of the casual observation suggest the quandary of behavioral theorists. Ever since Tylor laid the foundation for debate of the subject in 1873 by maintaining that "a minimum definition of religion must include a belief in Spiritual Beings" (Tylor 1965:11), analysts have struggled to identify religious ritual's defining characteristics.

Durkheim, for example, stressed the dichotomy of the sacred and the profane in attempting to classify various types of ritual. He insisted that acts which pertained to religion were sacred and public while magical acts were profane and privately conducted (Durkheim

1965:58). Malinowski and Talcott Parsons varied the argument by dividing religious from magical ritual on the basis of the specificity of their avowed goals—magical behavior having the most definite ends (Goody 1961:148).

Van Gennep broadened the discussion by reminding theorists that ritual was not confined to the magico-religious sphere but also included the political and social aspects of life (Gluckman 1962:4). Nadel's response was a definition of ritual which focused on its repeated character but continued to distinguish religious from secular acts on the basis of "a particular manner of relating means to ends which we know to be inadequate by empirical standards" (Nadel, in Goody 1961:158).

Monica Wilson next tried to solve the problem semantically, suggesting the term "ritual" for behavior which was "directed toward securing the blessing of some mystical power" and reserving "ceremony" for more secular activities (Wilson, in Goody 1961:159). Jack Goody supported this approach but used means-ends criteria like Nadel's to make the distinction between ritual and ceremony (Goody 1961:159). Edmund Leach countered, saying that the latter were points on the same continuum (Leach 1968:525).

More recently Martin Southwold has advanced a polythetic approach, providing a list of twelve attributes "some" of which must apply to cultural systems designated religious (1978:370–371). And as mentioned above, Geertz and others have advocated functional definitions of religion and ritual which are useful for analysis but not completely satisfying as means for distinguishing religious from secular behavior.

Having thus considered many of the major anthropological treatises on religion and ritual, I was only able to conclude that the *chaji* is an ideal example of the kind of behavior which makes it difficult to distinguish religious from secular ritual. The *chaji* confounds all the attempts at classification previously described. It does not require a belief in deities or mystical powers. It is privately held and its ends do not appear logically related to its means.

Further, Southwold's list of the attributes are split evenly down the middle. *Chado* does have an orientation towards salvation, ritual practices, an exalted oral tradition, a specialist elite, a moral community and association with an ethnic group. It lacks a concern with godlike beings, a dichotomization into sacred and profane, beliefs which must be held on the basis of faith with a supporting ethical code, supernatural sanctions against infringement of that code, and a mythology. Yet the most authoritative representative of the emic view, Sen Soshitsu XV (1978) suggests that tea ritual is religious behavior.

I endorse the grandmaster's interpretation because it is firmly grounded in a scholarly understanding of tea history and philosophy and I believe it can be reconciled with anthropological theory if we collaborate with our colleagues in religious studies. The problem of distinguishing religious from secular ritual can be solved by applying the criterion Girardot (1983:6) calls concern "with a means of transforming, temporally or permanently, some "significant ill" that seems to be part of the cosmological or existential order of human life" to behavior such as that seen at a *chaji.*

To the mind educated in the Judeo-Christian tradition, death is usually first perceived as the "significant ill" which requires a religious response. The concept of salvation is associated with a savior who overcomes death on behalf of humankind. As Girardot points out, however, "death may be viewed as only one phase of the total process of human life in time" (1983:6). Interpreted in the context of the Eastern concept of reincarnation, this would certainly seem to be the case.

A sense of chaos has broader cultural relevance as that "significant ill" which gives rise to an impulse to seek salvation through religious acts. Geertz defines "chaos" as "a tumult of events which lack not just interpretations but interpretability" (1973:100). He argues that man is so dependent on symbols and symbol systems that "the gravest sort of anxiety" arises at the suggestion that such systems are inadequate to cope with every aspect of experience. Girardot similarly maintains that religion exists to say that the felt chaos of life has meaning because it is interpretable. He believes that "Salvation . . . is concerned with healing human life in relation to the culturally perceived meaning and structure of the world" (1983:7).

If we think of the religious impulse as a response to a human sense of the potential for chaos, we must classify religious activity as ultimately consisting of soteriological attempts to order perception. Telling myths and performing rituals are satisfying responses to chaos, because they establish and confirm at least an illusion of cosmic order. Girardot says "Cosmos is the cultivated persona of chaos" (1983:5).

Figure 2.2 shows how a universal yearning for cognitive order has filtered through four major philosophical systems and is expressed in *chado*. To begin with, the Taoist philosophy reflected this desire in the ancient Chinese. Taoists were concerned mainly with promoting a general concept of universal order and exploring man's potential for integration with the cosmic (and chaotic) whole through ritual and alchemy.

Confucians inherited the Taoist idea of a unified cosmos but emphasized correct social conduct as the appropriate human reaction to a felt need for higher level order. Ch'an (and then Zen) Buddhists also subscribed to the Taoist model but influenced by Indian philosophy through Bodhidharma focused on the individual's response to perceived chaos rather than that of the group.

The Japanese solution to the need for order contrasted slightly with the Chinese. Their Shinto beliefs placed special emphasis on the integration of social, spiritual, and natural phenomena and expressed this as seeking closer fellowship with the spirits of social beings or natural objects (*kami*) (Ono 1962:28). The rituals of purification and exorcism which developed in both Taoist and Shinto ritual are vivid examples of ordering behavior.

As also indicated in Figure 2.2, a practitioner of *chado* usually conceives of and ritually expresses an emotional and intellectual requirement for cosmic order in a more immediate way. The concepts of harmony (*wa*), respect (*kei*), purity (*sei*), and tranquillity (*jaku*)[28] are all distillations of specific aspects of this need. They have become the central litany of tea values, the most commonly recognized and recited words in *chado*. Every symbol, every movement and every thought in tea ritual eventually relates back to one of these ideas and, through them, to a universal urge to order. Adherents of *chanoyu* invariably describe their ritual goals with reference to these four values.

Let us consider some of the general characteristics of religious ritual and the way in which the concepts just presented relate to it. Remember that such ritual functions to relieve the suspicion "that life is absurd and the attempt to make moral, intellectual, or emotional sense out of the experience is bootless" (Geertz 1973:108). Thus, effective religious ritual must always make sense out of parts of human life which otherwise seem uninterpretable and convince man that he can somehow affect his place in the larger scheme of things.

To achieve these goals, ritual practitioners must do four things: (1) establish their credentials; (2) identify the portion of the culturally defined cosmic model to be manipulated; (3) define the specific sphere of endeavor; and (4) project the results of the effort to those affected. In *chado*, the concept of purity (*sei*) relates to establishing the credentials of

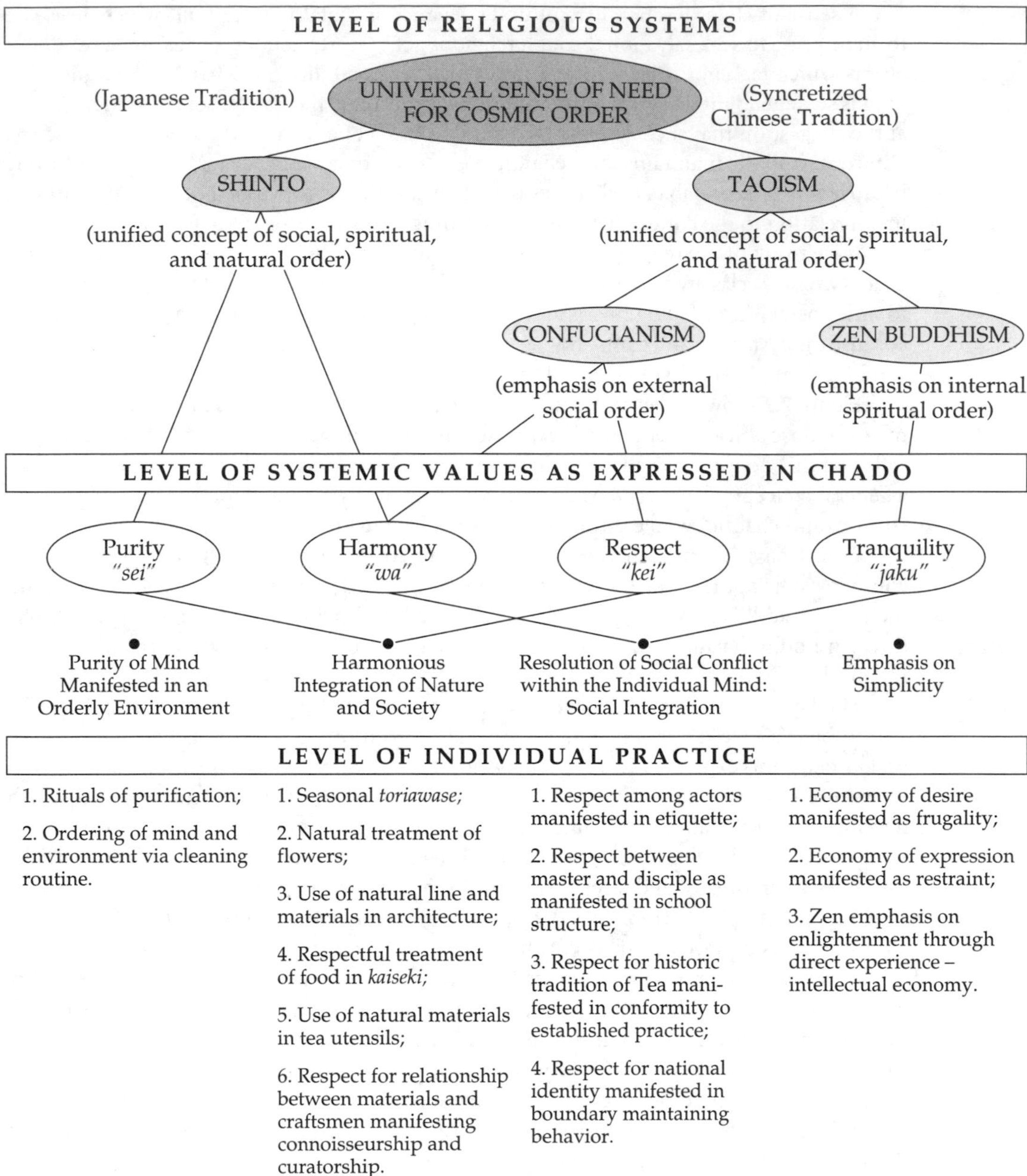

FIGURE 2.2

the practitioner and associating the ritual field with the cosmic model. Harmony (*wa*) and respect (*kei*) clarify the area of endeavor. A special kind of tranquillity (*jaku*) is the projected result.

As regards purity (in *chado* and any other ritual), the first priority of the practitioner must be to convince the individuals affected that by some right of lineage, character, vision, experience, knowledge, and/or training, he or she can perform an effective rite. If the ritual is an oft-repeated publicly visible behavior, its constituency may be conditioned to accept emblems of status such as vestments, masks, palms, staffs, ornaments, etc. as proof of such an authority. In Tea, kimono emblems and a special kind of jacket worn by senior instructors sometimes function this way. However, if the ritual is performed in private, for the first time, or for a group unfamiliar with the symbol system, acts of purification alternatively serve to establish the ritualist's identity.

There are other aspects to the ritual specialist's purificatory acts. For example, a fundamental assumption in *chado* (but not every ritual) is that the practitioner is a sincere participant who will share the spiritual benefits of the behavior. That is, a tea gathering is considered effective only if both host and guests are convinced of the validity of the cosmic model created and their relationship to it. Symbols of purity (washing, wiping, sweeping, etc.) serve not only to convince the guests of the host's ability ritually to create order but spiritually to integrate the host with his effort. The normative affect of purification varies, of course, among both individuals and rituals.

Acts of purification also help define the portion of the cosmic model manipulated in an individual ritual and convincingly link it to physical reality. By cleaning, sweeping, sprinkling water, etc., a ritual practitioner defines a physical area as his stage and sets it apart from everyday life. Thus, by washing his hands and sprinkling water around a basin in the garden, the host at a *chaji* demonstrates his credentials to his guests, orders his own mind, and draws a parallel between the path to enlightenment (the "dewy path") and the real setting in which the event will take place.

Creating such a metaphorical relationship between physical space and the cosmos is one of the most basic things a ritual can do. Usually, practitioners take the opportunity to add detail—complex models beget complex rituals. In Tea, for example, considerable effort goes into describing the spatial, temporal, and material aspects of the projected paradigm. The geomantic orientation of the tearoom identifies it with the celestial plane. Walls function both to define sacred precincts and to connect them to limitless space beyond. Architectural style also locates the ritual in a historic and ethnic milieu while seeming to affirm "the theory of non-existence of space to the truly enlightened" (Okakura 1956:60).

When considering the temporal dimension of this model, an observer noting the general archaism in dress, environment, and speech, may be tempted to say that ritual suspends time and negates space. Actually, both are used rather than denied by the ritualist. A skillful practitioner manipulates the sequential elements of a rite in a way which suggests that man can control time rather than being used by it. The seeming impossibility of such a feat as well as the power inherent in it may create an illusion of timelessness—hence, the unhurried pace of the *chaji*.

In addition to the spatial and temporal components just discussed, a cosmic model usually has a material element—because man perceives a material world and can conceptualize only a cosmos which mirrors it. The subtle use of physical commodities to create immediate sensation and, at the same time, to symbolize qualities of the universal model integrates reality with cosmos and makes "moods and motivations seem uniquely realistic" (Geertz 1973:90). At a *chaji*, for example, the texture of a bowl, the smell of incense, and the taste of tea all convincingly serve to blur the boundaries of a higher order of reality with that of man and nature. (I suspect tea practitioners are particularly sensitive to the material element in the cosmic model because of the Taoist interest in the metaphysical qualities of "the five elements.")

Once the practitioner has established his or her identity and reaffirmed that authority by demonstrating skill at the kinds of symbolic manipulations just discussed, the specific goals of the individual event can be clarified. If Girardot's view that religion seeks to transform "temporally or permanently, some 'significant ill' " and recover "a condition of original wholeness, health, or holiness" (1983:7) is accepted, then all religious ritual may be characterized as curative. This seems a useful mode of analysis because rituals of supplication and exorcism focus on reintegrating man with powers greater than his own while rituals of initiation and group maintenance heal the social corpus by drawing on symbols of a higher order as both model and sanction.

In *chado,* the concepts of harmony (*wa*) and respect (*kei*) define the ritual's specific area of endeavor. The idea of *wa* ascribed to in Tea developed out of the Taoist concept of universal harmony and attained an ethical character when used by Confucians in discussing the effect of interaction between humans and the cosmic order. Japanese consider it the basis of their social system since Prince Shotoku made it the basis of their "first constitution" in A.D. 604. Daisetz Suzuki suggests that it be defined as "gentleness of spirit," a sense of unegotistical spiritual integration pervading all that can be perceived (Suzuki 1959:74).

Kei, the Confucian quality of respect, imposes order on the model of integration represented by harmony (*wa*). Together they represent a balanced (and therefore benevolent) cosmos and suggest a mode for human interaction with it. A sense of harmony with nature is established in tearoom construction and utensils through the careful use of wood, clay fiber, etc. It is enhanced by the use of seasonal symbolic motifs, flowers, and food. In this symbol-laden environment, participants act out an ideal relationship to nature, the artists who have contributed to the atmosphere through their work, their forebears in *chado,* and their fellows. This interaction is satisfyingly ordered by formal etiquette, the codification of respect.

A *chaji* differs from more public rituals such as *okucha* and *okencha* because everyone in the tearoom is a participant. Usually the majority of those present (if not all) are tea practitioners. In such a case, it is not necessary for the host overtly to project the result of the ritual. By carefully constructing the atmosphere and judiciously manipulating the symbol system, the goal of the ritual has been subtly communicated. In rituals where the population affected is not familiar with the symbolic language employed by the specialist the goal may have to be more directly stated.

Conclusion

Whether directly stated or symbolically expressed, the goal of including a satisfying human element in high-level cognitive model formation is the object of all religious ritual (see Geertz and Girardot quoted earlier). Specific rituals may deal with all or part of the cosmic model and concern themselves with integrating individuals or groups in a variety of ways. The type of healing that occurs varies similarly and can be described by those affected in many different ways.

Because a *chaji* is an inclusive ritual, that is, it deals very broadly with the cosmic model, its projected result is described in a very comprehensive way. This is expressed in the Buddhist concept of *jaku. Jaku* literally means "the death of a priest." It is used in *chado* to indicate a special state of tranquillity which probably comes from a shortening of the phrase *Jaku metsu iraku* which means "the joy of entering Nirvana." In a poem attributed to Sen Rikyu it is described this way:

The garden path, the hunt,
The host and the guest—
All are whipped together
In the tea and are without distinctions.
(Sen Rikyu, in Tsutsui 1981:39)

This is the essence of the way a tea master uses the many symbolic aspects of a *chaji* to recreate a cosmic model which includes a human factor. Tea becomes the symbolic medicine for man's angst and he is restored to "original wholeness, health or holiness" (cf. Girardot 1983:7). Tea philosophers state this fact directly: "Through concentrating on *chanoyu* both guests and host can obtain salvation" (Sen Rikyu from the *Namboroku* quoted in Tanikawa 1981:41).

As illustrated throughout this analysis, the symbolic vocabulary of *chado* is complex and has been drawn from a broad variety of historical and philosophical traditions. Nevertheless, tea ritual seems to be interpretable if analyzed in the light of a soteriological definition of religion. Sen Soshitsu XV was able to say "Tea is the practice or realization of religious faith, no matter what you believe in" (1978) because he accepted the comprehensiveness of Tea's identity as religious ritual.

Even those who participate in the most abbreviated of tea rituals and lack any knowledge of its symbol system sense that it fulfills deep human needs. *Chado* has proved satisfying to a variety of people over a long time because the tranquillity it emanates affects everyone—be their understanding sophisticated or cursory. This analysis has barely touched upon tea ritual's rich intellectual resources but I hope that it will stimulate more anthropologists to share my interest in *chanoyu*. In the words of the Zen masters: *Kissa ko*—Do drink tea!

Notes

This analysis of *chanoyu* is based on my continuing experience as a student of Urasenke. I consider myself a committed practitioner of the way of Tea (thus participant as well as observer—and not an unbiased observer; see discussion in text). My ethnographic data pertain solely to the practices of the Urasenke school. While it seems likely that other tea schools (having emerged from the same historical and cultural milieu as Urasenke) fundamentally share its philosophical orientations, symbolic language and basic practical routine, the traditional rule that a student must join only one school precludes generalization. (Correspondence is welcomed at the following address: 740 E. Bel Mar Drive, La Selva Beach, CA 95076.)

1. *Chanoyu* is a general term for Japanese tea ritual. *Chado* means the "Way of Tea" and refers to the practice and philosophy of Japanese tea ritual. When "tea" is capitalized in this article it refers to *chanoyu* or *chado.*

2. My Ph.D. dissertation (Anderson 1985) treats the subject more extensively.

3. *Michi* or *do* are, respectively, the native Japanese (*kun*) term and the Japanese interpretation of the Chinese reading (*ou*) of the character for Tao. It also means road or way in Chinese.

4. Geertz does explain elsewhere that the "set of moods and motivations" created by ritual does include "an image of cosmic order" (1973:118).

5. Botanists fail to agree on the geographic origins of tea. There seem to have originally been two distinct species *Thea sinensis* and *Thea assamica.* The beverage offered to Lao Tze may have been *t'u* (sow thistle).

6. The definition of *wabi* has been the subject of much debate but all definitions stress the positive virtues of insufficiency and imply rustic simplicity.

7. The seven main kinds of *chaji* are the noon tea (*shogo chaji*); the yobanashi chaji held at night in the winter; the *akatsuki chaji* held at dawn in winter; the *asa chaji,* conducted very early on hut summer mornings; *hango chaji,* an abbreviated gathering held around noon at busy times of the year; *atomi chaji* held after another *chaji* at the request of a second group of guests; and the *rinji chaji* which is given spontaneously or on short notice. Kondo (1985) relied heavily on the sequence of the *shogo chaji* for her analysis, failing to note that the gathering's internal segments could be abbreviated or rearranged with no significant change in meaning. It is possible that she misinterpreted the concept of a "standard *chaji*" in the absence of data on its variants.

8. Night and dawn gatherings are considered the province of the expert because gatherings held at those times have special problems of mood and logistics.

9. I have tried to avoid the use of the word "formal" because of the ambiguity which results from using it to mean "solemn" and "ritualized." I use the terms "formal," "semi-formal," and "informal" as the equivalents of the *shin, gyo,* and *so* designations applied to Tea behavior and utensils. The concept of "formality" is culture-specific. Kondo's (1985) indiscriminate use of the term led her to misunderstand and misrepresent some important aspects of Tea behavior. It is, for example, quite possible to conduct a semiformal (*gyo*) *temae* during a relatively "informal" (read relaxed) segment of a *chaji.*

10. Sen Soshitsu XV enjoys using tea utensils of foreign manufacture and encourages non-Japanese students of Tea to look for suitable utensils among their own native handicrafts.

11. Kondo (1985:290) errs in saying that the host "begins to smooth the ashes in the brazier into a pattern" in *shozumi.* Ash is arranged outside the tearoom because it is a messy activity. Only charcoal is arranged during *shozumi.*

12. Rikyu advised drawing water at dawn because he believed this was the beginning of its *yang* period. He called it the "flower of the well." In contrast, water drawn from dusk to midnight was *yin* and considered poisonous. Special *temae* (*meisuidate*) exist to feature famous waters drawn from Shinto shrines or wells famous in tea history.

13. Proper *kimono* are attractive seasonal indicators and give clues to rank, family identity, marital status, and tea school affiliation. Tea people are more comfortable in them because they contain convenient places to put things such as fans and papers.

14. Kondo's pairing of *machiai* and tearoom for theoretical purposes (1985:295) is like trying to compare the sanctuary of a church with the cloakroom. There is no requirement that the *machiai* have *tatami,* a scroll, or be small and enclosed. The *machiai* has no structural symbolic importance while the tearoom functions as a complex cosmic model. They are not a homologous pair.

15. Kondo's opposition of strong and weak substances in *machiai* and tearoom (1985:299) is compromised by the fact that *sake* or something like plum wine may be properly served in the *machiai* at night gatherings in winter.

16. Contrary to Kondo's contrived concept of binary opposition, there are no strict rules which relate to the disposition of moss, trees, ferns, and flowers in inner and outer *roji.* Their distribution is a matter of taste.

17. The spatial diagram Kondo (1985:294) provides of a "typical tea garden" is fanciful at best. Even considering the ornamental character of the *setchin* it is inappropriate to locate it directly next to the main guest's seat. The drawing also ignores standard *tatami* mat dimensions, omits the *tokonoma* and preparation area of the tearoom, makes no provision for the host's entrance door, and shows the outer *roji* penetrating what is normally a solid wall of the *koshikake machiai.*

18. Contrary to Kondo (1985), mallet and board are not used here. Nonverbal signaling (the use of the gong and the wooden clapper, dropping chopsticks, closing doors) is only necessary when host and guest are physically

located so that shouting over distance or through doors is inconvenient. She also errs in asserting that the preparation of *koicha* and *usucha* are "always performed in complete silence."

19. *Tsukubai* comes from the verb *tsukubau* meaning to crouch or squat. Rikyu devised this low basin to encourage a humble attitude toward purification in the *roji.*

20. Rikyu also provided a sword rack (*katanakake*) outside the tearoom door. Fans are substituted for swords when making formal greetings in the tearoom.

21. There are several standard mat sizes. In Rikyu's day mats were about 6.5 feet in length and 39 inches wide. Today's mats are closer to six foot by three foot.

22. Today, honored guests may sit with their back to the *tokonoma* on this mat segment but the custom is a survival of etiquette developed in larger *shoin*-style rooms. The emperor always sat with his back to the north in the Imperial palace, hence it became the place of honor in any room.

23. For more advanced *temae,* a *daisu* and bronze utensils (*kaigu*) may be used. Allan Palmer has suggested that the same directional scheme applied to the tea house is pertinent to the manipulations of the *daisu* (Allan Palmer, personal communication 1983). Certainly, on the bottom (earth) board we find the brazier located in the section identified with fire in Rikyu's time and the water jar in the area associated with that element. Other connections between utensils and their symbols seem more tenuous but I do not practice Tea at this advanced level.

24. Sandalwood chips (*byakudan*) are used with the *furo* as both are considered Chinese in origin. With the Japanese winter hearth (*ro*), native Japanese kneaded incense (*neriko*) is used.

25. Four-corner examining (*yohosabaki*) calms the mind. When examining each edge the host is supposed to concentrate on emperor (or nation), family, teacher, and friends or the Buddhas of Four Directions.

26. Kondo described *usucha* as a less concentrated form of the same tea used for *koicha* (1985:291). This is not true. The two are named, sold, packaged and priced independently. *Koicha* comes from older tea bushes than *usucha* and the leaves are picked and handled differently. The same tea is never properly used for both *koicha* and *usucha temae.*

27. It is usual to give the tea scoop a name which evokes seasonal images.

28. Murata Shuko established *kin* (reverence), *kei, sei,* and *jaku* as the primary values of *chado.* Sen Rikyu substituted *wa* for *kin* (Sadler 1962:102).

References

Anderson, Jennifer (1985). *Chanoyu: An anthropological approach to Tea.* Thesis, Stanford University.

Beardsley, Richard K., Hall, John, & Ward, Robert (1959). *Village Japan.* Chicago: University of Chicago Press.

Blofeld, John (1985). *The Chinese art of Tea.* Boston, MA: Shambhala Publications.

Boas, Franz (1943). Recent anthropology. *Science, 98,* 311–314, 334–337.

Bodart, Beatrice M. (1977). Tea and counsel: The political role of Sen Rikyu. *Monumenta Nipponica, 32,* 49–74.

Burke, Patrick (1979). *The fragile universe, an essay in the philosophy of religions.* New York: Harper & Row.

Cooper, Michael (1970). The early Europeans and chanoyu. *Chanoyu Quarterly, 11,* 36–50.

Dore, Ronald P. (1958). *City life in Japan: A study of a Tokyo ward.* Berkeley: University of California Press.

Dore, Ronald P. (1967). *Aspects of social change in modern Japan.* Princeton, NJ: Princeton University Press.

Durkheim, Emile (1965). The elementary forms of the religious life. In W. A. Lessa & E. Z. Vogt (Eds.), *Reader in comparative religion: An anthropological approach.* New York: Harper & Row.

Feleppa, Robert (1986). Emics, etics, and social objectivity. *Current Anthropology, 27,* 243–255.

Firth, Raymond (1973). *Symbols: Public and private.* Ithaca, NY: Cornell University Press.

Frake, Charles O. (1962). The ethnographic study of cognitive systems. In T. Gladwin & W. C. Sturtevant (Eds.), *Anthropology and human behavior.* Washington, DC: Anthropological Society of Washington.

Geertz, Clifford (1973). *The interpretation of cultures.* New York: Basic Books.

Giradot, N. J. (1983). *Myth and meaning in early Taoism: The theme of chaos.* Berkeley: University of California Press.

Goodenough, Ward H. (1970). *Description and comparison in cultural anthropology.* Chicago: Aldine.

Goody, Jack (1961). Religion and ritual: The definitional problem. *British Journal of Sociology, 12,* 142–164.

Gluckman, Max (1962). Les rites de passage. In Daryl Forde and others (Eds.), *Essays on the ritual of social relations.* Manchester: University Press.

Guthrie, Steward (1980). A cognitive theory of religion. *Current Anthropology, 21,* 181–194.

Harris, Marvin (1976). History and significance of the emic-etic distinction. *Annual Review of Anthropology, 5,* 329–350.

Hayashiya Tatsusaburo (1970). Historical review of *chanoyu,* Part II: Tea among the Heian aristocracy. *Chanoyu Quarterly, 3,* 37–50.

Hayashiya Tatsusaburo (1971). Historical review of *chanoyu,* Part V: Zen and the Samurai. *Chanoyu Quarterly, 6,* 48–60.

Hsu, Francis L. K. (1965). *Jemoto: The heart of Japan.* New York: John Wiley.

Ishikawa Takashi (1984). The origin and essence of shinto festivals. *The East, 204,* 9–15.

Ito Teiji (1976). Sen Rikyu and Taian. *Chanoyu Quarterly, 14,* 7–20.

Kondo, Dorinne (1985). The way of Tea: A symbolic analysis. *Man (NS), 20,* 287–306.

Leach, Edmund (1968). Ritual. In *International encyclopedia of the social sciences* (vol. 13). New York: Macmillan.

Lebra, Joyce, & Elizabeth Powers (1976). *Women in changing Japan.* Boulder, CO: Westview Press.

Lu Yu (1974). *The classic of Tea* (Francis Ross Carpenter, Trans.). Boston, MA: Little, Brown.

Munn, Nancy (1973). Symbolism in a ritual context: Aspects of symbolic action. In John J. Hinigman (Ed.), *Handbook of social and cultural anthropology.* Chicago: Rand McNally.

Nakane, Chie (1970). *Japanese society.* Berkeley: University of California Press.

Okakura Kakuzo (1956). *The book of Tea.* Rutland, VT: Charles E. Tuttle.

Ono Sokyo (1962). *Shinto: The kami way.* Rutland, VT: Charles E. Tuttle.

Ortolani, Benito (1969). Iemoto. *Japan Quarterly, 16,* 297–306.

Plath, David W. (1980). *Long engagements.* Stanford, CA: Stanford University Press.

Sadler, A. L. (1962). *Chanoyu: The Japanese Tea ceremony.* Rutland, VT: Charles E. Tuttle.

Sanjonishi Kinosa (1977). The way of incense, Part I. *Chanoyu Quarterly, 20,* 31–43.

Sen Soshitsu XV (1978). Cha no sugata (Tea as it really is). *Urasenke Newsletter, 15.*

Sen Soshitsu (1979). *Chado: The Japanese way of Tea.* New York: John Weatherhill.

Southwold, Martin (1978). Buddhism and the definition of religion. *Man (NS), 13,* 362–379.

Suzuki, Daisetzu T. (1959). *Zen and Japanese culture.* Princeton, NJ: Princeton University Press.

Tanikawa Tetsuzo (1981). The esthetics of chanoyu: Part III. *Chanoyu Quarterly, 26,* 33–49.

Tsutsui Hiroichi (1981). The role of anecdotes in the transmission of Tea traditions. *Chanoyu Quarterly, 29,* 28–36.

Tylor, Edward B. (1965). Animism. In W. A. Lessa & E. Z. Vogt (Eds.), *Reader in comparative religion: An anthropological approach.* New York: Harper & Row.

Vogel, Ezra F. (1968). *Japan's new middle class: The salary man and his family in a Tokyo suburb.* Berkeley: University of California Press.

Williams, C. A. S. (1974). *Outlines of Chinese symbolism and art motives.* Rutland, VT: Charles E. Tuttle.

Young, John (1970). Tea for the west. *Chanoyu Quarterly, 1,* 28–38.

Ritual Hierarchy and Secular Equality in a Sepik River Village

SIMON J. HARRISON

Introduction

A recurring theme in the literature on Melanesian male cults is that these institutions are symptoms of "polarized" relations between the sexes and, in some cases, maintain the dominance of adult men and the subordination of women and juniors (Allen 1967; Herdt 1981, 1982; Langness 1967, 1974; Meggitt 1964; Read 1952–53; A. J. Strathern 1970). The aim of this article is to test this view against a particular ethnographic case: the male initiatory cult at Avatip, a community of some 1300 Manambu speakers (see Laycock 1965) situated on the Sepik River in the East Sepik Province of Papua New Guinea (see Harrison 1982a, 1982b, 1983, 1984, 1985).

My starting point for the analysis of this cult is the observation that much of its lore and activity has the key characteristic of being kept, at least in theory, secret. By definition, the existence of this "esoteric" sociocultural domain requires the parallel existence of a world of "public" social and cultural forms. This is also a practical requirement: if initiated men are to preserve their ritual secrets in everyday social interaction, there must exist a body of social and cultural conventions sufficient for the purposes of general social life. An irreducible feature of these systems and, I would argue, one from which any analysis of them must begin, is this: that they are based on a dichotomy between two sociocultural domains, one esoteric and the other exoteric, and that these two domains must in some sense *differ*. From the viewpoint of the initiates, I might add, the more they differ the more effectively is initiatory secrecy maintained.

In a system such as this, what one would normally regard as the "cultural order" in fact consists, minimally, of two distinct orders: one available to the society at large and the other available only to cult initiates. In practice, most systems are more complex than this, the esoteric order itself being differentiated into a further hierarchy of successively more secret levels. Characteristically, constructs belonging to one domain are revealed to be partly or wholly "fictional" on initiation into the next. At Avatip, for instance—as in many Melanesian male cults—spirits that supposedly "cry" within the men's cult-houses during rituals turn out, upon initiation, to be pairs of bamboo flutes played by men as a "trick" (*rək*). Barth (1975) has given an excellent analysis of one such corpus of culturai knowledge among the Baktaman of the West Sepik, comparing its "nested" structure to a Chinese box and describing a kind of epistemological vertigo which it induces in its bearers.

What I wish to show is that "public" and "ritual" culture at Avatip differ in their ideological content and contain, in effect, two opposed formulations of the nature of social relations between the sexes and between senior and junior males. The formulation governing the activities of the male cult I have elsewhere (Harrison 1985) called "ritual hierarchy." The alternative formulation, "secular equality" (Harrison 1985), prevails in nonritual contexts, preeminently in the sphere of kinship and domestic relations.[1] I argued there that these two ideologies, though antithetical in many respects, hinge upon and are reducible to ambiguities in the indigenous concept of "person." Here, I would like to extend this analysis by arguing that the hierarchical and male "elitist" values expressed in the men's cult are not culturally "definitive." The cult does not affirm the community's "cultural" values but its *ritual* values, and these differ from those prevailing in secular life. If Avatip religion serves to reinforce everyday social values, it does so by antithesis.

Second, the power and status men enjoy in ritual contexts are not in any sense an expression of, or pattern for, their role in the society in general. Male cult ritual is no more, or less, a "paradigm" for social action as a whole than is secular life. Like everyday life, it *is* a particular form of social action, but one employing specifically *ritual* structures of exclusion and hierarchy not employed in secular contexts. Avatip social structure has two alternative but conceptually coexistent dimensions, which manifest themselves in two contrasting forms of social action.[2]

Everyday Life and Secular Equality

In one of the most incisive contributions to the anthropological study of gender, Ortner (1974) has argued that male dominance is a universal fact of human culture, and that a basic element of this is a symbolic relegation of women and domesticity in some degree to the realm of "nature." Much of the material on Melanesian male cults seems to accord fairly well with this thesis. Read (1952–53, 1954), for example, described the male cult of the Gahuku-Gama as an attempt by men to redress, by "artificial" means, the perceived superiority of women's "natural" powers of growth and fertility; and Bowden (1983) has recently cited Ortner's argument with approval in his analysis of the art and ceremonial of the Kwoma men's cult. It does indeed appear that in many Melanesian societies men regard their religious activities as embodying something interpretable as the essence of "culture"; a fundamental antithesis exists, reinforced by innumerable regulations and taboos, between the ritual sphere of men and the female sphere of domesticity and child-rearing (see, for example, Herdt 1981; Newman 1965; Salisbury 1965). The business of ritual is, so to speak, to "create" men out of the products of women's "natural" fertility; and this requires removing boys at an early age from the debilitating influence of the female domain and exposing them to the central mysteries of male "culture." The men's cult at Avatip is quite amenable to an interpretation of this kind, as I shall show below.

But there is a problem with applying Ortner's thesis to the interpretation of Melanesian male cults, and it can be revealed most clearly if one returns for the moment to the terms of her argument. It seems from her argument that the main factor responsible for the identification of men with "culture," and women with "nature," is this: their associations with the political and domestic domains, respectively. One question that this raises is how the domestic roles of men are viewed. The logic of her argument would seem to imply that when men act in their capacity as members of familial groups they experience themselves to some degree as contextually "marginal" to culture. Similarly, if women assent to the view that domesticity is peripheral to culture, it would follow that women, in their domestic relations with men, view their menfolk situationally as to some extent "infracultural" like themselves. The argument seems to lead, in other words, to the conclusion that men, in the setting of their domestic lives, perceive themselves and are perceived by women as less than fully "social" beings: a conclusion that would contradict the original terms of the hypothesis, according to which this "marginal" status was reserved exclusively for women.

What is wrong here, I suggest, is that Ortner has implicitly identified "culture" with the political domain, and in this way seems to have fallen victim to the same ideological forms that she has so elegantly analyzed. Even if, as she argues, men in their capacity as political officeholders universally consign women and domesticity to an "infracultural" status, it is still essential to recognize that the "locus" of this idea is the *political* domain. That is to say, there would still be a fundamental distinction to be made between constructs employed *in* the domestic domain, and constructs used in political contexts *about* domesticity. To assume that these political values are culturally definitive is to succumb to the ideological devaluation of domesticity which, M. Strathern (1980) has argued, characterizes our own cultural tradition but can distort our understanding of others.

There is, I think, a widespread assumption in anthropology, of which Ortner's thesis is only one example, that *significant* formulations of the social order derive only from the public or political sphere. What this assumption ignores is the possibility of *alternative* symbolic or ideological forms through which both sexes put forward the claims and interests of the domestic sphere—quite possibly in opposition to those of the political domain—and express a distinctively familial vision of their social relations. I think this problem is particularly acute in the case of societies, such as Avatip, in which the central political institution is a male initiatory cult. At Avatip, at least, "exoteric" culture has its structural basis in the familial sphere, and it could most accurately be described as the cultural system of the domestic realm. To ignore this system would be to ignore the cultural regime under which everyday life is conducted and under which men and women lead most of their social existence.

I would like now to describe some of the salient contrasts between the "mundane" and "ritual" domains of Avatip culture, and to show that the first has its institutional locus in "familial" principles of social organization and that the second has its locus in the men's cult. Borrowing a term from Schutz (1967), I will call the mundane sociocultural sphere "everyday life"; I wish to avoid the term "domestic domain" as it has misleading connotations in the Avatip context. Domesticity at Avatip, as I will try to show, is not so much a domain of social action as a form of social action; it is not so much "enclosed" within political structures as it is an alternative to them, and in the context of everyday life the men's cult has much the same "private" significance as domesticity has in the context of ritual. Although it is possible to distinguish other contexts of social action at Avatip besides everyday life and ritual, I would like to concentrate on these two here. For they form the opposed institutional and ideological "poles" of the sociocultural system, and from them derive the two ideological countercurrents that comprise Avatip "culture."

The institutions around which everyday life at Avatip revolves are the household and conjugal family, and the networks of kinship and affinity that link these units together in exchanges of food, wealth, and labor. The main concerns of the community in everyday life are with the essentially "domestic" activities of food production, child-rearing, and the creation and maintenance of kinship relations. Because Avatip is largely endogamous most individuals can trace kin or affinal ties with each other, and in many cases these ties are multiple. In fact the "density" of kin ties within the community is such that, paradoxically, kinship has something of the character of a free contract. All of an individual's effective kin ties are based on exchanges of gifts and services; and most of his or her other social relationships are simply "unactivated"—but always potentially "operable"—kin relations. As a result the individual has considerable freedom to establish, maintain, or suspend effective kinship with others. An enterprising man or woman can set up and operate a very large kinship network; and this, in fact, is virtually the villagers' definition of a "good" (*viyakət*) person. Interpersonal kinship is not, in a sense, a structurally "limited" social universe; its only limits are those of the individual's initiative and energy.

It has sometimes been suggested (for example, Keesing 1982) that male cults in Melanesia serve in some sense to validate the exploitation of female labor by men. At Avatip this kind of expropriation occurs neither in everyday contexts nor, as I shall show later, in the performance of ritual. The main subsistence activities at Avatip are fishing and the production of sago-starch, with yam cultivation and hunting having secondary roles in the economy. Hunting is a male specialization, while fishing is almost exclusively a female task; yam gardening, on the other hand, is a collaborative activity involving no very rigid sexual division of labor except in the process of planting (see Harrison 1982b). In some neighboring Sepik River groups—the latmul (Bateson 1932, 1958; Hauser-Schaublin 1976) and Chambri (Gewertz 1983; Mead 1935) for example—women exchange surplus fish for the sago of inland groups. Avatip, however, is self-sufficient in sago and, while Avatip women do sometimes hold fish-for-sago markets with "bush" villages like their latmul and Chambri counterparts, this is not necessary for subsistence and much of the sago supply at Avatip is home-produced. Men and women contribute an approximately equal amount of labor to the production of sago: the husband fells the palm, cuts open the cortex, and pounds the fibrous pith to break it up; the wife then separates the flour from the pith in a special leaching apparatus.

An important point about the organization of production at Avatip is that it gives women a potential economic independence that it does not give to men. In order to support herself and her children, all a woman needs to do in principle is to fish and trade the surplus for sago. To have the economic collaboration of her husband saves her labor and provides her with a greater range of foods, but it is not actually *essential.* A man, on the other hand, cannot subsist adequately even in the short term without the assistance of a woman, for the only important food he can obtain solely through his own labor is game. Women consequently have a significant degree of power in the domestic economy and can force their husbands to meet their productive obligations in a way that men cannot do with their wives. If a woman is dissatisfied with her husband's work effort, she can simply withdraw her labor by laying conditional curses upon collaborating with him in food production and upon providing him with food. These curses are legitimate and powerful sanctions of a woman's domestic rights and would bring affliction on the entire household if the husband failed to respect them. A shiftless or exploitative husband simply finds himself—until he makes amends—reduced to a kind of domestic pariah scavenging for fallen coconuts and edible leaves, while his wife and children continue to subsist at more or less their usual level.

I am not suggesting here that Avatip men are the economic dependents of their wives in the way, for example, that Mead (1935) portrayed the neighboring Chambri (cf. Gewertz 1983). It is a basic ideal of the domestic ethos, and by and large an actuality, for husbands and wives to have equally important roles in food production and joint control of the products of their labor. But my point is that women have, in their latent economic self-sufficiency, a much greater power than men to ensure that this equitable collaboration is maintained.

It is largely for this reason that polygyny does not, as it does, for example, among the Tiwi of North Australia (Hart & Pilling 1960), enable a man to live off the labor of his domestic group and devote himself to ritual pursuits. A man with two wives does not, let us say, need to do only half the work of a man with one; his work is roughly *doubled* and as a result polygyny is an option which many Avatip men prefer not to take up. Polygynists are regarded with something of that uneasy respect we accord in our society to workaholics; they are, and have to be, men of exceptional productive energy.

Everyday life at Avatip is governed by values in which differences of power and status are minimally institutionalized; the aspect of social relations viewed as centrally significant is their moral and affective content. According to this scheme of values, which I have elsewhere (Harrison 1985) called "secular equality," the basis of sociality lies in the broadly conceived capacity of persons to "hear" (*wukəna*)—that is, to comprehend and empathize with—one another. The key values of secular equality have to do with marriage viewed as a cooperative partnership, with an ethos of parental nurture, and with an active sense of reciprocity between kin. From the perspective of secular equality the domestic sphere is the *core* of human culture; and people's commitment to their familial roles is the public measure of their "full" humanness.[3] The household sphere is the symbolic focus of "society," and all social relations take their ideal moral idiom from it.

The antithesis of society, from this viewpoint, is a conceptually amalgamated "extrasocial" world consisting of ghosts, spirits, wild animals, and foreigners. All such beings are regarded, in varying degrees, as hostile, as outside the scope of morality, and in some broad sense as "powerful." Power—whether manifested in the form of a ghost's malice, the ferocity of a wild boar or crocodile, or the sorcery or physical aggression of enemy villages—is viewed as a phenomenon emanating from beyond the "social" universe. That is to say, it is treated as a defining attribute of nonsocial beings and as ideally absent from *social* relations. The men's cult is accordingly a "marginal" institution in everyday life. For its primary activity is precisely that of contacting sources of "power"—spirit beings—and introducing them into human society. The morally ambiguous status of the cult gives it, in everyday affairs, a kind of structurally "private" significance, and domestic groupings are the focus around which public life is carried out.

The organizational forms of everyday life reproduce themselves autonomously and are not in any sense functionally dependent on the men's cult. The cult does not, for example, regulate marriage in any way, or the developmental cycle or productive activities of domestic groups. The only way in which the cult does intervene in familial life is by disrupting it, as it does, for instance, when the performance of a ritual requires the segregation of men from their wives and children. The values of "secular equality" are invoked and reaffirmed, sometimes openly but more often tacitly, as a continuous and integral part of "practical" day-to-day social interaction. They appear to be reproduced quite effectively in this way, and collective (Durkheimian) ritual affirmations of them would be superfluous; they certainly do not receive such reinforcement in any case, as Avatip ritual has an entirely different ideological message.

The Men's Cult and Ritual Hierarchy

The male initiatory system at Avatip is similar in type to many others reported from Melanesia and its basic features will, I think, be quite familiar. It is what Allen (1967), in his definitive survey of Melanesian cult systems, calls a "compulsory" association, all males being expected to enter it. The cult has a series of initiatory stages, at each of which the novices undergo various ordeals and privations, and have secret ritual objects, techniques, and knowledge revealed to them. All the rituals of the cult involve the initiates in impersonating spirit beings in one way or another, as supposed "deceptions" practiced on women and juniors.

The central concerns of the men's cult are with the maintenance of the cosmic order by men, and with their assertion of their individual and collective strength in warfare. In the cult ideology, which I have elsewhere (Harrison 1985) called "ritual hierarchy," society is conceptualized as a series of ritual categories graded in status according to their supposed proximity to the sources of supernatural power. According to this formulation, the core of human culture is the male cult and the secret knowledge and practices associated with it, while women, children, and the domestic sphere are accorded—very much along the lines of Ortner's argument—a virtually infracultural status. But I should point out that there is no simple nature/culture dichotomy here. Human society, according to the ritual ideology, is a hierarchy set between *two* "nonsocial" orders: the world of mystical powers "above" society, and the domesticity "beneath" it.

The decision to hold a ritual is made entirely by the ritually senior men. They sequester themselves in their cult houses, pronouncing themselves in a "tabooed" state of ritual potency; they purportedly summon spirit agencies and assume the dangerous supernatural power of these beings. Staging the ritual is, in other words, an entirely unilateral act, and this asymmetry is a central feature of "ritual hierarchy."

I will try to show that the hierarchical values celebrated in the men's cult have few repercussions on mundane social activities, and that it is primarily in the circumscribed setting of ritual itself that these values are publicly expressed. Although "ritual hierarchy" is an essentially "esoteric" doctrine, expressed in a body of ritual symbolism inaccessible to women and juniors, inequality is nevertheless manifested publicly in ritual at two distinguishable levels. First, it is represented, in a somewhat "disguised" form, as a value or ideal; and second, and more importantly, it is established temporarily as a *fact*.

The initiatory grades are associated with particular sets of named spirit beings, graduated in supernatural "potency" according to the ritual status of each grade. When a ritual is performed, the men of the relevant grade "summon" their associated spirits into the village and "install" them in their cult house, and in fact much of what the men do in the ritual they publicly attribute to these beings. For instance, during first-stage initiation the initiators cicatrize the novices, an operation meant to foster the novices' growth by purging them of "maternal" blood (cf. Salisbury 1965). But publicly the initiators claim that the novices are "gored" by spirits, whom they portray as anthropomorphic beings with tusks; and this device is, I think, a partial disavowal by the men of their own responsibility for the ordeal. It is a concession to the values prevailing outside the ritual sphere, made necessary because the ideology of ritual is at odds with the ethos of everyday life. The "public" symbolism of a ritual signifies hierarchy in a somewhat "weakened" form and is a kind of compromise-formation, to borrow a Freudian term, between two conflicting schemes of values.

When men attribute their own acts to spirits, they are not as disingenuous as might seem on first sight. They by no means regard these beings as fictional, and to men, in fact, one of the central secret "mysteries" of Avatip religion is that in ritual they themselves in some sense *incarnate* the spirits. This is not a "possession" cult in Lewis's (1971) definition of the term, and in ritual men retain their usual personalities. But men do, nevertheless, regard the spirits as in some loosely conceived sense "immanent" in themselves as a group. In a certain respect, this accurately reflects the sociological ambience of ritual: to the men, ritual is a highly "non-normal" form of social experience involving, temporarily, a felt change in their social identities.

The values of the male cult manifest themselves in "public" culture in the idea that men, in ritual, entertain spirit beings and while doing so take on something of the dangerous potency of spirits. The special status this gives to initiated men is viewed as consisting essentially in the privilege of contacting supernatural forces in ritual. The ritual status of initiates is conceived, accordingly, as "actualized" only in the performance of ritual itself; it has a largely nominal significance in mundane contexts, and the system of initiatory grades remains by and large a merely *potential* organizational principle.

I said earlier that Avatip ritual not only "communicates" inequality as an idea but also temporarily establishes it as a fact. By this, I mean that although women and uninitiated males are excluded from cult rituals, they nevertheless play an essential role in these events. Their role, of course, is the vital one of *being* excluded. During a ritual, the women and noninitiates cannot have direct contact with the performers and must avoid the cult building in which the ritual is taking place. At certain points in the ritual they may have to remain in their houses in silence or even leave the village altogether for a few hours. From a sociological perspective, this behavior is of course an absolutely integral part of the ritual; and the crucial point here is that it is enforced, ultimately, by the initiated men through their conjuring of spirits inimical to noninitiates. In effect men do indeed—and with perfect clarity—communicate to women and juniors the hierarchical values of the initiatory system: they do so by *implementing* these values.

In ritual, men suspend their "ordinary" social identities and arrogate to themselves, to some degree, the power of spirit beings. The implication here is that, while exercising power, men must temporarily become something "other" than themselves. This is, again, a compromise with the values of everyday life. Men assume in ritual a persona from which they dissocjate themselves in everyday life; and one which makes them, from the perspective of "secular equality," contextually "marginal" to human society.

This is in an important sense a basic weakness of the ritual ideology, for the ritual persona of men cannot by its very nature be maintained permanently. An elementary point here is that the performers of a ritual cannot fulfill their roles in the domestic economy, and Avatip rituals are limited in their frequency and duration ultimately by constraints inherent in the organization of production. Cult rituals tend to be mounted in the period between December and March, when the yam gardens are being harvested and there is little horticultural work to be done (see Harrison 1982b). Before any ritual of more than a few days' duration, the household must lay in a sufficient store of sago flour to last it until the end of the performance. While the ritual is taking place, each performer is supplied daily from this stock by his domestic group. His wife also provides him with fish each day, just as she does at other times. In addition, the men hold large-scale hunts during the longer rituals, and supply themselves (and also, supposedly, their spirit "guests") with considerable amounts of game. Ultimately, the time limits on ritual are set by the performers' need to resume, with their wives, their subsistence activities, particularly sago production and the cultivation of the swiddens. So, far from the men's cult being a means of disguising the expropriation of female labor, as Keesing (1982), for example, has suggested, it is precisely the impossibility of such exploitation that limits the activities of the cult. Ritual gives men no power over the sphere of domestic production; on the contrary, it is an attempt by men to periodically *escape* their implicitly inferior position within it.

In ritual men impose a hierarchical structure on the community through their control of the means of large-scale public acts of signification, and this structure is essentially disarticulated with the organizational forms within which production and exchange take place. But the weakness of a system of political relations sustained by the power of signification is that it rapidly "dissolves" once it is no longer actually being signified. At the end of every ritual men carry out ceremonial acts publicly "detaching" themselves from their ritual personae and announcing their return to everyday life; at this point the social system "lapses" rapidly back into an egalitarian register. Because the values of secular equality are reaffirmed through *practical* everyday social activity—marriage negotiations, exchanges of agricultural labor, the productive cooperation of spouses, and so forth—these values have a fundamental resilience and rapidly reconstitute themselves once these activities are resumed.

In the final analysis, the power of men simply *is* the power to constitute, occasionally and for limited periods, an altered social reality in which women and junior males are subordinate to them. Ritual is the social reality within which this domination exists; it does not reaffirm a power men hold in everyday life, for the power of men is in one sense far narrower and yet in another respect far more profound than this would imply. The cult simply does not give men any special coercive powers over women and juniors in secular life. What it does give them is the far more fundamental power to *negate* the mundane social order and replace it with a politico-ritual hierarchy. It is impossible for men to exercise power without at the same time bringing into being a specifically "ritual" milieu, and in this way transforming the ground rules of social action. And when men cease, at the end of a ritual, to exercise and display this power, the community resumes secular and egalitarian forms of social organization; it is impossible for men to operate as social actors in everyday life without forgoing their ritual powers over women and juniors. While men do, sometimes, appear implicitly to claim that ritual is a definitive representation of the social order, this claim is at one level excessive and at another level too modest: modest, because their ritual acts do not simply represent but contextually *create* a structure of social relations; and excessive, because their rituals do not correspond to the everyday social order but temporarily suspend it. Ritual, in effect, is men's power of veto over the egalitarian conventions of secular life.

The structural and ideological "disjunction" between male ritual and everyday life indicates that the cult cannot be fully understood if one focuses only on its role *within* the social system. To understand the significance of the cult, one needs to adopt a regional perspective and look to the community's external relations. In the past, Avatip existed in a more or less chronic state of war with most of its neighbors, punctuated by short-term and separate truces for trade and military alliance. A good deal of mutual hostility and suspicion still exists between them, primarily regarding land, and these rivalries are played out in intervillage brawls, sports contests, sorcery feuds, and, sometimes, litigation. Here I would endorse a view put forward by a number of authors (for example, Langness 1967): that Melanesian male cults and their associated values of male elitism are responses to the real and perceived exigencies of warfare. But a point on which I would differ from Langness is that, at Avatip, these values do not, as it were, pervade the totality of social life but have to do specifically with the political rhetoric of intervillage rivalry. I would argue that the cult ideology in fact describes the way in which the villagers—at least adult men—want their society to be viewed by outsiders. It is a model of the social order not primarily intended for "home use" but for consumption by the outside world. It is a response to the perceived need, pertaining to the "political" field of *inter*village relations, for men to delimit, as Ardener (1972) puts it, themselves-and-their-women from identically conceived neighboring groups. The important point here is that the ritual "model" is based on a principle of power and status ranking. To have a more elaborately or more rigidly ranked initiatory system is a bid for prestige in the intervillage political arena. Avatip men, for example, pride themselves (correctly or not, I am unable to say) on having one more initiatory grade in their cult than do their Tatmul neighbors. The values of the male cult are the values of the regional political system and not, in basis, those of the internal social field of the village.[4]

The cult has nevertheless quite real sociological effects within the village. One of the most important is that it provides the village with a political integration which the secular structures probably could not. Tuzin (1976) has argued that the complex ritual organization of another Middle Sepik society, the Ilahita Arapesh, is a response to the problems of integration faced by a large social system under pressure from warfare. I think a similar argument can be applied to Avatip, also a sizable community by Sepik standards though with a population a little less than Ilahita's 1500: that is, that the cult organization counterbalances the tendencies toward fission in this uncentralized social system and thereby maintains the military strength that lies in size. A point I would stress, however, is that these structures exist largely as *ideas* in secular contexts and are fully "actualized" only in the setting of ritual.

On the one hand, Avatip is part of a wider political universe in which villages communicate with each other, through their adult men, primarily by means of ritual and (in the past) warfare. The ideological message of Avatip ritual is that "society" is this intervillage universe presided over by senior men, and that Avatip itself is a kind of huge domestic "cell" confining women and juniors to a structurally inferior status. On the other hand, Avatip is in demographic, political, and economic respects very largely an autonomous social system; and from its "internal" perspective, society is the universe of the village itself, its people socially (that is, morally) equal in relation to the enemy (*mam*) groups beyond it. This is the view governing everyday social practice. There is, then, a kind of relativity of perspectives within the social system, and it is this issue I would like to examine a little more fully in the next section.

The Problem of Models

All that I have said so far about the ideology of the men's cult would seem to mark it indelibly as what Ardener (1972, 1975) calls a "male" model. It pertains to an exclusively male institution; its main relevance is to the male-controlled field of intersocietal relations; and, as I have tried to show, it represents one "half" of cognized social reality. However, if one tries to derive the ritual and secular conceptions of the social order from the dichotomy of the sexes, a number of problems arise. Men are quite aware that social relations outside the setting of ritual are governed by an egalitarian ethic and are capable of subscribing situationally to these values. The same is true of women in regard to the cult ideology: they are quite conscious that they are ritually unequal to men and, in appropriate contexts, are by no means incapable of endorsing the values of the ritual system. The ritual and mundane "models" are not in any simple sense gender-linked but are rather, as Milton (1979:51) puts it in her critique of Ardener's argument, "models appropriate for expression in particular situations." "Ritual hierarchy" cannot be interpreted as a "male" model in Ardener's sense of the term, because it is certainly neither subscribed to exclusively by males nor is it the only model men employ. But there is a different and rather more significant sense in which it is a sociologically "male" model; and this, as I have explained, is that men alone have the power to bring about the "realization" of this model in social action. In other words, one needs to take a rather different approach from Ardener's to the nature of actors' constructs of their social world.

The proposition that Ardener's argument is based on is undeniably true: as a result of their (no doubt always) different social experience, men and women must in some sense visualize their society differently. An assumption here is that the conceptions people hold of their society are subjective responses to their own social being, so that the locus of these models is, in short, the individual consciousness. Individuals whose social experience coincides to a significant extent (they have, for example, the same social status, or the same gender, or belong to the same class, and so forth) will tend to subscribe to significantly similar models of their society; while individuals with disparate positions in the social system will tend to construe their society in correspondingly different ways. But one of the problems with this approach is that there can *never* be an exact correspondence between the social experience of different individuals, no matter how similar their social positions or how homogeneous their society. As Ardener himself observes (1972:153), one can distinguish sociologically not only women from men, but also "inarticulate classes of men, young people and children." The difficulty here is precisely that the number of analytically significant categories distinguishable by the observer is in principle limitless. Indeed, the logic of Ardener's argument requires us to continue these discriminations down to the level from which his argument began: the level of the individual consciousness. We would be forced to recognize that there were in all truth as many "models" in a particular society as there were minds within it. This would certainly, as Ardener (1972:155) puts it, "split apart the very framework" of our discipline, but it would not put anything constructive in its place.

If Ardener is arguing, as I think he is, for a revision of the way in which we interpret social reality (and I agree with the need for such a revision) then his approach will not, as it stands, take us very far. He cogently makes the case that sociocultural systems—viewed in the functionalist tradition as more or less integrated and self-consistent wholes—encompass contrasting models reflecting different and even opposed social interests. But the assumption vitiating his argument is that the locus of these models is the consciousness of the individual. The assumption I adopt in this paper is that these models are not phenomena of subjectivity but, to use Schutz's (1967) term, of *inter*subjectivity. That is to say, they are not simply a means whereby the individual makes sense of his or her social world; they are a means of communicating with others and belong to a shared communicative universe. If different social structural models coexist in a given social system it is because they belong, not to different individuals or to different categories of individuals, but to what Schutz (1967, vol. 1:230) calls different provinces of meaning. Because my concerns are sociological rather than phenomenological in emphasis, I would rather speak of domains of social action or social experience. I have tried to show that at Avatip, ritual is one such domain and everyday life is another. This approach makes it possible to recognize the coexistence of a variety of models in a given society, but without reducing the analysis—as Ardener's assumptions logically commit one to doing—to a form of psychology or biography.

Ardener criticizes an older anthropology for implicitly treating "male" conceptions of society as definitive and argues that the analysis of ritual and other symbolic forms can reveal perspectives held by politically disadvantaged groups such as women. The assumption here, itself quite valid, is that consciousness experiences the social world as a kind of external reality (see Berger 1969). But Ardener's mistake is to treat ideology, ritual, belief—in short, the symbolic order—as simply this institutional reality reflected, from various perspectives within it, in the products of subjectivity. What this approach fails in the end to take account of is that the intersubjective nature of these constructs makes them the means not only of rendering the social world intelligible but of constituting it in the first place. The division of Avatip society into politically subordinate and superordinate groups is not an "absolute" property of Avatip social structure. It is one of two alternative ways in which the villagers formulate their social order, and it is "actualized" in social action by senior men in the context of ritual. These two formulations involve different forms of social classification and contrasting principles of social organization; they cannot therefore be "explained" by positing a logically "prior" division of the society into groups and categories. The secular and ritual spheres of Avatip society are alternative configurations of one and the same social universe, and the basic structural dichotomy in the social system is therefore not between initiates and noninitiates, men and women, seniors and juniors, or any other social categories. It is between those contexts in which these divisions are salient and those in which other organizational forms are employed. That is to say, it is not a dichotomy between social groups but between different conceptions of the nature of social relations.

So far as Avatip is concerned, I agree with Ardener that an interpretation of the society based solely on the statements of adult men would be incomplete and distorted. But this is not because men harbor models different from those of women. It is because men are likely to select, of the two formulations at their disposal, the one with which they tend to identify their political interests and which is meant for communication with outsiders: this is the formulation I have called "ritual hierarchy."

If one treats actors' models as creations merely of their own individual subjectivity, it would indeed seem unlikely that each actor would develop several conflicting models of his or her society. It is for this reason, I think, that Ardener tends to regard such models as belonging,in the end, to different social groups rather than to different contexts of social action. But this stumbling block is removed once one recognizes the essentially intersubjective nature of these constructs. Adults at Avatip have no difficulty whatever in conceiving of men and women, for instance, as morally equal yet ritually unequal. The models that I call ritual hierarchy and secular equality are two distinct, but simultaneously quite *thinkable,* dimensions of the villagers' cultural order. What they are not, however, is simultaneously *livable.* It is because of this that ritual and everyday life exist as two quite discrete fields of social action. And it is also because of this that the power of initiated men is both highly circumscribed yet radical: for it is the power, in effect, to periodicaily compel the community to "live" hierarchy within the delimited context of a ritual.

All properly socialized individuals at Avatip acknowledge the mundane and ritual models are equally "real." But individuals do differ—and in fact the same individual can differ from one occasion to another—in the way they *evaluate* these constructs. Some initiated men tend to speak of everyday life, in ritual contexts at least, as a state of political disorganization pervaded by a cloying and barely "social" domesticity. Some women, in everyday situations, tend to regard the rituals of the men's cult as an abrogation of many of the moral norms of kinship and potentially oppressive if continued for long. But these kinds of evaluations and there are others—are labile and contextual, and are not "tied" rigidly to gender, age, or any other criterion. They are a most interesting subject, and statistical patterns would no doubt emerge from an analysis of them. What I would emphasize, however, is that they cannot "explain" anything at all about Avatip culture or social structure. They are subjective responses to a particular social milieu and therefore presuppose its existence. What is important is that the nature of Avatip society is such as to present all individuals, to some degree or other, with a recurring dilemma of values in which their only guides are, ultimately, the ritual and secular ideologies themselves. This dilemma is a basic social fact; how individuals negotiate it is an important but analytically separate issue.[5]

Conclusion

I said at the beginning of this paper that in societies with male initiatory cults, the "cultural order" consists, minimally, of two distinct orders: one accessible to the society as a whole and the other accessible only to initiated males. One general suggestion I would like to put forward is that in cultural systems such as these, there will tend to be systematic differences in the way in which social relations between initiates and noninitiates are formulated symbolically at different "levels" of the cultural corpus. Specifically, the "esoteric" levels will tend to emphasize social and cosmological polarities between the sexes and between seniors and juniors; moving "down" the hierarchy of representations toward those of a "public" nature, these polarities will tend progressively to diminish. The reason for this, I would argue, is that each symbolic domain expresses a particular social perspective specific to the category of persons with access to that domain. Men of a senior grade "perceive" a greater differential in ritual status between themselves and noninitiates than do men of a more junior grade, and it is *this* perspective that is crystallized in the religious representations exclusive to their initiatory level. Conversely, wholly "public" constructs—everyday "secular" folk models of kinship, descent, domestic roles, and so forth—will have a more egalitarian character, because they will tend to reflect what is common to the social experience of everyone, irrespective of their differences in ritual status.

A second and related suggestion has to do with the social contexts in which mundane and ritual knowledge are used. To the extent that power is based on the control of ritual knowledge, it is likely, I suggest, to have a characteristic limitation. Social inequality will tend to manifest itself only in those contexts in which ritual knowledge is relevant, and in which the institutionalized exclusion of particular social categories from this knowledge is salient: that is, primarily in the setting of ritual itself. In contexts to which mundane knowledge applies—in situations calling for everyday, "practical" knowledge—social inequalities will tend contextually to "dissolve" because these forms of knowledge are not subject to, and therefore do not "register," the structures of exclusion on which inequality is based. "Practical" and "ritual" discourse in these societies carry different metamessages about the nature of social relations: in one case an "egalitarian" metamessage, and in the other a "hierarchical" one (cf. Bloch 1977).

If these suggestions are valid, a corollary is that in their everyday dealings with women and juniors, initiated men must perforce use relatively "egalitarian" forms of discourse. The hierarchy of ritual grades "exists" and everyone is aware of it, but the "language" of concepts the society uses (and must use) in mundane contexts is unable to "express" this in social action. The converse of this, I would argue, is also true. That is, that relations between the sexes, and between senior and junior males, actually *are* relatively relaxed, informal, and egalitarian in "secular" contexts; but that this fact is "muted," to borrow Ardener's (1975) term, in the symbolism of initiatory ritual, which is a language capable only of more or less extreme expressions of the idea of hierarchy.

My third suggestion has to do with the role of ritual secrecy. One function of secrecy is, of course, to preserve the "scarcity value" of ritual knowledge. But secrecy may also be required in some cases because the ideological content of this knowledge is to some degree normatively *counter* to the secular cultural ethos. Institutionalized secrecy is a prerequisite for the formulation and transmission, in specially "restricted" domains of the cultural order, of models contrary to the public normative system; and wherever such secrecy exists it is, I think, worth exploring the possibility that the ideology of ritual is in fact a *counter*ideology. Avatip, like most Melanesian societies, is an uncentralized, small-scale polity without formal political office or hereditary rank; and, apart from the male cult itself, it is characterized by a generally "weak" development of structural inequality. My argument in this paper is that its male initiatory system is a political hierarchy existing in a permanent tension with, or antithesis to, an institutional and ideological bias toward egalitarianism in secular contexts.

I have suggested that the symbolism of initiatory ritual is discordant with everyday social life. But there is one context in which social reality does correspond to the ritual "model": that is, when the ritual in question is actually being held. When men of the highest ritual grade perform a ritual at Avatip, for instance, the vision of "maximum hierarchy" contained in their shared ritual lore is "realized," temporarily, in social action. The society is polarized rigidly into ritual categories; an array of powerful taboos and prescriptions subordinate women and noninitiates to the performers and enforce a maximum of social distance between them. The spectrum of models—ranging from the mundane and "egalitarian," to the esoteric and "hierarchical"—are all equally "true": what they correspond to are different states of the social system along a processual cycle.

What I want to entirely disavow here is a notion, encountered sometimes in anthropological interpretations of religion, that ritual simply "says" something about social or political relations, as though ritual merely reflects or validates an independently existing institutional order. My approach is that an Avatip ritual brings into being a structure of social and political relations specific to that particular ritual; a structure altogether as "real" as the structure of everyday life, but simply *different* from it. The central privilege conferred by high ritual status is this: the privilege of periodically taking part in ritually *altering* social reality into a form which "realizes" one's high status.

From this point of view, ritual and everyday life are in one important respect entirely equivalent: they are both systems of collective action having a meaningful, communicative, or symbolic dimension. As a descriptive convenience, I have used the term "ritual" in this article to refer to the activities of the Avatip men's cult; but I nevertheless endorse the view of Leach (1954:12) that ritual, as an analytical category, is the communicative aspect of all or virtually all social behavior. Secular life at Avatip is a consensually maintained system of action and its symbolic dimension is "about" equality; rituals are systems of action imposed on the community by men of a particular initiatory grade, and their symbolic dimension is "about" inequality. Everyday life at Avatip is just as much symbolic or expressive action as is ritual: it simply has a different *meaning*.

There is a tradition in anthropology according to which ritual and religion affirm axiomatic and collectively shared values. My argument is that these male initiatory cults call for quite a different paradigm. I suggest that the rituals of these cults are by their very nature dissonant, to some degree, with the social and cultural actualities of "normal" social life, and that this "skewing" increases as one considers successively more esoteric rituals within any given initiatory system. The reason for this is that the performance of a ritual is not a manifestation of collective consensus, but of the coercive, yet highly circumscribed, power of a small group of men. The values displayed in ritual are distinctive to the cult itself; they are not, in any simple sense, subscribed to by the society as a whole or even by initiated men themselves outside the setting of ritual itself. Senior men may, in certain contexts, attribute an "ultimate" validity to their religious sacra (be these myths, cosmological notions, ritual techniques, and so forth) or speak of ritual as though it were an authoritative "model" of the social order. But it is important to treat these claims as simply part of the total range of sociocultural facts to be explained, and not as a premise of one's own analysis. Otherwise, one misses their *ideological* significance and, indeed, succumbs to it.

Notes

Acknowledgments. The fieldwork on which this article is based was carried out for 22 months between 1977 and 1979 under a Ph.D scholarship in the Department of Prehistory and Anthropology of the Australian National University. I should like to express my gratitude to that institution for its financial support and many facilities.

1. A social system with a number of striking parallels with Avatip has been described by Hill (1984) in an ethnoecological analysis of the Wakuénai of Venezuela. Hill argues that Wakuénai society alternates between two organizational modes, which the terms "social equality" and "ritual hierarchy," in response to severe seasonal fluctuations in environmental resources. I hope to discuss elsewhere the applicability of Hill's analysis to Avatip, with its similarly riverain adaptation.

2. There are indications that comparable patterns may exist in some other Sepik societies. Tuzin (1982), for example, writing of the Ilahita Arapesh, speaks of domestic and cult life being governed by antithetical moral codes and of permanent ethical dilemmas this poses for initiated men; and Losche (1984) writes of Abelam husbands and wives sharing, in the privacy of their conjugal relations, utopian visions of a sexually egalitarian social order.

3. M. Strathern (1980) makes a similar point concerning women's domestic roles in Mount Hagen in the New Guinea Highlands, in a discussion to which the present article owes much stimulus.

4. For an account of the regional system of some of the societies downriver from Avatip, see Gewertz (1983).

5. This dilemma is implicitly recognized as a primary datum of personal existence in the indigenous conception of personhood, a key construct of Avatip culture and one crucial to an understanding of Avatip social organization (see Harrison 1985). In effect, the conflict between "ritual hierarchy" and "secular equality" is represented as an opposition between two aspects or proclivities of the self; in other words, as an "inner" contradiction within human personhood and therefore as a part of an immutable "human nature." Society is simply apprehended as conforming to the unalterable constitution of the human personality.

References

Allen, Michael R. (1967). *Male cults and secret initiations in Melanesia.* London: Cambridge University Press.

Ardener, Edwin (1972). Belief and the problem of women. In J. S. La Fontaine (Ed.), *The interpretation of ritual* (pp. 135–158). London: Tavistock.

Ardener, Edwin (1975). The 'problem' revisited. In S. Ardener (Ed.), *Perceiving women* (pp. 19–27). London: Malaby Press.

Barth, Fredrik (1975). *Ritual and knowledge among the Baktaman of New Guinea.* New Haven, CT: Yale University Press.

Bateson, Gregory (1932). Social structure of the Iatmul People of the Sepik River. *Oceania, 2,* 245–291, 401–453.

Bateson, Gregory (1958). *Naven* (2nd ed.). Stanford, CA: Stanford University Press.

Berger, Peter L. (1969). *The social reality of religion.* London: Faber and Faber.

Bloch, M. (1977). The past and the present in the present. *Man (NS), 12,* 278–292.

Bowden, Ross (1983). *Yena: Art and ceremony in a Sepik society.* Oxford: Pitt Rivers Museum.

Gewertz, Deborah B. (1983). *Sepik River societies: A historical ethnography of the Chambri and their neighbors.* New Haven, CT: Yale University Press.

Harrison, S. J. (1982a). *Stealing people's names: Social structure, cosmology and politics in a Sepik River village.* Ph.D. dissertation, Department of Prehistory and Anthropology, The Australian National University.

Harrison, S. J. (1982b). Yams and the symbolic representation of time in a Sepik River village. *Oceania, 52,* 141–162.

Harrison, S. J. (1983). *Laments for foiled marriages: Love-songs from a Sepik River village.* Port Moresby: Institute of Papua New Guinea Studies.

Harrison, S. J. (1984). New Guinea highland social structure in a lowland totemic mythology. *Man (NS), 19,* 389–403.

Harrison, S. J. (1985). Concepts of the person in Avatip religious thought. *Man (NS), 20,* 115–130.

Hart, Charles W., & Pilling, Arnold R. (1960). *The Tiwi of North Australia.* New York: Henry Holt.

Häuser-Schäublin, Brigitta (1976). *Frauen von Kararau.* Basel: Museum für Völkerkunde.

Herdt, Gilbert H. (1981). *Guardians of the flutes: Idioms of masculinity.* New York: McGraw-Hill.

Herdt, Gilbert H. (Ed.) (1982). *Rituals of manhood: Male initiation in Papua New Guinea.* Berkeley: University of California Press.

Hill, Jonathan D. (1984). Social equality and ritual hierarchy: The Arawakan Wakuénai of Venezuela. *American Ethnologist, 11,* 528–544.

Keesing, Roger M. (1982). Introduction. In Gilbert H. Herdt (Ed.), *Rituals of manhood* (pp. 1–43). Berkeley: University of California Press.

Langness, L. (1967). Sexual antagonism in the New Guinea Highlands: A Bena Bena example. *Oceania, 37,* 161–177.

Langness, L. (1974). Ritual power and male domination in the New Guinea Highlands. *Ethos, 2,* 189–212.

Laycock, D. C. (1965). *The Ndu language family (Sepik District, New Guinea).* Canberra: Linguistic Circle of Canberra.

Leach, Edmund R. (1954). *Political systems of highland Burma.* London: Athlone Press.

Lewis, J. M. (1971). *Ecstatic religion: An anthropological study of spirit possession and shamanism.* Harmondsworth: Penguin.

Losche, Diane (1984). *Utopian visions and the division of labour in Abelam Society.* Paper presented at Wenner-Gren Symposium, "Sepik Research Today: The Study of Sepik Cultures in and for Modern Papua New Guinea," Basel, August 1984.

Mead, Margaret (1935). *Sex and temperament in three primitive societies.* London: Routledge.

Meggitt, M. J. (1964). Male-female relationships in the highlands of Australian New Guinea. *American Anthropologist, 66* (4, Pt 2):204–224.

Milton, Kay (1979). Male bias in anthropology? *Man (NS), 14,* 40–54.

Newman, Philip L. (1965). *Knowing the Gururumba.* New York: Holt, Rinehart & Winston.

Ortner, S. (1974). Is female to male as nature is to culture? In M. Rosaldo and L. Lamphere (Eds.), *Woman, culture and society* (pp. 67–87). Stanford: Stanford University Press.

Read, Kenneth E. (1952–53). Nama cult of the Central Highlands, New Guinea. *Oceania, 23,* 1–25.

Salisbury, Richard F. (1965). The Siane of the Eastern Highlands. In P. Lawrence & M. J. Meggitt (Eds.), *Gods, ghosts and men in Melanesia: Some religions of Australian New Guinea and The New Hebrides* (pp. 50–77), New York: Oxford University Press.

Schultz, Alfred (1967). *Collected papers.* 2 vols. The Hague: Martinus Nijhoff.

Strathern, A. J. (1970). Male initiation in New Guinea Highlands societies. *Ethnology, 9,* 373–379.

Strathern, Marilyn (1980). *Domesticity and the denigration of women.* Ms. in files of author.

Tuzin, Donald F. (1976). *The Ilahita Arapesh: Dimensions of unity.* Berkeley: University of California Press.

Tuzin, Donald F. (1982). Ritual violence among the Ilahita Arapesh. In Gilbert H. Herdt (Ed.), *Rituals of manhood* (pp. 321–355).

Dancing with Corpses Reconsidered: An Interpretation of Famadihana *(in Arivonimamo, Madagascar)*

DAVID GRAEBER

In September of 1990 I was talking with a woman named Irina about something an ancestor of hers had done some 60 years earlier. Like all the *andriana* or nobles of Betafo (a community to the north of the town of Arivonimamo, in Imerina, Madagascar) she was descended from a certain Andrianambololona, whose body, together with those of his wife and daughter and of three of his retainers, was buried in a large white tomb in the center of the village of Betafo, a five-minute walk across the rice fields from her house.

This particular ancestor, she was telling me, has long had the custom of appearing to his descendants in dreams to announce when the occupants of the tomb felt cold and needed to have a *famadihana* performed: that is, to be taken out and wrapped in new silk shrouds. When this happened in 1931, his descendants quickly gathered and organized the ritual. But, in their hurry perhaps, they forgot to exhume the bodies of the three retainers buried at the foot of the tomb somewhat apart from the rest. "The afternoon after they'd finished," she said, "the town suddenly caught fire and burned to the ground. And the next morning he came once more to the person"—the individual who had originally had the dream—"and said, 'If you don't wrap us all, next time I'll kill you outright....' So they got the tombs ready again and rewrapped them."[1]

This story is a good place to begin a discussion of the Merina practice of famadihana, if for no other reason than because it shows how high the stakes involved can be. Admittedly, it was the worst such disaster of which I ever heard, and Irina was doubtless justified in concluding that her ancestor was unusually "arrogant and cruel." But stories like this were hardly unusual. Rural communities in Imerina were, I found, largely organized around the memory of ancestors whose presence in the lives of their descendants made itself felt largely through the constraint and violence they were capable of inflicting on them. The dangers surrounding famadihana—and these were said to be great—only marked them as the culminating moment in an ongoing relationship between memory and violence implicit in the organization of everyday life, here played out over the very bodies of the ancestral dead.

Maurice Bloch, author of the classic analysis of famadihana, was also the first to point out the connection between memory and violence within it (1971:168–169). Pursuing that connection, however, leads one to focus on a very different side of Merina ritual life than the one emphasized in most of Bloch's subsequent work. Inspired by an ongoing interest in the legitimation of authority, his research has focused on how ritual creates the image of a timeless, idealized ancestral order, identified with death and the past and set apart from the practical contingencies of human existence (Bloch 1982, 1985, 1986). My own theoretical interests are more concerned with questions of how authority works itself out in practice: in the ways representations of death and the ancestors are continuous with everyday life.

Among people I knew in Arivonimamo, such representations were profoundly contradictory. Older men—almost anyone, in fact, who held a position of authority—would tend to become distinctly uncomfortable whenever the theme of ancestral violence arose. Most did their best to avoid the subject entirely—at least, they avoided it in front of me. Instead, they echoed the terms of formal rhetoric, in which ancestors were always represented as benevolent guardians of the moral unity of the community of their descendants, the very embodiments of moral good.[2] This is the view emphasized not only by Bloch but in most of the existing ethnographic literature on Madagascar (with exceptions: Astuti 1991; Feeley-Harnik 1991:56–60), and I certainly did not know anyone in Arivonimamo who would have openly challenged it. At the same time, however, it was difficult to reconcile with stories such as Irina's, and people seemed aware of the discrepancy, if not entirely sure what to make of it. To get at the roots of the contradiction, and to understand why it is that memory should have become identified with violence in the first place, one has to go beyond questions of ideology to consider how local authority actually works itself out in practice and the role famadihana play in reproducing it.

The Ritual

The word *famadihana*[3] is nowadays used to refer either to rituals held for the purpose of transferring a body from a temporary grave to its ancestral tomb, or from one tomb to another, or simply to open a tomb and remove the bodies temporarily for the purpose of wrapping them in new *lambamena,* or silk shrouds. While famadihana of this last kind appear to have become commonplace only in relatively recent times (at least, they are never mentioned in accounts of famadihana written in the 19th century: Callet 1908:272–273; Cousins 1963:79–81; Haile 1891; cf. Raison-Jourde 1991:717–738), everyone I talked to between 1989 and 1991 from the region of Arivonimamo,[4] and for that matter from elsewhere, took for granted that the rewrapping of ancestral bodies was the basic purpose of famadihana. Although the frequency of such ceremonies varied from tomb to tomb, most individuals said that the ceremony should be performed at least every six or seven years. This held true even if no ancestor—like Andrianambololona—appeared in a dream or vision to complain of being cold, as the ancestors were often said to do.

The overwhelming majority of famadihana about which I have information fell into one of two categories. Either they were held in order to return the body of an individual who had died away from ancestral lands, or else they were organized in honor of a local ancestor, dead some four to ten years, who had never before been the object of a famadihana (see Bloch 1971:146, 157–158). The sponsors of famadihana of the first sort—almost always families no longer living in the area—always made a point of rewrapping other ancestors in the tomb as well, and at times such "return famadihanas" (as Bloch calls them [1971:146]) could become quite elaborate. But the most celebrated and important famadihana of any given year were almost always of the second kind. Since it was considered important to honor each of the local ancestor's own immediate ascendants (mother, father's mother, mother's father, and so on), these might involve opening three or four different tombs—but the focus was always on the last one, from which the ancestor around whom the ceremony was organized was always the very last to emerge.

When people described a typical famadihana to me, they always emphasized the same basic sequence of events, starting with the calling of the ancestors' names, and ending with the ritual locking of the tomb. What follows, then, is my own version of such an account. The framework and order are based on participants' descriptions. The details are drawn from my observations of seven famadihana I attended between June 1989 and January 1990, all in the region of Arivonimamo, and the majority in Betafo itself.

The night before the tomb was to be opened, the sponsor and a few companions would mount the tomb and call out the names of the ancestors to be rewrapped, asking them all to return if they happen to have strayed. This stage is always important in accounts of famadihana, but it is conducted by a few close kin largely outside the public gaze. I never witnessed it myself.

The famadihana proper would begin the next day with a procession from the sponsor's hometown or village to the tomb. Between the *zanadrazana*—the "children of the ancestors"—and their guests and neighbors, there were usually at least several hundred people in attendance. An astrologer always led the way, usually accompanied by men carrying photographs of the most important ancestors, and always by one bearing the Malagasy flag (its presence confirmed that the ceremony was legally authorized). Musicians, and women carrying rolled papynus mats, followed close behind.

On arrival the flag was planted on the roof of the tomb, and men began digging away the earth that covered the buried stone door. The atmosphere was festive and informal, though marked by a certain feeling of anticipation: there was music, some people danced, others carried shovels and other tools back and forth or milled about and talked.

Once the door was fully uncovered some of the diggers splashed it with rum and then began to move it aside; others readied candles or lamps and then began to descend the stairs leading to the inner vault. As they disappeared inside the female zanadrazana (their numbers sometimes augmented by young men or boys) arranged themselves in rows, sitting with legs extended near the entrance to the tomb. Inside, the men would find the most ancient body, splash a bit of rum over it, make a brief invocation asking for its blessing, and then begin to roll it from its place onto a papyrus mat. Then three or four men would carry it up the stairs, calling out the ancestor's name as they emerged and the crowd whooped and shouted its enthusiasm. The music would usually pick up at this moment, and other men would help carry the body around the tomb three times, their abrupt stops and starts leading to its being twisted and crushed inside the mats.

After all the bodies had been carried out in order of seniority and had been placed on the laps of the women, the next phase of the famadihana began. Men and women produced bottles, some full of honey and rum, others of cow fat or occasionally cologne. There were also plastic bags full of honeycombs or pastel-colored "Malagasy" candies, pieces of ginger, and coins. Some moved from body to body, pouring rum and honey over each; others handed the bottles to the seated women (often after taking a sip or swig themselves). Sometimes a widow would produce a stick of tobacco and, putting half in her mouth, would place the remainder inside the tatters of her dead husband's lamba. Others broke off pieces of honeycomb or produced coins, ginger, and pieces of candy to place inside the folds of cloth around where the ancestor's head or chest would lie.[5]

This sequence of giving, taking, and sharing—invariably called a *fangatahana tsodrano* or "request for the blessing" of the ancestors—was always a moment of great emotional intensity. Women—particularly if they held the remains of a close relative on their lap—were clearly frightened, sad, and disturbed by what they were doing. Many appeared in a virtual state of shock, barely managing to hold back tears, and in every famadihana I attended at least one such woman did begin to cry. People quickly crowded around to do their best to reassure, comfort, or distract her, always reminding her, "This is an act of celebration, not of mourning" (*fifaliana fa tsy fahoriana ity*).

Next, men divided into teams around each ancestor to begin the actual wrapping. The initial stages were performed while the body lay across the women's laps, since it was very important that at no time should an ancestor touch the earth. Old layers of cloth were never removed; instead, all the remains were rolled first into a white sheet, then into one or more thicker and more durable lamba. There were almost always at least two layers of cloth in all: bright silk lambamena for the more important ancestors, polyester for the rest. While women watched and often gave advice, men were responsible for actually wrapping the bodies and then tying the resulting bundle together with cords or strips of cloth. They spared no effort to roll and bind the ancestral bundles as tightly as possible.

Once again the music picked up in volume and tempo, and the final, joyous part of the ceremony began. Mixed groups of men and women carried the bodies, borne in mats, one by one around the tomb, this time stopping and starting and dancing even more vigorously than they had before—even violently—with all sorts of roughhousing, shouts, whoops, and cries. People generally threw themselves about in a sort of delirious abandon, and the razana were twisted and crunched about a great deal before finally being returned to their places inside.

With this the business was basically finished. If there were more tombs to be opened, a procession would form behind the astrologer once again. If this was the last, the sponsor and some local elders or politicians would mount the head of the tomb to deliver brief orations summarizing the day's events and thanking everyone who had come. Afterward, as the crowd began to drift off, a group of men took shovels and began to pile back the dirt removed from the door to the vault.[6] Later still, often around nightfall after everyone had long since left, the astrologer and a few assistants would return to make a *fanidi-pasana*—a "lock to the tomb"—by burying a few magical objects in or around its doorway. If placed correctly, a *fanidy* should ensure that the ghosts of those within would remain there, unable to emerge again and trouble the living.

Descent Groups

Merina society is divided up into a number of named undifferentiated descent groups, which Maurice Bloch called "demes" because they tend toward endogamy and are closely identified with ancestral territories. About a third claim andriana, or "noble" rank; the rest are *hova,* or "commoner" demes. In addition, perhaps a third of the population of Imerina are descended from people brought there in the 19th century as slaves. These *mainty,* or "black people," are not organized into demes and do not usually intermarry with the *fotsy,* or "whites," though in most other respects their social organization was the same as that of the latter. (Betafo was made up of andriana and mainty in roughly equal numbers, but what follows is based on material from other andriana, hova, and mainty groups in the region of Arivonimamo as well.)[7]

Each deme has its history, usually beginning with an account of the origins of its founding ancestor, how he came to the territory on which his descendants now reside, how by his various movements he defined its boundaries, how he created its villages named various prominent aspects of its landscape, and so on. In most cases the stories go on to tell how he subdivided the territory by giving each of his children (or occasionally wives) a village or territory: that of the eldest always furthest to the east, with the others ranging westward in order of seniority (see, for instance, Condominas 1960:199–203; Rasamimanana and Razafindrazaka 1957:9–13).

Most people, I found, could tell me from which of these branches they considered themselves to be descended; but this was not because they could trace any genealogical link to the founder. Genealogical memory was in fact extremely shallow. I met very few people who could remember further back than their grandparents, or to people they personally remembered from their youth. Nor are deme divisions in most cases any longer identified with clearly bounded territories—if indeed they ever were. What mattered was not where one lived, but the location and history of one's tomb.

In rural Imerina, tombs are everywhere. In most villages there is literally no place one can stand without a tomb being somewhere in sight. Ancient ones, now little more than grassy mounds of earth, sit next to whitewashed stone and cement tombs topped with wreathes and stone crosses, now and then—if a particularly wealthy family lives in the neighborhood—flanked by brightly painted palatial structures on wide platforms, their doorways shielded by metal lattice gates. Whatever their size, their granite solidity is meant to contrast with houses, which are never built of stone but are usually made of mud brick. Clearly, tombs were meant to be symbols of permanence, constant reminders of the enduring presence of the ancestors.

Tombs were also organized into a hierarchy. It was this hierarchy of tombs that formed the real physical framework of the deme and provided the terms of reference by which people could place themselves within it. Most people I knew had only the haziest idea of their deme's history, but all could point out their family tomb.

Andrianambololona was buried with his wife and daughter in an impressive stone tomb to the east of the village of Betafo.[8] In the western part of the same village were four tombs, each said to hold the body of one of his four eldest sons, and half an hour's walk further to the west was a fifth tomb, that of his youngest son. (The youngest son is said to have quarreled with his seniors and moved away.) Each of the deme's divisions was said to be descended from one of these brothers, whose relative rank is remembered even if their names have long since been forgotten. And while only a handful of the present-day inhabitants actually expected to be buried in one of these ancient tombs, each new tomb was linked to one of them by the affiliation of its founder. In other words, what really knits a deme together is not a human genealogy but a genealogy of tombs. Older tombs are seen as generating younger ones, and the organization as a whole inscribes a pattern of historical memory in the landscape in a way that makes it seem one of its most permanent features.

The Organization of Tombs

This is not to say that this framework is in any sense really permanent or unchanging. In fact it is continually being transformed and redefined through human action. New tombs are always being built, old ones emptied and abandoned. Bodies are transferred back and forth, broken apart, and combined with one another. And in a purely practical sense, this is what famadihana can be said to *do*.

Whatever their outer appearance, inside, Merina tombs are much the same. The doorway always faces east; the door itself is a huge buried slab of stone. Below it a stair descends into a single large chamber from whose northern, western, and southern walls emerge stone "beds" (*farafara*) or shelves, set one above the other. Typically there are three shelves on each wall, making nine in all, but people are rarely willing to place bodies on the bottom shelves, so that in most tombs the number available is effectively six.

In principle everyone who has the right to be buried in a given tomb is descended from a single individual, known as that tomb's *razambe* (or "great ancestor"). The bodies of razambe are always placed on either the highest shelf to the north or the highest to the east, usually together with their firstborn children. The other children are allotted different shelves on which they become, as it were, minor razambe, and on which only their descendants have the right to be buried. Sometimes, individual shelves are further subdivided by the same means. Shelves and spaces on the shelves thus become a form of property. I have even heard of a case of a man in extreme financial trouble who tried to sell his space in a prestigious tomb, although I am not sure whether anyone would have dared to buy it from him; his relatives eventually talked him out of the idea.

In practice, however, one can draw on a variety of other connections—marriage, fosterage, blood brotherhood, and so forth—to gain access to a tomb, so that most men and almost all women have a range of choices over where they intend to be buried.[9] Informants often emphasized, however, that each tomb has its own regulations on such matters: children linked through women are not allowed on the upper shelves of one tomb; in another only actual descendants of the razambe, but not their husbands or wives, may be interred. Such regulations can take many forms but are always negative in their phrasing; in fact, they are usually called the tomb's *fady,* or "taboos," and are not distinguished as such from rules against wearing clothes with buttons inside some tombs or giving tobacco to the dead in others.

When I started going inside Merina tombs, the thing that continually surprised me was how few bodies most seemed to contain. In many ancient ones only two or three of the shelves held bodies at all. Even where the majority were occupied, there might be only three or four bodies on any given shelf—remarkably few, when one considers that some of these tombs had been in continual use for over a century. There were, I found, a number of reasons why this should be so. For one thing, new tombs were constantly being built. On completing a new tomb, it was customary to take at least one ancestor from one's former tomb to be the new one's razambe. If one can get permission from all the owners, a whole shelf's worth of ancestors might be cleared out and divided up among those of the new tomb.[10] And since the division of shelves in the old one was considered to have been fixed by ancestral decree—which made people very reluctant to rearrange the bodies—whole walls of shelves might end up lying empty as a result.

A more important reason, however, is that the number of bodies is kept limited by the habit of consolidating them. Here the reader should understand that these bodies—the Malagasy term *razana* actually means both "ancestor" and "corpse"—are not really "bodies" at all in any sense suggested by the English word.[11] They certainly did not look anything like human bodies, but resembled wrapped bundles of red earth.

No razana can take part in famadihana until the corpses are considered "dry"—that is, until they had been in the tomb for several years, by which time little but dust and bones are likely to remain. During famadihana, bodies are subjected to a great deal of rough handling: they are made to dance with living partners, pulled and tugged, wrapped and bound with extreme force, and then dragged into a still more tumultuous dance before being returned to their shelves. After 20 years and several famadihana, they have been quite literally pulverized; even the skeletons have largely crumbled, and there is little left to serve as a reminder that the thing has once had human form. People say that the deceased have turned into "dust" (*vovoka*): it is usually impossible to tell what was once body from what was once cloth, both having turned the same brick-red color that is, incidentally, the same as that of the lateritic Malagasy soil.

Bodies can only be combined after their first famadihana—that is to say, after they have already largely been reduced to dust. It is relatively simple to rewrap two such bodies in the same cloth. Indeed, if one does not, ancestors—unless they are regularly rewrapped in very large numbers of shrouds—tend to become ever thinner until they eventually look like mere tubes of cloth, no thicker than a human arm or leg, and with a bulge in the middle. On the other hand, *razana ikambanana*, or "combined ancestors"—which for all anyone knows may be comprised of the remains of a dozen different individuals and their accumulated lamba—can often attain a size two or three times that of a living human being.

The most frequent practice was to wrap husbands with their wives and to wrap children in one lamba together with their parents. (Despite the frequency of this practice I was often told that two siblings could never be combined.) Apart from this it is difficult to generalize, since as in so many things different families and tombs have different customs. But the ancestors combined together are almost always those on the verge of being forgotten—that is, contemporaries of the parents or grandparents of the tomb's oldest living descendants. Usually children who have died at an early age are the first to be so treated (these are incorporated in their parents); next come adults with no living descendants to provide them with lambamena during future famadihana (they are combined with ancestors who do). The names of such minor razana are for the most part quickly forgotten. In the end, however, except in those rare instances when the tomb's owners make a point of marking certain razana with written labels or keep family notebooks, all but two or three of the most famous older names will inevitably pass from memory. Most older tombs end up containing at least one and often several large bundles known only as a razambe ikambanana ("combined razambe") since none of the current owners have the slightest idea what the name of any of its component ancestors might be.

Since none of these razambe—named or nameless—can ever be removed to another tomb, no tomb, however old, can ever be entirely stripped of bodies. But as some of the branches of descendants die out and others build new tombs and remove their own immediate ancestors, many reach the point where they are no longer used for burial. (They are said to be "full," although in fact they are more likely to be largely empty.) Most such tombs will occasionally still be opened and one or two bodies rewrapped during elaborate famadihana. At least in my experience, however, this is usually the occasion of much confusion, as the zanadrazana inspect the half dozen or so ancestral bundles left in the tomb, trying to identify their own. And even these connections are not remembered forever. Hillsides are dotted with the remains of ancient tombs which often look like nothing more than low mounds with a few worked stones visible here and there through the grass; their remaining occupants have long since been forgotten. The most prestigious ancient tombs, seen as key nodes in the hierarchical framework of the deme, may really be merely the oldest ones that have managed to avoid oblivion.

The whole process of pulverizing and then consolidating bodies can be seen as the concrete or tangible aspect of a process of genealogical amnesia. Ancestral bodies are gradually dissolved at the same time as their identities are gradually forgotten; both are ultimately destined to become absorbed into those of more famous razambe. Something of this sort occurs wherever genealogies are important, but in the Merina case the whole issue of remembering and forgetting becomes much more of a tangible problem, if only because "ancestors" are conceived in so tangible a way. If remembering ancestors becomes a matter of handling corpses, forgetting them has to be made an active process rather than something that can just happen by default.

Similarly, while ancestral names played an important role in famadihana—they were called out from the tomb the night before, called out again as the bodies emerged, and, usually, listed a third time in the speeches that closed the ceremony[12]—almost no one has made the slightest effort to preserve these names in writing. There was no reason why they could not be preserved: illiteracy is almost unknown in rural Imerina. With very few exceptions, however, they are not. It is a central irony of famadihana that, while participants regularly call them "memorials" (*fahatsiarovona*) for the dead, what they actually accomplish is to make descendants actively complicit in forgetting them.

Cursing and Taboo

Most of the practices surrounding tombs and bodies have little impact on people's everyday affairs. When ancestors intervene directly in their descendants' daily lives, it is largely through the imposition of fady, or taboos. One might well say that "cursing," or imposing fady on one's descendants, is the quintessential mode of ancestral action; in the same way, the quintessential ritual action undertaken by the living is to ask the ancestors for their *tsodrano* or "blessing," that is, to ask them for release from such restrictions.

A good deal has been written about Malagasy fady (Lambek 1992; Ruud 1960; Standing 1883; Van Gennep 1904). For present purposes, the important thing to emphasize is that, unlike Polynesian *tabu,* for example, fady are not primarily concerned with ideas about the sacred or pollution; they are always placed on an action rather than a person or a thing. Fady are, quite simply, things one cannot do. Throughout Madagascar, to be able to impose such restrictions on others is one of the most basic ways of demonstrating authority over them; sharing fady is one of the clearest ways of demonstrating solidarity.

Each deme had its own ancestral fady. The older men who were considered the ultimate authorities on such matters tended to describe these fady to me in moralistic terms: they were the means by which the ancestors maintained the harmony and integrity of the deme. As a result, they would almost always dwell on the same two or three examples: fady against stealing from one's kindred, those against selling the ancestral land to outsiders, and, sometimes, those against intermarrying with inferior groups (particularly the descendants of slaves). Though always attributed to a deme's particular ancestors, this list remained largely unchanged from group to group. But there were also more particular deme fady: other groups of equal status into which one could not marry, and certain animals and plants that one could not raise, grow, or eat. Tombs often had their own sets of fady, usually attributed to their respective razambe; even living parents could, if they so chose, "curse" their descendants never to eat a certain kind of meat or wear a certain type of clothing, thereby creating a taboo.

Often there were stories about the origin of important fady. People were much more likely to know these stories than the more formal deme histories, if only because they were usually much more entertaining. Many were explicitly comic and clearly meant to poke fun at their ancestral protagonists. A favorite theme has various ancestors gorging themselves so greedily on a particular delicacy that they burst apart and died, whereupon the survivors cursed their descendants never to eat such food again. One might argue that the absurdity is meant to underline the perceived arbitrariness of so many ancestral restrictions. But there was also a genre of very serious stories about fady that were perhaps even more widely known, and these concerned the consequences of a fady's transgression.

I heard such stories constantly. A rich andriana who married a woman descended from slaves suddenly lost everything he had and is now a pauper. Someone grew garlic in a prohibited place; his crops were destroyed by hail. Someone else tried to remove a body from a tomb in violation of its regulations; he was blasted by lightning and died. Anyone—young or old, male or female—could easily recount a dozen or more such stories. And it is almost exclusively these stories which described how the *hasina,* or invisible power, of the ancestors actually manifested itself to living people—or, in other words, how the ancestors continued to act and to play a direct role in their descendants' daily lives. Remarkably, the ancestors' presence was almost always reified in attacks on their descendants; had these actions been carried out by a living person, they would have been instantly condemned as the most reprehensible kind of witchcraft.

No one would openly suggest that ancestors were anything like witches. As I have mentioned, elders in particular tended to picture them as the benevolent guarantors of the unity and moral integrity of the group. On the other hand, many of these old men grew distinctly uncomfortable whenever anything touching on the question of ancestral retribution was mentioned just as they would have done at any mention of witchcraft. Within a community, it seems mainly to be women who transmit these stories. Most of the women I spoke to did not hesitate to express their opinions about the ancestors' behavior—in fact, the most common epithet they used, *masiaka,* means "savage," "violent," or "cruel." The older men's reluctance to talk about ancestral violence probably sprang in part from the fact that they were very close to being ancestors themselves and as figures of authority simply tended to identify with the ancestors' position. Like all parents, they also wielded the power of *ozona,* or "cursing," their own children. Ozona could be used as a weapon to punish offspring who had proved unerly resistant to advice or admonition and inasmuch, this was the ultimate bastion of parental authority.[13]

While I only heard of two or three instances in which people I knew had been cursed, people constantly alluded to the possibility. By all accounts, such curses always took a negative form: "You will never have any children," "You will never find prosperity in your life," or "You will never enter the family tomb." In other words, whatever the content of a curse, and whatever the means of its enforcement, it never took the form of a direct assault, such as inflicting a disease on someone or causing people to loose all their wealth, but instead specified something the victim would never attain.

While the stories of distant ancestors separate the imposition of restrictions and punishment for their transgression, one might say that the two are merged here in a single gesture. But this only underlines what I think to be a general principle: that the power to impose restrictions is ultimately continuous with the violence through which those restrictions are enforced.

An Initial Synthesis

One reason Merina ancestors were felt to be a constraint on the actions of their descendants was that the ultimate aspiration, at least of any man, was to become a prominent ancestor himself. To do so, however, he must manage both to overshadow the memory of his own ancestors and to constrain his children—particularly his sons—from either moving away or overshadowing him in turn. It is important to emphasize that the social divisions I have been describing are not said to have been instituted by divine beings or totemic animals in some distant mythological past. They were created by ancestors. Ancestors, while still alive, were simply people—people who were born, had children, built tombs, and died in the same way that people still do today.[14] In principle, there is no reason why anyone alive today could not become famous razambe, even—and I met plenty of people willing to entertain this possibility—razambe on the order of the founders of demes. If one cannot become such an illustrious ancestor, it is only because someone else already has done so.[15] In other words, the memory of the dead is itself a constraint on the ambitions of the living. This makes it much easier to understand why the presence of the ancestors is generally felt through a series of constraints.

Madagascar is one of those places that anthropologists have found troubling in the past owing to the lack of "stnucture" or rules (Wilson 1977). Authors have emphasized the degree to which even links of descent are seen as created rather than as received ("achieved" rather than "ascribed" in Southall's usage [1971, 1986]), and have underlined the importance of links like fosterage, adoption, blood brotherhood, or other kinds of "friendship" in creating links between people (Feeley-Harnik 1991; Kottak 1986; Vogel 1982). In Imerina, propeny and rights of group membership are conveyed as easily through men as through women, marital residence is flexible, and marriage easy to dissolve. Most people have a very wide range of options about how and with whom to live their lives. At the same time, however, tremendous emphasis is placed on parental authority and the role of elders, of which ozona is only the ultimate form. In other words, people's freedom of action is not seen as greatly limited or constrained by explicit rules, but rather as constrained by others, especially those in positions of authority. Those social groups that (unlike those organized around tombs) provide the context for people's daily affairs are for the most part organized around the personality of a single individual.

A Politics of Movement

Already in the 19th century, Malagasy folktales implied that there was nothing unusual in a young man's abandoning his home and family to travel in search of fortune (Dahle 1984). Deme founders such as Andrianambololona still tend to be represented as men who had left home "to gain a better living" (*mitady ravinahitra*). To become a famous ancestor, however, it was not enough simply to break with one's own family and come into wealth. One also had to ensure that one's own children did not do the same. There was, and apparently has long been, a radical contradiction between a father's interest and that of his sons. As a result, generational politics largely amount to a politics of movement, with fathers striving to keep their descendants from leaving and sons at least dreaming of being able to break away.

In a place such as Betafo, where migration had been taking place for well over a century, most "owners" of any given tomb were likely not to live there. Some resided in the capital, others were teachers, officials, or shopkeepers in other parts of Madagascar, and yet others had migrated to new lands in the west. Since almost all the men (and a fair number of the women) spent a good deal of their time away from their villages and engaged in petty commerce or some other financial activity, everyone was aware of opportunities elsewhere.

In the end this meant that only the wealthiest or most successful farmers had the means to keep any large proportion of their children around them. The less fortunate would see their children disappear one by one. Daughters married away. Sons might well do likewise or might follow their mothers, be adopted by wealthier relatives, or simply head west or to the capital, at first intending to stay only long enough to make a little money, but ultimately never returning. The effects of such migration, combined with the vagaries of demography, lead to a perception of tremendous instability: in the space of one or two generations whole villages could be emptied, and large, prosperous families vanish without a trace. On the other hand, the most successful could not only keep most or all of their own sons and even daughters at home but could add a whole range of dependents or semidependents: poorer brothers or sisters and their children, affines (endogamous marriage was often used to cement such ties), kin through adoption or blood brotherhood, and so on. The crucial factor was land. A father who wanted to keep his children and dependents around him had to be able to grant them enough rice fields to support a family when they were ready to get married, usually leaving only a modest portion for himself.

For the vast majority of people in a given rural community, groups organized around one such prominent individual provided the real framework for daily life. Again following Bloch (1971:81–86), I call these groups "local families."[16] Members continued to work their fields cooperatively even after the patrimony had been divided, fostering each other's children, sharing meals, and generally allowing a far more intimate circulation of people and things than they conduced with any of their other neighbors. Sometimes, such groups would break away from larger settlements entirely. Even when they did not, communities were seen as little more than agglomerations of such local families, each of which would often cohere under a nominal head for at least a decade after the death of its original founder.

In their own way, these dead founders were the most significant political figures in any given community. Certainly, their names were always cropping up in conversation. Time after time I would hear someone speaking of a certain Rakoto's field or Rabe's house, only later to find out that the Rakoto or Rabe in question had been dead for over a decade. Usually it turned out that the groups these men had founded still existed, headed now by the men's widows, by elder sons of less intrinsic authority, or by both. Often in such cases the final division of rights in land and houses had not yet been made. In other cases the speaker either was not quite sure who the current owner was or considered the owner insignificant. Similarly, whenever I asked people in a given community who could tell me about local historical traditions—a role which should properly go to the political leaders of a community—their immediate response was always to begin naming the most prominent people who had died over the last ten or fifteen years.

In principle, the leaders of a community are its elders, or *Ray amandReny* (literally "fathers and mothers"). In practice, I found, people almost never used the term to refer to living people. The Ray amandReny were mainly dead individuals. Almost all others were excluded.

The largest quarter of Betafo, Andrianony, was made up of three local families. In oniy one family was the founder still alive. Between them, these three groups accounted for all but five of the quarter's twenty households. The other families were all marginal or fragmentary in some sense; most were composed of a single elderly man or woman living with an unmarried adult child, or with a small number of younger children or grandchildren. Although the heads of such families might be respected for their age, they were usually quite poor, and no one would think of them as Ray amandReny. The same was true of elders who were dependents within other local families. Women could in principle be Ray amandReny, but in practice they were almost never considered so. Other men were disqualified by questions of character. In the end, of the roughly 118 people who lived in Betafo, there was really only one who everyone agreed could be considered an elder. Betafo, moreover, was unusual in having even one.

Not Being Forgotten

Most of the members of any local family would normally expect to be buried in its founder's tomb. Often this was a tomb the deceased had himself created; if not, it was usually because he had already succeeded in establishing himself as the exclusive effective owner of one of the most famous ancient tombs, with whose razambe he might be confused in the eyes of the neighborhood.

How can a man of local fame—whose grandchildren still recall him in their daily lives—assume the status of a famous razambe, who will be remembered and revered long after those grandchildren are dead? If one founds a tomb, one has to bring in at least one of one's own ancestors to be its razambe; in the case of an ancient tomb, one is often dealing with an ancestor whose fame is already so great (one of the children of the deme's founder, for instance) that the identity of the owner could hardly help be overshadowed by it. While it is impossible to speak with any real certainty about processes that can only be observed over several generations, in practice there are several possibilities. Even a razambe can be forgotten or can end up absorbed into some more famous successor (with whom he is often physically merged). On inspection of old documents,[17] I frequently discovered that the ancestor generally assumed to be the razambe of some tomb was in fact not its oldest ancestor at all but the man who built it.

This entailed a complex politics whose very existence was never openly admitted. The authority of most of the effective community leaders was derived from that of some more venerable ancestor—most often a father who was no longer alive. While everyone spoke of the need to remember and honor deceased parents, they also knew that the ultimate fame of a father almost necessarily meant the eventual oblivion of his sons (and vice versa).

In any community there were admittedly some people who were apparently seeking their immortality vicariously. But in my experience this was a strategy mainly adopted by prominent women and rarely, if ever, by men. A widow might promote the prestige and memory of her late husband (or a daughter those of her father) as razambe of a tomb, thinking little of her own name and reputation in comparison. But women had a very different position than did men in the politics of local families. The relation between fathers and daughters was not at all like the difficult and contradictory relation between fathers and sons. It was held to be particularly close. I often heard preferences for cousin marriage, for instance, explained as a simple matter of paternal sentimentality: fathers could not bear to see their daughters move too far away. And even a daughter who does marry far away knows her father will always be happy to welcome her back if he is at all able to do so, should she wish to leave her current husband, and all the more so if she has children who will add to the number of his local descendants. For most women a father's house was a potential refuge[18]; this doubtless contributed to the universal feeling that girls naturally form their closest emotional attachments with their fathers, just as boys always tend to remain primarily loyal to their mothers, in childhood as well as later on in life.

Gender and the Politics of Memory

I mentioned at the beginning of the article that the most prominent famadihana of any year was likely to be dedicated to a single person who had died some four or five years before. In my experience this person was always the head of a local family whose memory still dominated the lives of his descendants in the way I have been described.

A famadihana was held for Irina's father, Razafindrabe, in the winter of 1990. Razafindrabe had died in 1982 at the age of 66, only two years after having finished building his tomb. He had been a very successful man and his descendants now dominated two different villages near Betafo. The ceremony was sponsored by his widow and six surviving children. Three different tombs were opened. The first was that of Razafindrabe's father. Though the father's body itself had been removed to the new tomb, four other ancestors were rewrapped there and some unrelated people took the occasion to add two bodies that had been buried in temporary graves nearby. Next came his mother's tomb, where the family was also responsible for the ancestors of a rich but childless woman who had adopted Razafindrabe and left him her land. Even at these first tombs there was a certain feeling of fear and anxiety as the ancestors first emerged, a certain air of triumph and rejoicing as they were returned. But these were not the bodies of people any of the participants had actually known; to the contrary, most did not even know their names.

The final tomb, however, was Razafindrabe's own. By the time the last tomb had been opened the tension had built up to the point where many of the zanadrazana clearly found it almost unbearable. Some of the young men carrying the bodies out of the tomb appeared, although fortified by rum, so overwhelmed by what they were doing that their faces were those of people in physical pain, as if they were forcing themselves to carry out their parts in the ritual. Others seemed to have fallen into an almost trancelike state, stumblingly oblivious to what was happening around them. When Razafindrabe himself emerged—and was immediately surrounded by a press of descendants who flooded him with rum and other offerings—the emotional pitch had reached a climax; few were the women who did not at least choke back sobs when the ancestors were first placed on their laps, and several, including Irina, broke down in tears.

As the process of giving gifts and wrapping the ancestors continued people would always gradually regain their composure, and by the end virtually everyone took part in mood of celebration; after the ceremony, however, women always tended to remark on who had cried—particularly if they had done so themselves. "It's because you still remember the person so vividly," I was told on several occasions, always in more or less the same words, "and then you see just how little is still left." I once asked one of these women why, if famadihana were supposed to be such happy occasions, someone always burst into tears. She looked at me somewhat quizzically and pointed out that such people had often just had their father's corpse placed across their laps. "Well how would you feel?" I did not want to give anyone the idea that we foreigners were lacking in normal human sentiments, so I hurriedly assured her that anyone in the world would be likely to have a similar reaction to such a situation. Only later did it occur to me that I could have added that this is precisely why we never put dead fathers on people's laps to begin with. If in Imerina they do so, it can only be because the memory of the living individuals—or at least, of some—remains so powerful and so persuasive a presence in the minds of their descendants that only such a dramatic confrontation can really bring home the fact of their death.

Bloch has already noted that famadihana are largely concerned with transforming the memories of the living (1971:168–169); this he adds makes them quite different from the secondary burials made famous by Robert Hertz (1907), which are primarily concerned with freeing the souls of the dead person from their lingering existence halfway between this world and the next. But in a way the two are not so very different: here, too, the dead could be said to linger on in a kind of suspended half-life in the memories of their contemporaries.

In the ritual, it was women's memories that were most prominently brought into play, while the ancestors who are the real emotional focus of the ritual were almost always male.[19] This was quite in keeping with the emotional bonds between fathers and daughters (as also between mothers and sons), attachments that colored both women's and men's attitudes toward ancestors more generally. The same pattern—female ancestors boding ill, males boding well—appeared constantly, for instance, in accounts of women's dreams. And while I know a good deal less about the dreams of men than those of women, since men were less inclined to tell me about such things, my impression is that the terms were typically reversed. Fathers appeared mainly to chide their sons when they had been squabbling with each other or had otherwise strayed, or to warn of disaster. Razafindrabe himself is a case in point. Irina told me he had made a deathbed promise to his six sons that he would continue, even after his death, to counsel and admonish them when there was a quarrel in the family. On the other hand, Irina herself had been her father's favorite, as well as his only daughter. She had never married away from her father's village, instead bearing a number of children by a variety of partners and letting her father help her raise them. During the famadihana described above, she had been the most conspicuous with her tears over his body; a few days later, she told me that her father regularly appeared in her dreams as a kind of guardian spirit, protecting her from danger and giving her advice.

A remarkable feature of all such dreams was the way that images of living people become mixed up with images of death. Frequently, as in the following dream, reported to me by Irina, they appeared in or near their tombs; alternatively, the images recounted shifted back and forth between those of living human beings and those of frightening corpses.

> *I dreamed that I saw my father in 1989 (this was when he was already dead) to the north of Ambodivona. There are some trees there and we were talking among them [and I asked myself], "Is this daddy appearing to us here, still alive?" Then, "Give me your blessing," I said (because I wasn't well . . .) So we were talking, when he said, "You shouldn't do such things, Irina," and right there he plunged back into being dead and bound. Later I went up to the village where my older brother was, and he too just took off out of the village, and plunged into death like that. It was, like, disgusting and frightening.*[20]

On first seeing her father Irina wonders whether he is still alive, but when she asks him for his blessing he suddenly rebukes her and turns into a corpse. The image changes from that of a living person to that of an ancestor, bound head and foot by the ropes used to fasten on his shrouds. What happens in Irina's dream—confronting a vivid memory of an ancestor, asking for his blessing, and then suddenly seeing him transformed into a dead, bound corpse—is just what happens to women in famadihana,[21] except that in famadihana it is living men who bring about the confrontation by calling out the names of the dead and thus evoking memories of living persons in the minds of the women, before placing those persons' decomposed bodies on their laps. The memories evoked by these names are tied to physical objects—objects that gradually dissolve as the names themselves are gradually forgotten. The process as a whole can be viewed as effacing the individual identities of all the dead except the very few who are or will become a tomb's razambe.

Earlier I described this process as an active form of genealogical amnesia in which the living begin to combine the remains of ancestors about to pass from memory with others whose names are thought to be more likely to endure. But few endure for very long. In examining the names that were actually called out during famadihana at particular tombs I found that, aside from one or two razambe, almost all belonged to people who had died within the last 10 or 15 years. In other words, most names continued to be commemorated only so long as memories of the bearers themselves were likely to remain vivid in the minds of any number of the living; or, perhaps more to the point, as long as the social ties derived from those memories still have some reality in people's daily lives.

Names like that of Razafindrabe, however, remain enormously important—so much so that local society can be said to be largely organized around them. Local families continued to be called by the names of their founders as long as they held together; as I have noted, these names were regularly invoked in conversation about the ownership of houses, rice fields, and tombs long after their bearers had died. The expression most often used to refer to ancestors on one's father's side literally means "name of the father" (*anaran-dray*). It was also used to refer to what might be called "ancestral propeny": houses, tombs, and rice fields passed on through the male line (as was *anaran-dreny*, or "name of the mother" for the female line). As a number of scholars have remarked (Gueunier 1982:237, n.2; Razafindratovo 1980; Razafintsalama 1981), this is a curious expression, since Malagasy society does not use patronymics or, for that matter, matronymics of any kind. Why, then, should the most important elements of one's inheritance be identified with one of the few aspects of a father or mother's social identity that were not inherited?

The answer, I would argue, is that by using this expression one underlines the fact that such property does not entirely belong to the person holding it. In some cases this was quite literally true. If a group of brothers and sisters postpone the formal division of their parents' property, land and houses might remain legally registered in a dead ancestor's name for years. I was even told that descendants might decide to hold a famadihana for the express purpose of asking such an ancestor's "blessing" (tsodrano) before dividing up a joint estate. Even when descendants do hold legal title, however, possession is not without its obligations: if one holds a rice field inherited from a given ancestor, one is responsible for providing lambamena and otherwise contributing to the expenses whenever that ancestor is involved in famadihana[22]—an obligation that endures as long as does the memory of the ancestor. Here again, the logic of the ritual leads back to the dissolution of identity: several people told me that the reason why it was necessary to combine razana together was to keep such expenses down.

Although I certainly never heard it put in quite this way, one might conceptualize famadihana as a process of transferring ancestral names from an attachment to land and houses to an attachment to stones. Standing stones have always been the archetypal form of memorial in highland Madagascar.[23] Tombs are in a sense themselves memorial stones; in former times they were always crowned by a stela, which was said to stand directly over the head of the razambe (then called the *tompon'ny fasana*, or "owner of the tomb" [July 1896]) and which received any sacrifices offered to him. In contemporary tombs the stelae have become crosses, but the implication and position remain the same. The stone in effect represents the tomb as a whole, and both are ultimately identified with a single ancestor, whose name would in turn be attached only to the stone but not to any property shared by living people. In this sense, at least, the handful of ancestors whose names endure are those who manage to transfer their memory from property shared with the living to property peculiar to the dead.

Famadihana as Reversal

The difference between men's and women's attitudes explains the very different roles they respectively play in the ritual, particularly at the critical moment when the confrontation between ancestral bodies and human memories takes place. Women carry ancestors on their laps. The expression used for this is *miampofo*, which literally means "to nurse a child sitting on one's lap," and the candy, honey, trifling sums of money, and so on, are just the sort of thing one gives as treats to small children. Even the fact that the zanadrazana clothe the ancestors and carry them rolled like infants in blanket-like lamba could be seen as treating them like children. Assuming the ancestors are here conceptualized as symbolically male, this treatment reverses the relationship between fathers and daughters, turning it into a relationship between mothers and sons.[24]

The men's part, on the other hand, is to carry the ancestors, to wrap them, to bind them, and to lead the dancing at the end of the ceremony with which they are returned to the tomb. In effect, this means that it is the male role to destroy the ancestors, since the combination of these actions—none of which are carried out in a gingerly fashion—results in the dry body's being broken apart and turning to dust. One woman told me this was the reason it was men who must bind the ancestors: the binding has to be done with such "outrageous" (*mahatsiravana*) force that only men are strong enough to do it.

The word *famadihana* itself can also mean "reversal," or even "betrayal." And it could certainly be argued that the male role in the ceremonies involves a reversal of the normal relationship between the living and the dead. The living inflict on the ancestors precisely what the ancestors inflict on the living: a form of constraint continuous with a form of violence. This is perfectly encapsulated in the act of binding the bodies, each cord yanked so forcefully that the very bones are crushed. A particular emphasis is also placed on the politics of movement. Just as any father or grandfather would strive to keep his descendants from moving away, so the process of famadihana is largely one of containing the dead ancestors in space: after being called to return from their wanderings to the tomb at the start of the ritual, they are removed, bound tightly with ropes, and locked back in the tomb with magic charms.

Ancestral Blessings

Rural society in Imerina was thus largely organized around the identities of a handful of prominent elders who had succeeded in assembling descendants around them or at least in keeping them from moving away. The memory of such elders generally retains enormous social force long after they themselves have died—so much so that to overcome it requires a ritual of profound trauma and violence in which the relation between ancestors and descendants is turned completely on its head. By allowing women to transform their dead ancestors into children, living men can turn back on them the very forms of constraint and violence that constitute ancestral authority and, in so doing, set off a process by which the memory of the ancestors themselves will be largely effaced.

This is not an interpretation a participant would be likely to offer or even to agree with. When discussing famadihana in the abstract almost everyone tended to avoid mentioning violence. Instead, people placed great emphasis on a theme central to famadihana orations: that the living wish to give honor to the dead, and that by doing so they receive their tsodrano or blessing—a blessing that will ensure their continued health, prosperity, and fertility.[25]

On the face of it, the notion that the ancestors remembered in famadihana provide positive benefits for their descendants would appear to contradict my own interpretation directly. On closer examination, however, the "health, prosperity, and fertility" provided by the ancestors turns out to be only of the most abstract and unspecific kind. No one would normally sponsor a famadihana in order to cure someone who was ill, bring success to some financial project, or cause someone infertile to conceive. In any of these situations, one might make a vow at the tomb of an ancient king or Vazimba spirit, or one might consult a magical specialist of one kind or another; all my acquaintances in Madagascar had done at least one of these things at some time. People would never consider appealing to their own ancestors, however, unless, perhaps they thought their ancestors had been responsible for the problem from the start.

In Betafo, some people would more or less surreptitiously deposit offerings of rum, candies, or honey on the roof of a tomb, accompanying the gesture with a prayer. This too was called "asking for a tsodrano." But it was hard to get information on this practice since, although there were almost always one or two empty bottles or the remains of offerings on prominent tombs, I only found one person willing to openly admit to having put one there at any time.

The one exception was something of a social pariah, said to have fallen into abject poverty and debt as a result of having offended his razambe by violating a number of ancestral taboos. One night, while drunkenly celebrating an unexpected windfall, he declared to his neighbors that he had appealed to this same razambe for relief from his debts, and that his prayers had been answered. It was clear to everyone that his real motive was to broadcast as far as possible that the ancestor had forgiven him. (Few were convinced.) I strongly suspect that, in most (if not all) cases of offerings left on the tops of tombs "to ask for the ancestors' tsodrano," they were actually appealing for relief from some punishment those ancestors had inflicted, and that this was the real reason for their reluctance to speak of the matter.

The literal meaning of tsodrano is "to blow water." At its simplest it refers to a domestic ritual in which a child or younger person requests an elder's blessing and the latter responds by sprinkling the supplicant with water. The elder usually adds a few words of benediction, which, using a relatively conventionalized language, wish good health, prosperity, and many descendants on the person being blessed.

Two important points should be made here. The first is that elders never give such blessings on their own initiative. A tsodrano must always be requested. In the past, I was told, children had to "buy" their parents' blessing by presenting a coin or small piece of money to them as a token of request. (The giving of small change and other "tokens of request" to ancestors in famadihana would seem to echo this same ritual logic.)[26]

The second point is that the effect a blessing has on its recipient is the precise opposite of that achieved through cursing or ozona. By cursing, parents impose taboos and restrictions on their descendants. By "blessing," they remove them. In one village, for instance, I heard that the local elders gave such a blessing after a number of teenagers who were studying in Antananarivo approached them to complain that it was impossible to maintain their deme's fady on pork while living in the city. The elders blew water over them, thereby freeing the whole deme from the taboo. In almost every context in which I heard of someone asking for a tsodrano, giving it could be construed as releasing the recipient from some constraint or restriction on which the giver would otherwise have had the right to insist. The archetypal example was that of a young man who left home, whether to pursue his education or simply to "look for money." Such a person, I was told, will always go to his parents and ask for their blessing, particularly if he was leaving the country or going very far away. The same notion of release occurs in common speech. One can say that two lovers have "blown water over one another" (*mifampitsodrano*) if, on parting temporarily, they agree that each is free to see other people until they are reunited. Shortly before leaving Madagascar in December 1990, just as the war in Kuwait was heating up, I heard on the radio news that "the American Congress has given President Bush its tsodrano to use force in the Persian Gulf."

A War Against Death?

What I am arguing then is that, since there is no clear line between positive benefits and the benefits of simply being left alone, the notion of tsodrano can be used as a kind of euphemism. This became particularly clear when, instead of asking why one performed famadihana, I inquired what would happen if one did not perform them at all. While answers to the first question were usually preceded by a good deal of reflection and casting about for the right words, responses to the second were instantaneous: your children will die, your health will fail, or your family will fall ever deeper into poverty. The catalog of misfortunes could admittedly be seen as simply a negative image of the fertility, health, and prosperity tsodrano was said to bring; but since people were always much more concrete and specific in speaking of the misfortunes than they were of the benefits, it would make better sense to look at it the other way around.

People were in fact quite concerned with the danger ancestors posed to their infant children. Ghosts (*lolo, angatra, matoatoa*) were said to linger around tombs. Anyone unwise enough to come into excessively close contact with a tomb under ordinary circumstances should light a small fire in the doorway of the house and enter by stepping over it lest a ghost follow. The same thing was done after attending funerals. The major consideration in building and maintaining tombs was that of denying the dead access to the living; one knew with certainty that one had failed to maintain that separation when the young children in one's family began to die. Most of the people I knew could tell stories about waking in the middle of the night because they (or others in the same room) were in the middle of being strangled by malevolent ghosts that, when they appear in one's sleep, are characterized by their naked, black forms and huge size. In any marketplace one can always find two or three vendors selling charms to keep ghosts away or to get rid of them. These ghosts were anonymous, generic beings and contrasted in this with individualized, "good" ancestors who when they appeared in dreams and visions were usually robed in white. But even such relatively benevolent ancestors were at least troublesome. The most frequent reason for their appearance was to complain of being cold and to demand that their descendants perform famadihana; and I have already mentioned the probable consequences of their dissatisfaction with the results. When asked about the origins of the dark, murderous specters that disturbed children's sleep or otherwise plagued the living, most people immediately suggested they were ancestors whose descendants no longer "took care of them."

Since some would say that it was most often the recently dead who demanded famadihana, one might be tempted to look for a parallel to Hertz's (1907) secondary burials once again. In the societies Hertz discussed, the vindictive ghosts of the recently dead were believed to linger near their old habitations; the ritual served to release them into another world where they would be harmless to the living. Famadihana could be thought of as doing something similar: dissolving away the identities of the dangerous, recent dead, so they could ultimately be absorbed into that of a relatively benevolent razambe. As the story with which I began this article makes abundantly clear, however, even razambe are not necessarily benevolent.

One married couple from Betafo—after relating to me their own version of the story about the 1931 fire—mentioned that following the most recent famadihana for Andrianambololona's someone had broken into his tomb and had stolen several expensive lambamena bought for the ceremony, but unused. "That's odd," I said. "You would think a thief would be afraid to enter such a tomb." "Well this one must not have been," they said. "But he's supposed to be so powerful and fearsome! Isn't this the same one who burned down the town?" "Well" they both replied—more or less in unison—"he wasn't cold any more, was he? If he starts appearing to you, it can only be because he's cold. But in this case, there had just been a famadihana. He'd just been wrapped; he wasn't cold at all. And unless he was," the husband added, "he's really nothing but a pile of dust."

Heat did play an important role in the symbolism of famadihana. Honey, rum, cow fat, ginger, and even candies—all of which are prominent among the "tokens of requests for tsodrano" given to the ancestors—are all also things one eats when one has a cold, precisely because they are considered food with heating properties. They are thought to relieve the "coldness" in one's head or chest responsible for coughing or congestion. Indeed, these gifts were supposed to be placed roughly where the ancestor's head and chest ought to have been.

Fire, too, had a complexly ambiguous relation with the dead Ghosts were frightened by it Everyone knew that if one was in danger of being accosted by a ghost one should light a match; a flashlight, I was told, would not suffice because ghosts do not fear light but only actual flames. I have already mentioned that stepping over a candle or other flame when entering a house prevented ghosts from following one in. Charms to drive away ghosts almost always involve heat and flames. At the same time, however, people insisted that one should carry a candle or lantern—again, a flashlight would not do—when descending into a tomb during a famadihana, just as it was common practice to burn candles at the tombs of ancient kings or other benevolent Spirits, or while invoking them elsewhere.

A friend of mine called Ramose Parson, a biology teacher at the Catholic secondary school in Arivonimamo, told me that he always thought of the practice of famadihana as being basically the same as cremation, except that it is carried out over a much longer period of time. Cremated bodies are reduced to dust through the application of heat; afterward, the dust is encased in an urn which insures that it will never mix with the surrounding earth. All this, he pointed out, is also true of Malagasy mortuary ritual. The place of the urn is taken by the lambamena, which is valued for its hardness and durability, and by the care people take to insure the ancestral bundles never come in contact with the earth. This is of course one man's theory, and rather an eccentric one at that, but if nothing else—it would make the story with which I began this article all the more appropriate poetically: by forgetting to carry out the famadihana in its entirety, the hapless descendants of Andrianambololona brought the destructive fire on themselves instead.

Some Conclusions

The incident can also be interpreted to mean that remembering and forgetting are equally matters of violence; that it is only the direction of the violence that varies between the two. This is the argument I have tried to develop over the course of the present article. In practical terms, the ancestors' enduring memories mainly gave shape to social groups through the power to constrain and punish descendants by ancestral violence; famadihana, seen as the highest expression of group unity, were occasions on which descendants could turn a form of violence precisely modeled on that of their ancestors against those ancestors, and, by so doing could gradually obliterate those memories.

In Imerina, the rather commonplace dynamics by which genealogies are made and transformed, requiring a continual process of forgetting people's names (cf. Evans-Pritchard's work on the Nuer [1940]), are changed into a veritable struggle for existence between the living and the dead. This was true in the most literal sense. The dead, as a Malagasy proverb puts it, "wish to become more numerous" by murdering the living; the living respond by crushing and consolidating the bodies of the dead so as to keep their numbers low.

This is not to deny that famadihana were also memorials to the dead. But the memory of ancestors was double-edged, particularly from the point of view of the most important men in rural society. They wielded an authority and fame largely borrowed from ancestors who were ultimately their rivals, as well as being people they knew and cared for while they were alive. As I have said, the contradictions of their position often seem to put such men in a position of wanting to deny the existence of such violence altogether, even though, in describing the moral unity of the community that ancestors create, they are to all intents and purposes speaking of the effects of that violence itself. Women, whose position in relation to ancestors is very different (though equally complex), felt much more comfortable talking about such matters. But even women could not reconcile the "cruelty" of which ancestors were capable when enforcing moral principles with the sheer egotistical violence of ancestors who simply wanted to be remembered. It was presumably this dilemma that effectively caused images of the dead to split in two, and that was itself a transformation of the same central contradiction of authority. This division pitted benevolent elders who brought their descendants together in a moral community against rapacious ghosts who carried off their descendants' children to join them in the tomb.

Notes

Acknowledgments. Research was funded by a Fulbright/IEEE fellowship. I would like to thank Jean Comaroff, John Comaroff, Debra Durham, Gillian Feeley-Harnik, Arjun Gunderatne, Marshall Sahlins, Johanna Schoss, Raymond T. Smith, Debra Spitulnik, and Rebecca Tolen for their helpful comments and suggestions.

1. "*Dia vita ohatran'ny androany antoandro izao ny fonosan-damba, dia injany fd nirehitra ny tanana.... Dia may izany. Dia maraina dia iny niavy tamin'ny olona indray hoe ho taperiko mihitsy aza ny ainareo raha ohatra ka tsy mamono lamba fa avelao izahy fonosona, . . . Dia novonona indray ireo fasana ireo dia fonosina indray.*"

2. While several people with whom I spoke repeated Irina's story of her ancestor's wrath and the resulting fire of 1931, others clearly avoided discussion of ancestral violence. The few older men I asked about such stories flatly denied that anything of the sort had ever happened.

3. Mamadika is a verb meaning "to turn over," "to reverse," or "to betray"; famadihana is its nominalization.

4. I spent 20 months in Madagascar, carrying out both archival research and fieldwork, between June 1989 and January 1991. I did my fieldwork in the town of Arivonimamo and especially in the rural community of Betafo, although I made a point of gathering comparative material from a wide range of social contexts.

5. I have heard that some people leave small bottles of rum in the wrappings during one famadihana and drink them during the next, and I often heard about people who took dust from inside the wrappings and smeared it on their faces or gums as tooth medicine (although I never saw it done myself), or took a handful of beads from the ancient cloth to preserve for the same reason.

6. In theory it should be the oldest man among the local zanadrazana who removes the first shovelful of earth from the doorway at the beginning of the ceremony; the first returned at the end should, I learned, be done by a young man whose father and mother are both still living.

7. Despite occasional remarks that mainty were more prone to preserve some of the more elaborate or traditional ritual forms, I found little difference in the practice of famadihana, or in fundamental attitudes toward ancestors, between these groups.

8. Archival sources make it clear that the andriana of Betafo are descended from military colonists placed there after the Merina kingdom's conquest of Imamo around 1800. These colonists were from a famous andriana group called the Zanak' ("children of") Andrianamboninolona, and, while no memory remains of the circumstances of their arrival, andriana from Betafo regularly call themselves children of Andrianamboninolona; most, in fact, think it is Andrianamboninolona himself who is buried in the razambe's tomb.

9. A woman may have more options because she can always choose to be buried in her husband's tombs (or,

often, in one of several husbands' tombs), while only occasionally is a husband buried in his wife's family tomb. For statistics on actual choices see Bloch (1971: 115), Razafintsalama (1981:190–200), and Vogel (1982: 162).

10. All the shelves of a new tomb were properly expected to hold at least one body, since if one is left empty the spirits of the dead were likely to carry off a child or other family member in order to fill it. If human bodies were not available, the trunk of a banana tree was usually placed on the empty shelf as a substitute.

11. Nor were they necessarily ancestors: all the bodies in a tomb were called *razana* whether they had descendants or not.

12. Examination, however, usually revealed that these lists represented only a tiny proportion even of those ancestors involved in the ceremony.

13. This is not to say that women could not curse as well—in fact, a few very old and venerable women would put more of a moral slant on the ancestors' ferocity (complaining, for example, that the ancestor was merciless in the punishment of evildoers). Most, however, did not do so.

14. This emerges very clearly in deme histories, in which ancestors are never represented as having had powers of action or creativity basically different from those available to people in the present. Even when magical powers enter into these stories (and they only rarely do), they are powers one could acquire in the present day, if one had the skill or if one were willing to pay for the knowledge.

15. One might even see the stories about the origins of fady as being statements about the essence of this relationship "because our ancestor took this action [for example, ate caterpillars], therefore we, his descendants, are never allowed to take that action again."

16. While there is again no generic term in Malagasy for such groups, people usually would refer to particular local families after their founders; hence, for example, "the offspring of Ranaivo" (*ny terad-Ranaivo*). For this reason Vogel (1982) calls such groups *teraka* ("offspring"). But the term would never be so used by a native speaker.

17. These were mostly private papers from families in Betafo, but they also included records of contracts involving tombs in the AKTA series of the Malagasy National Archives.

18. When women talked about leaving their husbands they always, I noticed, spoke of "going home to father," never "to mother."

19. I only saw women crying and male ancestors being cried over, but I only witnessed four or five incidents firsthand.

20. "*Izaho izao ohatra tamin'ny 1989 nanofy izany izaho eto hoe hitako i dadanay—izy izany efa maty io—ary Avaratr'Ambodivona ary—fa misy hazo eo, dia niresaka aminy izahay" "fa ity dada ity ve mbola tsy maty?" hoy aho "mbola miseho eto indray?" Dia "omeo tsodrano aho" hoy aho fa izaho tsy salama. . . . Dia niresaka eo izahay mianaka: "tsy fanao izay Irina" hoy izy, dia iny izy dia nidaboka maty tamin'izy nafatotra iny. Dia izaho niakatra tamin'ny tanana misy an'ilay zokinay lahimatoa hafareny tery. Dia izy koa mba nikisaka niala an-tanana izy izany nidaboka an'iny fahafatesan'iny, Ohatran'ny hoe: mahatsiravana mampahatahotra.*"

21. This comparison is somewhat complicated by the fact that Irina had this dream at a time her siblings were all quarreling—which probably explains her father's sudden transformation from benevolent to stern and authoritarian. It is unclear whether Irina meant to imply that her illness was caused by her father's disapproval.

22. In Betafo, for instance, I heard of the case of several absentee owners living in the capital who upon converting to an evangelical sect that did not allow them to participate in famadihana, immediately sold off their rice fields in Betafo.

23. No postindependence Malagasy government has, to my knowledge, ever erected a statue in the European sense—that is, one bearing some kind of likeness. Public monuments always take the form of standing stones.

24. One elderly man made a great point of this, in speaking of his father, whom he resented for not having taken care of him as a child: "He never so much as clothed us then, but we still bring cloth for him now." As Gillian Feeley-Harnik (1989) reminds us, lamba are feminine products, and ideally should be the handiwork of the participants themselves.

25. While older men and figures of authority were particularly inclined to emphasize these themes, this was a familiar notion to everyone. The formal expression meaning "to ask for a tsodrano" (*mangataka tsodrano sy ranombavaka*) was the one piece of ritual language even the most ignorant person was guaranteed to know, and the term was constantly invoked in ritual contexts, or in

any other context in which a certain formality of speech was felt to be appropriate.

26. Generally speaking, every ritual gesture that involved giving something to the ancestors—for instance, pouring rum over the door of the tomb or over the bodies inside, giving gifts when the ancestors are placed on women's laps—was called a "request for tsodrano." Similarly, anything taken away by the zanadrazana—such as the pieces of mat which are said to bring fertility to women and the tooth medicine mentioned above—can be called "tsodrano."

References

Astuti, Rita (1991). *Learning to be Vezo: The construction of the person among fishing people of Western Madagascar.* Ph.D. dissertation, London School of Economics and Political Science.

Bloch, Maurice (1971). *Placing the dead: Tombs, ancestral villages, and kinship organization in Madagascar.* London: Seminar Press.

Block, Maurice (1982). Death, women and power. In Maurice Bloch & Jonathan Parry (Eds.), *Death and the regeneration of life* (pp. 211–230). Cambridge: Cambridge University Press.

Block, Maurice (1985). Almost eating the ancestors. *Man (NS), 20,* 631–646.

Block, Maurice (1986). *From blessing to violence: History and ideology in the circumcision ritual of the Merina of Madagascar.* Cambridge: Cambridge University Press.

Callet, R. P. (1908). *Tantara ny Andriana eto Madagascar.* Tananarive (Antananarivo), Madagascar Académie Malgache.

Condominas, Gerard (1960). *Fokonolona et collenivités rurales en Imérina.* (Fokonolona and rural collectivities in Imerina.) Paris: Berger-Levrault.

Cousins, W. E. (1963). Fomba gasy. (Malagasy customs.) H. Randzavola (Ed.), Tananarive (Antananarivo), Madagascar: Imarivolanitra. (Original work published 1876)

Dahle, Lars (1984). *Anganon'ny Ntaolo, Tantara Mampiseho ny Fombandrazana sy ny Finoana Sasany Nanganany.* (Folk-Tales of the people of old, Stories that show ancestral customs and various beliefs they had.) Lars Sims (Ed.). Antananarivo, Madagascar: Trano Printy Loterana.

Evans-Pritchard, Edward E. (1940). *The Nuer: A description of the modes of livelihood and political institutions of a Nilolic People.* Oxford: The Clarendon Press.

Feeley-Harnik, Gillian (1989). Cloth and the creation of ancestors in Madagascar. In Jane Schneider & Annette B. Weiner (Eds.), *Cloth and human experience.* Washington, DC: Smithsonian Institution Press.

Feeley-Harnik, Gillian (1991). *A green estate: Restoring independence in Madagascar.* Washington, DC: Smithsonian Institute Press.

Gueunier, Nöel Jacques (1982). Review of *Le Tsimahafotsy d'Ambohimanga. ASEMI, 13,* 235–241.

Haile, John (1891). Famadihana, a Malagasy burial custom. *Antananarivo Annual and Malagasy Magazine 16,* 406–416.

Hertz, Robert (1907). Contribution à une étude sur la représentation de la mort. (Contribution to a study of the representation of death.) *L'année Sociologique, 10,* 48–137.

Jully, Antoine (1896). Funerailles, tombeaux et honneurs rendus aux morts à Madagascar. (Funerals, tombs and honors rendered to the dead in Madagascar.) *Anthropologie, 5,* 385–401.

Kottak, Conrad Phillip (1986). Kinship modeling: Adaptation, fosterage, and fictive kinship among the Betsileo. In Conrad P. Kottak, Jean-Ainée Rakotoarisoa, Aidan Southall, & Pierre Vérin (Eds.), *Madagascar: Society and history* (pp. 277–298). Durham, NC: Carolina Academic Press.

Lambek, Michael (1992). Taboo as cultural practice among Malagasy Speakers. *Man (NS), 27,* 245–266.

Raison-Jourde, François (1991). *Bible et pouvoir à Madagascar au XlXe siècle.* (Bible and Power in Madagascar in the l9th Century.) Paris: Karthala.

Rasamimanana, Joseph, & Razafindrazaka, Louis (1957). *Contribution à l'histoire des Malgaches: Ny Andriantompokoindrindra.* (Contribution to the history of the Malagasy: The Andriantompokoindrindra.) Tananarive (Antananarivo), Madagascar: Volamahitsy.

Razafindratovo, Janine (1980). Noms passés, noms présents chez les Mérina. (Past names and present names among the Merina.) *ASEMI, 11*, 169–182.

Razafintsalama, Adolphe (1981). *Le Tsimahafotsy d'Ambohimanga: Organisation familiale et sociale en Imérina (Madagascar).* (The Tsimahofotsy of Ambohimanga: Familial and social organization in Imerina.) Paris: SELAF.

Ruud, Jørgen (1960). *Taboo: A study of Malagasy beliefs and customs.* New York: Humanities Press.

Southall, Aidan (1971). Ideology and group composition in Madagascar. *American Anthropologist, 73*, 144–164.

Southall, Aidan (1986). Common themes in Malagasy culture. In Conrad P. Kottak, Jean-Ainée Rakotoarisoa, Aidan Southall, & Pierre Vérin (Eds.), *Madagascar: Society and history* (pp. 411–426). Durham, NC: Carolina Academic Press.

Standing, Henry L. (1883). Malagasy "Fady." *Antananarivo Annual and Malagasy Magazine, 8*, 253–265.

Van Gennep, Arnold (1904). *Tabou et totemisme à Madagascar.* (Taboo and totemism in Madagascar.) Paris: Ernest Leroux.

Vogel, Claude (1982). *Les quatres mères d'Ambohibao.* (The four mothers of Ambohibao.) Paris: SELAF.

Wilson, Peter (1977). The problem with primitive folk. *Natural History, 81*, 26–35.

Blood, Oil, Honey, and Water: Symbolism in Spirit Possession Sects in Northeastern Brazil

DOLORES J. SHAPIRO

Spirit possession groups have often been analyzed as carriers of a sociopolitical posture in which resistance, rebellion, and status enhancement counter or compete with the extant power structure (Comaroff 1985; Lan 1985; Lewis 1971, 1986). This power structure may favor men over women and post- or neocolonial over indigenous politicoeconomic control, and often includes a history of slavery and a present system of rigid social stratification. Brazilian society is ideal for the study of spirit possession groups because of the plethora of group types there, and because the vast majority of Brazilians recognize, although to differing degrees, the belief systems that these groups espouse.

In contrast to the analysis of spirit possession groups in other areas, which emphasizes social change, resistance, or status enhancement (Bourguignon 1973; Comaroff 1985; Lan 1985; Lewis 1971, 1986), my work indicates that Brazilian groups are agents not only of resistance or rebellion but also of accommodation and status maintenance. When analyzed as relational rather than as conceptually "independent" entities with greater or lesser resemblance to each other, Brazilian groups comprise an arena in which social identity and the ideology that sustains it are defined, negotiated, and solidified. For a majority of the population these groups are the only institutions in which social negotiation can occur; and if access to resources is to be enhanced, social class and "race" are the elements of identity that must be negotiated with greatest care.[1]

Access to resources is grossly inequitable in Brazil. The Afro-Brazilians,[2] who occupy the lowest educational and occupational positions in the country despite the national ideology of racial democracy (Hasenbalg 1985; Silva 1985; Skidmore 1985), are most disproportionately disadvantaged by this inequity. According to the 1988 issue of *Veja,* a national news magazine celebrating the 100th anniversary of the abolition of slavery, blacks at birth have a 30 percent higher chance of dying before age five, twice the likelihood of illiteracy, a 21 percent lower life expectancy (50 years versus 63 for whites), and an earning capacity of 18–22 percent less as professionals, 11–22 percent less as skilled workers, and 40 percent less as secretaries—with 60 percent of all blacks earning a minimum salary or less (*Veja* 1988: 20–43).

Thus the pressure to "whiten" or to "stay light" is strong, and has a long history as a dominant ideology in Brazil (Skidmore 1985:13). This pressure is intensified by commonplace societal associations between African origin and negative traits thought to pervade Brazilian society, such as laziness, bad manners, lack of enterprise, and lasciviousness (Andrews 1991:48, 201). As I will show, race functions as a primary reference point for the symbolism of the spirit possession groups that codifies moral and ideological stances with distinct racial identities.

Brazilian Spirit Possession Groups

The various spirit possession groups in Brazil have been documented as catering to specific groups in Brazilian society. These groups are most often classified according to color—white, mixed, and black—as well as to social class. Possession groups are also classified according to origin of belief system: the poorer, darker groups—Candomblé, Xangô, Macumba—are of African origin (Carneiro 1986; Landes 1947; Lima 1977; Motta 1988; Ramos 1934; R. Ribeiro 1952; Rodriguez 1935; Santos 1986) and the whiter, middle- and upper-middle-class groups—Espiritismo, Mesa Branca—of European derivation (Greenfield 1987, 1992; Hess 1991; Shapiro 1992). Groups that attract individuals of intermediate social class status and mixed "racial" heritage—Umbanda, Batuque, Giro—have a belief system and ritual practice that draw from both African and European traditions, as well as incorporating elements from indigenous Amerindian tradition (Brown 1986; Leacock & Leacock 1972; C. Ribeiro 1983; Shapiro 1992).

In the groups I studied, the Keto Candomblé, Giro, and Mesa Branca, participants also ostensibly subscribed to the beliefs and practices of Roman Catholicism.[3] Catholic prayer, the saints, and often the Mass played an integral, if variable, role in their ritual life. While there were always exceptions to class and racial homogeneity in these groups, my data suggest that, for adepts, these exceptions did not persist over time and/or that they were sporadic, being based on perceived need and variable group function. The other exception to the rule of homogeneity occurred when a person was either middle class and black, or lower class and white; as these are exceptions in society overall, however, I observed such cases infrequently. I found that fluidity of both association and meaning was central to the analysis of these groups; thus, casual nonsystematic observation would belie the homogeneity I observed over time.[4]

While most recent authors situate Brazilian possession groups along a continuum of European to African, overall the analysis of the groups has been from an intragroup perspective. A significant exception is Roger Bastide. In *The African Religions of Brazil* (1978b) he analyzes the emergence of groups such as Umbanda—as well as the survival of the

African-derived groups—in the framework of the rigid class and color system that continues to characterize Brazilian social relations. Umbanda is a whitening religion, and the Candomblé has persisted for blacks to take refuge "in mystical values, the only ones they [whites] could not take away from him [the individual Afro-Brazilian]" (Bastide 1978b:66). While Bastide has been criticized from a variety of perspectives (Dantas 1988; Goldman 1985; Hess 1992; Motta 1988; Ortiz 1978), I take issue with two hitherto unexplored aspects of his analysis.

First, Bastide contends that newer spirit possession groups such as Umbanda functioned critically as one of the few avenues of social ascension for Afro-Brazilians. Second, he contends that the Candomblé functioned mainly in the service of Afro-Brazilians defending themselves against white prejudice and discrimination (Bastide 1978b:66, 378). I suggest, however, that those groups in Bahia that resemble Umbanda—especially Umbanda Pura, which, as Diana Brown (1986:130) has documented, is amply frequented by light middle-class Brazilians—function more to distance their members from Afro-Brazilian identity than to integrate blacks into the middle classes. My observations revealed that over generations whitening was the most common method of social ascension; when accomplished, it could then result in frequenting groups such as the Mesa Branca described below. Ideological whitening, however, did not afford greater access to lighter groups—only actual lightening did.

Indeed, Brown provided documentation that Umbanda's founders were predominately white and also challenged Bastide's position on this point (Brown 1986:40, 131).[5] I would further Brown's argument by questioning Bastide's position that the Candomblé is primarily a haven for the disenfranchised. I argue that it is, in fact, a central force, symbolically and practically, in an arena of possession religions that exist as much for the privileged as for the poor. In Bahia, the Candomblé and its symbols provide basic terms for all spirit possession traditions.

Groups such as Umbanda, Batuque, and Espiritismo are almost always placed in contradistinction to the Candomblé. This intellectual posture presupposes that the Candomblé is still considered alien and exotic vis-à-vis Brazilian society—even, if not especially, in terms of other religious social institutions. The exaggerated focus on the Candomblé as exotic, quaint, and African (Dantas 1988; Oliven 1984; Skidmore 1985) has recast the group as a co-opted national treasure. More important, this focus has also belied the very critical part the Candomblé plays in the maintenance and significance of all spirit possession group activities. Borrowing from Tambiah's (1970) analysis of the relationship between Buddhism and spirit possession groups in northeast Thailand, in this article I identify continuities and transformations among and between the different Bahian possession traditions.[6] Central to my analysis is the assertion that each spirit possession group relies through the use of symbolic forms on its evaluation and portrayal of other groups to maintain its own coherence and appeal.

The Research Groups

Early in fieldwork, a friend asked incredulously if the Brazilian professor of anthropology in whose home I was staying "really killed animals." This person, who described herself as an Espirita, threw into relief what was later to become a persistent theme: the attribution of gradations of morality to the practices of different groups. The blood of the animal sacrifice practiced in the Candomblé embodies the most dramatic symbolism in this regard. Salvador is renowned for its famous Candomblé houses and has been the setting for the study of Afro-Brazilian cult groups since the beginning of this century by Brazilian, French, and American scholars (Bastide 1978a; Braga 1988; Carneiro 1986; Herskovits 1966:226–266; Landes 1947; Lima 1977; Ramos 1934; Rodriguez 1935; Santos 1986; Verger 1980). Although less well known, many other types of groups extant in Brazil also flourish in Salvador.The most common ones, with the exception of Espiritismo, were the settings for the fieldwork and are described below.

Candomblé

The Keto type of Candomblé is an Afro-Catholic cult group specific to the city of Salvador, although groups that identify themselves as Candomblé can be found in other Brazilian cities such as Rio de Janeiro and São Paulo. While some adepts claim the Candomblé as their religion, the vast majority call it "the sect" (*a seita*). It is a complex and, for the most part, orally transmitted tradition traced by scholars to the Yoruba-speaking peoples of Africa. Participants consider the Candomblé to be an African-derived religion that provides continuity to the religion of their ancestors. It is characterized by complex rituals, the most important of which entail animal sacrifice, initiation (which establishes a fictive kinship), a strict status hierarchy, elaborate public ceremonies, differential access to knowledge, secrecy, and very elaborate ritual dress and ornaments, as well as the use of a probably archaic form of the Yoruba language in ritual discourse. The majority of participants are from the poorest socioeconomic strata and are phenotypically the most Afro-Brazilian.

The principal spirits venerated in the Candomblé are called *orixás*. These spirits are the messengers between the Catholic God and humans; each adept is initiated in honor of one orixá who has been identified as the owner of the person's head. The initiate thenceforth is the ritual daughter/son (*filha/o-de-santo*) of that spirit, as well as the son/daughter of the cult leader, who is known as *mãe/pai-de-santo* (mother/father of the saint). Belonging to a special category of orixás, *exús* are spirits that are variously described as devils, messengers, and slaves. The orixá of each initiate has its own personal exú who undertakes difficult tasks for the orixá. These tasks are called *trabalhos* (works) and are effected by the pai-de-santo when a client comes to him with a problem. Orixás, considered to be of African origin and syncretized with Catholic saints, are the spirits directly involved in the consultations that take place in the Candomblé. Possession by the orixás and control over their exús is what most distinguished the Candomblé from the other groups. The house in which I did my research was dedicated to the orixa Nanã, and the leader was male, a pai-de-santo whom I will call Raimundo.

Giro

Giro groups are based in people's homes, and the major activity is called a *reunião* or a *sessão*.[1] These meetings occur at night, last from three to four hours, and convene from one to four times a month. The centerpiece of the room in which the meeting is held is a table covered with a white tablecloth and glasses of water, flowers, white candles on plates (often with honey on them), and the bead necklaces (*contas*) of the leader. The stated objective of the Giro session is to work for good. This is accomplished through prayer and song that call the *caboclo* spirits to the center, where they possess the mediums and greet and consult with those in attendance.

Caboclos are the spirits of indigenous Indians, known for their bravery, wildness, and healing powers. Many of the caboclos in the two Giro groups studied have the names of two *orixás*—Ogum and Oxossi—with a modifier, such as Ogum de Cariri. The Giro groups varied in composition and ritual behavior, one led by Helena—Giro (GC)—resembling the Candomblé in selected aspects of ritual behavior and the social class and phenotype of frequenters, with the other led by Margarita—Giro (GMB)—where ritual activity and the phenotype of participants more closely resembled those of the Mesa Branca adherents. Thus, GC members were poorer and darker than those of the GMB. The GC leader was addressed as mother, and the mediums dressed in the long skirts characteristic of the Candomblé ritual dress; their caboclo spirits smoked cigars, drank beer, wore leather hats, and danced their trademark steps just as in a Candomblé caboclo ceremony. Mediums in the GMB dressed in white and stood around the table with their hands on its surface, just as in a Mesa Branca session.

Mesa Branca

Literally translated, Mesa Branca means "white table." Weekly meetings of the group were held in a small building from 3–5 P.M. on weekdays. Of the 60–100 in attendance, approximately 15 would be experienced mediums. The room was set up with a long table in the front, covered with a white tablecloth), vases of flowers, glasses of water, white candles on plates, and a long arrow traversing the length of the table. Around this table sat the (male) president of the session at one end, the (female) leader (*a chefa*) of the group at the other, and a group of mediums on either side. Mediums at the table kept their hands on its surface at all times, thus maintaining the *corrente* (described as the link of human union that provided all the forces uniting the good of something or someone). Another type of Mesa Branca medium is *a passista,* who performs consultations and passes on those who request them. Passes are hand movements the medium makes over the body of a person in order to remove negative, and transmit positive, energy.

Participants, the majority of whom are middle class and *moreno,*[8] come to the session to request consultations, receive passes, and pray. Everyone is expected to dress in white or at least light colors; those who do not are given white garments to put over their street clothes. Many spirits manifest at the session[9] and may include so-called old blacks (*pretos velhos*), caboclos, gypsies (*ciganos*), spirits of the dead (*espiritos dos mortos*), and slave spirits (*escravos*). These sessions are distinguished from the Giro by activities known as *solenes,* in which the spirits of the dead—often recently deceased—possess the mediums to exchange messages with their loved ones. Other spirits of the dead might communicate through a medium who stares into a glass of water and receives a message. Da Matta (1987:154) maintained that there is more concern in Brazil with the dead (*os mortos*) than with death. He claimed that his primary fear was not of death but of seeing a vision of the shadowy figures that people the night, dark corridors, deserted cellars, and cemeteries. It is commonly believed, he stated, that people from the other world can return to hunt or help those left behind.

Da Matta describes this commerce between the living and the dead as "ample and intense." It takes place through communications (*avisos*), presentiment (*presságios*), accidents, coincidences, and, above all, dreams and mediums (Da Matta 1987:158). Dealing directly with these spirits of the dead is a specialized function of the Mesa Branca session. Adepts and participants of all the groups acknowledged this. This can be best explained by examining the notion of reincarnation, a belief to which most of my informants subscribed regardless of group, but one most elaborated in the belief system of the Mesa Branca. They maintain that spirits continue to be incarnated as human beings until they are sufficiently purified to preclude the necessity of further incarnations. According to Fernanda, a chefa and my key informant in this group, to expect to achieve this highly evolved state in one lifetime—as Catholicism teaches—was unrealistic. Thus spirits of the dead might be tormented—such as the spirits of recently deceased relatives—and destined to future incarnations, or they might be purified, purveyors of good—such as spirits of long deceased physicians—who are thus freed from future incarnations.

While seemingly discrete groups with distinct emphases and functions, the Candomblé, Giro, and Mesa Branca interact significantly. Informants from all the groups, for example, thought themselves to be primarily *of* a certain orixá, although possession by this type of spirit was almost exclusively found in the Candomblé. Similarly, spirits of the dead figured in the Giro and the Candomblé belief systems, but it was only in the Mesa Branca where this type of spirit was a major focus of the session. Members of each group had an overall image of what typified other groups, and both knew of and/or visited them—albeit sporadically, surreptitiously, or through intermediaries. These images were maintained and codified through the agency of the symbols of blood, oil, honey, and water. No symbol is associated exclusively with a single group. Rather there is an intergroup symbolic system, casting one symbol as predominant, using others selectively, and perhaps denouncing the use of another.[10]

There exists a panoply of interpretations of a single symbol depending on the vantage point and circumstances of the actor. This variable interpretation may lead the same person either to avoid *or* to seek out the services of any one group, depending on current circumstances, with differential use also occurring simultaneously.[11] Thus, when analyzed as a system, Bahian possession group symbols constitute a domain in which one can creatively respond to social-structural imperatives—not just to constraints, but also to possibilities and privileges. As a symbol blood most dramatically demonstrates how this domain can be manipulated and transformed when one is choosing affiliation or association. It is in contradistinction to the Candomblé that all the other groups are best understood, and it is the blood of Candomblé rituals that most effectively symbolizes this.

Of the four groups only the Candomblé uses animal sacrifice, both in rituals and consultas. Blood, according to Raimundo, the Candomblé pai-de-santo, symbolizes life and is the principal element in, and reason for, the most important rituals. In his words, blood is the primordial factor (*o fator primordial*), and nothing can be done without it.

The history of the Keto Candomblé has been traced to the early 19th century in Salvador. According to Raimundo its religious practices were expanded to integrate Catholicism. For example, he said that by placing statues of the Catholic saints above ritual paraphernalia for the orixás, the slaves placated their masters who insisted that they practice Catholicism, but also showed the masters that slaves had power too. This was accomplished, Raimundo maintained, because the masters came to the slaves with their problems and the slaves resolved those problems through intercession of the orixá-saint. Thus, they inverted the power relation, if only temporarily. Over the years, the saint converged with the orixá so that now a connection between the two really does exist, the exact nature of which Raimundo was not sure. He maintained, however, that the saint was purer than the orixá because a saint was a purified orixá who had never possessed anyone. This constitutes a history of counter-hegemony on the part of the slave, but also of successful domination on the part of the master, as demonstrated by the incorporation not only of the saint in the Candomblé belief system but also of the superior status of the European Catholic image. The vast majority of my research respondents continued to find these Catholic images compelling.[12]

Both historically and currently, the Candomblé is definitively associated with the Afro-Brazilians. Although slavery was abolished in Brazil in 1888, its legacy is everywhere obvious. The notion that a racial democracy exists in Brazil still persists as a national ideology, coincident with the fervent, yet contradictory, belief in the ideal of whitening (Skidmore 1985). During my fieldwork in 1987–89 I commonly observed among lower-class black women, dark-skinned mothers with their lighter-skinned children. One of my principal informants explained that the tendency to whitening—which was visible—was not due to black discrimination against their own kind; they were just trying to give their children a fair chance, she explained. This heartrending situation has long been denied by attributing primacy to social class as the perpetrator of inequality among people of color (Harris 1964; Pierson 1967; Wagley 1963). There is a strong association between social class and color. Indeed, individuals with darker skin are more likely be very poor. And the poorer and darker one is, the more likely is attraction to, and involvement in, the Candomblé.

Animal sacrifice is the factor most cited by those outside the Candomblé as their reason for avoiding participation in it. For Brazilians, this is largely what makes the Candomblé so "heavy" (*pesado,* which implies savagery, primitiveness, and consort with evil). Thus, blood functions symbolically in quite different ways, depending on the vantage point of the person interpreting it. While within the Candomblé the sacrifice draws on the emotional power of death, it is the blood and the life that it symbolizes, according to Raimundo, that are the keys. For the adepts of the Mesa Branca–type groups, however, the sacrifice and resultant blood symbolize evil and savagery—albeit with all the attendant power implicit in that imagery. In the Candomblé the blood regenerates, fortifies, and creates kinship, and thus symbolizes hope for the future. For the Mesa Branca members it unleashes the forces of darkness that can take life, dissipate the natural flow of social relationships, and undermine the moral order.

Blood is also the primordial symbol of kinship ties. The use of kinship terms in reference and address is a major feature of the Candomblé. The leader is always "my father/mother"—both inside and outside ritual contexts—and the behaviors expected of the "children" parallel those of biological kinship. Thus, loyalty, respect, incest taboos, and deference to one's parents and elders characterize these kinship roles. The public ceremonial room (*barracão*) is called the "home for everyone," and, in fact, at no time during my fieldwork were there less than two group members living in the barracão and being supported by the *terreiro* (the center at which the various religious activities of each Candomblé group takes place).

While blood within the Candomblé symbolizes the positive, as well as the problematic, aspects of kinship, for the other groups blood symbolizes conflict and obligation. It also evokes negative racial associations. The attribution by non-Candomblé of savagery and primitiveness to the practice of animal sacrifice coheres with their belief that all negative characteristics of Brazilians can be attributed to historical African influence. Both inside and outside Candomblé circles, animal sacrifice is held to be the most significant feature of the group. The blood of the Candomblé rituals crowns this evaluation. The Candomblé can thereby be denounced without recourse to direct racial aspersions.[13]

The emotional power evoked by blood birth and death—translates differently for each group. For those who reject formal affiliation with the Candomblé blood symbolizes only the dark power of its members. Alternatively, these are the very elements Raimundo embraces and uses to reinforce his strong sense of self and group. In the process, however, he simultaneously perpetuates the myth of social inferiority ascribed to him by others. It is reminiscent of the dynamic that Taussig (1987) describes for the Colombian Indian shaman and the white patient who comes to him to be healed: "This imputation of mystery and the demonic by the more powerful class to the lower—by men to women, by the civilized to the primitive, by Christian to pagan is breathtaking—such an old notion, so persistent, so paradoxical and ubiquitous" (1987:215).

Perhaps the undisputed power of the Candomblé lies in the fact that it draws not only on the pagan, racial, and lower-class categorization, but also to a great extent on the notion that women are powerful, as most Candomblé leaders are women.[14] The blood condenses all this in a most economical fashion, throwing the other groups into sharp relief. The other groups are "lightweight" (*leve*) by comparison, and some informants speak of this lightness as their most outstanding attribute.

Oil: I Could Work with Azeite *and Slaves but I Don't*

The oil of the palm tree (*azeite de dendê*) is a dark reddish-amber in color and came to be used in Brazil during the slavery era, when it was imported from Africa. While used ritually in the Candomblé and Giro groups, its use is renounced by the Mesa Branca. In the Candomblé dendê oil is used in trabalhos as well as in the preparation of ritual meals for certain orixás associated with fighting and fierceness. Fernanda's Mesa Branca spirit told me that he *could* work in azeite and with slaves if he had to, but did not want to because he had become purified and did not wish to regress. This regression can be best understood as exposure to evil influences. If dendê is necessary, the implication is that something "heavy" is being undertaken—in this case working with slave spirits. If you "mess" (*mexer*) with dendê you then expose yourself to unpredictable forces and, in consequence, to danger.

Distancing oneself from dendê, as from blood, translates clearly into distancing oneself from the Afro-Brazilian. The vast majority of the Afro-Brazilian population is poor and, as a group, is held responsible for the more reprehensible aspects of national character. Women, such as Fernanda and Margarita, a Giro (MB) leader—both dark although middle class—reject practices that overtly involve dendê because of the connotations of slavery, witchcraft, and evil. Other Candomblé members embrace these connotations, if at times in a tongue-in-cheek fashion.

Traditionally, middle class Brazilian men are said to prefer darker women as lovers. It is often thought that these women use black magic to lure men away from their wives and families. In such a situation the wife's only recourse is to retaliate in kind. In fact, both

Fernanda's and Margarita's marriages were destroyed by their husbands' involvements with other women. While both women condemned aggression presumably sent by exú or slave spirits through their blood- or dendê-based practices, they clearly recognized the need to protect themselves. In Margarita's Giro group dendê was placed behind the door, together with water and honey, to remove irradiations from the street and the crossroads so that bad things would not happen (*o ruim não entra*). While dendê is not seen as being as heavy as blood—without its weighty symbolism—it is nearly as potent. Rather than life, birth, death, and kinship ties that blood symbolizes, dendê symbolizes strength, Africanness, and thus protection from danger without the kinship obligations and the association with the supreme occult power that blood engenders in the Candomblé.

The deep color of dendê, like blood, symbolizes darkness of skin color, but dendê draws on the attendant power of color in a defensive rather than an offensive mode. Although the Mesa Branca rejects all association with the Candomblé ethic—and thus rejects identification with what is Afro-Brazilian—Fernanda at one point consulted with a Candomblé pai-de-santo in her attempt to resolve a series of simultaneous family crises. She did this surreptitiously—using me as her contact person. For Fernanda, such an onslaught of misfortune could only have meant that the Candomblé had been used to send these grave troubles her way. Consequently only the power of the Candomblé could effectively address her difficulties. As a symbol in the Mesa Branca, dendê is almost equivalent to blood—it is in effect taboo. In the Giro and Candomblé groups it can be used, but for different purposes—in the former defensively, but in the latter offensively as well.

There is little ritual elaboration in the Giro groups outside the session itself. For example, during one session Simone (GMB)—Margarita's daughter and a Giro coleader—was possessed by her caboclo spirit Oxossi, who advised me to bring flowers and a specific food drenched in honey to the sea, but I was instructed to do this out of session, alone. Helena (GC) told me that she did Candomblé rituals called *ebós,* and water *borís,* but rarely.[15] She attributed this to lack of time. These leaders of the Giro sessions, however, were highly conversant with the Candomblé ritual world. Helena is a Candomblé filha-de-santo in addition to serving as a Giro leader. Simone thinks she should be initiated into the Candomblé, but resists it precisely because of the demands of the ritual requirements. Finally, Margarita (GMB) eschews any involvement at all in the Candomblé because she is certain that all Candomblé adepts are up to no good and that their misguided tendencies are empowered through their rituals.

Despite significant Giro resistance to the Candomblé, two of the three most important caboclo spirits in both Giro groups have the same names as orixás who are associated in the Candomblé with dendê. These are Ogum and Obaluayê, who, with Oxossi, the third principal Giro spirit, are all connected with combat, according to Raimundo. The exú spirit also uses dendê (*exú pega dendê*), but Giro groups do not admit him to their ritual space.[16] Although I was surprised when I first saw the bowl filled with dendê behind the door at Margarita's sessions and had not noticed it for several months, I came to understand this was not an uncommon practice. In addition to the honey and water that are more obvious to the casual observer, the Giro use dendê, either directly or indirectly, both in their spirit worlds and as a ritual fluid. Helena once told me pointedly that she worked only in honey; however, in her role as a Candomblé filha-de-santo she had an exú house and enacted rituals to this spirit. Moreover, the only major Giro festival she conducted on a regular basis was for Obaluayê. Thus, the healer and owner of pestilence and illness (Obaluayê), the god of war (Ogum), and the king of the hunt (Oxossi) all figure predominantly in these Giro sessions, but as caboclo, not orixá, spirits. This borrowing of Candomblé belief is the more subtle aspect of these groups to those Giro participants unfamiliar with the ritual world of the Candomblé, and who might be drawn by the symbolism of the honey, water, the color white, and the emphasis on prayer and healing.

In the context of Giro practice there is thus no need for the blood sacrifice to feed the orixá and its exú, as the orixá and exú do not possess the mediums. The dendê is thus the next best thing. As Raimundo said, it complements the magic that is needed for heavy works (*trabalhos pesados*). No works are done in the Giro context, but one of the functions of their sessions is proactive: to prevent the need for compensatory works by barring mishap or evil. The dendê has no kinship connotations and implies no obligation of the group leaders to the participants or of the participants to each other. As it draws on African imagery, it reaffirms the power that the blood provides, but without the kinship connotations. This power, held to derive from the African tradition and, by extension, from the Afro-Brazilian lower class thought to continue the practice of African sorcery, is modified in Margarita's group to preclude consort with evil. Her group avoids ritual use of blood because only blood effects and counters evil.

That evil practices exist, however, no one, regardless of group identification, would deny. Dendê is linked to aggressive slave spirits and their avenging ways in the Mesa Branca, and is associated with evil practices that have been disavowed by the group ideology. Thus, when evil action against a Mesa Branca member is suspected, Mesa Branca adepts have to look to the Candomblé for protection or retribution. This is one basis of counterhegemony for Raimundo and those like him, but it is also a source of considerable amusement. To paraphrase from an interview with Raimundo in the summer of 1991—at which time I was explaining my symbolic analysis to him—he explained that while Mesa Branca members were more sophisticated than he was,[17] they nevertheless had problems and tried to "escape reality" at Mesa Branca sessions. Some might frequent the Mesa Branca for a long time, only to come eventually to be initiated in the Candomblé. He maintained, however, that most only came to the Candomblé when they had to resolve something heavy that was not of the *altura* (literally, "height") of the caboclo spirit there—that is, that was beyond the spirit's powers. They come running, he assured me with a grin but also in a serious voice; they sneak through the back door (*pelo fundo*) and jump through the window (*pula janela*)—but they come.

According to Raimundo, Giro groups have more preparation because an initiated Candomblé adept might run the session. Those sessions that are not overseen by such adepts, Raimundo said, might be laughable as all their practices could be predicated on ignorance rather than on the spiritual force—*axé*—that the proper preparation ensures. In fact, Raimundo told me, the person who introduced me to him, and who lived on the same street as Margarita, laughed at her sessions. Although the derision was cloaked in ritual, spiritual terms—lack of *fundamento*[18]—another aspect of it might have been that Margarita, dark but the offspring of a marriage of a white man with a dark woman and herself the dark spouse of a white man, disdained the ethos of her mostly very dark neighbors, with whom she did not wish to be identified.

Margarita's children varied in physical appearance, ranging from very light with European features to dark with Afro-Brazilian ones. All her grandchildren, however, could be considered white or moreno. Her sessions, where those present were predominantly mulatto, most resembled the Mesa Branca in ritual practice, and her stated ideology, which emphasized good works and the rejection of evil practices, mirrored that of the Mesa Branca. When I informed her of my intended initiation into the Candomblé, she literally begged me not to proceed. In her use of the dendê she acknowledges her Afro-Brazilian ancestry and the complex position she is in vis-à-vis both whites and blacks in Brazil (cf. Degler 1971; Fontaine 1985). But this use is downplayed, while the honey and water that adorn the table of her sessions are given emphasis. The dendê symbolizes one of the correntes at her sessions that is red. Honey also symbolizes this red corrente and is much more visible than the dendê.

Honey: I Only Work in Honey

When I first met the Giro (C) leader Helena, I was intrigued by the fact that she was both a Giro leader *and* an initiated filha-de-santo in the Candomblé. Her status in the Candomblé was not yet that of a leader—mãe-de-santo—as she was not ritually prepared to open a terreiro of her own. *Before* becoming involved in the Candomblé, however, she frequented and had become one of the principal mediums at a Giro center, which was subsequently torn down after the death of the leader. Despite her status as a Candomblé initiate, as I have written, Helena firmly maintained: "I only work in honey."

Honey is specifically associated with the caboclo spirits of indigenous Amerindians who are characteristically either young and handsome, brave and obstreperous, hunters or cowboys, or wild and savage. They are the antithesis of slave spirits in that they epitomize freedom of action and will, and their ritual roles include healing and raucous fun and abandon. In the Giro centers, honey is also found on plates on which candles are lit.[19] In the Candomblé, honey is used ritually and in works (trabalhos) in which a love or relationship problem might be the focus. Thus, the honey would sweeten a person's feelings or path.

Honey is also light amber in color—neither dark like the blood and dendê, nor light like the water. It thus symbolizes mixture, healing, and reconciliation. Its symbolic power does not draw on physiological referents (cf. V. Turner 1970), nor does it have any overt symbolic connection with Africa or slavery. It is Brazilian, pure, sweet, and pleasing, and implies no definitive social relations. Honey transforms color from something that stains a person as poor and immoral to a sign of incorporation of positive attributes: healing, reconciliation, and acceptance. Helena's Giro group typifies this set of values, in which color is de-Africanized and nationalized into something of which to be proud. Interestingly, Helena began as a medium in a Giro group and only entered the Candomblé at a point in her life when she felt that she would otherwise die. She stated that she went from her failing marriage[20] into the *roncô* (initiation into the Candomblé).

While Helena did not claim mixed racial ancestry, she described her father and sister as being light (*claro*) in color, while her mother was very dark (*escuro*). Since honey is neither light nor dark but intermediate, I suggest that Helena identifies with it because of its symbolic associations. Although she was preparing for her seventh-year Candomblé ritual cycle at the time of my fieldwork, she does not totally identify with the Candomblé ethic. She went so far as to tell me that Raimundo was wrong in not working a regular job (as she did) and in expecting to support himself from his religious role alone. She did not expect Candomblé practice to solve all problems.

Margarita, on the other hand, is the child and progenitor of mixed marriages—both her father and husband were white, as I have already noted. While she is dark, her children—and especially her grandchildren—have "whitened" considerably. She thus associates herself more closely with the Mesa Branca ethic. In fact, one of Helena's caboclo spirits who is very "purified" (whitened?) only possesses her in sessions similar to the kind Margarita (GMB) holds where, according to Helena, there are "all those prayers."[21] Another advantage of Helena's basing all her practices solely on honey is the paradoxical position of being able to project one image while at the same time harboring all the attendant occult power of the Candomblé, as her filha-de-santo status was common knowledge. Whether or not she practiced Candomblé in her sessions was less significant than her Candomblé ritual status, which, as everyone knew, would have been high enough to be a Candomblé leader (mãe-de santo) had she decided to put on the appropriate ceremonies. In fact this attracted to her center a white, middle-class adept (Selene) who became one of my principal informants. What attracted Selene to Helena's center was the depth of Helena's Candomblé knowledge.

When I asked why she, white and middle-class, would frequent sessions where the vast majority were of a very different social, racial, and economic background, Selene laughed and implied that it was indeed peculiar. What prompted the decision, she told me, was that Helena had the "line" (*linha*) of the Candomblé as well as that of the caboclo and thus was prepared for anything. Two-and-a-half years after my initial fieldwork ended, however, the relationship between Selene and Helena, previously close, appeared to have been irreconcilably severed.

While each interpreted this situation differently, Selene made it clear that she felt Helena was not using her power for good. Her exact words were: "Helena understands more than most people, knows how to help. Why disavow this responsibility?" (*Ela entende mais do que qualquer pessoa, dar ajuda. Por quê negou?*). Helena was also suggesting to Selene that she should be initiated into the Candomblé. Selene's response to this was a dream in which the orixá lansä, the owner of her head, told her that no one would put hands on her head—in other words, that she did not belong with the Candomblé.

At this point, Selene was starting to hold sessions in her own home, and demonstrated to me the materials that she used. These included honey, water, sweet oil, and dendê. She claimed that she had learned her ritual craft through intuition, not from Helena, who had never showed her what was happening in the rituals to which Selene was not privy. When I queried her about the use of blood, she replied that she did not use it yet, but that if the entities told her to do so she would even though she was afraid. "It's a serious thing" that can bring *coisas indizíveis* (unutterable things that should not be present). Blood, according to Selene, can bring good or bad, and thus is different from dendê.

Dendê in Selene's conception is strong and works quickly, but incorporates none of the associations with evil. Honey and sweet oil are characterized differently—they attract good, sweet things, and thus complement the use of the dendê. While honey, sweet oil, and dendê have all been included in Selene's ritual world, it is water for which she now reserves the highest evaluation. Water according to Selene is energy. It washes, cleans, and purifies; it is a "font of energy which attracts good things." What can you do without water, she asked me, the force of nature without which no one can live? This emphasis on water as the primordial spiritual force for Selene is predictable and supports my thesis that different symbols will attract the same person at varying points in time.

For Helena the predominant symbol of her Giro group is honey. The mixture and reconciliation aspects of the honey's symbolism are not applicable to Selene, who is white, middle class, and fully aligned with that identification. Her social class status, while threatened because of financial difficulties when she sought out Helena's help, was firmly established. It was the healing aspect of the honey as a symbol, together with the occult power conferred through Helena's status as a filha-de-santo, which maintained Selene in Helena's group for so long—almost two years.[22] Whether they are black, mulatto, or simply very dark and subject to varying "racial" identifications, for those who are trying to maintain or improve their social status an ostensible posture of tolerance of white hegemony is crucial. When I first met Raimundo and inquired about racism in Brazil, both he and his sister assured me that racism used to be a problem in Brazil but was no longer. I found their responses peculiar, as the marginalization of the Afro-Brazilian in Bahian society was everywhere apparent.

It was not until much later that Raimundo and I were able to have more candid discussions on the topic. He later told me that, in effect, if he discerned racism on the part of any individual, he would thereafter simply avoid further contact. Neither Helena nor Margarita could afford to do that. They had to maneuver constantly either to maintain (Margarita) or to improve (Helena) their social and economic positions, not only with the socially superior but with almost everyone. We should here recall Helena's accusation that it was improper of Raimundo not to work but instead to send his wife onto the street to sell (like a person without other options?). Margarita, according to darker and poorer neighbors, kept her grandchildren "locked up" in the house (to avoid contact with those below her who comprised a majority on the street?).

Thus, for both Margarita and Helena honey was a predominant symbol, especially for public consumption, but it certainly was not the only one. By maintaining that she only worked in honey, Helena was telling me—on one level misleadingly—that she was working only with the caboclo spirit, and thereby admitted only the healing and reconciliative spiritual works in her ritual world. By identifying more with the caboclo spirit than the orixá, she was saying that she was more Brazilian than Afro-Brazilian, at least in ideology (her appearance was definitely Afro-Brazilian). Thus, she was more tolerant of racial differences and consequently less subject to, and less a perpetuator of, racial and social class divisions.

Margarita, on the other hand, actually had different options available to her. Although one of the currents operating at her Giro sessions was red, as symbolized by the honey as well as the dendê oil, she said that she also had a white current. This was symbolized by the many glasses of water on the surface of the table during her sessions, by popcorn, and by the requirement that all the mediums maintaining the current at the table be dressed in white.

No dendê could be found on the table, and even the honey used was not particularly visible as it surrounded the white candles on white plates that also adorned the ritual table. For all ostensible purposes, her sessions were almost identical with those found in the Mesa Branca. If an unruly caboclo spirit gained entry into the session, it was not welcomed, nor was it given a formal role to enact as would have happened in Helena's Candomblé group—where beer drinking, dancing, and joking were considered characteristic of the ritual behavior of caboclo spirits. Rather, upon entering a Mesa Branca session, the message to the spirit was that it had entered a place of goodness and light and must quickly conform to the behavioral ethic of the house.

That ethic was of white, or light, middle-class society, which abhors the supposed depravity and disorganization of the masses (*o povo*). All those forces that admit these disturbing elements must be kept at bay. As I have stated, Margarita is both a product and a progenitor of the whitening that is so characteristic of the striving for upward mobility in Brazil. The use of honey in her sessions is, like the use of the dendê, symbolic of the historical struggle to achieve her elevated social position and of the continued maneuvering necessary to maintain it. She does not hold Mesa Branca sessions because her position is not yet secure. In fashioning her ritual practices after the Mesa Branca she is demonstrating that the gap is closing, that she is the rightful architect of a better life for her children and grandchildren. The emphasis on the color white and water in her sessions symbolizes the success of her struggle as well as the elevated moral status she is entitled to claim. Water, as Selene so poignantly pointed out, is purity personified, the elemental force of life and all that is good about it.

Water: Water Is a Medicine, It Heals, but Blood Is Life

Water is a primary symbol for all the groups except the Candomblé. There are always many glasses of water on the table at the Mesa Branca and Giro sessions. They can be used as an aid during consultas by the incorporated medium, who might gaze into the water to gain insight or information. There are also pitchers of water on the table during the Mesa Branca session; the water is distributed to all present at the end of the session. Many consultations result in prescriptions for cleansing baths (*limpezas*) or offerings of flowers to the sea—all practices involving water.

Water embodies the lightness by which Fernanda characterized the Mesa Branca, in contrast to the "heavy" Candomblé. Fernanda told me that the only way one's spirit can be liberated is to fulfill (*cumprir*) its responsibility (*o cargo*), its suffering here on earth. Fulfilling what my informants called "karma" would eventually result in purification in the other world. Thus, Fernanda's use of the concept of karma revolves around the suffering one must endure when alive, until no more suffering or reincarnations are necessary.[23] This human suffering is a theme that Da Matta claims is most germane to the code of the other world, a code renouncing a world full of pain and illusions, with its suffering, struggles, injustice, and deceit (Da Matta 1987:52–54).

Death, the ultimate injustice, the signally inexplicable, is thus transcended through the belief in reincarnation, which clarifies and justifies not only suffering but also wrongdoing. The implication in this sad tale of the inevitability of human suffering is that to be human is to be subject to less than admirable tendencies—one's own as well as those of others. The emphasis on *esclarecimento* (translated as enlightenment or elucidation and symbolized in the physical properties of water) was the key element for Mesa Branca ritual practice. Water, according to Solange, a Mesa Branca medium, is a part of nature no one can live without. It is a strong symbol of spirituality and is used in the Catholic church to bless and bring positive energy. It is especially important to the mediums who lose energy when possessed. Thus water in the Mesa Branca symbolizes life as well as the transcendence of death. For Raimundo, however, water as a symbol cannot compare with blood. He told me emphatically that if you have faith, water is a medicine—it heals, but *blood* is life.

This evaluation by Raimundo of the efficacy of the symbols extends also to the groups. The Mesa Branca, he assured me, is fragile because their preparation is the most minimal possible. "They don't have the smallest fundamento," he told me, "or none at all, no force [*força, axé*]." He said that water, like honey or dendê, is used in Candomblé ritual to consolidate the axé that comes from the blood. When I ventured that many people might not be aware of this, he replied with pointed laughter, "They shouldn't know, they'll all die fools [*burros*]."

Because the vast majority of Mesa Branca participants I observed were light skinned with European facial features and hair type, I suggest the water also symbolizes these physical characteristics. References to skin color, in Bahia at least, are rarely dichotomized in terms of black and white. Instead, the terms dark and light (escuro/claro) predominate. This not only reflects a discreet handling of skin color but also the reality of a population the majority of which is of mixed genetic makeup. Distinctions based on the shade of skin color were often imperceptible to me and were situationally determined as well.[24]

It does not matter what color a person is, Raimundo informed me: whether black, white, or yellow, everybody dies. According to Raimundo death is God's justice, the ultimate equalizer. The Mesa Branca adepts do not see death as final as Raimundo does, but, rather, as the ultimate mechanism of moral improvement, which is singularly difficult to achieve in life. Water thus constitutes, on one level, the polar opposite of blood. It represents all those qualities with which Mesa Branca adepts distinguish themselves from those of the Candomblé: goodness of purpose, lightness of skin color, absence of complication in social relations, and control over death.

Symbol: Identity and Ideology

The symbolic system of the spirit possession groups described here has race as its most basic organizing concept. Race relations in Brazil have been the subject of much scholarly exegesis. When Ruth Landes went to study race relations in Brazil in the 1930s it was generally believed that Brazil's large "Negro population lived decently among the general population" (Landes 1970:120). This notion was the inspiration behind a large scale UNESCO project, involving Brazilian, American, and French scholars, that sought to explain the supposed harmony in race relations in Brazil. The American scholars—Marvin Harris (1964) and Charles Wagley (1952, 1963) among them—concluded that the sharp inequities in the Brazilian social polity were due to class more than race. This conclusion was consistent with the findings of Donald Pierson (1967), as well as the common belief of the Brazilian elites that in their society was a racial democracy. Thales de Azevedo (1975), Fernando Henrique Cardoso and Octávio Ianni (1970), and Florestan Fernandes (1969) countered these conclusions, maintaining that underneath the guise of a racial democracy festered a racism of the most pernicious kind.

Subsequent scholars have focused on this problem, emphasizing the importance of the ideology of whitening (Skidmore 1985), the social position of the mulatto (Degler 1971; Fernandes 1978), and the dominant class's adoption of some popular Afro-Brazilian artistic and religious forms (Dantas 1988; Oliven 1984). Contemporary Brazilian scholars have debunked the myths of racial democracy—that being mulatto provides a means of escape and that it is class more than race that governs socioeconomic mobility (Fontaine 1980; Hasenbalg 1985; Ianni 1987). Nonetheless, the ideology of a racial democracy persists in the general population alongside the perceived advantages of whitening (Skidmore 1985).

Disparities in income have been increasing over the past decade. Estimates by Hoffman for 1983 indicate that the poorer 50 percent of the Brazilian population earned 13 percent of the total income while that of the 10 percent who constituted the richest stratum earned about 46 percent of the total income (Hoffman 1989:224). Hoffman's conclusion is that as of 1986 "the huge social debt to the poorest in Brazil remains to be paid" (1989:226). Afro-Brazilians comprise a grossly disproportionate percentage of this group of the "poorest." While Hoffman's analysis of poverty and class in contemporary Brazilian social structure is compelling, its omission of any mention of the Afro-Brazilian presence is typical. This blindness is characteristic of the other articles in the same volume, as well as of much of the scholarship on Brazilian society as well as Latin American society in general (Fontaine 1980).

While the primacy of class versus race has provided the underpinnings of debate in Brazilian race relations scholarship, the fact that the majority of Brazilians are classified as neither white nor black is also enormously significant (Hasenbalg 1985:27). This demographic picture, together with the negative moral overtones associated with African heritage and the ideological value placed on racial tolerance as well as whitening, makes the negotiation of identity critical in Brazil. Much of the scholarship on "Afro-Brazilian" religion presupposes a constituency that differs from the "average Brazilian." The latter, however, is in some measure at least potentially identifiable as Afro-Brazilian.

It is in this fluid—and even, at times, volatile—situation that spirit possession groups are situated. The maximal fluidity of interpretation and association accrues in the Giro groups where oil and honey are key symbols. The class and "racial" composition of these groups is mixed and, thus, more social room is available for identity negotiation. In the groups in which water (Mesa Branca) and blood (Candomblé) are the dominant symbols, the negotiation of identity is either not imperative (Mesa Branca) or impossible (Candomblé) because of the combination of social class and color. Thus, the variable participation in different groups allows for an exquisite self-revelation, showing how specialization in function and symbol makes them a vibrant arena for social negotiation.

This variable participation is also what makes the relational analysis of the groups so important. Selene is an excellent example of this: a white middle-class woman seeking the ultimate spiritual power for what she perceives as grave problems. Her identification with the Giro (GC) group, however sincere at the time, is doomed to be short-lived. From the outset she is uncomfortable with the "level" of the average person there, the fear that she will be exploited. This uneasiness is eventually transformed into a profound distaste, in which she attributes to the Giro (GC) leader Helena an intentional corruption of Helena's spiritual knowledge and power. Selene does not explicitly accuse Helena of evil but instead implies it, asking why she does not help instead of rejecting this responsibility. The paradox is that Selene chose this group precisely because of Helena's known association with the Candomblé and its reputation for occult power.

Conclusion

The religious scene in Brazil, like the racial one, has long been of interest to scholars because of its diversity, its retention of allegedly "pure" African forms, and the proliferation of European traditions such as Catholicism and Kardecian Espiritismo as well as the emergence of syncretic traditions, such as Umbanda, considered distinctly Brazilian. The symbolic analysis of these varying traditions suggests that they are inherently interrelated and therefore best not interpreted as functioning solely in the service of one group's ideology or identity. Hess (1992) makes a similar argument for the interrelationship between Macumba and various types of Umbanda in southern Brazil. All groups can be tapped into by most actors for various outcomes. To analyze only one tradition as an isolate distorts knowledge of all the others.

The key or dominant symbols of these spirit possession religions comprise a system that mediates an action orientation, guiding the actor through an arena of spirit possession groups. Each symbol has the potential to embody a power ploy, a race/class identification, and a moral and social ideology, and can be employed differently depending on the person's life stage, life circumstances, and stage of group involvement. These three aspects of each symbol are interrelated in that the moral and social norms are often presented in terms of race and class, and the power orientation is derived either from the lower-class and African-derived forms of addressing the occult or from the status and privilege that light middle- and upper-class society claims for itself. Depending on one's social, physical (health), economic, and political status and commitments at any given point, the symbolic meaning given to each symbol may vary.

This system of symbols thus lends itself well to situational interpretation, often simultaneously possessing different meanings for interacting parties from different social strata, as well as different meanings at different times for the same person. While my data suggest that adepts' ultimate group identifications will gravitate to those groups that most effectively represent their class, racial, and moral identities and ideologies, examining each group in isolation would fail to reveal this high degree of contingency.[25] The exceptions to group homogeneity are most often short-lived and opportunistic and the advantages dissipate over time, either because they have been fully exploited or because the whole enterprise begins to backfire, or both. Once the negotiation of the ritual relationship starts to lean too far in the direction of one or the other party, the fragile hold begins to break down.[26] This might—and often does—involve the expectation of greater financial or social support, increased ritual commitment, and, by extension, public identification with a social and moral order that is antithetical to standard social relations.

The symbols can also be manipulated quite consciously, as is the case in the Candomblé, where the pai-de-santo exploits the attribution of sorcery-derived power that the blood represents. He knows this attracts lighter, middle-class clients who are currently in trouble;

he nevertheless laughs at their misguided notions of his intentions, if not his capability. Thus, the symbolic system embodies temporal, transformative, and evaluative features in which group members can manipulate meaning. Spiritual and aesthetic features probably also influence group affiliation over time. This is a matter for further research.

The analysis of Brazilian spirit possession groups as autonomous, or as being more African, European, or Brazilian in nature, has missed the interrelations among and between them and the network of ideological and situational contrasts in which they operate. This has been especially true for the interpretation of the role of the Candomblé in the overall religious scene. Its symbolism, ideology, and practice are central to the understanding of those of the other groups, not solely from a historical perspective or in terms of the ideological and social class shift that whitening allows but also because of the role of the Candomblé in contemporary religious affiliation and the negotiation of identity that is so central to Brazilian social life.

Notes

Acknowledgments. I would like to express my gratitude to the late Libbet Crandon for her guidance and inspiration while I was first working out the details of this analysis. Thanks are also due to Barbara Price, David Hess, and Kathy McDermott for their suggestions and critiques, to Alan Swedlund for inviting me to present this paper at a University of Massachusetts, Amherst, Department of Anthropology Colloquium, and to John Cole and Brooke Thomas for their comments at that time. Three anonymous reviewers provided critiques that were constructive, and I thank them for the time and attention they gave this article. This research was supported by a National Research Service Award predoctoral grant from the Division of Nursing, U.S. Department of Health and Human Services, a Columbia University Traveling Grant, and a Fulbright IIE award. Words are inadequate to express my appreciation for the kindness and trust of so many in Brazil. I thank them for their patience and most of all their friendship.

1. I use the term *race* in the sense that my informants did. It is said that Brazil is composed of three races: the black, the white, and the Indian. Assigning racial categories to self and others, however, is hardly straightforward. Not only do people fail to classify themselves and each other consistently, but they also do not define racial terms in the same way. For example, while Harris (1970) defines *sarará* as half-breed of the Amazon area, most of my informants describe sarará as light-skinned and blond, but with frizzy hair (*cabelos crespos*).

2. I use the term *Afro-Brazilian* to encompass a complex of physical features including dark skin color, a broad nose, full lips, and specific hair type referred to in Bahia as hard hair (*cabelos duros*) or bad hair (*cabelos ruins*). These are the characteristics my informants maintained when speaking of Brazilian blacks, who in Portuguese would be referred to as *negros* or *pretos*.

3. The fieldwork on which this research is based took place in the city of Salvador, in the state of Bahia, Brazil, over a period of two years in 1986 and 1987–89. The names of all informants have been changed.

4. There are no survey data available on the racial composition of these groups in Bahia to the best of my knowledge. Brown (1986) is the only author who provides systematic data on race for Umbanda groups. She, however, does not distinguish among group types—that is, whether or not Umbanda Pura is different from Quimbanda in this regard. Similarly, Prandi (1991) notes that about one-third of the 60 Candomblé houses he studied in São Paulo have white leaders, but he does not characterize the group members in this regard, nor does he attempt to estimate the racial composition of the Candomblé overall in São Paulo, where he states there are 2,500 houses. It is much more common to observe white and lighter Brazilians, as well as foreigners, at the large, renowned Candomblé centers in Salvador, such as Gantois and Casa Branca, than in average houses. Both Motta (1988) and Dantas (1988) mention this phenomenon, Motta going so far as to say that it was fairly com-

mon in Recife's Xangô houses to find a symbiotic relationship between university researchers and cult leaders whereby information was exchanged for certificates of orthodoxy. This pattern is also documented by Prandi (1991), who suggests that changes in affiliation between Candomblé groups in São Paulo are to garner prestige, the greatest of which accrues to those who can claim ritual ancestry from the Candomblé house of Gantois in Salvador. Outside these more august settings, however, the Candomblé population was overwhelmingly Afro-Brazilian in the ten houses I frequented, many on a fairly regular basis. In the Mesa Branca center, the most blacks I counted at any one time were 6, when the number present ranged from 60 to 100.

5. On the other hand, Brown challenges the notion that upwardly mobile blacks and mulattoes would dissociate themselves from their African cultural heritage, their participation in Umbanda would seem to support this view. This is nonetheless a somewhat contradictory stance as she has clearly classified Umbanda as "whitened." My data do not support her findings. Upwardly mobile mulattoes were most commonly encountered in the Giro (MB) group, and the Candomblé was denounced as dangerous or, at best, regressive.

6. I omit Catholicism from the focus of this article as I have no systemic data on which to draw and because there appeared to be little distinction among groups with regard to Catholic practice. All group members interviewed practiced Catholicism to some extent, baptism and marriage being the two most important rituals. Catholicism did not compete with the groups in the manner in which the groups competed with each other, but rather was used as an adjunctive measure—going to Mass at the end of Candomblé initiation, or having a special Mass dedicated to the Catholic saint counterpart for a caboclo spirit at an annual Giro session. Also, practicing or adhering to Catholicism was not a marker for race or social class, and this further reduced its role as a social marker. A compelling account of the differential appeal of contemporary Catholicism versus Pentacostalism and Umbanda in a Rio suburb can be found in Burdick (1993). Burdick concludes that active involvement in extraritual church life such as base communities is not characterized by the participation of the less educated and poor, whom he also recognizes as most often being darker. I also do not include Espiritismo, again because of lack of systematic data; Espiritismo, however, can be viewed as lying at the other end of the spectrum from Candomblé. Like the Mesa Branca, the color white and water are primary symbols, but spirits such as caboclos and gypsies are not a part of its spirit world—only spirits of the dead can belong there.

7. While the most common meaning for these words is meeting and session, respectively, the Michaelis dictionary also translates both as séance.

8. *Moreno* translates as dark, brown, tawny. It is commonly used to describe persons of dark skin but European facial features and hair type. Skin tone may vary considerably, and the term is also used to mark a difference from someone who is mulatto as well as someone who is white.

9. I will use the words *manifest* and *incorporate* rather than *possess* to represent more authentically my informants' verbal style. Although they understand the words *possess* and *possession*, they rarely use them. Instead, to characterize possession, they use the verbs *manifestar-se* and *incorporar-se*, and the nouns *manifestação* and *incorporação*.

10. These are not the only symbols found in the groups, nor are they the only ones that could be analyzed in the intergroup context. They are, rather, those mentioned by all group leaders and by many members in their discussions of group practice and belief with me. They were the ones most often employed to emphasize or make a point, or to distinguish between groups, and were the most emotion laden. They are aspects that, as both Sherry Ortner (1979) and Victor Turner (1974) maintain, characterize the key or dominant symbols of a group. Thus, I am not exhausting the range of possible explanations for religious behavior in this article, but am instead presenting the most compelling ones and my analysis of them.

11. The persons most likely to attend two groups on a regular basis were Giro members. They would often, for example, invite me to join them at Candomblé, Mesa Branca, and Umbanda ceremonies. They were also more likely to attend Mass on a regular basis. Helena, one of the Giro group leaders, for example was an initiated Candomblé adept. This situation can occur when an adept is not yet fully ritually prepared to open a Candomblé house but has the potential to do so in the near future; a following, meanwhile, becomes established.

12. There is a movement to extirpate Catholic practice (going to Mass at the conclusion of a ritual cycle) and imagery (icons of and devotion to the saints syncretized with the orixá) from the Candomblé. Mãe Stella, of the

Candomblé house Ilé Axé Opó Afonjá in Salvador, is a strong advocate of this change (Guerreiro et al. 1994). The fact that three of the four symbols analyzed here are also key or dominant Catholic symbols suggests that they might have been adopted (water in the case of the Mesa Branca) or reinforced (blood in the Candomblé) as a means of co-opting the power of Euro-Catholic hegemony. Future research, including ethnohistorical inquiry, could no doubt shed more light on this question.

13. The racial referents of the symbols were not conspicuously expressed by any of my informants. This is rather my etic interpretation, based on the correlation of type of group membership with the most compelling descriptions of the meaning and role of the symbol in the belief and practice of all the groups.

14. Buckley and Gottlieb, in their introduction to *Blood Magic* (1988), point out that menstrual symbolism is also found to represent power, especially that of creative power. Although anthropological analysis of the taboos and pollution associated with menstruation and menstrual blood has predominated in the literature, the articles in their book attest to the variety and ambiguity of social responses to menstrual blood.

15. Ebós are cleansings done at various times in Candomblé religious practice. Borís are ceremonies that are an integral part of the initiation and obligation cycle in the Candomblé, and, as such, they involve animal sacrifice. One purpose of the borí ritual is to identify definitively which spirit is the owner of the initiate's head. The ritual is repeated throughout the seven-year initiation period. There is no connection between these rituals and the full-scale Hausa Borí cult studied and described by Besmer (1983).

16. On one occasion an exú spirit possessed one of the mediums at Margarita's sessions, but that was quickly expelled by surrounding the medium with lit candles and reciting repeatedly and emphatically the Catholic version of the prayer "Our Father" consonant with Catholic identity and practice in the region. Exús can be male or female, but are most commonly referred to as male.

17. By "sophisticated" he meant rich, middle class.

18. *Fundamento* is the word used in the Candomblé to describe a quality inherent in the practices, instruments, and knowledge that form the basis of religious legitimacy. Thus, by saying something does not have the least fundamento implies a lack of religious power as well as legitimacy.

19. Lévi-Strauss (1973:53) documents the association of honey with the native Amerindians of Brazil. He states that wild honey is a passion with the Indians and has an attraction that no other food can equal. Although his analysis of honey in native American Brazilian myths is not relevant here—he analyzes the origin myths of honey and ashes to signify a pathology in the marriage relationship—his understanding of the meaning of the substance corroborates the association of honey with the native groups symbolized in the caboclo spirits.

20. This is the usual scenario: a philandering husband who drank too much. Helena never got divorced subsequently, and told me with amusement, but quite determinedly, that she was waiting for her husband to die to go and collect his pension!

21. This is further evidence for the significant role Catholicism plays in these groups. Giro and Mesa Branca group practice is characterized by the repealed recitation of the Catholic prayer "Our Father." I never noticed more praying in the Giro (MB) group, but Helena did observe it and went so far as to assert that some spirits at least aspire to a "purer" atmosphere into which they can become manifest. No spirits would openly become manifest in a church, however.

22. In addition to her financial difficulties, which were endemic to most middle-class Brazilians at the time of the fieldwork, she was experiencing some very disturbing symptoms—acute anxiety, depression, and hallucinations—although she was at the time of my fieldwork and two-and-a-half years later functioning normally in a high-pressure job as executive secretary to the head of a civil service department. She told me two-and-a-half years after my fieldwork that one of the reasons she sought out Helena's group rather than psychiatric help was because she could not afford the latter. Certainly another reason was that she did not want to think of herself as "crazy," as she put it; she knew that this was an alternative explanation for the hallucinations, which she interpreted as spiritual.

23. The concept of karma as delineated by Fernanda is a little different from, although not incompatible with, Greenfield's (1989:10) definition of karma in Espiritismo. In this latter context, karma, accumulated through repeated reincarnations, is the cumulative balance of each spirit's previous experiences, viewed by some as a series of moral "pluses and minuses."

24. A friend's niece, for example, was described to me as mulata and morena on two separate occasions by her

aunt. On the first occasion Rosane called her niece a *mulata* and explained to me that her sister had married a black man. By using the term *mulata* she was expressing her disapproval, which she supposed I would share (Americans are considered very racist by Brazilians). Months later this same niece was at Rosane's house and Rosane then referred to her as morena. In this instance she was trying to minimize the social distance between them, as this niece was now a houseguest.

25. Involvement in spirit possession groups is one way of solidifying identity and ideological issues, but it is not the only one. Three out of eight new mediums whom I followed during my fieldwork chose not to become involved in any group, although they were clearly struggling with these issues. The importance of the groups in this regard is that they are the only *institutional* forums where identity and ideology can be negotiated. A young college-educated lawyer who is a mulata continues to struggle with these issues and, at last contact in 1993, was toying with participation in various groups ranging from Espiritismo to the Candomblé. Politically she identifies with the Afro-Brazilian population, as she maintains that she is so subject to racial discrimination, but involvement with the Candomblé frightens and confuses her. Her characterizations of the various groups was telling: Espiritismo is for *os burgueses* (the bourgeois), Giro for the *povo popular* (the popular masses), and the Candomblé for *os pobres miseráveis* (the wretched or abject poor).

26. The advantages of having white or black group members in the Candomblé and Mesa Branca, respectively, are more significant than in the other groups whose membership is more mixed in the first place, and where class and kinship mediate race more dramatically. For the Candomblé both prestige and resources accrue when someone like myself is initiated and maintains group membership over time. In the Mesa Branca, the ethic of charity and goodness is highlighted when someone of a different class/racial group is present and helped. In all four groups where the research took place, as well as all the groups that were related to these four in that we visited them or they us, homogeneity was the norm and exceptions were short-lived.

References

Andrews, George (1991). *Blacks and whites in São Paulo Brazil, 1888–1988.* Madison: University of Wisconsin Press.

Azevedo, Thales de (1975). *Democracia racial.* Petrópolis, Brazil: Editora Vozes.

Bastide, Roger (1978a). *O Candomblé da Bahia.* São Paulo: Companhia Editora Nacional.

Bastide, Roger (1978b). The African religions of Brazil: Toward a sociology of the interpenetration of civilizations. (Helen Sebba, Trans.). Baltimore: Johns Hopkins University Press.

Besmer, Fremont (1983). *Horses, musicians and gods: The Hausa cult of possession trance.* South Hadley, MA: Bergen and Garvey Publishers.

Bourguignon, Erika (1973). *Religion, altered states of consciousness and social change.* Columbus: Ohio State University Press.

Braga, Júlio (1988). *O Jogo de Búzios.* São Paulo: Editora Brasiliense.

Brown, Diana (1986). *Umbanda: Religion and politics in urban Brazil.* Ann Arbor: University of Michigan Research Press.

Buckley, Thomas, & Gottlieb, Alma (Eds.) (1988). *Blood magic: The anthropology of menstruation.* Berkeley: University of California Press.

Burdick, John (1993). *Looking for God in Brazil: The progressive Catholic church in urban Brazil's religious arena.* Berkeley: University of California Press.

Cardoso, Fernando, & Ianni, Octávio (1970). *Côr e mobilidade social em Florianópolis.* São Paulo: Editora Nacional.

Carneiro, Edison (1986). *Candomblés de Bahia.* Rio de Janeiro: Civilização Brasileira. (Original work published 1940)

Comaroff, Sheila (1985). *Body of power, spirit of resistance.* Chicago: University of Chicago Press.

Da Matta, Roberto (1987). *A casa & a Rua. Espaço, Cidadania, Mulher e Morte no Brasil.* Rio de Janeiro: Editora Guanabara.

Dantas, Beatrix (1988). *Vovó Nagô e Papai Branco.* Rio de Janeiro: Ediçoes Graal.

Degler, Carl (1971). *Neither black nor white: Slavery and race relations in Brazil and the United States.* New York: MacMillan.

Fernandes, Florestan (1969). *The negro in Brazilian society.* New York: Columbia University Press.

Fernandes, Florestan (1978). *A integração do negro na sociedade de classes* (Vols. 1 and 2). Sao Paulo: Editora Atica.

Fontaine, Pierre (1980). Research in the political economy of Afro-Latin America. *Latin American Research Review, 15*(2), 111–141.

Fontaine, Pierre (1985). *Race, class and power in Brazil.* University of California Special Publications, 7. Los Angeles: Center for Afro-American Studies.

Goldman, Mário (1985). A construção ritual da pessoa: A possessão no Candomblé. *Religião e Sociedade, 12,* 22–55.

Greenfield, Sidney (1987). The return of Dr. Fritz: Spirits healing and patronage networks in urban, industrial Brazil. *Social Science and Medicine, 24*(12), 1095–1108.

Greenfield, Sidney (1989). *Dr. Lacerda and the Casa Do Jardim: Innovative spiritist healing in southern Brazil.* Revised version of paper presented at the Symposium on Healing Systems in Brazil, Annual Meeting of the American Anthropological Association, Washington, DC.

Greenfield, Sidney (1992). Spirits and spiritist therapy in southern Brazil: A case study of an innovative syncretic healing group. *Culture, Medicine and Psychiatry, 16,* 23–51.

Guerreiro, Ana Maria, Gottschall, Carlota, & Berreto, Neilto (1994). Mãe Stella: Sacerdotisa e Guardiã do Candomblé na Bahia. *Entrevista, Bahia Análise & Dados, 3*(4).

Harris, Marvin (1964). *Patterns of race in the Americas.* New York: W. W. Norton.

Harris, Marvin (1970). Referential ambiguity in the calculus of Brazilian racial identity. In Norman Whitten & John Szwed (Eds.), *Afro-American anthropology.* New York: The Free Press.

Hasenbalg, Carlos (1985). Race and socio-economic inequalities in Brazil. In Pierre Michel Fontaine (Ed.), *Race, class and power in Brazil.* University of California Special Publication Series, 7. Los Angeles: Center for Afro-American Studies.

Herskovits, Melville (1966). *The new world negro.* Bloomington: Indiana University Press.

Hess, David (1991). *Spirits and scientists.* University Park: Pennsylvania State University Press.

Hess, David (1992). Umbanda and Quimbanda magic in Brazil: Rethinking aspects of Bastide's work. *Archives de Sciences Sociales des Religions, 79,* 135–153.

Hoffman, Helga (1989). Poverty and property in Brazil. What is changing. In Edmar Bacha & Herbert Klein (Eds.), *Social change in Brazil: 1945.* Albuquerque: University of New Mexico Press.

Ianni, Octávio (1987). *Raças e clases sociais no Brasil.* São Paulo: Editora Brasiliense S.A.

Lan, David (1985). *Guns and rain: Guerrillas and spirit mediums in Zimbabwe.* Berkeley: University of California Press.

Landes, Ruth (1947). *The city of women.* New York: MacMillan and Company.

Landes, Ruth (1970). A woman anthropologist in Brazil. In Peggy Golde (Ed.), *Women in the field.* Chicago: Aldine.

Leacock, Stanley, & Leacock, Ruth (1972). *Spirits of the deep.* New York: Doubleday.

Lévi-Strauss, Claude (1973). *From honey to ashes.* New York: Harper & Row.

Lewis, I. M. (1971). *Ecstatic religion.* Middlesex, England: Pelican Books.

Lewis, I. M. (1986). *Religion in context: Cults and charisma.* Cambridge: Cambridge University Press.

Lima, Vivaldo da Costa (1977). *A familia-de-santo nos Candomblés Jeje-Nagôs da Bahia: Um estudo de relações intra-grupais.* Salvador, Bahia: Dissertação de Mestrado, Universidade Federal da Bahia.

Motta, Roberto (1988). *Meat and feast: The Xangõ religion of Recife Brazil.* Ph.D. dissertation, Columbia University.

Oliven, Ruben (1984). The production and consumption of culture in Brazil. *Latin American Perspectives, 11*(1), 103–115.

Ortiz, Renato (1978). *A morte branca do feiticeiro negro.* Petrópolis: Editora Vozes.

Ortner, Sherry (1979). On key symbols. In William Lessa and Evon Vogt (Eds.), *Reader in comparative religion.* New York: Harper & Row.

Pierson, Donald (1967). *Negroes in Brazil: A study of race contact at Bahia.* Carbondale: Southern Illinois University Press.

Prandi, Reginaldo (1991). *Os Candomblés de São Paulo.* São Paulo: Editora da Universidade de São Paulo.

Ramos, Artur (1934). *O negro Brasilerio.* São Paulo: Companhia Editora Nacional.

Ribeiro, Carmen (1983). Religiosidade do Indio Brasilerio no Candomblé da Bahia: Influêcias Africana e Européia. *Afro-Ásia, 14;* 60–80.

Ribeiro, René (1952). Cultos Afro-Brasileiros do Recife: Um estudo de adjustamento social. *Boletim do Instituto Joaquim Nabuco de Pesquisas Sociais,* Número especial.

Rodriguez, Nina (1935). *O animismo fetichista dos negros Bahianos.* Rio de Janeiro: Civização Brasileria.

Santos, Joana Elbein dos (1986). *Os nagô e a morte.* Petrópolis: Editora Vozes.

Shapiro, Dolores (1992). *Symbolic fluids: The world of spirit mediums in Brazilian possession groups.* Ph.D. dissertation, Columbia University.

Silva, Nelson do Valle (1985). Updating the cost of not being white in Brazil. In Pierre Fontaine (Ed.), *Race, class and power in Brazil.* University of California Special Publications Series, 7. Los Angeles: Center for Afro-American Studies.

Skidmore, Thomas (1985). Race and class in Brazil: Historical perspectives. In Pierre Fontaine (Ed.), *Race, class and power in Brazil.* University of California Special Publications Series, 7. Los Angeles: Center for Afro-American Studies.

Tambiah, Stanley J. (1970). *Buddhism and the spirit cults in northeast Thailand.* New York: Cambridge University Press.

Taussig, Michael (1987). *Shamanism, colonialism and the wild man: A study in terror and healing.* Chicago: University of Chicago Press.

Turner, Victor (1970). *The forest of symbols.* New York: Oxford University Press.

Turner, Victor (1974). *Dramas, fields and metaphors.* Ithaca, NY: Cornell University Press.

Veja (1988). Centenário de um Mau Século. Edilora Abril, Ano 20, No. 19, May 11.

Verger, Pierre (1980). Orixás da Bahia. In *Iconografía dos deuses Africanos no Candomblé da Bahia.* Carybe: Editora Raízes Artes Gráfícas.

Wagley, Charles (1952). *Race and class in rural Brazil.* Paris: UNESCO.

Wagley, Charles (1963). *An introduction to Brazil.* New York: Columbia University Press.

Taboo as Cultural Practice among Malagasy Speakers

MICHAEL LAMBEK

The most important developments as regards social theory concern not so much a turn towards language as an altered view of the intersection between saying (or signifying) and doing . . . (Giddens 1984:xxii).

In the final analysis, social life is made possible by keeping a delicate balance between falling inward and falling outward (Murphy 1987:227).

Malagasy Negation

In a paper that was only half facetious Peter Wilson recounted his despair at locating social structure among a northern Malagasy group known as the Tsimihety The Tsimihety "prove difficult to describe because they don't take structure as seriously as anthropologists do" (1977:26). Wilson continues:

> *These are hardly the sort of tribes who can provide the anthropologist with a new model to be slotted into the anthropological repertoire or help him dazzle his colleagues with a virtuoso analysis of a new logic. The people of such tribes don't do things, don't think new thoughts, don't create new symbols:* they can, in a sense, only be described negatively, *by comparing them with neighbors who do believe in reciprocity or do practice elaborate rituals crammed with mysterious symbols; who do tell contrapuntal*

> *myths or prescribe their daily lives through kinship. But there is not much point in trying to write 200 pages or so listing all the things a tribe doesn't do (pp. 26–27, my emphases).*

And yet there are at least two lengthy books on Madagascar which do precisely that, Arnold van Gennep's *Tabou et totémisme à Madagascar,* published in 1904, and Jørgen Ruud's *Taboo: A study of Malagasy customs and beliefs,* published in 1960. Wilson's answer lies unheeded in his own words. Obsessed with positive signs and rules, he does not stop to consider that structure can be located in negation, in prohibition and restriction. Both Lévi-Strauss and Freud tell us that this is what underlies society (cf. Murphy 1972); the incest taboo is just that, a taboo, a negative injunction and an absence of a specific practice. Whereas Bryan Turner (1984:19–20) contrasts theories which see prohibitions at the heart of society and those which locate that heart in language, taboos themselves form a kind of language. Taboos transcend the distinction between language and act since they are both enunciated and lived out—the word made flesh, and the flesh made word. So perhaps Madagascar affords a privileged view of something that is basic to society.

Whether we wish to consider universal theories of Society or not, the fact is that a focus on negation provides a useful perspective on Malagasy societies. The very name of the Tsimihety, like that of a number of other Malagasy groups, contains the negative participle *tsy.* Tsimihety means "[those who] do not cut their hair." Not those who wear their hair long, but those who do not cut it. This is identification by negation; persons and groups are defined in terms of what they do not do. This process is not necessarily simply a pejorative evaluation such as might be imposed by one group on its neighbor, but something much more general, establishing axes of dissociation.[1] Rather than prescribing behavior, it merely sets the limits beyond which action is unacceptable. Moreover, what is circumscribed in narrow, specific terms is the other, not the self. Self-identity or self-knowledge is predicated not on substance, but on that which the other is not. Such negation, displacement or indirection is found frequently in Malagasy nouns; something similar occurs in verbs, which are most frequently uttered in a kind of passive voice.[2] Spirit possession, common in many Malagasy societies, is another vivid example of an indirect depiction of the self through the periodic abdication to and substantiation of an explicit other (cf. Boddy 1989; Crapanzano 1977; Giles 1987; Kapferer 1983; Lambek 1981; 1988b; Zempleni 1977). Working from Malagasy material Bloch (1986, 1989) has developed a whole general theory of the construction of ideology through the negation or devaluation of its contrary in ritual. At the heart of Malagasy identity, then, lies implicit affirmation by means of negation.

Negation can be most clearly articulated in the form of taboo, *fady* in Malagasy. In the case of the Tsimihety I do not know whether their name is merely a description or an explicit prohibition, a *fady,* but the fact is that *fady*s are extremely prevalent throughout Madagascar, a matter demonstrated encyclopedically in the two books mentioned above and addressed from a theoretical perspective in one of them. In focusing on *fady* I have no wish to reify the concept or even to suggest that my interpretation fits all usage of the term, which ranges from the nominal to the adjectival and which covers, as one reader has remarked, reference to such mundane matters as driving through a red light. On the other hand, little seems to be gained by excessively restricting the inquiry from the start. Suffice it to say that I will be treating *fady*s less as facts than as acts, less as lists of prohibitions than as a local means for constituting and marking significant relationships. In this endeavor van Gennep points the way.

van Gennep's *Tabou et totémisme à Madagascar* appears to have been extremely important in the development of his thinking, laying the foundation for the general insights in *The rites of passage* concerning the enactment and marking of status changes. van Gennep made a number of important points in the earlier work. He refused to succumb to the diffusionist tendencies which to this day bedevil Malagasy scholarship. He stuck resolutely to the view that taboos were a fundamental Malagasy institution, although he was quite prepared to admit that they were also basic to Judaeo-Christianity, Islam, and African societies. Although the book purports to deal with both taboo and totemism, van Gennep wrote almost exclusively about the former topic and very little about the latter. This is because there is virtually no positive identification with a totemic species. van Gennep concluded that "One therefore finds in Madagascar none of the characteristics of true totemism. . . . It thus seems excessive to speak of the animal tabooed by the Malagasy as a totem" (1904:314). Indeed, in Madagascar the taboo *is* the totem.[3] In a sense, of course, this is precisely Lévi-Strauss's point in *Totemism* (1963), namely that the central issue concerns the differentiation of self and other rather than the substantiation of the self.

van Gennep also argued staunchly against the animist interpretation of taboo (e.g., concerning the supposed fear of the dead) with its separation of body and soul. With the help of van Gennep we can see that the theory of animism is just another version of Cartesian or Christian dualism and thus quite ethnocentric when applied to other societies. van Gennep saw taboo as an expression of a sense of pervasive, nondualistic power, known in Malagasy as *hasina.* Taboos are thus acts of separation; they serve as boundaries, spatial and temporal, boundaries between or within persons and groups, boundaries which are marked on, or within, or by means of the body. In thus delimiting and differentiating persons and bodies they help to constitute them.

van Gennep's view, although somewhat more empiricist and intellectualist and less coherent, does not seem all that far from that of Mary Douglas as expounded in *Purity and danger.* Douglas follows van Gennep in linking boundary transgression to pollution and danger (cf. Douglas 1970:116). Both van Gennep and Douglas can be said to view taboo from a structuralist perspective. Unlike those of Douglas, however, van Gennep's boundaries are not between symbolic categories. Likewise, his position is not reflectionist; he does not distinguish the human body as a distinct order of classification which could be used to represent that of society at one remove from it. The taboo is not merely a symbolic representation of a boundary or ambiguity.[4] van Gennep would not, I think, have seen any point in searching for correlations between social organization and representation precisely because he does not distinguish them in the first place. Thus, for example, he argued that the taboo is an expression of social obligation and hence "creates social continuity" (1904:27). While van Gennep's understanding of social structure was rather weak and unsystematic (a problem he recognized and, in the Malagasy case, attributed to his unwillingness to generalize from insufficient and dubious enhnographic data), it also had a strength, which was that he viewed representation as inherent in social structure. Taboos do not reflect Malagasy society since they help to constitute it; they are part of its very substance.[5]

My argument begins with this insight of van Gennep. My own concern is less with the theory of power that lies behind the taboos than with the kinds of power and of persons they make possible. Similarly, I am less concerned with the content of specific taboos (why pork rather than beef, father's brother's offspring rather than mother's brother's) than with thinking about taboos as acts or practices and the consequences of such acts or practices for society and for the persons who carry them out. If the semantic content of the taboo elaborates who or what one is not, it is the practice of the taboo that substantiates who one is. This perspective also derives from the revision of psychoanalytic language from mechanism to agency (Schafer 1976, 1978). Instead of speaking about "having" taboos, we need a language of "being" or "doing," of verbs rather than nouns; taboos can then be seen as claims and disclaimers. This recognizes the fact that taboos are lived as well as thought and that the living out of taboos is a continuous product of human agency.

Taboos are produced and reproduced in a kind of dialectic of embodiment and objectification.[6] On the one hand, taboos are objectified negative rules (proscriptions) which people can acknowledge, share, dispute, reflect upon and choose to adhere to or to transgress, and in which anthropologists may discover structural order. Taboos may originate as culturally appropriate objectifications of either (Freudian) intra- or (Durkheimian) intersubjective experience or Lévi-Straussian play of the mind. But whatever their origins, taboos are also embodied, that is to say they become part of the lived experience of specific individuals. And hence, if taboos are the rules of society, one can say that society is embodied in the acts and experience of its members.

Following a taboo means both articulating a prohibition in words and shaping one's daily acts to conform to it.[7] In the most profound cases, one's very perceptions become organized around the taboo such that the absence feels right and natural, even unmarked, and the violation or possibility of violation causes distress. Incest taboos and other sexual restrictions are so well internalized by the majority of people that the lack of sexual interest in the relevant directions appears unproblematic and its appearance brings forth feelings of disgust, anxiety or guilt. The objective rule may appear secondary to the embodied perception. Likewise, there are Hindus and Jews for whom orthodox dietary rules no longer carry any objective value or meaning yet who cannot overcome a visceral reaction against eating the once forbidden substances. These are positions which in the normal course of events need not be articulated consciously but are held within the body.

But often taboos are followed deliberately and perceived consciously. In any given society we may inquire how various taboos are reproduced and what their consequences are for those who maintain them as well as for society in general. More basically, how do we describe the relationship of persons to their taboos? The remainder of this article addresses these questions, although focusing exclusively upon social rather than psychological aspects of the problem; without dismissing a Freudian approach, I leave the question of personal motivation in the adherence to taboo, as well as the psychic consequences of such adherence, to another context (Lambek n.d.; cf. Obeyesekere 1981). Most of my examples will be drawn from my fieldwork among Kibushy speakers of Mayotte.[8] Hence one of my concerns is to depict personhood in Mayotte as it is evident through the practice of taboos. For all kinds of reasons, the result can only be partial (cf. Lambek 1983, 1990b). Just as I de-emphasize the content of the taboos here, so I do not attempt to describe the content of personhood. The point is rather how personhood emerges as the product of a given kind of relationship with the world that the practice of taboos establishes and exemplifies. The anthropologist can locate structure; the content is left for the individual people of Mayotte to fill in.

Negation as Affirmation

If we are to consider taboos as acts as well as rules, it may be helpful to compare them with the positive rules and acts of exchange, of which, in Lévi-Strauss's theory, let us remember, taboo forms an intrinsic part. There are three well-recognized functions I wish to explore briefly, namely alliance, separation, and incorporation or union. If the first of these is generally considered the most significant dimension of exchange, the latter two may be the more relevant for an understanding of taboo. Turning to alliance first, while taboo might be seen as the inverse of exchange in the sense that it can enact the rejection of a social relationship, it does provide a means of affinity for those who agree to hold a taboo in common. In Madagascar members of a descent group, a locality or a polity often share taboos. In Mayotte, there is an inherited taboo, known as *rangginalu,* against hot substances. People who are *rangginalu* avoid food and bath water of high temperature as well as spicy foods. They have an affinity with cold things and it is likely to rain when they perform life crisis rituals. Most saliently, whether she herself is *rangginalu* or not, the pregnant wife of a man who is *rangginalu* must avoid hot and spicy foods, and especially the fire under the bed, the hot foods, drinks, and bath water that are normally prescribed for the postpartum period. This can be interpreted as a statement and legitimation of their joint parenthood of the new infant (somewhat akin to the couvade, but with the difference that it is the woman who takes the action); rain falling during a life cycle ritual is also a legitimation of *rangginalu* status. As an aside, it is an indication of the cultural bias towards negation that while *rangginalu* is defined as a taboo against hot substances, its obverse is referred to as *tsy rangginalu* ("not *rangginalu*"), hence as a double negative.[9]

Exchange not only links parties; a second function is to distinguish donor from recipient and to mark the space between them. A taboo clearly differentiates between those who must practice it and those who need not. Likewise, the distinction between the promulgator of a taboo and the person who is supposed to take it up is often significant.

Hence taboo forms a basis for hierarchical relationships, as is perhaps apparent in the co-parental relationship just described. Indeed, if exchange goods may be characterized as moving up the hierarchical ladder, the imposition of taboos tends to move down. In Madagascar taboos are often issued by royalty or ancestors; their observance by commoners or the living substantiates the power difference between them. It is in this light that Bloch (1986) argues that descent forms the negation of daily life. Yet the power dimension of taboo has many twists to it. Adhering to taboos is not just, or even primarily restrictive, nor simply a response to orders, but is creative and carries positive moral implications; thus the taboo grants value to the person who maintains it (cf. Lambek 1983). Likewise, as van Gennep argued, royalty themselves were often the ones most bound by taboo.[10]

In Mayotte there are no longer any living royalty nor any vestiges of kingship except what is found in spirit possession (Lambek 1981). Taboos are imposed on their human hosts by the spirits, especially the royal *trumba* spirits, who possess them. A common taboo imposed by the *trumba* spirits is that the hosts are no longer to eat chicken. At the beginning of a possession history the taboos indicate simply the superior power of the spirit over the host. Towards the end of the ritual sequence the taboos are negotiated; those that remain come to symbolize the contract between the spirit and the host, the ongoing nature of their relationship, and hence the power now *within* as well as simply imposed upon the host. Similarly, every medicine has an associated *fady* and virtually all local medical treatments are accompanied by taboos, for example, against eating such common foods as chili pepper, lemon, or fresh fish. Some time after the success of the treatment has been established, the client will approach the healer in order to have the taboos removed. If payment for the treatment is required it occurs at this time; hence the taboos can be said to signify the dependency and indebtedness of the client upon the healer and the medicine, conditions which end with the lifting of the taboo. Yet, because the taboos are embodied, lived out, they do more than signify the relationship; they are rather a constituent part of it. The client's continued commitment throughout the treatment is expressed through abstention. On occasion, the curative taboo is transformed into a prophylactic one and hence continues to be observed after the patient is declared well (cf. van Gennep 1904:54). Such vitally experienced commitment—a marked consolidation of energies—may, of course, also entail therapeutic effects.

One of the characteristics of a gift as opposed to a commodity is that it is essentially inalienable (Gregory 1982; cf. Parry 1986). Hence a third aspect of exchange, much discussed in the Melanesian literature, is that acceptance of the gift is a form of incorporation. An aspect of the self, albeit the public persona, is offered and, where the gift is food, literally consumed by the recipient. Thus, Fortes (1987:139) argues that "nothing so concretely dramatizes acceptance—that is, incorporation in the self—be it of a proffered relationship, of a personal condition, or of a conferred role or status, as taking into one's body the item of food or drink chosen to objectify the occasion [or, I would add, the donor]; and sharing or abstaining from the same food, means uniting in common commitment. The intangible is thus made tangible." Fortes here likens sharing and abstention. Like a feast or gift of food, a taboo can also objectify and embody status, relationship and union. It should be clear from the earlier discussion of alliance and separation that these functions are secondary to the primary function of taboo as a vehicle of incorporation. In Mayotte taboos mark the incorporation of a spirit within a host as much as the relationship of inequality and the contract established between them. In the long term, the enactment of the taboo serves to dissolve the differentiation of host and spirit (cf. Lambek n.d.). Similarly, the pre- and postpartum taboos suggest or index a shared substance which is uniformly vulnerable to a particular stimulus. Sexual taboos likewise identify the parties as kin.[11]

A brief discussion of one of the taboo conditions most salient in Mayotte may help to substantiate the general points made above. In *trambungu* medicine, applied when a couple has difficulty producing live offspring or maintaining them past infancy, the parents, especially the mother, must observe a whole set of taboos, often for a period of several years. They must refrain from attending funerals, from eating the food served at funerals, from washing the dead, from committing adultery, from quarreling, and the like.[12] The following example is typical.

> Fieldnotes, July 1980. *Amina's child has grown to toddlerhood and so she has come to the curer asking to have her* fadys *reduced as they are too hard to follow. But the curer replies that it is too early since Amina is pregnant again. Her* fadys *include the following—she must avoid funerals, she cannot eat at a ritual in which the food is cooked in many pots, she cannot eat chili pepper nor fish caught with fish poison, she*

must not get into arguments with anyone nor go watch others argue. . . . Normally one can have the taboos removed once the child starts to move around on its own, away from the mother; the toddler itself would not be able to maintain the fadys, *the argument goes, so why should the mother?*

In their symbolic content the taboos create a barrier or counterweight to the forces of destruction and excessively dispersive behavior. But more important are the relationships that the observation of the taboos establish. These are not restricted to the renewed sense of identity and common purpose between the prospective parents, nor to the identification of mother and infant, whose separation is subsequently recognized in the removal of the taboo when the child becomes ambulatory. The taboos are entered into through the mediation of a powerful senior curer, either an astrologer or a spirit who manifests itself in the body of a known medium. The curer establishes the taboos and serves as a kind of guarantor of the wager that the prospective parents make; a relationship of clientship is thereby established. Not only can the observance of the taboos last several years, but even when procreation has been successful and the taboos have been dismantled in a ceremony directed by the guarantor, the relationship continues. Guarantors, whether astrologers or spirits, ought to retain a benevolent, if rather distant, interest in the children born under their protection; they are notified at subsequent rituals of transition such as circumcision and marriage, their continued protection is urged, and they are sent a portion of meat. Most important, people born under a condition of *trambungu* must themselves reinitiate such a condition when they wish to have children. They will turn either to the original guarantor or to the guarantor's successor. In the case of a spirit, this means discovering a medium in whose body the spirit now appears. Like the *rangginalu fady,* which is also most saliently associated with childbirth, the need for *trambungu* may be passed on bilaterally, yet its observance is most critical for the procreative partner of a susceptible male. In this manner, relationships initiated and constituted through the imposition and observance of taboos are reproduced from generation to generation.

The Temporal Dimension of Taboos

The rejection of food can dramatize acceptance of relationship; it may appear to do so less concretely than ingestion, but its results can be equally incorporative, profound, and even longer lasting. In the positive case, the rule of consumption becomes relevant in the context of the significant object, that is, as an act it is episodic and context specific. Food is rapidly consumed and digested. Unless the moment of exchange is defined as part of a longer cycle, for example in those Melanesian societies in which feeding is the index of parenthood (e.g., Clay 1977), the message of the exchange and consumption may be quite transitory. But a taboo is relevant unless or until it is specifically dismantled. The principle of rejection requires a continuous stance; one must consistently stand on guard against the unwanted presence of the forbidden object and be ready to modify one's behavior accordingly. An adult in Mayotte takes care never to be left alone inside a house with a sibling of the opposite sex; a person who does not eat goat or chili pepper must inquire about the composition of every dish served outside the household or responds with nausea at the smell of the forbidden substance. The principle, relationship, or person which the objective rule of the taboo symbolizes in a relatively abstract fashion is simultaneously embodied in disposition. Daily practice and ordinary experience are shaped by taboo to a very fine degree.

My analysis presupposes a more performative than prescriptive view of society or "mode of symbolic production" (to turn Sahlins's terms [1985:xi, 29] to my own ends), in which action is as significant as rule. Moreover, the dialectic of objectification and embodiment is ongoing; Bourdieu's argument concerning the inherent temporality of exchange (1977) holds as well for taboo. There are moments at which specific rituals occur, including rituals which performatively initiate or terminate conditions of taboo, and hence one can speak of "before" and "after" states and periods. But I argue that a ritual dimension remains in effect for most, if not all, of the time, and hence that the boundaries and identities of bodies and persons (body-persons) are continuously vibrant. This is reminiscent of Leach's (1954) argument that ritual is the communicative dimension of activity and therefore omnipresent. The Leachian perspective on ritual was overshadowed by the power of Victor Turner's approach to rituals as transformative events and the focus upon the temporal and synaesthetic aspects of ritual, but speech act theory allows us to return to Leach now that it is clear that acts and statements may be unified phenomena.[13] Performative rituals such as the utterance of marriage vows bring a new state of affairs into being through communication. If some rituals, such as the wedding vows, are temporally discrete events, I propose that others may operate continuously. Thus, a man who dons a protective amulet is placing himself in a state of protection for as long as he wears it (Lambek 1990a), and not merely advertising that state to others as in the Leachian paradigm. The words of the spell, written and enclosed in the amulet, function in the manner that the words of an oral spell do. The act of wearing the amulet replaces or extends the act of speaking the words; although in one case the performance is momentary and in the other continuous, the illocutionary effect is the same, namely establishing and affirming a state of protection.[14]

To say this is not to attempt to weaken or trivialize Austin's notion of performative utterances (1965) but rather to use the insights developed from this approach in order to deepen our understanding of conventional acts. If Austin focused strictly on "cases . . . in which to *say* something is to *do* something; or in which *by* saying or *in* saying something we are doing something" (1965:12), he also recognized a close affinity between such performative utterances and conventional acts or ritual in general (1965:19, 69–70), and he concluded that some illocutionary acts could be accomplished by nonverbal means (1965:118). One of the problems with which I am concerned is how to characterize the ongoing acts that I take the observance of taboos to be. Taboos are not merely imposed or lifted in discrete ritual acts and utterances, but are also observed over time. The observance of a taboo, when it is maintained under the sorts of conventionally prescribed procedures and conditions that Austin describes as prerequisite (appropriate time, place, agents, etc.), is a kind of continuous performative act in the sense that it brings into being and maintains—embodies—a particular (contextually defined) moral state. While not necessarily conforming to all features of Austin's definition of a performative act, the observance of a taboo is often considerably more than the indexical trace of such an act.[15] Abstention itself is an act and not simply the bodily inscription of one. For example, during the month of Ramadan each day of fast is preceded by a pledge. The pledge is a perfect example of a performative utterance in the pure sense described by Austin. Yet it is the fasting, not the pledging, that ultimately sanctifies. Hence it is insufficient to describe the fasting as merely the fulfillment of the pledge; moreover this would not correspond to the much higher saliency of the fasting than the pledging for participants. Hence the pledge might be described as a meta-performative condition for the felicitous enactment of the fast. There is not a great logical jump from this example of an annual fast to a lifelong abstention from pork or alcohol.

Appropriate adherence to socially legitimated taboo exemplifies Rappaport's (1979) depiction of ritual as the union of the indexical with the canonical, together with the consequences of such conjunction that he elucidates. The canonical, in this case in the form of a "Thou shalt not . . . ," is rendered present because of the act of commitment to the rule by the individual whose body demonstrates restraint. If we ask what is the practical difference between sacrificing an animal and holding it taboo, it lies precisely in the fact that the taboo is "pervasively performative," being inscribed into the continuous practice of everyday life.

Body, Personhood, and Society

One of my arguments here is that persons as moral entities are performatively constituted in part through the practice of their bodily taboos, that is, through living them. A similar position has been articulated by Gell. Beginning with the idea that the taboo is an emblem of the self, he quickly realizes that:

> *outside the specific acts, observances—and taboos—which specify a self as* my *self, there is nothing for am emblem of the self to be an emblem of.*
>
> *To observe a taboo is to establish an identifiable self by establishing a relationship (negative in this case—not eating) with an external reality such that the "self" only comes into existence in and through this relationship. In phenomenological language, the self only comes about in 'intentional acts' and the observance of a taboo is such an "intentional act." It is nowhere except in what it accomplishes (Gell 1979:136).*

The relevance of Gell's argument for Madagascar is reinforced by Ruud's observation (1960) that every positive intention is accompanied by its taboo. In a sense, the taboo is the embodied and inverted sign of the intention. But more than a sign, it is also an act, less direct but more concrete and continuous than the verbal intention itself. While Gell refers to the "self" here, I prefer the term "person" in order to emphasize that the practice of taboo is, as van Gennep argued, primarily a social act, directed, though not determined, by collective imposition. The emergence of the self is a significant question, but complementary to the constitution of the person.[16] Taboos, as Gell argues, "establish and specify the individual at a number of levels" (1979:136). In Mayotte taboos are distinctive at every level of social inclusion from humanity viewed as a whole down to the individual. Some taboos identify or differentiate relationships between men and women, young and old, members of a specific locality, or a particular line of descent, or people subject to a particular political authority. Taboos also mark people undergoing specific rites of passage or curing rituals, or having particular relationships with spirits.

In general, women bear a heavier burden of taboo observance than men, although not markedly so. It is not so much the number or content of women's taboos that exceeds that of men, as the expectation that they will adhere to them more exactly. It is this adherence—again, practice more than symbolic content—which serves as a mark of gender. Thus, it is mothers rather than fathers who are the focus of the birth taboos. And while everyone is tabooed tenrec (*trandraka*) meat, it is recognized (and tolerated) that young men hunt and eat the hedgehog-like animals in the bush. Similarly, while more men than women carry out the positive Islamic injunction of prayer five times daily, women generally observe the fast better than men. The gender bias of taboos raises a complex of issues related to the paradoxical relations between autonomy and value that I cannot address here (cf. Boddy 1989; Lambek 1983).

Some taboos are individual. These may be established by means of astrology (Vérin & Rajaonarimanana n.d.), but they are often discovered or allocated in a manner not dissimilar to the way Westerners talk about having allergies. Thus, a healer expressed the view that each person is different and must be treated accordingly. This was illustrated for me when I unsuccessfully attempted to treat a small boy's sore with antiseptic ointment. Some months later the boy returned with another sore on his leg. When I offered the same ointment the boy's mother flatly turned it down, asking for an alternative medicine. It was not that she rejected the healing powers of the ointment or that she thought it was not suitable for treating sores (indeed she accepted some for her other children). But it was evident to her that it could not work on her son. The failure of my first attempt at cure had established a lack of fit between this particular kind of ointment and her son. The ointment was *fady* for him.

The totality of a person's taboos provide a summary of his or her current social status as well as a kind of retrospective account of that person's moral career, in much the way that, in Fortes's classic account (1983), individual Tallensi articulate particular constellations of ancestral guardians. Being both indices of present conditions and icons of past events, taboos may also be symbolic of intention, and therefore the future—for example the taboos engaged upon by a couple having trouble producing offspring. Thus, taboos provide both the grounds through which the person is distinguished from the wider context and hence comes to be a demarcated and coherent entity in the first place, and, as signs of status, history and intention, the means through which the person is constituted by selective incorporation and rejection of particular aspects of the context. As forms of negation, taboos provide the space within which individuality and personhood can be constructed at several levels of inclusion. The taboos at each level appear as choices within the more general level, even as they circumscribe the space within which further discrimination can take place.

Having argued that taboos are conventional acts, it is important to re-emphasize that this constitution of the person or self, of present status, past history and future intention, occurs by means of the body. Here we can observe a contrast with the Tallensi case in which taboos, though important, are less critical than the objectification of ancestral links in the spirit shrines. The body is not merely a handy set of signifying devices, a kind of alphabet, map, or forest of symbols used to encode a predetermined message, but a living, active, sensate, dynamic entity, a center. The experience of fasting cannot be reduced to the rule of abstention any more than the rule can be reduced to an expression of hunger or satiation.

As Gell argues, the body helps to constitute the very things of which it speaks. Jackson (1989:136) puts the point more strongly:

> *My argument is against speaking of bodily behavior as symbolizing ideas conceived independently of it. . . . it is misleading to see the body as simply a representation of a prior idea or implicit cultural pattern. Persons actively body forth the world; their bodies are not passively shaped by or made to fit the world's purposes. As Merleau-Ponty [from whose* Phenomenology of Perception *this position largely derives] puts it, "Consciousness is in the first place not a matter of 'I think that' but of 'I can' (1962:137).*

To the degree that this is so, we cannot speak of a mind/body or even a body/society distinction. It is insufficient to state, for example, that the categories of food and non-food represent society, precisely because it is the acts of eating and refraining from eating which constitute society. There is no realm of pure or primary social relations existing apart from meaningful acts of refraining from, engaging in, passing on, sharing and withholding food, sex, labor, comfort, knowledge and the like.

Indeed, what impresses me most about the Malagasy case is the degree to which body and society are understood to form a totality. The social nature of the body (or, conversely, the embodied nature of society) is quite explicit among Malagasy speakers in Mayotte. Before demonstrating this I need, at the risk of reintroducing dualism, albeit of a culturally contingent order, to describe briefly the concept of *rohu,* from which the body, or *nengin,* is chiefly distinguished. *Rohu* (from the Arabic *ruh*) shares features of the English "soul," "character," and "consciousness," though these words are partial and inadequate glosses. The *rohu* is the locus of the emotions; one's *rohu* may be temporarily happy (*rav'ravu*), sad (*malahelu*), or calm (*kutrulia*). But the *rohu* is connected to will, intentionality, as well as to emotion and may be described by others as essentially good (*tsara,* kind, well-disposed to others) or bad (*ratsy,* unkind, nasty, ill-disposed). Attributions of *rohu* include reference to: someone who keeps to him- or herself, doesn't raise children, or has no friends; someone so unselfish as to raise and care well for the children of a co-wife; someone who is lazy and cannot stick to cultivating, as opposed to someone who works hard but doesn't succeed.[17] As consciousness, the *rohu* is diffused throughout the body, hence insubstantial: no matter where you're cut, people explain, you feel it. Yet the *rohu* is also given a physical locus at the base of the neck just above the breastbone, and is evident in the physical signs of the breath or pulse. It remains attached to the body when you faint or are in trance (when it is surpassed by the stronger *rohu* of the spirit), but unlike the flesh, which rots, it survives after death.

I have claimed that through taboos we can see the embodiment of society. By pursuing the distinction between *nengin* and *rohu* we can add a political dimension to the argument. Embodiment is a primary means, perhaps *the* primary means, of legitimation. It does this by ostensibly naturalizing the social rule (or, conversely, naturalizing resistance to the rule).[18] This can be observed in the distinction Malagasy speakers in Mayotte make between not doing something because one cannot and because one does not feel like it. The first of these is often phrased as *nengin tsy mety,* literally "the body does not allow it, does not grant it the possibility." The latter is *rohu tsy tia,* literally "the *rohu* does not like it." In other words, the former is grounded in inevitable bodily constraint or consequence, while the latter is a matter of individual will or freedom. The constraint of the *nengin* is social as well as physical. The phrase is used to explain not only something whose impossibility is given in the nature of its physical source, say the inability of a cripple to walk, but also a *fady*, something impossible because of its negative consequences. Moreover, in the latter case the constraint of the *nengin* is socially significant and becomes a recognized part of one's social identity, while the taste of the *rohu* is idiosyncratic. Hence the constraints of the *nengin* are intrinsic and unquestionable while those of the *rohu* are subject to independent moral evaluation.

Given the bilateral basis of the kinship system in Mayotte, the inheritance of taboos, like succession to mediumship (Lambek 1988a), provides a basis for articulating kinship connections in successive generations. Thus, the members of a particular descent line (*razanga*) may share a taboo against a particular food substance, say octopus, claiming that to eat it makes their teeth fail out. Each descendant must decide whether to follow the taboo of the relevant parent or to ignore it, following instead the practice of an alternate ascendant or of none.

> Fieldnotes, October 1975. *Mdala remarks that his* razanga *is tabooed goat. He points out that this taboo originated in Madagascar. His mother's mother has it and so did her husband, his mother's father. When the latter ate goat, his wife, Mdala's grandmother, became sick. In fact, she won't go anywhere near where a goat is being slaughtered. When Mdala married, his grandmother warned him not to let goat meat into the house. Mdala's father does eat goat although the spouse of someone who is* fady *goat really shouldn't. The husband of Mdala's mother's sister also eats goat, though his wife doesn't. Two of their children have reactions when they eat it, while the others seem able to consume it freely. All the children in Mdala's family tried goat, but Mdala stopped as soon as it made him sick. He spat blood when he tried it. His mouth itches when the plate he is eating from has previously held goat meat. But some of his siblings do eat it.* "Kula ulung ndraka nenginy *(each person according to his or her own body),*" *he says. The bodies (*nengin*) of some people follow the taboos of their* razanga; *the bodies of other people do not. The children of people who have stopped observing the taboo are no longer subject to it themselves. [Note that X, Mdala's mother's brother, can eat goat meat; indeed, he says he cannot think of anything better, that he comes running when he hears there is a platter of goat.]*

Taboos can be activated or not in a myriad of ways, enabling (with some allowance for family politics and public opinion) individuals to cast their personhood for themselves, to have it emerge in the course of life and experience. If your body cannot tolerate goat meat, if every time you taste it you break out in a rash or become nauseated, this indexes a salient aspect of your identity, most probably linking you via the taboo to members of your mother's or father's or one of your grandparents' descent lines (cf. Lan 1985). Whereas if you just don't like the taste of something, it is socially insignificant. Maintaining the goat taboo, or conversely, ignoring it and suffering or not suffering the consequences, legitimates your identity, both to others and, perhaps even more significantly, to yourself. Eating goat freely without negative consequences may index—and legitimate—your relative autonomy from the descent line (though it cannot erase or revoke the connection), just as abstention demonstrates, and is an act of, commitment to it. Your action is not an insignificant whim or anti-social refusal to participate in a collective practice, but an expression through the *nengin*, of the way things are.[19] Persons are distinct entities but they are fundamentally social. Or rather, in Mayotte personhood is simultaneously social and natural, and socially acceptable because it is evidently natural, rather than individual and idiosyncratic.

In an interesting twist which serves to underline the basic point, there was a man who refused publicly to acknowledge his origins in a distant Malagasy group, yet continued to practice the food taboo characteristic of that group, thereby tacitly undermining his own conscious claims. The reverse process, where immigrants legitimate and naturalize their claims to a new identity by sickness cured through adherence to the relevant taboos is discussed by Sharp (1989) for the Ambanja region of Madagascar.

Taboos function to legitimate spirit possession in a manner similar to the way in which they regulate descent. People who are possessed often attempt to disregard the taboos their spirits have imposed. They then suffer the consequences, anything from mild nausea to serious illness. The bodily reaction not only demonstrates the presence and power of the spirit, but also the host's ostensible lack of complicity in the process of possession. By demonstrating the distinctiveness of host and spirit, the attempt of the former to evade the latter, and the lack of success at resistance, the process contributes to the naturalization of possession in general (spirits exist "out there" and can enter and harm people) and its legitimation in this instance (the host is a victim of possession). Hence in legitimizing convention embodiment simultaneously mystifies the human agency required for the ongoing production and reproduction of convention.

The following brief account gives a taste of the subtlety, and not infrequently the humor, of the role of taboos in the negotiation of identity and relationship in spirit possession. The occasion is one in which a woman named Mohedja has entered trance in order that I may greet one of her senior (male) spirits upon my return to the field after an absence of four years. The spirit is speaking through Mohedja, contrasting its relationship with her and with me:

> Fieldnotes, July 12, 1980. *The spirit tells me it is glad that we are good friends, that I haven't abandoned the relationship once I received what I wanted. The spirit stresses it is pleased that I have returned, that it wishes me nothing but good, that it follows me wherever I go. It then goes on to remark that it is* fady *chili pepper (*pilipily*) and will fight with Mohedja [the host] if she doesn't stop eating it. The spirit says that it feels sorry for her and so is telling her gently first; it does not want to cause her any more illness. Mohedja's husband has always treated it well and Mohedja should too. The spirit adds that it has many* fadys, *such as that Mohedja cannot eat from a disk that the children have eaten from, nor from any dish previously started and mixed [i.e., the sauce with the rice in order to start eating] by anyone else. But it ways it goes easy on these* fadys *since Mohedja is raising small children.*
>
> *Later, when Mohedja is out of trance, she says she ate* pilipily *yesterday and it made her ill. She really likes hot pepper and every once in awhile she cannot resist having some, but she is always sick afterwards. Mohedja insists that she cannot keep the spirit's taboos not to eat with the children. At first it made her very sick. She would drink a little cologne with white clay [spirit medicines] and feel a bit better. Now she is more used to it and does not get too ill. Chili pepper still always makes her sick, though it didn't before she was possessed by the spirit. . . .*

In this discussion I have had in mind Durkheim's distinction between the person and the individual, yet the *nengin/rohu* contrast provides a critical twist to Durkheim's argument. For Durkheim:

> *it is not at all true that we are more personal as we are more individualized. The two terms are in no way synonymous; in one sense, they oppose more than they imply one another. Passion individualizes, yet it also enslaves. Our sensations are essentially individual; yet we are more personal the more we are freed from our senses and able to think and act with concepts (1965:307–308).*

Following Kant, Durkheim associated the universal with reason and the individual with the body, and he argued that it was society which provided the means to transcend the individual body in favor of reason. "There really is a part of ourselves which is not placed in immediate dependence upon the organic factor: this is all that which represents society in us. The general ideas which religion or science fix in our minds, the mental operations which these ideas suppose, the beliefs and sentiments which are at the basis of our moral life, and all these superior forms of psychical activity which society awakens in us, these do not follow in the trail of our bodily states" (1965:307).

In contrast to this Western view which associates the body pole of the mind/body dualism with the mute rather than the articulate, the natural rather than the cultural, the asocial and individual rather than the social and personal, the discourse of taboo in Mayotte grants the body greater social value. It is the body which substantiates what is socially significant, whereas individual preferences and passions are linked more closely to the mind (*rohu*). The indexical, embodied qualities of both taboo observances and the manifest consequences of their violation form a means of substantiating, simultaneously "naturalizing" *and* "socializing," and hence legitimating, both public rules and personal departures from them. Although it is the body rather than the mind which ostensibly constrains the passions here, my argument still supports and draws inspiration from Durkheim in its focus upon constraint and moral transcendence. Hence taboos in Mayotte personify rather than individuate.

This is true even where the taboo is observed by a single person. As we saw in the case of the boy who could not use the antiseptic ointment, when a medicine that has alleviated a particular set of symptoms in many individuals fails to do so in someone new, it is neither the medicine which is seen to be at fault nor the individual (*rohu*). Nor need it be the meaning of the symptoms which is questioned. Rather, it is claimed that the medicine simply doesn't work for a certain patient, that it is incompatible with him (*nengin tsy mety*), and he will not be offered it again. It is the cause and effect relationship between the person (body) and the medicine rather than between the disease and the medicine which is naturalized.

There is thus a strong political dimension to the body in Mayotte. In a sense we are talking about how society constrains the body, but in the local ideology this is nicely inverted so that it appears to be the body that asserts or denies social connection. By a process that is at least partially mystified, it is the body which sets demands and constraints on the person. Bodily experience, whether nausea or breaking out in hives, supersedes the conscious will of the individual, thereby grounding events in ostensibly inevitable processes. This is naturalization; as both an indexical center and the site of experience (emotion, pain, illness), the body clearly provides a "natural"—and highly salient—symbol for naturalization.

The political dimension is most explicit where a distinct authority figure imposes its will on and through the body. In northern Madagascar this was apparent in the taboos imposed by monarchs on their subjects. In Mayotte, the royalty are all dead and external taboos come by means of dreams or spirits. Spirit possession is sometimes viewed in explicitly coercive terms. When I asked one man to describe what the experience of possession was like he suddenly reached out and gripped my arm tightly. "Coup d'état!" he exclaimed.

Yet it is important to recognize that the source of the power is diffuse. In some Malagasy societies at certain historical periods it has stemmed from coercive leaders (though only from those operating within the system), but the kinship example cited earlier locates the source within the person and the family. People who take on or ignore their descent line taboos are ultimately the agents of their own decisions, even though the explicit recognition of their autonomy in this regard is denied them and others. The taboo may also be a vehicle of resistance to external power. Feeley-Harnik (1984) has shown how the power of deceased kings has been used successfully in a political struggle against the French over the imposition of demands of work, both as regards the nature of the tasks and the time required to put into them. *Nengin tsy mety*... it is not that I don't wish to work, to accept your demand or offer, but that my body cannot tolerate it; if I accept, I will get sick. (Of course, as we all know from experience, sickness is a widespread form of everyday resistance; the association with taboos in Madagascar makes it a legitimate one.) Sickness is also social punishment for reneging on one's moral commitments to a social identity, as son, subject, or whatever. Here the manifest effects of ignoring the taboo again naturalize the underlying connection and force. Conversely, to the degree that one accepts the authority of the taboo-imposing force, or simply its greater power, submission to the demands may be onerous but will not necessarily encroach on one's self-esteem or sense of justice.

Taboo and the Constitution of Moral Persons

People in Mayotte possess social identity and value not only because of what they do but also because of what they reject or refrain from doing (cf. Lambek 1983). Rather than following prescriptive rules and automatically taking on or stepping into previously determined social positions, they carve socially relevant space for themselves by establishing acceptable boundaries. They legitimate these boundaries by embodying their limits.

Boundary crossing has, of course, moral implications. The old statement that taboos are made to be violated need not be understood through the current fascination with transgression and the culture of infinite consumption. Rather, the violation of a taboo (a double negation), and its consequent effects, are what legitimate it. Furthermore, the violation of taboo need not be viewed in terms of individual morality, according to a Judaeo-Christian-Islamic logic of divine proscription, temptation and sin. To the degree that the impositions and enactments of taboos form conventional acts, their violations are, in Austin's (1965) inimitable vocabulary, "infelicities," in the sense that they are interruptions of acts that by convention ought to be consistent and continuous. How given cultures interpret infelicitous acts is likely to depend on various contingent factors, including local context-specific judgements. Broadly speaking, in the Malagasy system the taboos need not serve to protect a universal positive ideal, transgression of which would be an instance of defilement.[20] Rather, as I have argued earlier, the taboo carves out a space for the self-construction of identity more than it ascribes identity *per se*. Generally speaking, then, one is not identified better or worse by the observance or neglect of Malagasy taboos, but as a more or less differentiated person. Some people simply have fewer taboos than others. Moreover, the incidental failure to observe a taboo that one does have may be more a matter of being unrealistic, inattentive, stubborn, defiant, skeptical, unserious, or out of context, than of being immoral. Similarly van Gennep argues that "in the last analysis the real meaning of *fady* is that of dangerous" (1904:23) rather than prohibited or wrong. Individual moral evaluation is precisely a matter of *rohu* rather than *nengin*, of disposition rather than prohibition, of freedom rather than perceived necessity.

In Mayotte ignoring taboo is immoral less when it concerns one's own body than when it consists in failing to observe the taboos surrounding the bodies of others. Transgressions of the taboos of violence and sexual conduct (which are also, of course, among the most generalized) are attributed to the *rohu*, and individuals are held accountable. When this violation of others' bodies is carried out indirectly or secretly it is *voriky*, sorcery or witchcraft.[21] Sorcery is a surreptitious attack on another person, most vividly symbolized as an attack on and into the body, in part by means of impure bodily substances, hence as an act that is a kind of anti-observance of taboo. The desire to commit sorcery, i.e. to violate such taboos, comes not from the *nengin*, the body, but from the individual *rohu*. The intention is not naturalized or legitimated—no taboo is initiated, nor is there any attribution of Zande-like bodily witch substance—but remains a matter of individual responsibility. The same is true for the violation of incest taboos and other sexual rules. In other words, the naturalization of choice does have its limits, and leaves a sphere of individual accountability.

The condition of sorcery as well as its removal are also expressed in concrete bodily idioms, indeed in graphic, visceral and often painful ways. Acceptance of an imposed taboo and rejection of imposed sorcery make similar use of the body. Again following Rappaport (1979) on ritual, we can conclude that the formal and explicit extraction of sorcery from the body is a necessary component both of the recognition of its passage from the person and of the acceptance of the set of ideas which underlie its reality. In other words, reality—publicly, socially legitimated views of how the world is—is established not simply through thought but through bodily action and experience: through posture, movement, desire, pain—and, most basically and significantly of all, through presence.[22]

Hence, if intentionality is ascribed explicitly to the *rohu*, the moral qualities of the embodied taboo stem less from intentionality than from the manner, in a Durkheimian sense, in which taboo provides a legitimate and indeed often required means towards self-transcendence, social commitment, and personhood. The ultimate antithesis of taboo is not evil but undifferentiated unity. Whether this is viewed as chaos, entropy, ecstasy, nirvana, or liminal creative flux depends on the context. In Mayotte, prior to the embodied marking which differentiates circumcised from uncircumcised boys and appropriately deflowered women from virginal girls, both boys and girls undergo what is generally agreed to be a more painful operation than either of these, in which their bodies are pervaded with a dense cloud of acrid smoke produced from the burning of a wide range of disparate ingredients. This, I think, is an antithesis of taboo. The body is opened out and suffused with the amorphous smoke. Initiates perspire, gag, and choke, their eyes and noses run, and they emerge black and stinking. The normal boundaries of the body are entirely transcended. What happens to the body indexes and constitutes what happens to the person. In classic liminal fashion, initiates are virtually stripped, enclosed, and hidden away, and reduced to undifferentiated equality. Completely pervaded, boundary-less, they lose their identities. Although subsequent rituals will definitively engrave adult, gendered, and sexual status during the smoking young boys and girls may be taken together and are not distinguished from one another in any way. Taboos frame the liminal space (for example, that one may not enter or leave the house during the smoking), but they do not compose it. Other taboos help to constitute, differentiate, and identify the persons who are created out of the amorphous mass of the liminal experience. Thus, the imposition of taboos serves to create persons, while their breakdown reduces personhood.

In sum, my argument has been that one cannot have a theory of the human person without the body (and vice versa). The body is the primary seat, the ground and signifier of the person. As Rappaport (1979) has argued, it is the presence of the body that renders ritual distinctive and powerful. Through their bodily presence persons commit themselves to the religious and social order of which the ritual action or event is a part and thereby help to create not only themselves but the social order itself. Commitment, which is a social and moral relation, is enacted or performed, hence it is physical, embodied. If, following Durkheim, the person is a moral entity, and if moral commitment is established by presence, then bodies are necessary for persons; there can be no fully disembodied persons.[23] Similarly for society. For Durkheim and Rappaport ritual lies at the heart of society; for Lévi-Strauss and Freud taboo does; I am merely pointing out that these are the same thing.

Whatever their generality, it is of course important to remember that these are ideal statements. In reality, not all societies are alike. From arguing that taboos are acts it follows that they are not abstractions or timeless processes but are situated in concrete historical contexts and with respect to specific discourses and practices which articulate with one another and with wider forces and more powerful dialectics of encompassment and resistance (cf. Jean Comaroff 1985). Taboos are but one kind of practice in a wider field of intersecting discourses in Mayotte, discourses which exist in some opposition to one another. As with totemism (Lévi-Strauss 1963), the validity of taboo as a general category needs to be kept in question. Not only may various taboos be more or less directly performative, but we need to keep asking in the name of whom or what, and at whose instigation, does renunciation take place, and whether the various instances are truly comparable with one another.

The picture of personhood and the body that I have drawn for Malagasy speakers shares certain features with the interpretation of the Kabyle house, and by extension of pre-colonial North African society more generally, proposed in Mitchell's (1988) recent re-reading of Bourdieu's account. Unlike the European "world as spectacle" in which order is understood as a framework

> *whose lines would bring into existence a neutral space in terms of which things were to be organised, [the North African] ordering does not work by determining a fixed boundary between an inner world and its outside, . . . it is not concerned with an order set up in terms of an isolated subject, who would confront the world at his or her object.*

> *Nor, finally, is it concerned with meaning as a problem for this individual subject of fixing the relation between the world and its plan or representation; or with truth as the certainty of such representation.... What we inhabitants of the world-as-exhibition would ordinarily take for granted as the elements of any order—framework, interior, subject, object, and an unambiguous meaning or truth—remain problematised and at play in the ordering of the Kabyle world (1988:50–51).*

Thus, the Kabyle house has "a life made up not of inert objects to be ordered but of demands to be attended to and respected, according to the contradictory ways in which they touch and affect each other, or work in harmony and opposition, or resemble and oppose one another" (1988:51). And, "rather than a fixed boundary dividing the city into two parts, public and private, outside and inside, there are degrees of accessibility and exclusion determined variously by the relations between the persons involved, and by the time and the circumstance . . . the dynamic relation between openness and closure . . . a city with no fixed exteriors, . . . without facades" (1988:56).

What Mitchell and Bourdieu describe so well for the North African house and city resembles my view of social life in Mayotte circa 1975. What exists is not a stable structure, a cast of discrete characters, but a play of forces and relations. The "person" is a continuously emergent product of these forces and relations; there are no "sovereign [essentialized] bodies," nor sovereign individuals.

And yet, of course, persons have agentive qualities which spatial structures do not. Taboos are not merely relations, but acts. Taboo is both the complement of exchange and its condition. Being a person entails the right and ability to refuse the total permeability of one's being, to reject the dissolution of identity in limitless exchange and interpenetration, and therefore, as Lévi-Strauss argued, the consequence of having nothing of value left to offer at the appropriate moment (cf. Lambek 1983). Being a person also entails resisting a total inward collapse, that is, resisting the rejection of all material or social connection with the outer world. Thus, exchange and taboo, openness and closure, engagement and resistance, must be understood conjointly. Taboos help to regulate the fluid boundaries of inner and outer worlds. They provide a concrete and material means to carve out and connect personal and social spaces and to grant such spaces the legitimacy offered by both objectified public rules and immediate bodily experience.

Notes

Research in Mayotte has been generously supported by the National Science Foundation, the National Geographic Society and the Social Sciences and Humanities Research Council of Canada. A version of the article was written while I was the recipient of a research time stipend from the SSHRC and the hospitality of the Department of Anthropology at Yale. Versions of the article were presented to the panel "Bodies and persons: the dialectics of objectification and embodiment in Africa" at the annual meeting of the American Ethnological Society, Atlanta, April 1990, and at the Department of Anthropology, University of Chicago, January 1991. I am very grateful to both audiences for their astute comments as well as to Paul Antze, Janice Boddy, Rory Crath, Mary Douglas, Joe Errington and Jacqueline Solway for their careful reading of earlier drafts. None of these people is likely to agree with all the arguments presented here.

1. The contrast between prescriptive and complex (proscriptive) marriage systems is obviously an example

of what I am talking about. The marriage system of Malagasy speakers in Mayotte is of the latter sort, specifying the categories of people whom one cannot marry rather than those whom one should.

2. Another kind of linguistic displacement common in Madagascar is word taboo. The forbidden word is replaced by a new or alternate word or by a metaphoric circumlocution.

3. I am indebted to Paul Antze for this phrasing of the point.

4. At the same time, *Purity and danger* is a brilliant attempt to rethink and synthesize the issues. The reflectionist strain in Douglas's work goes hand in hand with a strong concern for a holistic analysis in which symbols are constitutive of social worlds and basic to social action. Many of my arguments in this article are prefigured in her work although I do not follow her in the direction of social typology and systematic comparison.

5. Douglas (personal communication, June 1990) suggests that this argument can be taken much further; taboos negatively constitute not only society, but the cosmos.

6. By objectification I refer to features that are externalized, or that exist externally and at some degree of independence from particular bodies, as signs, rules, or constraints of personhood. Objectification as a process follows the path of bodies and persons into and within the public realm, for example, the legal status or change in name of a new mother, or the construction and manipulation of a statuette of a nursing mother and child. Embodiment refers to features that are internalized, or that exist internally or by reason of the fact that they are located within or as bodies. A woman who gives birth, who nurses and cares for an infant in a certain way, embodies motherhood, just as teknonymy or the exchange of cattle between affines objectifies it. Embodiment refers here not merely to the woman's body as an index of motherhood, nor just her iconic representation of the particular cultural construct of "motherhood," but also to the body as the locus through which the experience is integrated and to the complex of sensations and energies generated by the embodied experience which it then becomes the challenge of the objectified concepts to capture. The examples of cattle and statues suggest other kinds of complexity as embodied icons in the objectified realm. In fact, many acts and practices simultaneously embody and objectify; in general, this is true of ritual (cf. V. Turner 1967; Rappaport 1979) and also, perhaps, of precapitalist exchange (cf. Gregory 1982). My conceptualization of dialectics obviously owes a good deal to Berger and Luckmann's synthesis (1971). That work prefigures some of this discussion, elaborating the matter of public existence, for example, by distinguishing externalization from institutionalization, levels of legitimation, etc.

7. Janice Boddy (personal communication) has suggested that in a sense all embodied meanings are negations since they preclude alternative forms of action. Hence what is significant about taboo is not that it is an embodied negation but that the negation is marked, hence also objectified.

8. Kibushy is a dialect of Malagasy spoken on the French territory of Mayotte, an island in the Comoro Archipelago to the northwest of Madagascar. Fieldwork in Mayotte was carried out in 1975–76, 1980, and 1985 for a total of some 20 months.

9. Such a double negative, in turn, does have a positive content. The application of heat after birth is an aspect of humoral theory, hence the *tsy rangginalu* option may mark the penetration of Islam.

10. Although van Gennep realized that in the more complex polities the chiefs used the *fadys* against their subjects and as defense against invading strangers, i.e., as an instrument of state (1904:29), it was also the case that "in reality, the chief is the least free of all the individuals of a given group" (1904:78–79). The contradiction between the chief's subjection and his power was situated in the nation of *hasina,* sanctity (cf. Block 1989). The taboos on royalty are not, of course, conceptualized as originating lower down the ladder of secular hierarchy, but rather draw their source from a transcendental order. Violations by the kind of ancestral taboos bring calamity on the whole country. Royal family members, especially the kind, concentrate the vitality of the people within them. The chief "is precisely that individual who is the most social: far from being outside and above society, he is its incarnation" (1904:118).

11. More precisely, as Héritier (1982) notes, the brother-sister taboo marks both identity and difference.

12. One explanation offered locally concerning the content of the taboos has to do with a theory of contagion in which the fetus is felt to be extremely susceptible to the experiences encountered by its parents. This impression (*tuhingy*) is evident in stories such as the following: a man died with his eyes open and they were shut by the man who laid out the corpse. The latter's wife was pregnant at the time; subsequently their infant son was born with his eyes shut. Similarly, it was often suggested that the pregnant women among whom I spent time might give birth to infants with my complexion.

13. Speech act theory originates with Austin (1965); innovative applications within anthropology include Ahern (1979), Block (1989), Brown (1985), Tambiah (1985) and, most relevant for the present argument, Rappaport (1979).
14. The illocutionary effect is the same; the perlocutionary (persuasive) effect may be much stronger in a discrete immediate performance.
15. Similarly, an ostensible index of the violation of taboo, such as breaking out in hives, might also be analyzed as a performative act that establishes a moral state of impurity.
16. Another reason why I am reluctant to speak of the self here is that I am uncomfortably aware that the model elaborated in this article is essentially an external one, a "reading from without," rather than a "reading from within" (Boddy n.d.). While the external argument is structuralist in that it provides for a relational constitution of the person or subject, a reading from within would doubtless be more substantive, taking into account the particular meaning and relative importance of each kind of act of restraint for the subject. I attempt this elsewhere (Lambek n.d.). Fortes's work (1987), while centered primarily on the person, remains an important attempt to bridge the Durkheimian and Freudian perspectives.
17. Alternative and overlapping discourses of accountability make use of "destiny" (*nyora*) and "God's will" (*bok'an drangahary*).
18. Naturalization may be a general function of indexicality. Writing of the creative use of a linguistic index in order to bring an aspect of the context into cognitive relief, Silverstein remarks that, "Under these circumstances, the indexical token in speech performs its greatest apparent work, seeming to be the very medium through which the relevant aspect of the context is made to 'exist' " (1976:34).
19. Nevertheless, it is evident from the brief description from my field notes that *how* the taboo is accepted or rejected—compare the claim by Mdala to a violent reaction if his utensils have ever even come into contact with goat, and the exaggerated statement by his uncle that nothing tastes better—suggests that a strong psychological dimension often underlies the social choices.
20. In this sense the Islamic and non-Islamic prohibitions found in Mayotte are not commensurable.
21. van Gennep also notes that the most strictly prohibited things are referred to by the term *vorika* (1904:87).
22. That the presence of the body signifies the acquiescence of the person is most graphically displayed to the people of Mayotte in its violation, when the body is present but the person has been replaced by another, that is, by a spirit. But one could say too that the spirits only become real, social persons, through their embodied presence. Having no visible bodies of their own, they need to take on the bodies of humans, by *coup d'état*. And it is the bodily act o possession which signifies acceptance of the reality of spirits on the part of the temporarily absent host. Likewise, it is the interactions of other human persons with the spirit present in the body of a human host which constitute their own acceptance of the phenomenon.
23. Bodiless persons—gods, ghosts, etc.—are always special cases. While spirits act and are conceptualized as persons in Mayotte, they only become persons to the degree that they invade and are manifested in human bodies. Indeed, it is precisely such embodiment which differentiates possession from myth or the indirect propitiation of spirits at shrines. Moreover, the morality of spirits is problematic and becomes an issue precisely to the degree that the spirits are embodied. Murphy (1987) provides a compelling account of the effects on personhood of partial disembodiment.

References

Ahern, E. M. (1979). The problem of efficacy: Strong and weak illocutionary acts. *Man (NS), 14*, 1–17.

Austin, J. L. (1965). *How to do things with words.* J. O. Urmson (Ed.), New York: Oxford University Press. (Original work published 1955)

Berger, P. & Luckmann, T. (1971). *The social construction of reality: A treatise on the sociology of knowledge.* Harmondsworth: Penguin.

Bloch, M. (1986). *From blessing to violence: History and ideology in the circumcision ritual of the Merina of Madagascar.* Cambridge: University Press.

Block, M. (1989). *Ritual, history, and power: Selected papers in anthropology.* London: Athlone Press.

Boddy, J. (1989). *Wombs and alien spirits: Women, men, and the zar cult in northern Sudan.* Madison: University of Wisconsin Press.

Boddy, J. (n.d.) *Essential texts: On defending uterine blood in northern Sudan.* Paper presented to the American Ethnology Society, April 27, 1990.

Bourdieu, P. (1977). *Outline of a theory of practice.* (R. Nice, Trans.). Cambridge: University Press. (Original work published 1972)

Brown, M. F. (1985). *Tsewa's gift: Magic and meaning in an Amazonian society.* Washington, DC: Smithsonian Institution Press.

Clay, B. J. (1977). *Pinikindu: Maternal nurture, paternal substance.* Chicago: University of Chicago Press.

Comaroff, Jean (1985). *Body of power, spirit of resistance.* Chicago: University of Chicago Press.

Crapanzano, V. (1977). Introduction. In V. Crapanzano & V. Garrison (Eds.), *Case studies in spirit possession.* New York: Wiley.

Douglas, M. (1970). *Purity and danger: An analysis of concepts of pollution and taboo.* Harmondsworth: Penguin. (Original work published 1966)

Durkheim, E. (1965). *The elementary forms of the religious life.* New York: The Free Press. (Original work published 1915)

Feeley-Harnik, G. (1984). The political economy of death: communication and change in Malagasy colonial history. *American Ethnologist, 11,* 1–19.

Fortes, M. (1983). *Oedipus and Job in West African religion.* Cambridge: University Press. (Original work published 1959)

Fortes, M. (1987). Totem and taboo. In J. Goody (Ed.), *Religion, morality, and the person.* Cambridge: University Press. (Original work published 1966)

Gell, A. (1979). Reflections on a cut finger: Taboo in the Umeda conception of the self. In R. H. Hook (Ed.), *Fantasy and symbol: Studies in anthropological interpretation.* London: Academic Press.

Giddens, A. (1984). *The constitution of society: Outline of the theory of structuation.* Berkeley: University of California Press.

Giles, L. (1987). Possession cults on the Swahili coast: A re-examination of theories of marginality. *Africa, 57,* 234–257.

Gregory, C. A. (1982). *Gifts and commodities.* London: Academic Press.

Héritier, F. (1982). The symbolics of incest and its prohibition. In M. Izard & P. Smith (Eds.), *Between belief and transgression* (J. Leavitt, Trans.). Chicago: University of Chicago Press. (Original work published 1979)

Jackson, M. (1989). *Paths toward a clearing: Radical empiricism and ethnographic inquiry.* Bloomington, Indiana University Press.

Kapferer, B. (1983). *A celebration of demons.* Bloomington: Indiana University Press.

Lambek, M. (1981). *Human spirits: A cultural account of trance in Mayotte.* Cambridge: University Press.

Lambek, M. (1983). Virgin marriage and the autonomy of women in Mayotte. *Signs, 9,* 264–281.

Lambek, M. (1988a). Spirit possession/spirit succession: Aspects of social continuity in Mayotte. *American Ethnologist, 15,* 710–731.

Lambek, M. (1988b). Graceful exits: Spirit possession as personal performance in Mayotte. *Culture, 8,* 59–69.

Lambek, M. (1990a). Certain knowledge, contestable authority: Power and practice on the Islamic periphery. *American Ethnologist, 17,* 23–40.

Lambek, M. (1990b). Exchange, time, and person in Mayotte: The structure and destructuring of a cultural system. *American Ethnologist, 92,* 647–661.

Lambek, M. (n.d.). Toward a psychoanalytically informed reading of spirit possession in Mayotte. Paper presented to the Third Indo-Canadian Symposium, Mysore, January 1990.

Lan, D. (1985). *Guns and rain.* London: J. Currey.

Leach, E. R. (1954). *Political systems of highland Burma.* Boston: Beacon.

Lévi-Strauss, C. (1963). *Totemism.* Boston: Beacon. (Original work published 1962)

Merleau-Ponty, M. (1962). *The phenomenology of perception* (C. Smith, Trans.). London: Routledge & Kegan Paul.

Mitchell, T. (1988). *Colonising Egypt.* Cambridge: University Press.

Murphy, R. F. (1972). *The dialectics of social life.* New York: Columbia University Press.

Murphy, R. F. (1987). *The body silent.* New York: Henry Holt.

Obeyesekere, G. (1981). *Medusa's hair.* Chicago: University of Chicago Press.

Parry, J. (1986). The gift, the Indian gift and the "Indian gift." *Man (NS), 21* 453–473

Rappaport, R. A. (1979). The obvious aspects of ritual. In *Ecology, meaning, and religion.* Richmond CA: North Atlantic Books.

Ruud, J. (1960). *Taboo: A study of Malagasy customs and beliefs.* London: Allen & Unwin.

Sahlins, M. (1985). *Islands of history.* Chicago: University of Chicago Press.

Schafer, R. (1976). *A new language for psychoanalysis.* New Haven, CT: Yale University Press.

Schafer, R. (1978). *Language and insight.* New Haven, CT: Yale University Press.

Sharp, L. A. (1989). *Spirit possession as ethnohistory.* Paper presented at the American Ethnological Society annual meeting, Santa Fe, New Mexico.

Silverstein, M. (1976). Shifters, linguistic categories, and cultural description. In K. Basso & H. Selby (Eds.), *Meaning in anthropology.* Albuquerque: University of New Mexico Press.

Tambiah, S. J. (1985). *Culture, thought and social action.* Cambridge, MA: Harvard University Press.

Turner, B. S. (1984). *The body and society: Explorations in social theory.* Oxford: Basil Blackwell.

Turner, V. (1967). *The forest of symbols.* Ithaca, NY: Cornell University Press.

van Gennep, A. (1904). *Tabou et totéimisme à Madagascar: Étude descriptive et théorique.* Paris: Ernest Leroux.

van Gennep, A. (1960) [1908]. *The rites of passage* (trans) M. B. Vizedom & G. L. Caffee. London: Routledge & Kegan Paul.

Vérin, P. & Rajaonarimanana, G. N. (n.d.). *Divination in Madagascar: The Antemoro case and the diffusion of divination.* Ms. Paris: Institut National des Langues et Civilisations Orientales.

Wilson, P. J. (1977). The problem with simple folk. *Natural History, 86*(10), 26–32.

Zempleni, A. (1977). From symptom to sacrifice: The story of Khady Fall. In V. Crapanzano & V. Garrison (Eds.), *Case studies in spirit possession.* New York: Wiley.

From Saints to Shibboleths: Image, Structure, and Identity in Maya Religious Syncretism

JOHN M. WATANABE

Introduction

At the center of every Maya town in the highlands of southern Mexico and Guatemala stands the Catholic church, often referred to as the house of the saints' images that dwell inside. For the Maya, these saints have long served as local guardians of crops, health, and community well-being, whose benevolence hinges on proper homage from town residents. The people of Santiago Chimaltenango, a Mam-speaking Maya town in western Guatemala, even go so far as to say that their Catholic patron saint is a Maya like themselves. This article examines how and why these people have come to imbue a Catholic saint with their native "Mayanness" and, more generally, what this reveals about religious syncretism and the nativism underlying it among the highland Maya of southern Mexico and Guatemala.

Anthropologists have long characterized Maya religious syncretism as a seamless fusion of native and Christian elements (cf. Thompson 1954:5; Wisdom 1952:120). Ironically, however, they tend to see in this fusion either some enduring, if ineffable, Maya culture (cf. Thompson 1954:26; Vogt 1969:586–587), or a relative, yet decisive, Catholic evangelization (cf. Ricard 1966:274–282; Wolf 1957:166–167). On one hand, authors who take a primordialist perspective seek the essential Mayanness behind this folk religion. Eva Hunt's (1977) brilliant structuralist analysis of Mesoamerican symbolism posits a "symbolic armature" that, although now "buried," continues to motivate Maya religious life based on "a quadripartite, yearly, agrarian, solar calendric cycle . . . deeply embedded in a root paradigm of ecology, agrarian schedules and invariant astronomical events" (1977:248–249). Similarly, Victoria Bricker (1981) argues that Maya myth and ritual synchronize—and thus syncretize—episodes of ethnic conflict in Maya history according to the dictates of an enduring "substrate" in Maya culture of cyclical time and calendrical prophecy. On the other hand, historicists argue that Maya syncretism simply reflects the exigencies of Spanish conquest and colonialism. Robert Wasserstrom (1983:20, 77, 102–103) sees Maya Catholicism in Chiapas as a genuine, pragmatic response to imposed marginality, serving initially to establish and then to assert Maya rights as good Christian subjects of Castile, and later as a means of soliciting divine deliverance from rapacious colonial overlords. The Guatemalan historian Severo Martínez Peláez (1979) goes even further, asserting that no syncretism occurred at all; instead, colonial oppression alone "created the Indian" (1979:594; cf. Friedlander 1975; Hawkins 1984; W. Smith 1977).

Unfortunately, the terms of this debate obscure the very crux of syncretism, which lies precisely in its paradoxical conjunction of both persistence and conversion, nativism and opportunism (cf. Edmonson 1960:194). Consequently, in this paper I focus not on "globally determinant" cultural or historical patterns but on the dialectical process of Maya syncretism itself (cf. Rojas Lima 1983). I take this process to be grounded in the social context that most immediately motivates it—the local community—much as Nancy Farriss does in her masterful history of colonial Yucatan (1984). She argues there that syncretism pertained more to the realm of public community religion than it did to personal observances or universal cosmology. She infers that the Yucatec Maya conceptualized life as a collective enterprise of survival based on public rituals of reciprocity between mortals, gods, and nature (1984:6). When Christian evangelization banished the old gods from public purview, the Yucatec Maya of necessity turned to the tutelary Catholic saints allowed them by the missionaries in order to sustain the community rituals that they considered so basic to their survival. Through a "creative process of reconstruction," and the normalization of these innovations from one generation to the next, the saints gradually lost their status as surrogates for Yucatec gods, but the idea of community-based devotions, not divine salvation, continued to govern Maya relations with their saints (Farriss 1984:309–314, 324–333).

Of course, any attempt to rectify primordialist or historicist reifications of Maya religious syncretism by focusing on the importance of community risks succumbing to equally reified assumptions about "community." Far from denoting some insular, homogeneous whole, however, I see community as a problematic social nexus within which people constantly negotiate the immediate existential concerns and possibilities of their lives, conditioned by the wider economic, political, and natural ecology of which they are a part. In the Maya case, two features ground community, although they never absolutely bound it: first, Maya communities center strongly on circumscribed local places in which presumed ancestral affinities, primary access to land, and immediate interpersonal familiarities inhere; and second, the historical coincidence of ethnic Spaniard and Maya with the hierarchy of conqueror and conquered, master and servant, Ladino (hispanicized *mestizo*) and Indian, motivates opposed social categories that, when seen in light of one another, obscure very real internal variability and equally real external conjunctions between the two groups. That is, local Maya community places also entail antagonistic racist stereotypes of self-ascribed, as well as other-attributed, distinctiveness that tend to elide both actual differentiation within communities and abiding commonalities between them. I take Maya religious syncretism to be at least in part constituted by, and thoroughly constitutive of, the cultural conventions by which Maya negotiate these community-cum-ethnic boundaries with themselves and with others.

To develop this argument, I first examine the cultural construction of contemporary Maya saints in the highland Guatemalan town of Santiago Chimaltenango. I then contrast these patterns with their antecedents in 16th-century Spain, drawing on comparative evidence from saint cults in other Maya communities (Fig. 7.1) to substantiate the historically emergent—rather than timelessly enduring—"Mayanness" evidenced by such syncretism.[1] Second, I relate saints to other Maya images of community, especially ancestors and "earth lords," to explore in greater detail precisely how the Maya have appropriated these once-Catholic figures and what this syncretism implies about Maya conceptions of their own identity. In this way, I hope to demonstrate that the particulars of both image and structure in Maya religious syncretism attest to ongoing, opportunistic struggles for local identity that have forged Catholic saints into the shibboleths of a paradoxical, yet nonetheless genuine, Maya ethnicity.

Why Santiago Is an "Indian"

The people of Santiago Chimaltenango, or Chimbal, as they call their town, live on the rugged southern slopes of the Cuchumatán Highlands in western Guatemala. They eke out a livelihood by subsistence corn farming and local cash-cropping in coffee, petty trade, and migratory wage labor on Guatemala's coastal plantations. The town's 3500 or so souls speak Mam, one of Guatemala's 20-odd Maya languages, and, in contrast to other Maya, reside mostly in a nucleated town settlement rather than in dispersed hamlets. Local public and economic life lies firmly in Chimalteco hands, with Ladinos constituting less than five percent of the town's population—many of them transient schoolteachers and their families. Charles Wagley (1941, 1949) first carried out research in the town in 1937, and I did so in 1978–80, with brief return trips in 1981 and 1988 (Watanabe 1981, 1984, in press).

Like many Maya towns, Chimbal first appears in Guatemalan history as a tribute-paying village and later as an administrative and ecclesiastical subjurisdiction of the colony (Watanabe 1984:47–50). Despite this past, however, the town today evinces an emphatic local identity, reflected in its own particular style of Maya speech, ethnic dress, and local custom. Although these patterns have undergone rapid, increasingly repressive change during this century (Watanabe in press), Chimbal remains highly endogamous, and Chimaltecos retain an abiding sense of ethnic distinctiveness. The town's patron saint, Santiago (Saint James), constitutes an important expression of this local sovereignty. In the guise of a sword-wielding figure mounted on horseback, Santiago Matamoros ("Saint James the Moorkiller") originally served as the saintly protector of Guatemala's 16th-century Spanish conquerors, but Chimaltecos no longer associate their Santiago with the Spanish conquest, instead regarding him with a virtually exclusive proprietary eye.

N
0
80
160 km
0
50
100 mi.
Caribbean Sea
Chan Kom
Yucatán Peninsula
MEXICO
GUATEMALA
BELIZE
Belmopan
Usumacinta River
Chamula
Zinacantan
Amatenango
Chiapas Highlands
Presa de la Angostura
San Miguel Acatán
Santa Eulalia
Todos Santos
Santiago Chimaltenango
Colotenango
Aguacatán
Lago de Izabal
Gulf of Honduras
Momostenango
Chichicastenango
San Andrés Semetabaj
Motagua River
Guatemalan Highlands
Lago de Atitlán
Santiago Atitlán
Chinautla
San Luis Jilotepeque
Jocotán
Guatemala City
HONDURAS
Tegucigalpa
EL SALVADOR
San Salvador
PACIFIC OCEAN
Gulf of Fonseca

Chimaltecos possess two wooden images of Santiago, a large one that presides permanently over the altar in the church, and a smaller white-skinned, black-bearded figure riding a burro-like white horse. They dress this smaller image in the typical men's garb of the town, and they say that, like any good Chimalteco, he has a "wife," Saint Ann, whose feast day closely follows his in late July. Appropriately, her image wears the handwoven red blouse and navy blue skirt of a good Chimalteco woman. Chimaltecos pray to these saints in Mam, not in Spanish. During important fiestas, they carry the images in processions around the town church and plaza. Each year, Santiago visits two neighboring towns to pay his respects to their patron saints on their feast days, just as these saints return the courtesy at Christmas, Corpus Christi, and the feast of Santiago.

Formerly, Chimaltecos performed extensive rituals for the saints, both publicly to validate their local sovereignty and individually to ensure personal health and well-being (Wagley 1949). A strong sense of reciprocity infused Chimalteco relations with Santiago. In return for his protection, Chimaltecos would feed their saint ritual offerings of incense, flowers, candles, and shot glasses of rum, so that he would not starve (cf. Wagley 1949:69). Although many of the old devotions have now given way to more worldly pursuits and to the orthodoxies of Catholic and evangelical Protestant missionization, Chimaltecos still claim the special protection of Santiago. Some even say that it was the repeated visitations of their saint, mounted on a fearsome white charger, that delivered Chimbal from the Guatemalan army's counterinsurgency occupation of late 1982–83 and spared them the brutal massacres suffered by towns all around them (cf. Manz 1988).

Consequently, Chimaltecos continue to celebrate processions with their saint. During fiestas, the small image of Santiago on horseback still sallies forth from the church to survey his domain. The way that the figure moves serenely above the crowd on the shoulders of

FIGURE 7.1 (left) The Maya communities that constitute the major sources for this study (numbered roughly from west to east).

Language	Town and Principal Ethnographic Source
Trotzil	1. Zinacantan (Vogt 1969, 1976)
	2. Chamula (Gossen 1974, 1975)
Tzeltal	3. Amatenango (Nash 1970)
Kanjobal	4. San Miguel Acatán (Siegel 1941)
	5. Santa Eulalia (LaFarge 1947)
Mam	6. Todos Santos (Oakes 1951)
	7. Santiago Chimaltenango (Wagley 1941, 1949; Watanabe 1984)
	8. Colotenango (Valladares 1957)
Aguacatec	9. Aguacatán (Brintnall 1979; McArthur 1977)
Quiché	10. Momostenango (Tedlock 1982)
	11. Chichicastenango (Bunzel (1952)
Tzutujil	12. Santiago Atitlán (Mendelson 1965)
Cakchiquel	13. San Andrés Semetabaj (Warren 1978)
Pokomam	14. Chinautla (Reina 1966)
	15. San Luis Jilotepeque (Gillin 1951)
Chortí	16. Jocotán (Wisdom 1940)
Yucatec	17. Chan Kom (Redfield and Villa Rojas 1934)

his celebrants, bowing ceremoniously to the other saints, presents Santiago as an active participant in, not merely the object of, these devotions. Although no Chimalteco ever said as much to me, it is almost as if they are helping him to perform the old prayer rounds that mortal Chimaltecos now forgo—bearing him from station to station, playing his music for him, making his prayers and offerings, launching his skyrockets into the heavens. Despite the creeping disenchantment of everyday Chimalteco life, processions still precipitate a sense of closeness between townspeople and their Santiago—and thus among themselves as well.

Chimaltecos further naturalize Santiago through accounts of how he came to live in Chimbal. They tell of when the first Chimaltecos found Santiago in the mountains, in a place where even today no one lives because it has no water. After building the church that still stands at the center of town, these ancestral Chimaltecos fetched Santiago to his new home. The next morning he was gone. Searchers eventually found him back where they had first encountered him and once more returned him to the church. Again he fled to his old place but this time, when they tried to carry him back to town, Santiago made himself so heavy that no one could lift him. Exasperated, the ancestors beat him with whips to get him into the church, leaving gouges on his back that can still be seen today. Santiago has dutifully abided in the church ever since (Watanabe 1984:82–83). Although he is neither the mythic founder of the town nor even originally Chimalteco, Santiago attests to those ancestral Chimaltecos who first discovered him, built his fine house for him, and finally domesticated him. Older than living Chimalteco memory, saint and church substantiate otherwise shadowy Chimalteco ancestors for their living descendants.

Santiago has thus come to look, act, and belong in the community like any Chimalteco. The exact import of this transformation, however, in itself remains unclear. On one hand, Chimaltecos iconographically and mythologically repudiate saint and church as images of the Spanish conquest, yet, at the same time, their devotion to Santiago testifies to their utter encompassment by a Catholic evangelization predicated on that conquest. Given this contradiction, Chimalteco patterns of saint worship must be compared with their antecedents in Spain as well as with saint cults in other Maya communities in order to clarify both the nature of this evangelization and the meaning of Maya syncretic accommodation to it.

Castilian and Maya Saints

Contemporary Maya saint cults originated with the Spanish conquest of the New World and have their roots in the local worship of Catholic saints in 16th-century Spain, since Catholic evangelization of the Maya occurred mostly during that century. By the early 17th century, basic parish structure and administration of Maya towns had been firmly established, and American-born and -ordained creoles, not *peninsulares* from Spain, made up the majority of the Guatemalan clergy (Oss 1986:45, 65, 159–160, 181). Given George Foster's (1960:232–234) observation that initial adaptations in situations of culture contact exert a kind of "founder effect" on subsequent cultural developments, such "cultural crystallization" of the colonial Guatemalan church would suggest that 16th-century patterns of Spanish Catholicism most directly influenced the formation of Maya saint cults.

William Christian (1981) argues that religion in 16th-century Spain constituted a local, as opposed to a universal, Catholicism concerned with the welfare of relatively small agricultural communities afflicted by epidemics, pests, droughts, and tempests. Such misfortunes bespoke God's wrathful intervention in human affairs, which saints or the Virgin Mary might assuage to varying degrees—although at times townspeople apparently suspected disgruntled saints themselves of inflicting the harm.

Villagers established covenants with the saints in two ways, through vows and through shrines. In times of crisis, villagers collectively vowed devotion to a particular saint in return for saintly intercession before God. Such vows committed the community to fasting or refraining from work on the saint's day, to constructing a new image or chapel for the saint, or to sponsoring processions or public charities in the saint's honor. These corporate vows and annual acts of reciprocity and commensality reaffirmed the community's covenant with the divine, while also literally enacting the community's solidarity with itself: celebrations for the saints "actualized, put into physical form, the juridical entity of the community that met in the first place to make the vow" (Christian 1981:59). Townspeople came to call particularly effective or powerful local saints their town "patrons," a status formalized by the Church in 1630 (Christian 1981:92).

If votive devotions served to express local allegiances to certain saints, saint shrines conventionally expressed the affinity of saints themselves for particular local places. After the introduction of saints' images into Spain during the 11th and 12th centuries, devotions formerly restricted to actual saint relics in cathedrals, monasteries, and parish churches proliferated at more proprietary shrines dedicated to local miraculous images (Christian 1981:21). The origin legends associated with these shrines reflect a leitmotif of the "found" saint, most often Mary. In these stories, a saintly apparition or image repeatedly returns to the place where it first appeared or where villagers first discovered it, until finally officials build a shrine there, usually in the countryside remote from town and parish church (cf. Foster 1960:161–162).

These legends entail what Christian (1981:73–75) calls "encapsulated devotional charters"—dialogues between saint and community in which the saint, not ecclesiastical prescription, ultimately dictates the circumstances of local worship. Because the saint is often found by poor or dispossessed shepherds, children, or women, who, together with the saint, finally triumph over town authorities, these legends further validate a local Christian populism by affirming that "the saint has come to serve everyone; that the bond set up between the saint and the town is also a direct bond between the saint and each person of the town, beginning with the powerless" (Christian 1981:82). Castillian saint cults in the 16th century thus appropriated and embraced particular saintly guardians and imbued the local landscape, whether urban or rural, with a sacred geography of shrines known and proven for divine deliverance from disaster. In forging covenants with the divine, saint worship also expressed for many Castilians their equally binding commitment to the lands and people that sustained their communities.

In the New World, Franciscan, Dominican, and Mercedarian missionaries aspired to instill in the Maya a similar Christian humility and Spanish civility by resettling the largely rural Maya into *congregaciones*—nucleated, Spanish-style communities centered on church, plaza, and town hall (cf. Farriss 1984:158–164; Lovell 1985:76–94; Oss 1986:14–37). The friars met with some success, for by the early 17th century the Dominican chronicler Antonio de Remesal could note the industry with which the Maya of Guatemala produced altarpieces and saint figures for their churches. Many churches housed ten or more images—doubtless testament to Maya faith, Remesal presumed, especially since Guatemala was "less rich than the rest of the Indies" (1966:181; cf. Oss 1986:121, 150–152).

Nonetheless, the historical circumstances of the Mayas' initial encounter with Christianity clearly distinguished these cults from Castilian ones. First, unlike Castilian devotions, Maya covenants with their saints originated neither in vow, sign, nor miracle, but were dictated to them by the founding missionary-friars (cf. Farriss 1984:310; Oss 1986:109; Wasserstrom 1983:28, 30–31). At the same time, a chronically shorthanded clergy left many Maya communities without resident priests, placing primary responsibility for Christian instruction and supervision on minimally trained native *fiscales* or *maestros* (cf. Clendinnen 1987:47; Orellana 1984:197–199, 203–205; Ricard 1966:97–98; Watanabe 1984:57–58). In contrast to Spain, where priestly presence in town and parish church left local saint cults to claim countryside shrines, absent priests enabled many Maya to claim for their own their local churches and the saints inside them. Given the triumph of their saint-worshiping conquerors, the Maya needed little doctrinal sophistication to recognize—and come to value—the apparent efficacy of the saints. Indeed, saint images in themselves undoubtedly proved more compelling to the Maya than did garbled sermons on transubstantiation, the Holy Trinity, or Christ's passion—subtleties often well beyond either missionary mastery of Maya tongues or neophyte predisposition to discern (cf. Gage 1958:236–237). The resulting cults made neither formal Christian doctrine more intelligible nor its necessity more apparent.

Not surprisingly, then, Chimalteco devotions to Santiago, like saint cults in other Maya communities, today evince a more profound parochialism than did saint worship in 16th-century Spain. Cosmologically, Maya saints have become decidedly local personages relatively independent of the remote, almost inaccessible figure of God. Many Maya still regard their saints in part as *abogados* ("advocates") who intercede for them before God, but instead of Christian divine grace, these saints tend to represent "genuinely creative or protective powers" in their own right (Bunzel 1952:267; cf. Gillin 1951:83; Valladares 1957:192). Local myths clearly depict the saints, and often Christ, as local culture heroes or creators notably lacking in Christian virtues (cf. Gossen 1974:313, 316, 337, 343–344; LaFarge 1947:50–65; Mondloch 1982:119–123; Nash 1970:198–210; Reina 1966:2; Valladares 1957:29–30; Vogt 1969:356–360; Wagley 1949:51–52; Warren 1978:35–39). Maya saints also appear to intervene in earthly affairs mostly to punish transgressions against their persons—usually some real or supposed ritual neglect—rather than to uphold universal Christian principles or to enact divine covenants (cf. Bunzel 1952:166; Redfield & Villa Rojas 1934:108; Wagley 1949:53–54; Wisdom 1940:417, 420; Vogt 1969:361).

Although Maya may suggest that images with the same name could be "brothers" (Wagley 1949:52–53; Wisdom 1940:413), or that all saints are kinsfolk of Christ (Gossen 1974:43), the saints of different towns constitute distinct personages who exercise territorial sovereignty over their own communities and moral suasion and sanction over their townspeople (cf. Gillin 1951:83, 85–86; LaFarge 1947:104–107; Nash 1970:198, 204–206; Redfield & Villa Rojas 1934:107–110; Reina 1966:18; Wagley 1949:53–54; Vogt 1969:361). Consequently, Maya rarely pray to saints of other towns, and Maya dealings with their egoistic saints have never given way to more universalistic devotions to Mary and Christ, as did local religion in Spain after the 16th century (Christian 1981:182, 185, 199, 206). Instead, Christ and Mary have entered local cosmologies as the sun and the moon, with images of the Virgin often characterized incongruously as the "consorts" of local male saints (cf. Colby & Colby 1981:38–39; Gossen 1974:21; LaFarge 1947:104, 106; Mendelson 1965:103; Mondloch 1982:120; Nash 1970:198–203; Valladares 1957:192; Vogt 1969:367–368; Wagley 1949:52–54; Wisdom 1940:392, 399*n*, 400*n*, 411–412).

Ritually, Maya saint cults further emphasize local sociality over divine covenants. Like Chimaltecos, other Maya dress and care for their saints, sometimes arraying them in the typical Maya garb of their town (cf. Gillin 1951:83; Vogt 1969:353; Wisdom 1940:449). Similarly, they attend their saints in annual processions (cf. Bunzel 1952:252; Valladares 1957:193), while some towns also take their patrons to visit one another on the host saint's feast day (cf. Farriss 1984:151, 331–332; Gillin 1951:97–100; Valladares 1957:175, 193; Vogt 1969:362–365; Wagley 1949:82–83; Wasserstrom 1978). Maya feed the saints offerings of incense, flowers, candles, and rum, and they sponsor ceremonial meals of which the saints symbolically partake (cf. Bunzel 1952:251, 292–293, 302; LaFarge 1947:73–74; Moore 1973:84; Nash 1970:208, 302; Vogt 1969:361, 486, 495). Although Maya may offer money to the saints (Nash 1970:302), food—both actual and metaphorical—remains the primary ritual medium, emphasizing the mutual sustenance on which the survival of both saint and Maya depends (cf. Farriss 1984:321–324).

None of these devotions, however, stems from vows to the saints in any penitential sense. Whatever penance there is lies in the ongoing obeisance to the saint of the community as a whole and in the future oblations of its members that this ensures. Personal prayers beg forgiveness for past offenses and deliverance from future ones, but they promise nothing beyond the usual offerings that accompany the entreaties themselves (cf. Bunzel 1952:292–293; Laughlin 1980:250–252; Vogt 1969:361–362). Similarly, public devotions to the saints reflect neither individual nor collective vows but rather the obligations prescribed by each community's annual cycle of fiestas. Responsibility for the saints remains "standardized" (Nash 1970:207) and "utterly impersonal" (Reina 1966:163)—literally *cargos* or "burdens" that individuals must shoulder because they live in the saint's town, not because the saint personally inspires them to serve (cf. Bunzel 1952:164–165; Farriss 1984:329; Watanabe 1984:163–164). Maya appeals to their saints thus serve more to affirm an ethic of local reciprocity, social propriety, and moral accountability in this world than to seek the divine grace of redemption in the next (cf. Bunzel 1952:162, 293–294; Colby & Colby 1981:122–123, 138–141; Farriss 1984:328; Koizumi 1981:21–56; Mendelson 1965:96–101, 116; Nash 1970:287–288; Redfield 1941:115–116, 127–131; Reina 1966:163; Vogt 1969:222; Wagley 1949:67; Warren 1978:65).

Maya myths of saintly origins complete the localization of these once-Catholic figures. As in Chimbal, the Castilian motif of "found" saints abounds. In some cases, the saint simply appears (Reina 1966:172) or falls from the sky (Wisdom 1940:415). In others, God or Christ sends the saint directly to the town (Gossen 1974:316; Warren 1978:49)—often without mention of the Spanish conquest (Gillin 1951:77; Nash 1970:5) but not always (Warren 1978:40–41). In still other tales, the hapless, wandering saint arrives and asks local Maya authorities, whether mortal (Vogt 1969:356) or supernatural (LaFarge 1947:61, 63), for permission to live in the town. Such acquiescence to local sovereignty also transpires in the seemingly more typical tales of Maya who find the saint in the countryside and bring it into the town. As with the discovery of Santiago, these accounts often end with villagers punishing the saint to make it "behave" properly. In Zinacantan, town elders pour hot water over San Lorenzo to silence him because they dislike "talking saints" (Vogt 1969:356); in Amatenango, they throw their evil image of San Pedro out of the church and then behead him for his witchcraft (Nash 1970:205).

These narratives systematically invert the canons of Castilian saint legends. First, although saints originate in the "wilds" in both genres, Castilians interpret this as God's "divine participation in the landscape" (Christian 1981:208); for the Maya, it signifies the saints' alien origins. Second, Castilian saints eventually settle into countryside shrines, whereas Maya saints take up residence in churches at the centers of towns: saintly comings situate Maya Catholicism centripetally in particular communities, not centrifugally in nature wherever divine providence chooses to manifest itself. Third, Castilian villagers build shrines where the saints—not church authorities—dictate; Maya literally and mythically "encapsulate" (cf. Vogt 1969:582, 586) the saints within the moral compass of their communities. Finally, Castilian tales associate "found" saints with the poor or powerless, not with ancestors or other primordial sovereigns, as Maya tales do. Rather than reiterate a populist covenant forged by the saint between the meek and the divine, Maya encounters between saint and mortal substantiate the social and moral sovereignty of the community. Maya transformations of Spanish hagiology clearly emphasize the social over the sacred, the local over the transcendent, the immediate over the eternal.

Maya saint cults thus contrast in two ways with the 16th-century Castilian devotions from which they spring. First, Maya saints themselves appear to be at once more accessible and at the same time more worldly and willful than Castilian saints. Rather than Christian vice or virtue, they display all-too-human idiosyncrasies. Second, Maya devotions localize the saints by socializing this saintly willfulness through the very ethic of local reciprocity and commensality that the Maya trust to affirm their own ongoing but contingent relations with one another. Confronted by stranger-saints who turn up in the mountains or who arrive unheralded in their communities, Maya use cult ritual and legend to make the saints live in their towns in plain view of everyone, just as they themselves must do. More than just divine intercessors for their communities, Maya saints conventionalize the immanent sociality—and moral authority—of the communities that incorporate them into their midsts. Largely shorn of any Christian eschatology of divine salvation, the community enactments that served as the means to deliverance in Castilian saint worship have become an essential end of Maya devotions.

Santiago's transformation from Christian saint to Chimalteco shibboleth thus exemplifies a more pervasive parochialism that cosmologically, ritually, and mythologically differentiates Maya saint cults from their antecedents in 16th-century Spain. These differences, however, reflect neither sterile negations of the Church Triumphant that engendered them in the first place nor anachronistic Maya worship of "idols behind altars" (cf. Brenner 1929). Instead, the ongoing "Mayanness" of these cults derives from the fact that despite—or perhaps because of—a sovereignty decreed for them by conquest of "fire and sword," the immigrant-saints could never freely occupy the Maya landscape as they had done their

Spanish homeland. From the very beginning, Maya conventionalizations of the saints involved local Maya ancestors and earth lords who simply refused to leave.

Ancestors

Chimalteco myths of Santiago's origin suggest an intimate relationship between the ancestors who initially discovered and then socialized him, and the saint's enduring Chimalteco nature. In many other communities, ancestors constitute an equally vital link between saint and living Maya. The Maya call these ancestors "mother-fathers" or "grandfathers,"[2] although these figures rarely represent named ascendants of specific kin groups—evidence of the general attenuation of Maya blood relations beyond the immediate extended family. Ancestors most often betoken social affiliations based on land and locale rather than on strict descent (cf. Bunzel 1952:18, 269–270; Davis 1970:83–84; LaFarge 1947:24, 114–116; Reina 1966:227; Vogt 1969:144, 301; Warren 1978:67). Many Maya consider these generic community forebears the primordial claimants of lands now held by the living, and periodic offerings to them validate rights to these estates as well as ensure the land's fertility (cf. Bunzel 1952:17–18; Davis 1970:84; McArthur 1977:17; Vogt 1976:111–112). In some places, ancestors further serve as "terrible avengers of all kinds of wrongdoing" (Bunzel 1952:268; cf. McArthur 1977:11; Vogt 1969:300–301; Warren 1978:67), watching over their descendants from nearby mountain peaks (Vogt 1969:298), from caves (LaFarge 1947:59; Nash 1970:19, 22), or even from the large crosses that stand before local churches (Brintnall 1979:91). Hardly blameless paragons, however, ancestors are often said to have committed innumerable unexpiated wrongs against the "World" and each other, for which their descendants suffer the consequences of sickness and misfortune (cf. Bunzel 1952:146; Koizumi 1981:25–27; Tedlock 1982:142; Valladares 1957:258; Wagley 1949:76).

Despite their vague genealogical status and all-too-human failings, Maya ancestors still evoke the essential continuity and regenerative power of their communities: some Maya regard children as "substitutes" or "replacements" for deceased relatives whose souls the ancestral gods have reincarnated in the newborn (Vogt 1969:272–273); others name infants after their grandparents so that they may respect, remember, and emulate them (cf. Colby & Colby 1981:53*n*; Warren 1978:57); still others identify the ancestors' earthly remains with the spiritual "breath" that lives on in their descendants (Tedlock 1982:41–42). As keepers of the land and givers of life, as the dead in the grave, ancestors fuse local affinities and generational continuity to the very landscape itself.

This nexus of place and past in turn joins ancestors to saints. Just as the saints came long ago to inhabit ancestral places, so the ancestors came first to associate with these strangers. Out of this primordial encounter arose *costumbre*, a term literally meaning "custom" but used generally by Guatemalan Maya to refer to the ritual precepts originally set down by the ancestors (cf. Warren 1978:56–57, 67–73). By reenacting the devotions that first bonded ancestor to saint, saint to community, *costumbre* in the present affirms ancestral acts in the past. The ritual advisors who school each year's cargoholders in their responsibilities to the saints constantly invoke ancestral precedents to justify the strictures of *costumbre* (cf. Bunzel

1952:230, 249; Mendelson 1965:53–54; Nash 1970:102; Reina 1966:112–113, 119–120; Warren 1978:66–69; and, less explicitly, Cancian 1965:42–44; LaFarge 1947:134; Oakes 1951:57–60; Wagley 1949:85 ff.). It often becomes impossible to tell whether these rituals serve more to honor the saints or to obey the ancestors (cf. Brintnall 1979:92; Bunzel 1952:249–250; McArthur 1977:6; Mendelson 1965:94; Reina 1966:18, 108, 120).

Ruth Bunzel (1952:250) once pondered why such continuity should be "reiterated in the one aspect of life in which the break with the past has been so dramatic." Far from reflecting some "false consciousness" conjured up by colonial Catholicism, however, this conflation of saint and ancestor in fact reflects actual historical convergence: one of the most widespread practices in colonial Maya Catholicism involved individually sponsored saint cults called *guachibales,* in which wealthy Maya bequeathed to their heirs both the responsibility and the wherewithal to perform annual celebrations for a particular saint in their memory (cf. Hill 1986:64–67; Oss 1986:89). Although the fees charged for masses said during these celebrations constituted a major source of parish income and thus clearly served priestly interests (cf. Gage 1958:234–241; Oss 1986:111–112), this fusion of saint worship with public remembrance of the dead also fit well with a corporate Maya religiosity in which personal salvation, however defined, depended on collective memorials performed by one's descendants (cf. Farriss 1984:322, 328; Wasserstrom 1983:77). Robert Hill (1986:66–67) has even speculated that the term *guachibal,* derived from the Cakchiquel "to take another form," may itself have alluded to a deeper association between saint image and the soul of the deceased sponsor. Indeed, some Maya today explicitly liken their long-suffering ancestors to "saints" in their own right (Menchú 1984:81; cf. LaFarge 1947:46).

Equally suggestive, the Maya continue to honor their dead each year during the Catholic feasts of All Saints and All Souls on November 1 and 2. On these days, Maya everywhere entertain the dead with food, music, and drink. At altars in their homes and at gravesides in the cemetery, the living feast their dead in ready, often drunken, communion (cf. Bunzel 1952:213, 272; Fought 1972:291–294; LaFarge 1947:77–78; Siegel 1941:72; Vogt 1969:481; Wagley 1949:109–110). Although some communities follow more closely the Spanish custom of commemorating only the recent or remembered dead rather than the ancestors in general (Nash 1970:136; Reina 1966:171; cf. Foster 1960:201; Wisdom 1940:455), it remains unclear to what extent this reflects purposeful disregard of the ancestors or simply the biases of living memory (cf. LaFarge 1947:78). In any event, one essential difference distinguishes Maya from Catholic observances: Maya prayers and oblations engage the dead directly rather than offer penance on behalf of their souls in purgatory (Bunzel 1952:273; Wisdom 1940:454–455; cf. McArthur 1977:12–13). The living present the dead with food; then, having partaken of its essence, the dead in turn "leave" food for the living. Cosmologically, such commensality enacts recurrent cycles of mutual nurturance between living community and generative ancestor rather than the soul's final progress toward eternal salvation. As with the saints, the ritual intent remains immediate, social, and regenerative, not eternal, ethereal, and redemptive (cf. Farriss 1984:322–323; Mendelson 1965:93–94; Taussig 1980:157, 167).

Thus, while Maya ancestors clearly anchor local communities to place and past, they embody less a primordial Mayanness than a sense of enduring continuity between the dead and those now living. Within this continuity, the opposition between Maya ancestor and Christian saint ceased long ago to be absolute—Maya ancestors became "Christians" as much as Catholic saints became "Indians"—and Maya conventions duly reflect this. Nonetheless, despite the *costumbre* that binds them, Maya saint and ancestor persist as distinct images of community: saints occupy church and town, whereas ancestors both figuratively and literally inhere in the place where church and town stand. Neither figure, however, can now do without the other: alone, each contradicts itself—the stranger-saint who precipitates community, the life-giving ancestor whose now lifeless bones lie in the cemetery on the edge of town. Mythically, ancestors appear to antedate the coming of the saints, yet only when the saints arrive are towns founded, churches built, and orderly social life established (cf. Gossen 1974:140, 320, 324; LaFarge 1947:61–62; Reina 1966:172; Vogt 1969:356; Warren 1978:39–40); experientially, saint rituals and churches now constitute the most immediate proof of past ancestral accomplishments. Thus, neither the ongoing sociality of the town and saints nor the self-generative fecundity of the land and ancestors by itself composes a sufficient image of community. Eternal land and ancient church, saint's image and ancestor's grave, all must serve as indispensable conventions of Maya community.

Earth Lords

The seemingly unholy, or at least incongruous, alliance between saint and ancestor derives, of course, from Maya confrontations with the new forms of mortality, morality, and community instituted by Spanish rule after the conquest. Catholic evangelization and forced resettlement imposed, then polarized, contrasts between town and place, saint and ancestor, Christian civility and native devilry. Maya iconography reflects this social and cultural encompassment in a third image, one of capricious power and unbridled egoism: that of the earth lord. Also referred to as "owners" or "guardians" of the mountains, these figures invariably appear as fair-skinned Ladinos, rich in money, clothing, livestock, and land. They dwell in caves, inside mountains, or under the earth, controlling water and rainfall, the land and all its products. Ritual offerings must compensate them for any use of these resources. Ever needful of workers, these earth lords enslave Maya souls by making Mephistophelean promises of worldly success or, more rapaciously, by inflicting on the living illness, chronic misfortune, and death (Mondloch 1982:111–112; Nash 1970:18, 23–24; Oakes 1951:74–77; Siegel 1941:67; Vogt 1969:302–303; Wagley 1949:56–58, 60; cf. Gillin 1951:106; Reina 1966:181–182; Wisdom 1940:408).

In Chimbal, townspeople know the earth lords as *taajwa witz,* Mam for "owners" or "masters" of the mountains. From nearby peaks, these *witz* (or "mountains," as Chimaltecos most often call earth lords) once presided over Chimalteco field and forest as the givers of maize and the rain that made it grow. Snake, cloud, and lightning symbolism clearly identified them with old Maya rain gods (cf. Vogt 1969:302). As personifications of the enduring landscape, Chimalteco *witz* also once served to validate Chimbal's territorial sovereignty through the yearly rituals performed for them by town officials (Watanabe 1984:157–160). Despite associations with land and livelihood, however, Chimalteco tales invariably characterized *witz as tii moos* ("imposing Ladinos"), often dressed in colonial-style Spanish clothing and speaking only Spanish. Whether accosting Chimaltecos on lonely mountain paths far from town or confronting shamans at midnight seances, these *witz* evinced an unpredictable, often ruthless nature. Their great wealth enabled them to intrude in Chimalteco affairs only when it suited them—at times capriciously benefiting poor, humble Chimaltecos, at others greedily spiriting away human souls to work for them inside their mountains. As with the saints, recent years have witnessed a waning in Chimbal of many rituals that formerly beseeched *witz* or sought their leave to farm or hunt on their land, but *witz* remain familiar images—if perhaps no longer vital personages—to Chimaltecos, images enlivened by the Ladino demons that still haunt nightly darkness and dreams, and by the felt proximity of the *witz*-like Ladino Devil himself (cf. Wagley 1949:56*n*).

Thus, just as Santiago has become a Chimalteco and Chimalteco ancestors have become good, saint-worshiping "Christians," so Chimalteco *witz* have metamorphosed into imperious Ladinos closely resembling Ladino plantation owners in status, speech, wealth, and their preemptory—or at best paternalistic—attitudes toward Chimaltecos. Whatever their guise in pre-Hispanic times, *witz* have perhaps always embodied the impassive, contingent—and therefore morally indeterminate—providence of the actual mountains on which rain falls, corn grows, and the living abide. The Ladinization of these presences, however, clearly precipitates the latent ambiguities of nature into more purposive negations of social, moral, and material reciprocity—a transformation that in itself dramatically conventionalizes the Maya experience of conquest and colonialism (cf. Taussig 1980).

This transformation also reflects the more immediate indifference, if not outright hostility, that Chimaltecos have come to expect from outsiders—from the Ladino bureaucrats and schoolteachers who intrude in their community; from the Ladino overseers on Guatemala's coffee and cotton plantations where Chimaltecos toil as migrant laborers; from the Ladino shopkeepers in the cities who sell them needed goods; and most recently, from the Ladino commanders of Guatemala's counterinsurgency army. The history of Chimalteco, indeed of Maya, relations with the Ladino world chronicles a living conquest of intrusion, extraction, and expropriation in which Ladinos more often than not have dictated the conditions—if not the actual outcome—of Maya survival (cf. Lovell 1988). Consequently, Ladinos tend to presume a categorical superiority over all "Indians," regardless of local cultural or linguistic differences among Maya themselves, while Maya tend to make more concentric distinctions between their individual communities and all other outsiders—but especially dominant Ladino authorities (cf. Colby & van den Berghe 1969:179–180; C. Smith 1987:208–211). These boundaries entail abiding ethnic antagonisms that imbue purely cultural differences in language, dress, livelihood, and residence with mutually derogatory racist stereotypes: to Maya, Ladinos are categorically lazy and untrustworthy; to Ladinos, all Maya are brutish and uncivilized.

Despite such obvious and pervasive antipathy, however, the double transposition of Catholic saint into Chimalteco shibboleth and local *witz* into Ladino devil implies neither that all Chimaltecos are saints nor that all Ladinos are devils. Instead, close scrutiny reveals that Chimalteco saint and *witz* differ little in their essential natures. Both, after all, are white-skinned foreigners who come from the mountains, and neither represents a paragon of unmitigated good or evil: Santiago can be cranky and unresponsive, just as *witz* can exhibit a capricious generosity. What differentiate saint and *witz* most clearly are the social relations that Chimaltecos deem possible with each. Santiago lives in the church at the center of town, readily accessible to townspeople. Chimaltecos can actively engage him, tacitly sanctioning their demands with the ritual offerings and assistance on which he depends. Far from innate or inherent, Santiago's Chimalteco-ness emerges from the mutual sociality between saint and town that makes this otherwise imperious figure open to Chimalteco appeal.

TABLE 7.1 Distinctive Features of Saint, Ancestor, and Earth Lord.

	Saint	Ancestor	Earth Lord
Social contiguity	+	–	–
Ethnic continuity	–	+	–
Moral reciprocity	+	+	–

In contrast, *witz* brood inside solitary mountaintops, intervening in local life only when they, not Chimaltecos, please, impervious to the moral suasion of reciprocity. Consequently, *witz* become Ladinos not necessarily because Ladinos are naturally evil, but because, like Ladino strangers, *witz* dwell outside the community, indifferent—if not actively inimical—to the local sociality of Chimalteco life. That is, like Santiago's Chimalteco-ness, the Ladino nature of *witz* remains relational, not essential. As conventionalized social interlocutors, both Chimalteco saint and *witz* polarize, without epitomizing, the disparity between social relations within and outside of the community. Their ethnic transposition dramatizes the moral accountability—and its limitations—that living as neighbors should at once rightfully presume and promote.

Iconographically, then, Chimalteco *witz* suggest that Maya earth lords at once sharpen the respective meanings of saint and ancestor while at the same time uniting them against a backdrop of negative sociality. On one hand, earth lords are Ladino foreigners like the saints, but unlike the saints, they refuse encapsulation into the community. Their amoral intractability parodies the willful but domesticated nature of the saints, accentuating both the moral imperatives of town life and the dangers that lurk beyond its bounds. On the other hand, earth lords dwell in the mountains like the ancestors, at least partially associated with natural powers of regeneration, yet they remain ethnically distinct Ladinos. Unfettered by bonds of blood or local reciprocity, earth lords caricature ancestral powers of life and death, consuming Maya souls rather than nurturing them. The amorality of their ethnically ascribed Ladino-ness emphasizes the significance of ancestry in Maya communities. In sum, earth lords circumscribe the realm of saint and ancestor by opposing the saints spatially, inverting the ancestors ethnically, and negating both morally (Table 7.1). In the world beyond the town dwell neither saints nor ancestors, only mockeries of them.

Recombinant Patterning in Maya Syncretism

Close examination of Maya saints, ancestors, and earth lords reveals historically relativized images that inextricably bind Maya to where and with whom they worship. Furthermore, the syncretism linking these images constitutes neither a simple rearrangement of discrete symbols within some fixed cultural structure nor an indiscriminate seamless fusion of images. Instead, the syncretism of Maya saint, ancestor, and earth lord involves an emergent symbolic reassortment that continually alters the very cultural structure in which it occurs.

On one hand, initially foreign saints have come to precipitate what I would call Maya "cults of community." Territorially, the saints conventionalize ethnic and jurisdictional boundaries, not the immanent divine; morally, cult rituals affirm local standards of propriety, not universal Christian virtues; politically, Maya incorporation of the saints into church and chapel at the center of town dramatizes the moral—if hardly political—sovereignty of their communities, not unequivocal Christian faith. The mere presence of the saints in town and church thus conventionally substantiates a saintly conversion to local bonds of reciprocity that at once attests to the ability of the community to socialize these powerful strangers and at the same time authenticates the community's moral authority to do so.

On the other hand, Maya ancestors originated the *costumbre* that first mastered the saints and so established local community life, but in so doing they also converted themselves and their descendants to saint worship. That is, Maya myths depict the ancestors embracing the saints not necessarily as surrogates for old Maya gods but as new presences who first entered Maya towns as wandering strangers or figures found in the mountains. The ancestors then built them the very churches around which present communities coalesce. In a sense, then, rather than dictate the present from the past as primordial Mayas, ancestors more often simply recapitulate—and thus validate—present circumstances as rooted in the past. The continuity that they embody remains more emergently historical than mythical or even genealogical.

Lastly, earth lords personify the Ladino-cum-natural world over which communities of saints and ancestors never exercise final control. Although irreducible, the distinction here between local communities and the larger world remains to a certain extent relative and self-limiting, because the same mountains that oppose earth lord to saint also belong to the ancestors, whose presence there qualifies purely centripetal notions of sociality; nor can the surrounding land harbor only evil when it is also the sacred *Mundo* ("World") that nurtures all life (cf. Bunzel 1952:264; Carlson & Eachus 1977:41–42; McArthur 1977:16; Mendelson 1965:93–94; Tedlock 1982:41–42). That Maya should nonetheless still liken earth lords not only to Ladinos but also to the absolute malevolence of the Christian Devil attests to the perceived disjunction between community and Ladino morality (Hinshaw 1975:124–125, 127; Wagley 1949:56*n*; Warren 1978:47; cf. Taussig 1980:96).

The syncretism of saint, ancestor, and earth lord thus serves to situate Maya communities morally, historically, and physically. Saints substantiate the ongoing vitality of local life; ancestors anchor the ever-changing present in the undeniable precedents of the past; and earth lords personify inescapable encompassments by natural as well as human realities. Having themselves been transmuted from 16th-century Catholic saints, deceased Maya forebears, and eternal "spirit owners," however, these images remain neither static nor immutable, but constantly interpenetrate one another (Fig 7.2). For example, Maya prayers to the ancestors often come to address earth lords as well (cf. Bunzel 1952:310; Vogt 1976:111–112), just as prayers to the saints are sometimes made at mountaintop shrines otherwise dedicated to ancestors and earth lords (cf. Mondloch 1982:116–117).

In the Quiché town of Chichicastenango, ancestors have actually come to resemble earth lords as the implacable owners of family lands and houses—proprietors from whom the living must constantly implore protection and forgiveness for domestic transgressions (Bunzel 1952:269–270). The Tzeltal of Amatenango go even further and characterize similar punitive house spirits not as ancestors but as earth lord-like Ladino children. Like ancestors in Chichicastenango, these spirits require offerings to protect the souls of house occupants from evil, especially witchcraft (Nash 1970:11–18). The Tzotzil Maya in Zinacantan also

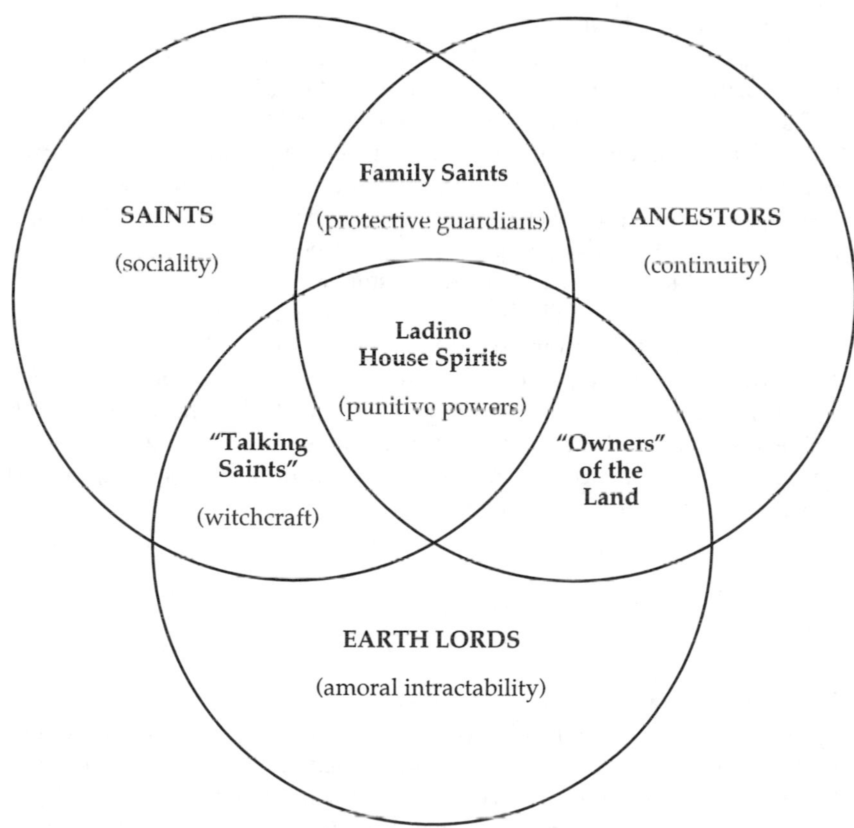

FIGURE 7.2 Recombination of images in Maya syncretism.

conflate ancestors and earth lords by saying that their ancestral gods live inside nearby sacred mountains in earth lord–style Ladino houses (Vogt 1969:384). This systematically inverts both the terms and the relations found in the other two cases: Quiché and Tzeltal houses with spirits inside them become transformed into the sacred abodes of Zinacanteco ancestral spirits themselves, while the Ladino-like behavior of house spirits becomes the Ladino house style of Zinacanteco-like ancestral gods.

Saints also figure in such permutations. While saints in Chimbal and elsewhere serve implicitly as metonyms for Maya ancestors, guardian family saints explicitly take the place of ancestral or Ladino house spirits among the Chortí of eastern Guatemala (Wisdom 1940:414–415, 417). Similarly, in Zinacantan again, individually owned "talking saints" contrast with publicly held saints in church and chapel; these "talking saints" emerge from the earth associated with earth lords, prognostication, and personal welfare rather than with God, Christ, and the common good (Laughlin 1969:175–177; cf. Vogt 1969:365–366). Finally, in Santiago Atitlán, a distaff saint called Maximón—a masked wooden figure dressed in local

Maya style but identified with Judas Iscariot and the Spanish conqueror of Guatemala, Pedro de Alvarado—has come to embody sexuality, fertility, and natural cycles of regeneration, while "earth owners" have taken on the guise of "angels" bearing the saints' names of Martín and María (cf. Mendelson 1965; Tarn & Prechtel 1981).

Far from random confusions, such apparent anomalies at once mediate and further relativize saint, ancestor, and earth lord by dissociating and then systematically recombining their spatial, ethnic, and behavioral attributes. This ongoing reassortment of symbolic features into new images demonstrates how indispensable—yet elusive—the proper constitution of local Mayanness actually is: ancestors without reciprocity become Ladino house spirits; saints without sociality become witches; remote ancestral "owners" verge on becoming earth lords. Hardly an indiscriminate seamless fusion, the recombinant patterning of Maya syncretism situates ethnic distinctions between Maya and Ladino in the emergent morality of social accessibility, mutual familiarity, and the enduring associations that ancestral places circumscribe. More than some quaint or arbitrary index of Maya ethnicity, the syncretism of saint, ancestor, and earth lord constitutes an essential property as well as expression of these local Maya identities.

Conclusion

Maya images of saint, ancestor, and earth lord clearly reveal that syncretism here constitutes a highly selective recombination of symbolic forms, not simply an indiscriminate homogenization of Maya and Catholic faiths. In one sense, syncretism does indeed relativize any "pure Maya" versus "imported Hispanic" distinctions: native ancestors become Christian ritualists; local earth lords metamorphose into diabolical Ladino devils; Catholic saints take on Maya garb, speech, and temperament. Despite this, such symbolic reassortment reflects highly motivated conventionalizations of local place, propriety, and permanence, not merely innate congruencies between Maya and Hispanic religion. The recombination of saint, ancestor, and earth lord systematically molds the Maya cultural and social landscape into ethnic enclaves of community and country, neighbor and stranger, Maya and Ladino. More than fortuitous accretion or amalgamation, Maya syncretism purposively engenders as many meaningful contrasts as it subsumes.

Such recombinant syncretism in turn suggests the emergent rather than determinant nature of the cultural structure linking saint, ancestor, and earth lord. This structure remains inclusive, open to transformational incursions from the likes of saints, God, the Devil, and creeping doubt. Moreover, even the most canonical images often appear to subvert the very relations linking them. Ancestors socialize stranger-saints into the community, but they themselves commit sins against the *costumbre* that they lay down. Saints, despite their incorporation into the community, retain a transcendent willfulness that sanctifies yet also relativizes the sociality that binds them to ancestral places. And finally, the brooding presence of earth lords at once confirms and threatens the communitarian ethic articulated by saint and ancestor.

Contrary to those who give primacy to an underlying "deep structure" of Maya culture (cf. Bricker 1981; Hunt 1977), I would see in these indeterminacies the conditional rather than generative nature of such inherited constructs: "structure" circumscribes possibilities but constitutes a constantly emerging process rather than its own primordial essence. What endure for the Maya are the immediacies of a struggle for meaningful social existence—that is, for a community—rendered in local languages of received but continually reinterpreted conventional forms. It neither denies the relevance of structure to say that it emerges only through historical circumstance nor belittles Maya religion to say that it abides in the hazards of trust, decency—and hope—in Maya life.

Recombinant image and emergent structure bring me, finally, to the Maya identity embedded in both. Syncretism reveals this Mayanness to be neither the direct survival of primordial Maya attachments nor the ordained outcome of colonialist domination. Instead, the ritual conflation of saint and ancestor, and the ethnic transposition of Maya saint and Ladino earth lord, conventionalize an historically emergent social identity precipitated by moral propriety in the here and now of particular local places. Such propriety, however, remains relative rather than absolute, as images of willful saints and capricious earth lords attest. Far from being homogeneous, the ethnic communities that result each constitute at best a problematic consensus of individual wills and contingent affinities. Yet images as well as individuals remain bound up in compelling local concerns and commitments, if for no other reason than to fend off greater, or simply unknown, perils in a larger world that has always taken and seldom given. The dialectical process of syncretism mirrors as well as motivates this oppositional stance of Maya ethnic identity.

The syncretism evident in Maya saint, ancestor, and earth lord thus proves neither so seamless nor so spurious as some have supposed. Although indubitably shaped by both tradition and hegemony, syncretism proves that the Maya have survived an often perilous, always uncertain world as more than tradition-bound anachronisms of a long-vanished civilization or as helpless victims of class oppression. In an inconstant world where even saints lack altruism, the Maya have pragmatically and opportunistically sought their worldly salvation in the ever-contingent affinities of place and past that so long ago made Catholic saints the shibboleths of enduring local identities.

Notes

Acknowledgments. I gratefully acknowledge the Frederick Sheldon Fund of Harvard University and the Michigan Society of Fellows of the University of Michigan, Ann Arbor, for support during the various phases of research, reflection, and writing that led to this article. For comments and encouragement, I thank Evon Z. Vogt, Jr., Ruth Behar, Barbara Smuts, Tom Gregor, and three anonymous reviewers, one of whom's relentless critical eye but appreciation for this article's potential inspired me to make it better.

1. I need to issue two caveats here. First, the use of sources so disparate in both time and space intends neither to imply nor to substantiate the existence of some pan-Maya culture. I do assume, however, that these communities share basic historical and cultural affinities (cf. Vogt 1964, in press) as well as formal similarities in world view (cf. Watanabe 1983) that justify such comparisons. As used in this article, "Maya" refers to the peoples speaking genetically related languages of the Maya Family, living in communities ranging from the Yucatan Peninsula on the north to the Pacific piedmont of Guatemala on the south. Second, this article attempts to outline the cultural space within which Maya religious syncretism occurs, and as such it constitutes neither a full ethnographic analysis of the place of religion in Maya life and history nor an exhaustive treatment of Maya religion

as a whole. In addition to the "public" saint cults discussed here, there exists what I would call a "cult of the soul" (Watanabe 1987:300–301; cf. Farriss 1984:287–289, 296) that focuses on such things as crops (cf. Wagley 1941:31–44), divination (cf. Tedlock 1982), and curing (cf. Fabrega and Silver 1973), which I have dealt with in part elsewhere (cf. Watanabe 1989).

2 León Valladares (1957:195) suggests that the Coloteco (Mam) term *Man-Txu* ("Father-Mother") refers to a supreme deity who, being of both sexes, "has no sex and is [therefore] an absolute being." Miguel León-Portilla (1963:80–103) argues the same thing for *Ometeotl* ("God of Duality"), one manifestation of the supreme god of the Nahua, but he also notes that such duality makes this god the creator of all—including human—life, in a sense, then, perhaps a "cosmic" ancestor.

References

Brenner, Anita (1929). *Idols behind altars: The story of the Mexican spirit.* New York: Payson and Clarke.

Bricker, Victoria Reifler (1981). *The Indian Christ, the Indian King: The historical substrate of Maya myth and ritual.* Austin: University of Texas Press.

Brintnall, Douglas E. (1979). *Revolt against the dead: The modernization of a Mayan community in the highlands of Guatemala.* New York: Gordon and Breach.

Bunzel, Ruth (1952). *Chichicastenango: A Guatemalan village. Publications of the American Ethnological Society, No. 22.* Locust Valley, NY: J. J. Augustin.

Cancian, Frank (1965). *Economics and prestige in a Maya community: The religious cargo system in Zinacantan.* Stanford, CA: Stanford University Press.

Carlson, Ruth, & Eachus, Francis (1977). The Kekchi spirit world. In Helen L. Neuenswander & Dean E. Arnold (Eds.), *Cognitive studies in southern Mesoamerica* (pp. 38–65). Dallas: Summer Institute of Linguistics Museum of Anthropology.

Christian, William A., Jr. (1981). *Local religion in sixteenth-century Spain.* Princeton, NJ: Princeton University Press.

Clendinnen, Inga (1987). *Ambivalent conquests: Maya and Spaniard in Yucatan, 1517–1570.* Cambridge: Cambridge University Press.

Colby, Benjamin N., & Colby, Lore M. (1981). *The daykeeper: The life and discourse of an Ixil diviner.* Cambridge, MA: Harvard University Press.

Colby, Benjamin N., & van den Berghe, Pierre L. (1969). *Ixil country: A plural society in highland Guatemala.* Berkeley: University of California Press.

Davis, Shelton H. (1970). *Land of our ancestors: A study of land tenure and inheritance in the highlands of Guatemala.* Ph.D. dissertation. Department of Social Relations, Harvard University.

Edmonson, Munro S. (1960). Nativism, syncretism, and anthropological science. In *Nativism and syncretism. Middle American Research Institute, Pub. 19* (pp. 181–204). New Orleans: Tulane University.

Fabrega, Horacio, Jr., & Silver, Daniel B. (1973). *Illness and shamanistic curing in Zinacantan: An ethnomedical analysis.* Stanford, CA: Stanford University Press.

Farriss, Nancy M. (1984). *Maya society under colonial rule: The collective enterprise of survival.* Princeton, NJ: Princeton University Press.

Foster, George M. (1960). *Culture and conquest: America's Spanish heritage. Viking Fund Publications in Anthropology, No. 27.* New York: Wenner-Gren Foundation for Anthropological Research.

Fought, John G. (1972). *Chorti (Mayan) texts, (1).* Sarah S. Fought (Ed.). Philadelphia: University of Pennsylvania Press.

Friedlander, Judith (1975). *Being Indian in Hueyapán: A study of forced identity in contemporary Mexico.* New York: St. Martin's Press.

Gage, Thomas (1958). *Thomas Gage's travels in the New World.* J. Eric S. Thompson (Ed.). Norman: University of Oklahoma Press.

Gillin, John (1951). *The culture of security in San Carlos: A study of a Guatemalan community of Indians and Ladinos. Middle American Research Institute, Pub. 16.* New Orleans: Tulane University.

Gossen, Gary H. (1974). *Chamulas in the world of the sun: Time and space in a Maya oral tradition.* Cambridge, MA: Harvard University Press.

Gossen, Gary H. (1975). Animal souls and human destiny in Chamula. *Man (NS), 10,* 448–461.

Hawkins, John (1984). *Inverse images: The meaning of culture, ethnicity, and family in postcolonial Guate-*

mala. Albuquerque: University of New Mexico Press.

Hill, Robert M., II (1986). Manteniendo el culto de los santos: aspectos financieros de las instituciones religiosas del altiplano colonial maya. *Mesoamérica, 7*(11), 61–77.

Hinshaw, Robert E. (1975). *Panajachel: A Guatemalan town in thirty-year perspective.* Pittsburgh: University of Pittsburgh Press.

Hunt, Eva (1977). *The transformation of the humming bird Cultural roots of a Zinacantecan mythical poem.* Ithaca, NY: Cornell University Press.

Koizumi, Junji (1981). *Symbol and context: A study of self and action in a Guatemalan culture.* Ph.D. dissertation. Department of Anthropology, Stanford University.

LaFarge, Oliver (1947). *Santa Eulalia: The religion of a Cuchumatán Indian town.* Chicago: University of Chicago Press.

Laughlin, Robert M. (1969). The Tzotzil. In Evon Z. Vogt (Ed.), *Ethnology,* Part 1 (pp. 152–194). *Handbook of Middle American Indians,* Vol. 7. Robert Wauchope (Gen. Ed.). Austin: University of Texas Press.

Laughlin, Robert M. (1980). *Of shoes and ships and sealing wax: Sundries from Zinacantan. Smithsonian Contributions to Anthropology, No. 25.* Washington, DC: Smithsonian Institution Press.

León-Portilla, Miguel (1963). *Aztec thought and culture: A study of the ancient Nahuatl mind* (Jack E. Davis, Trans.). Norman: University of Oklahoma Press.

Lovell, W. George (1985). *Conquest and survival in colonial Guatemala: A historical demography of the Cuchumatán highlands, 1500–1821.* Kingston and Montreal: McGill-Queen's University Press.

Lovell, W. George (1988). Surviving conquest: The Maya of Guatemala in historical perspective. *Latin American Research Review, 23*(2), 25–57.

Manz, Beatriz (1988). *Refugees of a hidden war: The aftermath of counterinsurgency in Guatemala.* Albany: State University of New York Press.

Martínez Peláez, Severo (1979). *La patria del criollo: Ensayo de interpretación de la realidad colonial guatemalteca.* 6th ed. Costa Rica: Editorial Universitaria Centroamericana.

McArthur, Harry S. (1977). Releasing the dead: Ritual and motivation in Aguacatec dances. In Helen L. Neuenswander & Dean E. Arnold (Eds.), *Cognitive studies in southern Mesoamerica* (pp. 3–34). Dallas: Summer Institute of Linguistics Museum of Anthropology.

Menchú, Rigoberta (1984). I . . . Rigoberta Menchú: An Indian woman in Guatemala. Elisabeth Burgos-Debray (Ed.). (Ann Wright, Trans.). London: Verso.

Mendelson, E. Michael (1965). *Los escándolos de Maximón: Un estudio sobre la religión y la visión del mundo en Santiago Atitlán. Seminario de Integración Social Guatemalteca,* Pub. 19. Guatemala: Tipografía Nacional.

Mondloch, James (1982). Sincretismo religioso maya-cristiano en la tradición oral de una comunidad quiché. *Mesoamérica 3*(3), 107–123.

Moore, Alexander (1973). *Life cycles in Atchalán: The diverse careers of certain Guatemalans.* New York: Teachers College Press.

Nash, June (1970). *In the eyes of the ancestors: Belief and behavior in a Mayan community.* New Haven, CT: Yale University Press.

Oakes, Maud (1951). *The two crosses of Todos Santos: Survivals of Mayan religious ritual.* Princeton, NJ: Princeton University Press.

Orellana, Sandra L. (1984). *The Tzutujil Mayas: Continuity and change, 1250–1630.* Norman: University of Oklahoma Press.

Oss, Adriaan C. van (1986). *Catholic colonialism: A parish history of Guatemala, 1524–1821.* Cambridge: Cambridge University Press.

Redfield, Robert (1941). *The folk culture of Yucatan.* Chicago: University of Chicago Press.

Redfield, Robert, & Villa Rojas, Alfonso (1934). *Chan Kom: A Maya village. Carnegie Institution of Washington, Pub. 448.* Washington, DC: Carnegie Institution.

Reina, Ruben E. (1966). *The law of the saints: A Pokomam pueblo and its community culture.* New York: Bobbs-Merrill.

Remesal, Fray Antonio de, O. P. (1966). Historia general de las Indias Occidentales, y particular de la gobernación de Chiapa y Guatemala, Pan 2. Biblioteca de Autores Españoles, Vol 189. P. Carmelo Saenz de Santa Maria, S. J. (Ed.). Madrid: Ediciones Atlas. (Original work published 1619)

Ricard, Robert (1966). *The spiritual conquest of Mexico: An essay on the apostolate and the evangelizing methods of the Mendicant orders in New Spain, 1523–1572.* (Leslie B. Simpson, Trans.). Berkeley: University of California Press.

Rojas Lima, Flavio (1983). El sincretismo cultural: Un enfoque sincrético. *Anales de la Academia de Geografía é Historia de Guatemala, 57,* 89–122.

Siegel, Morris (1941). Religion in western Guatemala: A product of acculturation. *American Anthropologist, 43*(1), 62–76.

Smith, Carol A. (1987). Culture and community: The language of class in Guatemala. In Mike Davis, Manning Marable, Fred Pfeil, and Michael Sprinker (Eds.), *The year left 2: An American socialist yearbook* (pp. 197–217). London: Verso.

Smith, Waldermar R. (1977). *The fiesta system and economic change.* New York: Columbia University Press.

Tarn, Nathaniel, & Prechtel, Martin (1981). *"Eating the fruit": Sexual metaphor and initiation in Santiago Atitlán.* Paper read at the XVII Mesa Redonda of the Sociedad Mexicana de Antropología, San Cristóbal de las Casas, Chiapas, Mexico.

Taussig, Michael (1980). *The devil and commodity fetishism in South America.* Chapel Hill: University of North Carolina Press.

Tedlock, Barbara (1982). *Time and the highland Maya.* Albuquerque: University of New Mexico Press.

Thompson, Donald E. (1954). Maya paganism and Christianity: A history of the fusion of two religions. In *Nativism and Syncretism.* Middle American Research Institute, Pub. 19 [1960]. pp. 1–35. New Orleans: Tulane University.

Valladares, León A. (1957). *El hombre y el maíz: Etnografía y etnopsicología de Colotenango.* Mexico: Editorial B. Costa-Amic.

Vogt, Evon Z. (1964). The genetic model and Maya cultural development. In Evon Z. Vogt & Alberto L. Ruz (Eds.). *Desarrollo cultural de los Mayas* (pp. 9–48). Mexico: Universidad Nacional Autónoma de México.

Vogt, Evon Z. (1969). *Zinacantan: A Maya community in the highlands of Chiapas.* Cambridge, MA: Belknap Press of the Harvard University Press.

Vogt, Evon Z. (1976). *Tortillas for the gods: A symbolic analysis of Zinacanteco rituals.* Cambridge, MA: Harvard University Press.

Vogt, Evon Z. (in press). On the application of the phylogenetic model to the Maya. In Raymond J. DeMallie & Alfonso Ortiz (Eds), *The social anthropology and ethnohistory of American tribes: Essays in honor of Fred Eggan.* Norman: University of Oklahoma Press.

Wagley, Charles (1941). *Economics of a Guatemalan village. Memoirs of the American Anthropological Association, No. 58.* Menasha, WI: American Anthropological Association.

Wagley, Charles (1949). *The social and religious life of a Guatemalan village. Memoirs of the American Anthropological Association, No. 71.* Menasha, WI: American Anthropological Association.

Warren, Kay B. (1978). *The symbolism of subordination: Indian identity in a Guatemalan town.* Austin: University of Texas Press.

Wasserstrom, Robert (1978). The exchange of saints in Zinacantan: The socioeconomic bases of religious change in southern Mexico. *Ethnology, 17*(2), 197–210.

Wasserstrom, Robert (1983). *Class and society in central Chiapas.* Berkeley: University of California Press.

Watanabe, John M. (1981). Los cambios económicos en Santiago Chimaltenango, Guatemala. *Mesoamérica, 2*(2), 20–41.

Watanabe, John M. (1983). In the world of the sun: A cognitive model of Mayan cosmology. *Man (NS) 18,* 710–728.

Watanabe, John M. (1984). *"We who are here": The cultural conventions of ethnic identity in a Guatemalan Indian village, 1937–1980.* Ph.D. dissertation. Department of Anthropology, Harvard University. Ann Arbor: University Microfilms.

Watanabe, John M. (1987). Maya religion. In M. Eliade (Ed.), *The encyclopedia of religion,* Vol. 9 (pp. 298–301). New York: Macmillan Publishing Co.

Watanabe, John M. (1989). Elusive essences: Souls and social identity in two highland Maya communities. In Victoria R. Bricker and Gary H. Gossen (Eds.), *Ethnographic encounters in southern mesoamerica: Essays in honor of Evon Zartman Vogt, Jr.* (pp. 263–274). Albany: Institute of Mesoamerican Studies, State University of New York at Albany.

Watanabe, John M. (in press). Enduring yet ineffable community in the western periphery of Guatemala. In Carol A. Smith (Ed.), *Guatemalan Indians and the state: 1530–1988.* Austin: University of Texas Press.

Wisdom, Charles (1940). *The Chorti Indians of Guatemala.* Chicago: University of Chicago Press.

Wisdom, Charles (1952). The supernatural world and curing. In Sol Tax (Ed.), *Heritage of conquest: The ethnology of Middle America* (pp. 119–134). Glencoe, IL: The Free Press.

Wolf, Eric (1957). *Sons of the shaking earth.* Chicago: University of Chicago Press.

Salāt *in Indonesia: The Social Meanings of an Islamic Ritual*

JOHN R. BOWEN

Among the world's major religious rituals, surely the Islamic ritual of worship, the *salāt*, has been one of the most intractable to anthropological analysis. Although it is central to the Muslim's religious repertoire, it is usually accorded only a brief mention in studies of Islamic communities.[1] Part of the difficulty may be, as Tapper and Tapper (1987) have argued, that anthropologists and Islamicists alike have neglected "ordinary" Islamic rituals as having more to do with a "Great Tradition" than with local social meanings. But in Islamic societies of Asia, Africa and the Middle East, discourse about *salāt* often takes on broad and deeply felt religious, social and political significance. The task facing anthropologists studying these societies is to account for the particular ways in which the *salāt* ritual takes on local social meanings. I develop one approach to understanding *salāt* significance through the analysis of disputes about the ritual in three Indonesian societies. I then suggest a general model for the study of the *salāt* and its implications for current theories of ritual meaning.

The *salāt* ritual is one of several activities included in the category of *'ibādat*,* the rites and practices through which one worships God. Narrowly interpreted, *'ibādat* is the domain of explicitly prescribed activities of worship, most notably the "five pillars," which are the confession of faith, the *salāt*, fasting in the month of Ramadhan, almsgiving and the pilgrimage to Mecca. Broadly interpreted, *'ibādat* encompasses all the activities of life, from

*The initial accent in the word *'ibādat* (also present in the terms *du'ā* and *jama'ah*), is represented in this article by an inverted comma.

specific rites to everyday dress to the conduct of science. In between the five pillars and "life as '*ibādat*" lies a wide range of Islamic activities from which Muslims in particular societies have constructed distinctive, local ritual repertoires that include rites of passage, sacrifice, recitations of the Qur'an and the commemorations of births and martyrdoms.[2]

Most Muslims would agree that, regardless of the degree of their own conformity, regular performance of the *salāt* is required of all Muslims.[3] The ritual begins with ablutions, after which the worshiper, either alone or in congregation, performs two, three or four ritual cycles (the number depending on the time of day) in the direction of Mecca. In each cycle the worshipper executes a fixed sequence of movements (standing, prostrating, kneeling, sitting), each accompanied by a fixed Arabic recitation. The recitations include praises of God affirmations of His oneness, a general request for divine guidance, and, at the beginning of each cycle, two or more verses from the Qur'an. They may also add private prayers (*du'a*) to their recitations. The *salāt* should be performed five times daily in normal circumstances, and the Friday noon worship, which includes a sermon, should be held in congregation (*jama'ah*). My analysis is limited to the social meanings attached to these obligatory *salāt* performances. Special *salāts* are held on the two major feast days of the year (after the fasting month and during the pilgrimage) after burial, and as a part of other rituals of supplication (see Wensinck 1953).

The structure of the *salāt* ritual is derived from traditions (*hadīth*) regarding the statements and actions of the Prophet Muhammad. Disputes over ritual procedure usually turn on differing interpretations of these prophetic traditions.[4] Some Islamicists (Graham 1983; Denny 1985:98) claim that the distinctive characteristic of Islam is precisely this concern for correctness in ritual practice (orthopraxy) based on conformity to the historical precedent of the Prophet. But local understandings of ritual are as much shaped by social and cultural context as by scriptural disputations. A properly anthropological approach to the *salāt* must study its links to other beliefs and practices in particular Islamic societies as well as its place in Islamic doctrine (Eickelman 1982). A more complete analysis than that offered here also would extend to the emotions and thoughts that accompany worship.

I have selected three cases from Indonesia to explore the social meanings of the *salāt*. In each case a dispute over ritual procedure was motivated by larger debates about the nature of community and society: in the provinces of Aceh, a debate about political unity; in highland Gayo society, a debate about the limits of proper ritual communication; in the capital, Jakarta, a debate about urban forms of sociability. All three cases were shaped in part by a broad movement of Islamic reform in which scholars have rethought the form and meaning of Islamic rituals. The modernist movement that emerged in Cairo in the late nineteenth century soon attracted advocates in Indonesia (Noer 1973). Different Indonesian reform-oriented associations developed particular critiques of traditional religious practices. Some, such as the self-styled "young group" (*kaum muda*) in West Sumatra, emphasized the appropriateness of modern schools and science for Muslims throughout Indonesia; others such as the Aceh reform movement POESA discussed below, placed regional unity in the forefront. These movements shared a call for a return to scriptural sources, the Qur'an and *hadīth*, as the major or even sole guide to ritual practice. Confrontations between reform-oriented Muslims and those Muslims who defend older procedures have lent a particular urgency to local discussions of the *salāt* in twentieth-century Indonesia.

Salāt *as Struggle among the Acehnese*

In the province of Aceh, on the northern tip of Sumatra, the *salāt* has shaped the language of religious dispute by supplying the idioms in which alternative socioreligious models have been evaluated. Provincial leaders have viewed the *salāt* as providing the image of the ideal society and of the impediments to its realization.

Aceh came under Dutch control only after a protracted struggle between 1873 and 1910, a struggle in which some traditional rulers allied themselves with the Dutch against forces led by Acehnese religious leaders *'ulamā*). In the face of dissension, collaboration, and the economic crisis of the 1930s, a group of scholars came together in 1939 to form the Union of 'Ulama throughout Aceh (POESA, *Persatoean Oelama Seloeroeth Atjeh*). POESA leaders began a campaign for social and religious reform in public meetings and in newspapers that circulated throughout Aceh. Members of the movement dominated the provincial leadership of Aceh in the Japanese period (1942–45), through the Social Revolution of the late 1940s, and on both rebel and loyalist sides in the Darul Islam rebellion of 1953–62.[5]

POESA leaders urged other Acehnese to unite and awake to the threat posed by the true enemies of Islam, which they identified not as external forces but as the passions and self-interest of individuals. They argued that the means to overcome these enemies were the duties of *'ibādat*, and particularly the *salāt*. By punctually carrying out these duties one would increase one's power of reason (*aql*) and the ability to control one's behavior (Siegel 1969:115–119). Only when individuals had first improved themselves would the perfect society be realized. It would rise from the joint submission of all its members to God in a mechanical solidarity of universal *salāt* performance.

If the *salāt* provided the means to realize that society, it also provided, in fleeting moments, its visible model. Individuals who came together for the congregational *salāt* best exemplified the "profound moral egalitarianism" (Kessler 1978:212) of the reformist vision.[6] Consider the address by the Aceh governor, Daud Beureuéh, to 6,000 worshipers after the *salāt* celebrating the day of pilgrimage in 1964 (Siegel 1969:263–266):

> *The entire community must, five times a day, face toward Mecca and, at the proper time, pray the daily prayers. So, too, for the whole Islamic community, we must come together. We are with God, we face toward Mecca. When we pray in assembly (*ber-jama'ah*), we are face to face with each other after the prayer. The poor confront the rich, the evil confront the learned, the weak confront the firm, and the humble confront the proud.*

POESA leaders highlighted just those features of the *salāt* that supported their political project: the this-worldly discipline it imposed on the individual and the egalitarian and universal character of the congregation. They played down other possible interpretations of the ritual, such as its power to place the worshiper in a direct relation with God. Given this particular construal of social meaning on the *salāt*, the reformists saw as politically threatening local particularisms in ritual performance. Such particularisms were not difficult to find, because, in the words of one POESA commentator, "the inhabitants of each region [of

Aceh] took pride in 'having their own '*ulamā*' " (Nyo Neunan, quoted in Morris 1983:86). As long as the "local '*ulamā* confined themselves to such minor matters as fixing the time for the fasting month, POESA could tolerate them. A few of them promoted alternative ritual repertoires, however, and had to be opposed. One leader singled out for particularly sharp criticism from the 1930s onwards was the Habib Seunagan on the west coast of the province.

The first Habib had established himself as a local religious figure in the Seunagan area in the 1860s. He was succeeded by his son's son, called the Young Habib, some time in the 1920s and then by the latter's son, Habib Quraish, in 1971.[7] The first Habib based his claim to spiritual authority on two kinds of transmission: genealogical descent from the Prophet Muhammad and the direct transmission of spiritual exercises from the founders of the Naqsyabandiyyah Sufi order (*tariqa*). He proclaimed himself the *kutub* (Arabic *qutb*, "axis, pole") for worshipers along the west coast, with a four-level hierarchy of religious authorities reaching down to the village prayer leaders.[8]

The Habib's followers engaged in a number of idiosyncratic ritual practices (and continued to do so in the 1980s), including chewing betel and "drinking water while submerged" during the fasting month (on the grounds that neither counted as a normal act of taking liquids), substituting chants for the special *salāt* prayers performed during the fasting month, and circumambulating the grave of the first Habib on the tenth day of the month of pilgrimage as a local substitute for the *tawaf*, the circumambulation of the Ka'ba in Mecca. The Habibs held that these practices brought the worshiper closer to God by increasing his or her inner knowledge and made the performance of outer ritual unnecessary.[9] Other practices emphasized the role of the Habibs as spiritual mediators between worshipers and God. The first Habib promulgated a distinct confession of faith that proclaimed "There is no God but Allah, this Habib is truly the body of the Prophet" (Snouck Hurgronje 1906:14). The second Habib substituted for the cry of *Allahu akbar* ("God is great") his own version, *Allahu ku akbar* ("God and myself are great") (Tengku Zakaria Yunus, interview 1981).

These ritual innovations diverted the religious attention of the Habib's followers from the *salāt* toward the Habib himself. They did so by emphasizing one of the features of the *salāt* that had been neglected by POESA, namely, the relation of the individual worshiper to God. This centered ritual orientation had political implications as well. It channeled authority towards the Habib rather than the provincial authorities and POESA. It also discouraged the regular practice of *salāt* and thus prevented the provincial unification through ritual unity hoped for by the POESA leaders. By 1939 POESA had begun to send speakers to Seunagan to denounce the Habib (Pauw 1981). The Habib was able to maintain control of the West Aceh religious hierarchy through the 1960s, however. He fought the POESA-led province-wide rebellion of the 1950s and opposed the Islamic political parties. The provincial Islamic leadership was never able to prohibit the organization but has issued decrees condemning its practices.

The focus of criticism by POESA and the Aceh Council of '*Ulamā* has been the social and political implication of these local ritual innovations, not their ritual property *per se.* Indeed, the first POESA leader in Seunagan (and a great-grandson of the first Habib) declared that temporarily relaxing fasting rules in order to encourage conversion to Islam had been appropriate. His criticism was of the Habib's neglect of regular *salāt* (Tengku Zakaria Yunus, interview 1981). Similarly, the Council of '*Ulamā* has objected less to the ritual innovations themselves than to their substitution for the *salāt*. Ali Hasymy (the head of the Council since 1981, a former PUSA leader, and former governor) approved of the efforts by Naqsyabandiyyah Sufi orders to seek inner strength through meditation and chanting, but criticized the social consequences of abandoning the regular performance of obligatory worship (interview 1981).

> *These movements [such as the Habibs'] think that man can approach God and become one with him, since man and God are the same in being. Now, once you have climbed to a level close to God, you do not have to perform* 'ibada *in an external way any more, but only in an inner way. This idea can lead to extreme deviations, such as the leaders marrying and having sex with the wives of their followers, on the grounds that the latter marriages are only external, but that their own relationships with these women are inner.*

At issue in the conflict between the Acehnese leadership and such local movements as that of the Habib Seunagan has been not doctrine or even orthopraxy, but the political importance of universal and uniform *salāt* performance throughout the province. This pattern of political discourse about Islam has continued with regard to new movements. The Council of 'Ulama banned an East Aceh movement in 1984 because the group taught that "the Friday *salāt* could be performed at home."[11] An outbreak of religious violence on the north coast in May 1987 was traced to a group in West Aceh that had been banned by the Council for teaching that *salāt*, fasting and the pilgrimage need not be performed by those who had attained the level of gnosis (*ma'rifat*). The moral bankruptcy of this movement was supposedly proven when some of its followers were unable to perform the *salāt* correctly.[12]

Salāt *as Communication among the Gayo*

In the next case ritual form itself became the object of dispute. While Acehnese religious leaders have considered the *salāt* as instilling proper attitudes in the individual and thereby leading towards a better society, most of the 200,000 Gayo in the central highlands have perceived it as an act of communication between worshipers and God. Its performance anchors—repeatedly, daily—a view of ritual as communication. This view underlies many other less frequently performed rituals. Gayo village ritual has profound moral importance in that it maintains links in a community consisting of living humans, ancestors, spirits, and God. Reformist Muslims, whose influence has been limited to the major town of Takèngën and environs, have challenged this idea of community and threatened the ritual basis of the village moral universe.

In the village-complex of Isak, where I lived for two years (1978–80), virtually all men and women performed the *salāt* from time to time, some quite regularly, others less so. Because Isak Gayo see the *salāt* as a set of communications from humans to God, they reason that it should be performed in an audible way, just as people must speak out loud when talking with one another. When a religious teacher explained the difference between his views and those of the town-based reformists, he criticized the practices of the latter on the grounds that they failed to fulfill the conditions for proper communication as set out by the Prophet Muhammad. When townspeople recited the obligatory texts of the *salāt,* he noted they said them quietly and quickly:

> *At the end of worship, when one ways "subhanallah" twelve times, they just run through the repetitions in their minds, going much faster than you could say them [out loud]. They really just say "semelah, semelah," they do not enunciate it correctly to themselves.*[13]

> *They are wrong, because the Prophet Muhammad said that the tongue and heart should work together, not the heart by itself. If I say something to you without making a sound, can you hear me? Of course not. You have to talk out loud for anyone to understand you.*

In the late 1920s Gayo began to study under reform-oriented teachers in Aceh, Minangkabau, or Java, and many became convinced that village religious practices represented deviations (or "illegitimate innovations," *bid'a*) from the example and teachings of the prophet Muhammad. Gayo reformists tended to live in or near the town of Takèngën, and their religious orientations were partially shaped by their association with traders and educators from elsewhere in Sumatra, many of whom also held reformist views. These views were similar to those of POESA, although the Gayo tried to maintain their distance from the lowland Acehnese leadership. In their critique of *salāt* practice they interpreted certain scriptural passages to the effect that the *salāt* worshiper should say neither the Qur'anic verses nor the initial *bismillah* out loud. Villagers generally have stuck to their view that they must pronounce clearly the words of the *salāt* if God is to hear them. The audibility of *salāt* recitation became an issue throughout Islamic Indonesia in the 1930s and 1940s. Advocates of each position wrote prayer manuals in which they marshalled *hadīth* to buttress their case.[14]

In the late 1930s these disagreements led to mass exoduses from some villages. In Isak a group of about thirty households (of about 200 total), swayed by the reformist argument but rebuffed by the rest of the community, decided to build their own mosque in which to perform the *salāt* in their own fashion. The village religious leadership complained to the Dutch authorities and their local Gayo representative, who (correctly) saw Islamic reformism as incipiently anti-colonial and prevented the construction of the mosque. The reformist families left Isak for uninhabited territory north of Takèngën where they established new villages. In the 1980s the reformist *salāt* was performed mainly in the town and in new districts, while a modified version of the older form was retained in older villages. The issue continued to lead to disputes whenever a new mosque was opened and a protocol had to be established.

Why would the issue of an audible *salāt* have led to these deeply felt and long-lasting local disputes? The answer lies in the importance of a theory of ritual communication to village ritual practice as a whole. The reformist attack on the village way of performing the *salāt* was perceived as an attack on that theory and a threat to the moral community of the living and the dead that it sustained. Reformists, for their part, considered a wide range of Gayo rituals to involve illegitimate communication between humans and spirits. Their attacks on audibility in the *salāt* were motivated by the implications villagers drew from it for other rituals. They accused villagers of improperly assuming that ritual speech was in some way like everyday speech, and of failing to follow strictly the Prophet's own exemplary conduct.

The area of disputed ritual thus came to include all activities in which communication was at issue. In the performance of funeral ritual the moral quality of the dispute becomes apparent. The Gayo see their community as including spirits of deceased men or women who interact in various ways with the living (Bowen 1984). The living begin reconstructing social relations with the spirit of a deceased person on the nights immediately following the death. Relatives and neighbors of the deceased gather to chant Qur'anic verses. These sessions, called *shamadiyah* (Arabic *shamad,* "eternal"), last until well after midnight, and food is served at intervals. Sometimes incense is burned. In the 1980s nearly everyone in Isak participated in *shamadiyah,* and participants agreed that verses were sent (somewhere) when they were chanted, that the number of reciters times the number of repetitions yielded the amount of merit (*pahla*) transmitted, and that the torment experienced by the spirit of the deceased was correspondingly lessened. Participation in these sessions was felt to be the moral responsibility of all neighbors and relatives towards the deceased because it had a direct practical effect on his/her well-being.

Villagers differed with respect to how they thought the chanting functioned, but these differences remained in the implicit (or whispered) background of ritual life; they were not aired in public. Some villagers, in private conversations, said that the spirit of the deceased directly experienced the merit of the chants and the taste of the food. The incense created a path along which the food and the chants travel, they claimed. Other villagers presented a sharply different interpretation of the same ritual. They considered a chanting session to be merely one of many occasions on which humans pleased God by reciting scripture. They pointed out that the most important verse for *shamadiyah* chants was Sura 112, al-Ikhlas (known as the "Kul hu" after the first two syllables) because it contained the name of God and emphasized His uniqueness. (It is also one of the verses most frequently recited in the *salāt* because it is one of the shortest.) Because God heard His name He was pleased and therefore well disposed towards the deceased, they said. Even some religious scholars who disapproved of many village rituals participated in *shamadiyah.* They viewed the chants as identical to any other occasion on which scripture was recited. The local government religious official, for example, participated but was particularly careful to distance himself from the food-and-incense interpretation of the ritual. "If food happens to be offered, we can eat it," he said, "but if not we cannot ask for it." If there is food without prayer, he added, he would not attend.

The *shamadiyah* thus constituted a shared practical framework within which individuals were able to retain the private certainty of their own, differing theological convictions. What united them was the belief that by doing whatever it is they did by chanting, they sent something somewhere with the effect of benefitting the deceased. Audible recitations, channels of the communication to the unseen world, and the welfare of the deceased were linked.

This link was denied by reformist teachers. They forced the issue by publicly denying (in sermons and in everyday discussions) that the dead could be part of a community. They quoted *hadīth* to the effect that the dead could neither hear nor receive presents of chants or food. In their view, to attend a *shamadiyah* session was to act as if the dead did have these powers, and thus to commit the offence of "illegitimate innovation" (*bid'a*). The dispute over mortuary ritual form made it necessary for high public officials to hold two kinds of rituals: one for the reformists and one for the traditionalists among their following (Bowen 1984).

Now we can better understand the full force of the argument about the *salāt*. Seemingly unimportant in themselves, the small details of *salāt* performance have been taken by Gayo on both sides of the debate to imply particular ideas about the nature of communication. The reformist critique of village *salāt* practice was aimed at a broad range of village rituals of which *shamadiyah* was only one (others included rituals of planting and healing). But their warrant for demanding reform of *salāt* necessarily was the failure of that practice to conform to the prophet's example, not its implications for other rituals. The same is true for "traditionalist" villagers such as the religious teacher quoted above: he based his argument that *salāt* must be pronounced audibly on a claim about the prophet's own position. Broad issues of the nature of the socioritual community were disputed in terms of faithfulness to the historical example set by the prophet.

Salāt *as Boundary-Maintaining in Jakarta*

Disputes about the *salāt* in the third case centered on the threat posed by a closed congregational community for pluralistic and urban forms of sociability. In Jakarta, the nation's capital, most people live in small tightly packed neighborhoods called "[urban] villages" (*kampung*). Each neighborhood is composed of people from many different ethnic groups, from different parts of the country and speaking different languages. One focus of community for the Islamic majority in Jakarta has been congregational *salāt* performance in the neighborhood mosque or prayer-house. Worship brings together all residents overriding other distinctions. Mosque youth groups (*remaja mesjid*) organize festival celebrations and may serve as an informal police force. In a few cases the mosques have been the points of assembly for antigovernment rallies. More often, they have been the place for relatively open discussions on current social and political issues. The mosque, and the congregational *salāt*, is able to serve as the center of community in mobile, polyethnic Jakarta precisely because it is open to all.[15]

In the 1970s some urbanites perceived the open character of the mosque to be threatened by a movement called Islam Jamā'ah[16] The name came to be applied to any and all exclusivist tendencies, especially as made manifest in a refusal to perform the *salāt* with others. The founder of the movement, Nurhasan Ubaidah (1908–1982), had spent several years in Mecca where he claimed to have been inspired to reformist ("Wahhabi") teachings. In the 1950s he opened a series of religious schools in different parts of Java. By the late 1970s he had created at least twenty schools in East Java alone. In Jakarta and other large cities Nurhasan created prayer groups, with the Jakarta membership estimated at 23,000 by 1976.[17] Although the Attorney General prohibited the organization in 1971 it continued to thrive through the 1970s until a flare-up of publicity in 1979 led to widespread public demands for its suppression. Nurhasan's death in 1982 spelled an end to the central organization, although the schools continued to function in the 1980s.

Islam Jama'ah spokesmen described the goals of the movement as reconstructing correct procedures for the *salāt* and other acts of worship by imitating the conduct of the Prophet.[18] Nurhasan forbade any books other than the Qur'an and *hadīth* from his schools lest his pupils be led astray, and directed that sermons be held only in Arabic. These practices were not themselves unusual; many traditional teachers have given sermons in Arabic in Indonesia despite the near-total lack of Arabic comprehension, and the mainstream reformist groups also advocated reliance on Scripture over subsequent works of interpretation. Islam Jamā'ah worshipers reportedly performed their *salāt* in a manner identical to that of other reformist groups (Thayib & Zuhdi 1979:33).

The feature of Islam Jamā'ah ritual that aroused alarm in Java was not the sequence of steps in their *salāt*, but their exclusion of nonmembers from congregational worship. They erected their own mosques in villages and cities and forbade their use by others. In at least one village they shaved their heads and did not wear the otherwise ubiquitous Indonesian black cap, distinguishing themselves in a way that bore directly on the techniques of the *salāt*, in which the forehead is supposed to touch the ground directly without the intervention of hair or headcovering.

The exclusion of outsiders from the *salāt* was based on two general features of the movement: a strict internal religious hierarchy and boundary-maintaining norms of personal purity. A spokesman for the movement declared in 1979 that there could be no proper *salāt* outside of a congregation (*jamā'ah*) and that a congregation was only legitimate if it was based on an oath of allegiance (*bal'at*) to a leader (*amir*).[19] The movement also taught that the *salāt* was only valid if the worshiper had successfully avoided physical contact with those not involved in the movement. A follower was forbidden to eat with outsiders. Clothing had to be rewashed for *salāt* use if it had been washed by an outsider. Sexual intercourse was seen as particularly polluting, and there were reports of divorces based on the refusal of one partner to join the group.[20]

All Muslims must observe purification rituals (*tahara*) for their other rituals, including the *salāt*, to be valid. "Purity is half the faith," said the Prophet (Tritton 1953), and the rules and conventions that distinguish the pure from the impure are important features of everyday Muslim life. But from the mainstream point of view purification rituals also make possible universal social intercourse among all Muslims. They guarantee—indeed sanctify—the purity of all persons who execute them. By creating a new, more restrictive code, Islam Jama'ah denied the possibility of such universal sociability, a denial others found morally offensive and socially dangerous.

Islam Jama'ah rules and behavior went beyond ritual purity to imply the permanently polluted status of all outsiders. Many felt the refusal to eat with others, or even to shake hands, as an attack on pan-Indonesian symbols of sociability. The exclusiveness of the group was viewed as symbolic of the most dangerous form of Islam: exclusive and un-Indonesian in spirit, rigid, and potentially subversive in doctrine, and potentially anti-Chinese and inflammatory in action, summed up in the phrase "Islam fanatic." By the late 1970s village and urban youth groups began to act against the group, pulling down the separate village mosques and sending "education teams" to argue interpretations of Scripture with the Islam

Jamā'ah leaders. As of late 1987 the government continued to receive demands from other Islamic organizations that it close down the Islam Jamā'ah schools.[21]

Because of the publicity surrounding Islam Jamā'ah their name began to be used for any individual or group who performed the *salāt* in a closed setting. It was applied to a number of highly visible and successful Jakarta "personalities" in the music and film industries who, perhaps moved by a renewed sense of Islamic piety, had built their own prayer houses where they invited teachers to lead worship and give educational speeches (*da'wa*). The mosque youth groups in the communities saw the prayer houses as signs of Islam Jamā'ah affiliation and took action against several of the artists. In September 1979 the youth group in the neighborhood of the popular actor and singer Benyamin S. boarded up the front of his house. They complained to the press that he had brought an Islamic teacher to lead prayer inside the house for seventy to ninety people rather than pray in the nearby mosque with everyone else, thus "going on his own" (*menyendin*) rather than "being with the people" (*bermasyarakat*). These two expressions are particularly culturally loaded in Indonesia; the latter is included in the state ideology of Pancasila. The following Friday, Benyamin showed up at one of the two community mosques for the congregational *salāt*. After participating in worship, he publicly gave the keys to his house and to the prayer-house behind it to "the people" (*masyarakat*) of the neighborhood. The context for the return was as significant as its content: prayer was returned to the public sphere. In an interview, however, Benyamin was indignant at the public criticisms:

> *I used to drink beer, having dancing parties at my house, no one said anything. Now, nothing's happened yet, people attack—you want I should just get drunk all the time? Just want to* da'wa *and people attack. I get anonymous letters; it gets scary!*[22]

Neighborhood mosque groups in Jakarta and other cities have interpreted Islamic boundary-creating conduct (in *salāt* or in, for example, dress style) not as emblems of allegiance to a universal Islam but as claims that one is better than "the people." Whether or not, as was alleged, the Jakarta artists were members of Islam Jamā'ah (and the question occupied Jakarta's investigative journalists for many months), separate *salāt* congregations were seen as indicative of an exclusivist social orientation. Benyamin and others suspected of being Islam Jamā'ah followers routinely parried journalists' queries by stating that they "performed *salāt* anywhere at all," thus claiming to be "of the people" by joining in open worship.[23] In this way the *salāt* has become a test of one's willingness to join the community to participate in new urban forms of sociability through worship.

Salāt *and Society in Indonesia*

In each of the three Indonesian cases a social group has emphasized certain features of the *salāt* in its efforts to define or maintain a particular social form. The disputes that ensued have implicated wider social, political and religious values, but they have been argued explicitly as competing interpretations of the role and form of the *salāt* itself.

The reformist leaders of Aceh held up the congregational *salat* as the perfect icon of a perfect society: religiously conscious individuals heightening their reason through acts of submission to God. These leaders highlighted two features of the *salāt* that provided a model and a means for realizing that society, namely, the egalitarian character of the congregation and the everyday discipline that worship imposed on the individual.[24] They found the negative image of these features in the religious hierarchy and ritual laxity of communities such as that in Seunagan. The larger issues at stake were the recovery of the province from decades of division, but the religious warrant for the criticism of local communities was their purported neglect of their religious obligations and, in particular, of the *salāt.*

For Gayo villagers, by contrast, communication between worshipers and God was a focus for the interpretation of *salāt.* Worship, so viewed, served as a legitimating model for communication with all manner of unseen, morally significant interlocutors, including spirits of the dead, "owners" of the farmland various prophets and God. Gayo reformists objected to such broad-based communication as tantamount to polytheism; their concern focused their objections to village *salāt* practice on its communicative aspect, the audible recitation. Both sides to the disputes over *salāt* justified their positions not in terms of the local sociocultural importance of communication, however, but in terms of the importance of following the prophet's example. Because debates about worship were perceived as Islamic matters (rather than specifically Gayo ones), they took place in a framework where the interpretation of scripture was of highest authority.

Members of the Islam Jamā'ah sect sought to create a religiously pure congregation within a pluralist society. They did so by carefully protecting their performance of the *salāt* from impurities. They limited physical contact with others, demanded strict obedience of the sect leader and prohibited the consultation of sources other than scripture. These actions all contributed to maintaining the group's boundaries. Here, as in the other two cases, those opposed to the sect were troubled by the social and religious implications of *salāt* performance. They objected publicly to the exclusiveness of Islam Jamā'ah worship as socially (and politically) damaging to the solidarity of "the people."

All three disputes were deeply intertwined with national politics. In the post-1965 New Order, Acehnese provincial leaders, Gayo reformists and the mosque groups in Jakarta have been strong supporters of the nationwide Islamic party. The Habib Seunagan and Islam Jamā'ah have equally strongly supported the state party, Golkar, for fear that a strongly Islamic government would seek to compel uniform ritual conduct.[25] Indonesian Islamic politics involves a wide array of issues, ranging from economic development to corruption to the control of educational policy, but, at least in some instances, disputes about the nature and form of the *salāt* have become foci for these broader disputes.

The power of the *salāt* as a central social model in Indonesia comes from its obligatory and, when performed in congregation, public character. It makes public particular ideas about the arrangement of men and women in social life: about hierarchy, social boundaries and the nature of communication. Other Islamic obligations have taken on similarly salient sociopolitical roles in particular parts of the archipelago: mortuary ritual in Japanese (Geertz 1959) and Gayo (Bowen 1984) societies; the alms (*zakāt*) in Malaysia (Scott 1987); sumptuary rules in nineteenth century Minangkabau (Dobbin 1983). But the *salāt* appears to serve as a generally prominent intersection of religious disputation and political discourse in Islamic Indonesian life.

Towards a General Model of the Salāt

Our discussion of the Indonesian cases returns us to the issue raised at the beginning of this article, namely, how can we understand the meaning of the *salāt* in the broader comparative studies of Islam and ritual? I suggest that discourse about *salāt* is one possible focus for the comparative study of Islamic societies. But the *salāt* is much more than discourse. Worshipers experience a wide array of thoughts and emotions when engaged in *salāt,* and they face choices and constraints in constructing each worship event. The depth and force of the worship experience contributes to the importance attached to debates about worship form.

Worship may have quite different effects on the individual's thoughts and feelings and no general description of this dimension of worship is likely to be valid. The range of worship experience is apparent even from written accounts of worship. For some Sufis, for example, the *salāt* provided a means of union with God; for others, it was an interruption of their concentrated rapture (Schimmel 1975:148–155). Some described a heightened awareness of submission and intimacy with God: "The prostration of the body is the proximity of the soul," wrote the poet Rumi (quoted in Schimmel 1975:153). Al-Farid wrote of the union with God during the event: "both of us are a single worshipper . . ." (Schimmel 1975:153). Prescriptive writings often emphasized the importance of humility before God. Al-Ghazzali made humility a felicity condition for the ritual: "If a man does not know humility, his *salāt* is invalid" (Wensinck 1953:499; see also von Grunebaum 1951:12). The term "*salāt*" literally means: "to bow," and the bows and prostrations (*sujud*) of the ritual may engender emotions of pious submission in many worshipers (Padwick 1961:6–11). The gestures of prostration and feelings of submission together construct a "religion of worship and dependence" (Gilsenan 1973:184) or *islām* (lit: "surrender, submission").

But other Muslims have emphasized the self-control and discipline that follows from regular performance of *salāt.* Many Acehnese saw the *salāt* as a source of strength for reason (*aql*) in its struggle to control passions. Regular worship thus became a sign of another's rationality and was one basis for trust and co-operation in business affairs (Siegel 1969:98–198). (Compare Weber 1958 on worship as a sign of trustworthiness in U.S. Protestantism.) Gayo men also attested to feelings of self-control derived from *salāt* performance, especially at times when they were engaged in spiritually dangerous pursuits, such as studying esoteric subjects or learning spells. They spoke of the activity of worship, physical as well as linguistic, as ordering their thoughts and keeping them from "becoming dizzy" in the face of new, powerful knowledge.[26] Other Gayo men and women said that they worshiped primarily because it was required of them, or because they feared the consequences on the Day of Judgement if they did not worship.

Areas of choice within the *salāt* framework allow for the ritual expression and reinforcement of particular emotional and cognitive orientations. The worshiper (or, in congregation, the worship leader, *imam*) may choose any Qur'anic verse for recitation in each ritual cycle (*rak'a*) after the obligatory verse, *al-Fatiha.* A worshiper may choose to recite one or more of the shorter verses, either because of limitations of time or knowledge, or because of its content. Some Gayo mentioned a preference for verse 112 (*al-Ikhlas*) because it affirmed God's oneness (see also Padwick 1961:108–119). For many worshipers, however (especially non–Arabic-speaking worshipers, including nearly all Indonesian Muslims), the semantic meaning of these verses may be of secondary ritual importance to their sacred quality as the words of God. The worshiper repeats back to God his own words. If the *salāt* is an "intimate conversation with God," as the Prophet is said to have characterized it (Wensinck 1953:498), then for many the subject of the conversation is the worshiper's humility and submission rendered in stereotypic terms. The worshiper may lengthen (and deepen) his experience by choosing a particularly long verse and drawing out its recitation silently or aloud, perhaps in an elaborate melodic pattern.

A worshiper also may add a prayer (*du'a*) near the end of worship, often drawn from the Qur'an or from a stock of "traditional" prayers (Padwick 1961:209–219). Some Gayo men and women consulted books in which the distinctive efficacies of particular prayers were explained: one prayer kept away torment after death; another kept away Satan during sleep. The worshiper may shape the ritual in other ways as well: performing the optional *qunut* prayer in the morning worship (or not), adding a midday prayer to the Friday congregational service, worshiping alone or in congregation at other times.

The individual structuring of worship in turn shapes and is shaped by public discourse about its proper form. Three modes of this discourse (among, surely, others) may be indicated here: the historical, the diacritic and the iconic. By "historical discourse" I mean discussion of the relative faithfulness of particular practices to the example set by the prophet Muhammad and elaborated in later commentaries. For centuries Muslim scholars have analyzed, justified and disputed the form of *salāt* by sifting through the numerous reports (*hadīth*) about the prophet's statements and actions. Their disputes have turned on the reliability of particular reports (or, more precisely, of the person transmitting it), not the beauty of a recitation or the symbolic quality of a gesture. If the Prophet recited a particular verse or stood in a particular way during worship then it should be replicated by his followers; if not, then it must not be performed. "Illegitimate innovation" (*bid'a*) is not tolerated in acts of *'ibādat*. This historical discourse has its more and less "learned" variants, as the Gayo example indicates. Villagers who were not schooled in *hadīths* nonetheless referred to the prophet's example as a way of justifying their positions on worship form.

The historical orientation of much Muslim discourse contributes to what Graham (1983:63) calls its "fundamentally *ritualist* orientation," by which he refers to an overriding concern with conformity to ritual norms in carrying out central ritual duties. In designing *salāts*, individual worshipers, prayer leaders and teachers justify their selection of gestures and recitations by reference to Muhammad's example. The personal sense of submission to God and to Muhammad reported by worshipers corresponds to this discourse of conformity.

The particular historicity of *salāt* discourse distinguishes it from that of other Islamic rituals, for example, the pilgrimage (*hajj*). The pilgrimage contains multiple instances of commemoration of past events. The pilgrim is directed to remember Hagar's search for water, Abraham's willingness to sacrifice his son, and Muhammad's first pilgrimage from Medina to Mecca as he/she carries out particular steps of the ritual sequence. These commemorative meanings are known to many Muslims throughout the world; they are also indicated in pilgrimage manuals and taught to prospective pilgrims before their journey.[27] Muslims not on the pilgrimage commemorate Abraham's obedience to God by sacrificing an animal on the tenth day of the pilgrimage month. Gayo spoke of this commemorative meaning. (Some also stated that the animal sacrificed would be available for transport to Jerusalem for the Day of Judgement.) By contrast, a worshiper does not commemorate Muhammad's first *salāt* when he worships; he performs it as Muhammad eventually came to prescribe it. This is not to say that some worshipers may not have Muhammad in mind when they worship (although I did not hear of such imaginings in Gayo or Acehnese discussions of *salāt*), but that discussion and teaching about the ritual celebrate it as conforming, not commemorating.

But conformity and "ritualism" alone do not explain the rich social significance that we found attached to the *salāt* in Indonesia. There and elsewhere Muslims construe the *salāt* to bear on contemporary society in at least two ways. In a *diacritic* bestowal of meaning Muslims take differences in the performance of the ritual as signs of social distinctions, without the ritual differences themselves taking on a semantic or representational value. Members of such categories or groups also may impute an *iconic* meaning to an aspect of worship, in which they take the form of the ritual to model or diagram features of society. These modes of discourse often are supported by demonstrations of their historical well-foundedness based on *hadīth* interpretation. Thus the historical and the social discourses often intertwine.

The most elemental diacritic reading of the *salāt* is one that identifies worshipers as Muslims over and against non-Muslims. As an obligatory, frequently performed, and sometimes public ritual, worship functions in many Islamic societies as a primary sign of Muslim identity. Ritual practice as the basic text of affiliation allows an expanding religion to be maximally inclusive; this aspect of Islam has been most extensively studied along its West African frontier. The Hausa, for example, query a newcomer's religious affiliation not with "Are you a Muslim?" but with "Do you pray?" (Trimingham 1968:62; see also Nadel 1954:235).[28] In the Volta basin a three-tiered category system developed of "learned" Muslims who were somewhat literate in Arabic, "those who pray [*salāt*]," and pagans, allowing chiefs to enter the second category and yet retain earlier beliefs and practices (Levtzion 1968:108–109). Within the category of Muslims, the greater or lesser frequency of *salāt* performance may be a badge of social identity *vis-à-vis* another Muslim group. In Java, for example, conscientious *salāt* performance was taken to distinguish "purer" Muslims (*santri*) from others (Geertz 1960:127). Relative degrees of attention to *salāt* may also be important elements in ethnic self-definition. Writing of tribally organized pastoral societies in Iran and Afghanistan, R. Tapper (1984) describes the way Pashtu-speaking Durranis claim that their attention to worship marks them off from all "Uzbeks" (non–Pashtu-speaking Sunnis). Basseri, by contrast, distinguish themselves from the settled, "mullah-dominated" Persians by referring to their own *neglect* of ritual observance.

Details of the *salāt* also can take on socially distinguishing meaning. In eastern Indonesia, for example, the daily frequency of worship divides the Sasak people into two categories: the "Five Timers" and those who are less observant, the "Three Timers" (Bousquet 1939). As such distinctions become the raw material for political struggles they may appear to turn on ritual details that are without intrinsic social meaning. In northern Nigeria in the late nineteenth and early twentieth centuries crossing the arms during the *salāt* (rather than letting them hang at the sides) became the major distinguishing mark for both a Sufi reform movement in Kano and the messianic (Mahdiyya) movement in neighboring Sokoto, causing "widespread confusion" among Nigerians and British (Paden 1973:200–201, 179). In Ibadan such distinctions in *salāt* became emblems of Hausa and Yoruba identity (Cohen 1969:152–156).

As well as serving as differentiating emblems, *salāt* details may be the focus for struggle within a social or cultural domain. In such cases the parties to a dispute may represent issues of local power and identity as if they were primarily, or even entirely, issues of conformity to the prophet's directives and example. *Hadīth* scholarship, which purports to transcend local imperatives, then takes on immediate local import. For example, along the border between Afghanistan and then British India a major dispute erupted in 1896 between the followers of two religious leaders (*mullahs*). At issue was whether the index finger should be raised during worship. The eminent mullah of Hadda had declared, based on his perusal of the relevant *hadīth*, that the finger should be raised at a certain point in the ritual. He was opposed by the mullah of Manki (who interpreted the traditions differently) but also by the Emir of Afghanistan, who, desirous of any means of undercutting the Hadda mullah's authority in the area, issued a prohibition against finger-raising. The eventual victory by the Hadda mullah increased his influence in the struggle against the British in the frontier region.[29] As these two examples suggest, it is on the frontiers of Islam that such diacritic meanings ("indexing" authority) are most prominent.

Differences in *salāt* procedure take on iconic as well as diacritic meaning when they are seen as diagrams or depictions of a wider set of social or ritual relations.[30] This diagrammatic relation becomes socially or politically important when it is taken to imply those wider relations as well as depict them (as a "model for" as well as a "model of"). The three Indonesian cases involved such a perceived implication, Aceh leaders view *salāt* as a template for the future society. Gayo villagers and reformists alike perceived audible recitations in worship as implying a general channel of communication between humans and spirits. Similarly, followers and opponents of Islam Jamā'ah saw its closed, hierarchical congregations as standing for a general image of hierarchical authority and social exclusiveness. These and other cases suggest that congregational worship is particularly likely to be taken as implying a specific form of society at large. When worshipers join in congregation, they must translate multiple, and normally separable, orderings by rank, age, gender and wealth into a single, public social arrangement (see also Cohen 1969:136–138). (Thus future research might focus on how gender and rank distinctions shape the *salāt* over space and time.)

As the above examples indicate, arguments about *salāt* involve combinations of historical, diacritic, and iconic models of discourse. A certain degree of rhetorical primacy is accorded to historical arguments, in that debates about the "design criteria" of the *salāt* center on issues of historical accuracy. Parties to the Gayo and Afghan debates, for example, although motivated by a variety of considerations and interests, presented their cases as "applied historiography": how to interpret the historical (*hadīth*) material.

Islamic Worship and Ritual Theory

The case of the *salāt* may help to indicate the limits of recent general formulations of the nature of ritual. Among the richest and most comprehensive of these studies have been the analyses by Bloch (1974:1986) and Tambiah (1968;1981) of ritual meaning. Bloch, Tambiah, and others (Barth 1987; Munn 1973) have expanded the scope and power of earlier symbolic (Turner 1967) and pragmatic (Malinowski 1965) approaches by incorporating the history, variation, and political role of rituals into accounts of their meaning. These studies provide a rich historical and symbolic framework for the comparative study of ritual. At the same time, they may have prematurely limited the domain of ritual meaning to a subset of existent ritual forms: those in which a stable symbolic or propositional core can be identified. Tambiah (1981:153), for example, refers to the "duplex existence" of ritual as:

> *. . . an entity that symbolically and/or iconically represents the cosmos and at the same time indexically legitimates and realizes social hierarchies.*

This approach is usefully (and, in the cases Tambiah studies, convincingly) pluralistic. But it is also dualistic: it separates two domains of ritual's "existence"—semantic and iconic, on the one hand, and pragmatic and political, on the other. In their case studies Tambiah and Bloch have given the semantic domain a communicative and historical primacy over the pragmatic. In his analysis of Trobriand magic (1968), Tambiah argues that the semantic content of the spells, their "inner frame," provides a "blueprint and a self-fulfilling prophecy" (1968:200) for practical activities, their "outer frame." The native semantic interpretation of the spells makes possible their pragmatic value. Similarly, he discovers in the Thai topknot-cutting ceremony (1981:155–160) a constant semantic and iconic core, the central feature of which is an image of the mountain abode of Shiva. On this core is constructed a variable indexical, political message when officiants indicate the rank of the individual by varying the size of the image.

In quite similar terms Bloch (1986:157–195) bases the politicoeconomic power of the Merina circumcision ritual on its stable symbolic or propositional core. He shows how the political uses of the Merina circumcision ritual changed over a two-hundred-year span while the "central symbolic structure" remained essentially the same (1986:157–165). Ritual's power lies in its ability to represent the world as unchanging and as beyond the creative powers of the individual actor (1986:189–191). One must not confuse Bloch's argument that ritual language, being "impoverished" (1974:60), should not be treated as an explanation to be decoded (1974:178–182) with his argument that participants do in fact decode the ritual as if it were a representation of reality. For Bloch, ritual can be an instrument of control precisely because it misrepresents reality to social actors (1974:77–79, 1986:189).

Tambiah and Bloch disagree over the political functions assumed by representation, but they converge strikingly on a model in which the ritual "says something" and on the basis of its propositions "does something." Both writers rely explicitly on a particular theory of language use, namely, Austin's (1962) studies of performatives (Tambiah 1981:127–128; Bloch 1974:67). The Austinian approach has been criticized for its construal of speech functions or pragmatics as dependent on, or secondary to, their transparent semantico-referential value (Siiverstein 1987).

The approach demands that one explain the apparent loss of semantic clarity in rituals. Bloch asserts that ritual words "drift out of meaning" (Bloch 1974:74). Tambiah (1981:165) suggests that rituals may undergo "ossification." Whereas initially participants in rituals are able to perceive the representation of cosmological ideas in rituals, over time this semantic transparency is lost as rituals undergo "meaning atrophy" (1981:163). Rituals increase in "tedium" (1981:161) as participants repeat modules of a ritual over and over with relatively little relation to immediate context and little appreciation of semantic content. Tambiah holds out hope for a reclarification of semantic meaning to participants: movements of religious revivalism, he argues (1981:165), attempt to render rituals semantically clear. Semantic and pragmatic meanings take on opposite ethical tinges. Semantic meaning is "the fragrant," "messianic hope," "religious revival and reform," whereas pragmatics is "the fetid," "indolent routine" and "the pragmatic interests of authority, privilege, and sheer conservatism" (Tambiah 1981:165–166).

Leaving aside the issue of the advisability of making an ethical case even implicitly, for one mode of meaning over others, I find the analyses by Tambiah and Bloch of their respective cases elegant and convincing. Other anthropologists as well have assumed that rituals possess an intrinsic, semantic core, even if that core has yet to be found.[31] Among Islamic rituals, some do possess a set of constant symbolic and iconic representations. The pilgrimage is one such case, for reasons mentioned earlier (its commemorative emphasis); the Shi'i *ta'ziya* (dramatization of the martyrdom of Hosain) is another. And, at least in Turkey, the Prophet's birthday recitations (*mevlud,* Arabic *mawlid*) also have a central symbolic component concerned with gender and salvation (Tapper & Tapper 1987).

As a general model of ritual, however, the formulations advanced by Tambiah and Bloch only reinforce the general tendency in Islamicist circles to favor rituals with a highly symbolic content. Dramas, sacrifices, and other commemorative rites smell more "fragrant" to the social anthropologist than does the apparent "tedium" of the *salāt* and other worship activities (a "tedium" that is, in fact, seen by many Muslims as the repeated obedience of God's commands). The prostrations and recitations in the *salāt* do not have the intrinsic symbolic richness of the Ndembu milk-tree, Trobriand spells or any circumcision rite. Movement of Islamic reform and revival often have attempted to purify the historical links between the prophet's *salāt* and current practice by opposing symbolic elaboration (thus an exception to Tambiah's [1981:165–166] general association of revivalism with semantic interpretation). Some anthropologists of Islamic societies thus have looked elsewhere for suitably rich domains to analyze. Barth (1961:135–153), for example, failing to find in Basseri ritual a symbolically adequate representation of society, complains of their "poverty of ritual," and Peters (1984:214) elevates ritual sacrifice, a type of ritual more familiar to the social anthropologist, to the status of "the core of Islam."[32]

The *salāt* is not structured around an intrinsic propositional or semantic core. It cannot be "decoded" semantically because it is not designed according to a single symbolic or iconic code. In particular times and places Muslims have construed the *salāt* as conveying iconic or semantic meanings, but as part of particular spiritual, social, and political discourses. The three Indonesian cases, and the brief perusal of examples elsewhere, suggest the wide variety of *salāt* meanings. These cases also suggest the importance of the historical discourse within the field of "speaking about *salāt*." The further comparative study of Muslim worship may broaden the general anthropological picture of the place of rituals in social life.

Notes

I pursued fieldwork in Gayo society in 1978–80 and in several short trips since that time and in West Aceh in 1981. Gayo fieldwork was funded by the Social Science Research Council and the Fulbright-Hays Program, and sponsored by the Universitas Syiah Kuala in Banda Aceh. An earlier version of this article was delivered to the Department of Anthropology, University College London; the Southeast Asia Studies seminar, University of Kent, Canterbury; and the American Ethnological Society meetings, St. Louis. I should like to thank participants at those sessions and Lois Beck, David Edwards, Dale Eickelman, Peter Heath, Bruce Kapferer, Nancy Tapper and the reviewers for *Man* for their comments.

1. Among the exceptions are Siegel (1969) on Aceh and Cohen (1969) on Nigeria. Both studies focus on the changing political significance of *salāt*. Brief references to *salat* are included in other monographs, e.g., Nadel (1954) for Nigeria, Geertz (1960) for Java. Fernea and Fernea (1972) discuss gender-based variation in overall

ritual participation in the Middle East, and R. Tapper (1984) analyzes the relation of ritual to social identity in three tribal societies.

2. Islamicist discussions of Islamic ritual emphasize the more orthoprax and universal traditions (Denny 1985; Graham 1983; von Grunebaum 1951) whereas anthropologists emphasize locally specific rituals that have a greater degree of symbolic content; see especially Tapper and Tapper's (1987) fine, detailed study of the Prophet's birthday ritual in Turkey. I find the tension between those two approaches to be indicative of the tension in Islam itself between local elaborations and transcultural Islamic traditions (see Roff 1987).

3. I use the Arabic term *salāt* throughout the article. The Persian and Turkish equivalents is *namaz*; the term *sembahyang*, "worship," is often used in Indonesia. All three terms connote submission through prostration before God. The following description of both Islamic attitudes and *salāt* performance attempts to capture the broad area of consensus among Muslims of different doctrinal orientations and cultural traditions. Differences within this area of consensus stem from, *inter alia*, the existence of four distinct schools of law (*madhhab*), Sunni/Shi'i contrasts, individual interpretations of ritual norms and sociocultural variation (e.g., in the roles of hierarchy, gender distinctions and self-styled orthopraxy in constituting local identity). Wensinck (1953) surveys the forms and history of *salāt*; further descriptions are to be found in Lane (1860) for Egypt and Juynboll (1930) for Indonesia. Beyond the orthoprax consensus are interpretations, particularly by Sufi thinkers, of *'ibādat* as merely external activities which may be discarded once a level of gnosis is reached.

4. Wensinck (1953) lists several such disputes and their corresponding *hadīth*; Robson (1963) is a translation of a standard compendium of prophetic traditions on worship. In Indonesia, as in other Islamic countries, the authors of worship manuals compile and translate *hadīth* that support their particular positions. The most frequently consulted manuals in the Acehnese and Gayo regions, where the bulk of my fieldwork has taken place, were those by Abbas (1976), who follows the Shafi'i law school, and Hassan (1979), who advocates the direct, "rational" interpretation of scripture.

5. Siegel (1969:98–133) places POESA in the context of socioeconomic change in Aceh; Morris (1983:75–93), in the context of the struggle by the province for regional autonomy.

6. Siegel (1969:108–115). For similar ideas elsewhere see Nakamura (1983:135–139), on Java, and Kessler (1978), for Malaya. See also remarks on the pilgrimage in Siegel (1969:260–275) and Kessler (1978:217–218).

7. *Quraish* indicates the family's claim to descent from the tribe of the prophet Muhammad. In Aceh the word *habib* also indicated a claim to descent from the Prophet. Information on the early history of the movement is found in Nota (1935); all other information and quotations, unless otherwise specified, were gathered with the assistance of two students from the Universitas Syiah Kuala during two short trips to Seunagan in August and November 1981.

8. Such hierarchies were found in Sufi orders throughout the Islamic world. For comparable cases see Schimmel (1975:199–200). On the Naqsyabandiyyah order see Margoliouth (1953).

9. Valuing inner (*bāthin*) experience over outer (*zāhir*) behavior is a basic Sufi teaching, although not all Sufis agree that outer ritual may be neglected. Indeed, Sufi practice has varied from exactingly frequent performance of *salāt* to its neglect in favor of other means of obtaining religious ecstasy (Schimmel 1975:148–155).

10. The *ku*, "me," is a Malay insertion into the Arabic phrase.

11. *Tempo*, May 30, 1987, p. 16.

12. *Tempo*, May 23, 1987, p. 13.

13. In Gayo, "semelah" means "one-half"; the reformist, rather than praising God, is rattling off irrelevant Gayo phrases.

14. Among the most important Indonesian writers on the topic, Abbas (1976:229–244) concludes that, because the Prophet is reported to have uttered the opening statement of intent to pray both audibly and inaudibly at different moments, the matter is up to the individual. Hassan (1979:91–95), arguing for the strict reformist position, claims that only the reports of silent intent-declarations by the Prophet are reliable and that, because we may only worship as did the Prophet, anyone who pronounces it out loud has committed *bid'a*, "illegitimate innovation," and will burn in hell. See also Robson (1963:165–168). Gayo also argued over whether a normal noon worship should follow the Friday service.

15. Virtually nothing has been written on Islam in Jakarta. Krausse (1978) provides a useful geographical overview of kampungs. I have based the above description on my own observations in a number of different Jakarta kampungs, including eight months' residence in one mosque-centered lower-middle-class neighborhood.

16. Jama'ah is used to refer to the broad consensus of Muslims (as in the phrase, *Ahli Sunnah wal Jamā'ah*, the

"people of custom and of the community") or to designate a congregation of worshipers.

17. *Tempo*, September 15, 1979, p. 48. In the absence of any study of the movement, information on Islam Jama'ah unfortunately is limited to press reports: *Tempo*, September 15, 1979, pp. 48–54 and April 10, 1982, pp. 61–62; Thayib & Zuhdi (1979).

18. Drs. Nurhasyim in *Tempo*, September 15, 1979, pp. 51–52.

19. Ibid. It was rumors of plans to establish a shadow government for Indonesia, with Nurhasan as the supreme *amir*, that led to the prohibition of the organization in 1971.

20. The Islam Jama'ah movement could be compared to the urban Sufi orders that are of major sociopolitical importance in other Islamic cities, e.g., Cairo (Gilsenan 1973) and Ibadan (Cohen 1969). Both types of movement enable people to create or maintain a sense of religious identity within a larger, heterogeneous population. I find it perplexing, and worthy of further study, that Sufi orders, although prevalent elsewhere in Indonesia, are relatively unimportant in Jakarta.

21. *Jawa Pos*, November 10, 1987.

22. *Tempo*, September 15, 1979, p. 54. Benyamin's reactions were echoed by other artists alleged to be members of Islam Jamā'ah. They contrasted their formerly dissipated lives in discos and bars with the moment when they "became aware" of Islam and began to pray and study enthusiastically.

23. *Tempo*, September 15, 1979, p. 53.

24. It is precisely on this point that Acehnese contrast their own behavior to that of the Gayo. They claim that Gayo allow their kin ties to interfere wit their business acumen, whereas Acehnese remain rational individualists thanks to their *salāt* and thus are better businessmen (Siegel 1969:249–250).

25. As a result, those villages in the Seunagan subdistrict that were controlled by the Habib Seunagan at the time of the 1977 national election voted 70 to 90 percent for Golkar, while those outside his control voted for the Islamic party with similar majorities (Seunagan Subdistrict Office vote tallies, 1977).

26. As the use of "men" indicates, even less study has been made of women's worship than of men's. For an exemplary analysis of a different Islamic ritual from a gender-sensitive perspective see Tapper & Tapper (1987).

27. Husain (1972) is a particularly rich example in English; in Indonesia Shiddieqy (1983) is widely used.

28. The use of ritual compliance as the main test of religious affiliation is, of course, hardly unique to Islam. Wilfred Cantwell Smith (1978:21) has made a similar argument regarding the Roman identification of *religio* with ritual.

29. David Edwards, personal communication (1989) based on letters in Peshawar District Archives. See also Churchill (1976:807*n*.1).

30. An additional ionic reading of *salāt* has been proposed by some Muslims, particularly Sufis, in which the physical positions assumed in the ritual stand for the letters of the name Adam and the entire ritual is seen as a momentary sacrifice of the worshiper to God (Schimmel 1975:148–155).

31. In highland New Guinea studies the difficulty of eliciting consistent semantic exegeses from local actors has led to a debate over the necessity of such exegesis (Gell 1975; Brunton 1980; Barth 1987) without challenging the assumption that such a comprehensive symbolic account of ritual could be obtained eventually (Wagner 1984). The *ur*-house where these accounts will be found serves as a sort of Holy Grail trope for partisans of the "cultural account" (Wagner 1984).

32. On the relative neglect of Islamic ritual in anthropology see Antoun (1976:163), Peters (1984:187), and Tapper and Tapper (1987:7).

References

Abbas, K. H. S. (1976). *40 masalah agama* [40 religious issues]. Jakarta: Pustaka Tarbiyah

Antoun, R. T. (1976). The social anthropologist and the study of Islam. In L. Binder (Ed.), *The study of the Middle East*. New York: John Wiley.

Austin, J. (1962). *How to do things with words*. London: Oxford University Press.

Barth, F. (1961). *Nomads of South Persia*. Boston: Little, Brown.

Barth, F. (1987). *Cosmologies in the making*. Cambridge: University Press.

Bloch, M. (1974). Symbols, song, dance and features of articulation. *Archives of European Sociology, 15*, 55–81.

Bloch, M. (1986). *From blessing to violence: History and ideology in the circumcision ritual of the Merina of Madagascar.* Cambridge: University Press.

Bousquet, G. H. (1939). Recherches sur les deux sectes musulmanes (Waktou Telous et Waktou Lima) de Lombok. *Reves Etude Islam, 13,* 149–177.

Bowen, J. R. (1984). Death and the history of Islam in highland Aceh. *Indonesia, 38,* 31–38.

Brunton, R. (1980). Misconstrued order in Melanesian religion. *Man (NS), 15m,* 112–128.

Churchill, R. S. (Ed.) (1976). *Winston S. Churchill: Companion Volume 1.* Part 2, 1896–1900. Boston: Houghton Mifflin.

Cohen, A. (1969). *Custom and politics in urban Africa.* Berkeley: University of California Press.

Denny, F. M. (1985). *An introduction to Islam.* New York: Macmillan.

Dobbin, C. (1983). *Islamic revivalism in a changing peasant economy: Central Sumatra, 1784–1847.* London: Curzon Press.

Eickelman, D. F. (1982). The study of Islam in local contexts. *Contributions to Asian Studies, 17,* 1–16.

Fernea, R. A., & Fernea, E. W. (1972). Variation in religious observance among Islamic women. In N. R. Keddie (Ed.), *Scholars, saints, and sufis.* Berkeley: University of California Press.

Geertz, C. (1959). Religion and social change: A Javanese example. *American Anthropologist, 61,* 991–1012.

Geertz, C. (1960). *The religion of Java.* Chicago: University Press.

Gell, A. (1975). *Metamorphosis of the cassowaries.* London: Athlone Press.

Gilsenan, M. (1973). *Saint and sufi in modern Egypt.* Oxford: Clarendon Press.

Graham, W. A. (1983). Islam in the mirror of ritual. In R. G. Hovannisian & S. Vryonis, Jr. (Eds.), *Islam's understanding of itself.* Malibu, CA: Undena.

Hassan, A. (1979). *Pengajaran shalat* [Salat Manual] (2nd ed). Bandung: Diponegoro.

Husain, S. A. (1972). *A guide to hajj.* Lahore: SH. Muhammad Ashraf.

Juynboll, Dr. Th. W. (1930). *Handleiding tot de kennis van de Mohammedaansche wet.* Leiden: E. J. Brill.

Kessler, C. S. (1978). *Islam and politics in a Malay state: Kelantan 1838–1969.* Ithaca, NY: Cornell University Press.

Krausse, G. H. (1978). Intra-urban variation in kampung settlements of Jakarta: A structural analysis. *Journal of Tropical Geography, 466,* 11–26.

Lane, E. W. (1860). *An account of the manners and customs of modern Egyptians* (2nd ed.). London: John Murray.

Levtzion, N. (1968). *Muslims and chiefs in West Africa.* Oxford: Clarendon Press.

Malinowski, B. (1965). *Coral gardens and their magic,* 2 vols. Bloomington: Indiana University Press.

Margoliouth, D. S. (1953). Nakshband. *Shorter Encyclopedia of Islam.* Ithaca, NY: Cornell University Press. Morris, E. (1983). *Islam and politics in Aceh.* Thesis, Cornell University.

Munn, N. D. (1973). Symbolism in a ritual context: Aspects of symbolic action. In J. J. Honigmann (Ed.), *Handbook of social and cultural anthropology.* New York: Academic Press.

Nadel, S. F. (1954). *Nupe religion.* Glencoe, IL: Free Press.

Nakamura, M. (1983). *The crescent arises over the banyan tree.* Jogjakarta: Gajah Mada University Press.

Noer, D. (1973). *The modernist Muslim movement in Indonesia, 1900–1942.* Kuala Lumpur: Oxford University Press.

Nota (1935). Nota van toelichting betreffende het landschap Seunagan, 25 July 1935.

Paden, J. N. (1973). *Religion and political culture in Kano.* Berkeley: University of California Press.

Padwick, C. E. (1961). *Muslim devotions: A study of prayer-manuals in common use.* London: S.P.C.K.

Pauw, J. (1981). Mailrapport no. 193/40, 1939. In *Laporan Politik.* Banda Aceh: PDIA.

Peters, E. (1984). The paucity of ritual among Middle Eastern pastoralists. In A. S. Ahmed & D. M. Hart (Eds.), *Islam in tribal societies.* London: Routledge and Kegan Paul.

Robson, J. (Ed.) (1963). *Mishkat-al-masabih* by Wali ad-Din Muhammad al-Khatib at-Tibrizi. Vol. 1. 1st Arabic ed. 1335–36. Lahore: SH. Muhammad Ashraf.

Roff, W. R. (1987). Islamic movements: One or many? W. R. Roff (Ed.), *Islam and the political economy of meaning.* Berkeley: University of California Press.

Schimmel, A. (1975). *Mystical dimensions of Islam.* Chapel Hill: University of North Carolina Press.

Scott, J. C. (1987). Resistance without protest and without organization: Peasant opposition to the Islamic *zakat* and the Christian tithe. *Comparative Studies in Social History, 29,* 417–452.

Shiddieqy, T. M. H.A. (1983). *Pedoman hajji* [Guide to the Pilgrimage]. Jakarta: Bulan Bintang.

Siegel, J. T. (1969). *The rope of God.* Berkeley: University of California Press.

Silverstein, M. (1987). The three faces of "function": Preliminaries to a psychology of language. In M. Hickman (Ed.), *Social and functional approaches to language and thought.* New York: Academic Press.

Smith, W. C. (1978). *The meaning and end of religion.* New York: Harper & Row.

Snouck Hurgronje, C. (1906). *The Achehnese* (vol. 1). Leiden: E. J. Brill.

Tambiah, S. J. (1968). The magical power of words. *Man (NS), 3,* 175–208.

Tambiah, S. J. (1981). A performative approach to ritual. *Proceedings of the Britain Academy, 1979, 65,* 113–169.

Tapper, N., & Tapper, R. (1987). The birth of the prophet: Ritual and gender in Turkish Islam. *Man (NS), 22,* 69–92.

Tapper, R. (1984). Holier than thou: Islam in three tribal societies. In A. S. Ahmed & D. M. Hart (Eds.), *Islam in tribal societies.* London: Routledge & Kegan Paul.

Thayib, A. T., & Zuhdi, M. N. (1979). *Musim heboh Islam Jama'ah* [Period of fame for Islam Jama'ah]. Surabaya: P. T. Bina Ilmu.

Trimingham, J. S. (1968). *The influence of Islam upon Africa.* New York: Praeger.

Tritton, A. S. (1953). Tahara. *Shorter Encyclopedia of Islam.* Ithaca, NY: Cornell University Press.

Turner, V. (1967). Symbols in Ndembu ritual. In *The forest of symbols.* Ithaca, NY: Cornell University Press.

von Grunebaum, G. E. (1951). *Muhammadan festivals.* London: Curzon Press.

Wagner, R. (1984). Ritual as communication: Order, meaning and secrecy in Melanesian initiation rites. *Annual Review of Anthropology, 13,* 143–155.

Weber, M. (1958). The Protestant sects and the spirit of capitalism. In H. H. Gerth & C. W. Mills (Eds.), *From Max Weber: Essays in Sociology.* New York: Oxford University Press.

Wensinck, A. J. (1953). *Salāt Shorter Encyclopedia of Islam.* Ithaca, NY: Cornell University Press.

Communitas Reconsidered: The Sociology of Andean Pilgrimage

M. J. SALLNOW

Victor Turner's model of pilgrimage has proved widely influential in the recent upsurge of interest in the phenomenon among social anthropologists. As Werbner (1977:ix) has noted, ritual activities which confound political or ethnic boundaries are inherently problematic for a discipline whose strength has always been the intensive study of the little community. Furthermore, the conventional mode of ritual analysis still turns largely on the identification of those aspects of the social structure to which it corresponds and which it legitimates. Given this perspective, pilgrimage, and the regional cults of which it is the devotional expression, at best tend to be depicted as residual phenomena and at worst are ignored altogether.

Turner's model, propounded in a series of publications (1969; 1974; Turner & Turner 1978), seems to offer a solution. His point of departure is the analytical dichotomy between *structure*, the organization of society in terms of roles and statuses, and *communitas*, the ". . . direct, immediate, and total confrontation of human identities" (1969:131), along with which "... there tends to go a model of society as a homogeneous, unstructured communitas, whose boundaries are ideally coterminous with those of the human species" (1969:131). Structure and communitas stand in a dialectical relation to each other. The purest form of communitas Turner labels "existential," but in order to persist this must itself develop a structure to mobilize and organize people and resources. Thus there emerges what he calls "normative" communitas—existential communitas ". . . organized into a perduring social system" (1969:132).

Pilgrimage, according to Turner, is a form of normative communitas. It represents . . .

> *the ordered anti-structure of patrimonial feudal systems (1974:182). Though pilgrimages strain in the direction of universal communitas, they are still ultimately bound by the structure of the religious systems within which they are generated and persist (1974:205–206). Nevertheless, it may be said that, while the pilgrimage situation does not eliminate structural divisions, it attenuates them, removes their sting (1974:207). The social mode appropriate to all pilgrimages represents a mutually energizing compromise between structure and communitas; in theological language, a forgiveness of sins, where differences are accepted or tolerated rather than aggravated into grounds of aggressive opposition (1974:208).*

I assess the usefulness of this model for understanding pilgrimage in the central Andes, an especially pertinent exercise in that the Andean material bears a number of similarities to the Mexican data on which Turner bases his ideas. My debt to Turner's seminal writings on pilgrimage will be readily apparent. I shall argue, however, that ultimately the concept of communitas is dispensable for an understanding of the phenomenon, and that in fact it tends to inhibit an appreciation of the contradictions and emergent processes in Andean regional devotions.

The setting is the Cuzco area of southern Peru, where research was carried out in 1973–4. The region is heterogeneous ecologically, economically, and ethnically. Ecologically, it may be broadly characterized in terms of four zones: the *puna* or high pasture zone, above 4,000 meters; the upper *keshwa* tuber zone, between 3,500 and 4,000 meters; the lower *keshwa* cereal zone, between 2,500 and 3,500 meters; and the *montaña,* below 2,500 meters, where a variety of subtropical crops are cultivated. The region displays a mixed agricultural and pastoral economy, with forms of production ranging from relatively highly capitalized, market-oriented estates to small peasant farms producing primarily for subsistence. Ethnic diversity is cast in terms of the opposition between Indian and *mestizo,* the former connoting Quechua monolingualism and "traditional" cultural *mores,* the latter a knowledge of Spanish and a "Western" cultural orientation. Religion is nominally Roman Catholic though heavily syncretized with pre-Columbian elements in rural areas. A number of shrines in the Cuzco region regularly constitute the foci for penitential pilgrimage, and I shall characterize these in general terms below. The subject of this article, however, is not the regional shrine system as such but the sociodynamics of pilgrimage. For this my data derive mainly from observations among the people of Ccamahuara, an upland community of peasant cultivators and pastoralists which at the time of fieldwork numbered some 500 souls.

The farmsteads of Ccamahuara, together with those of its neighboring communities of Occoruro and Siusa, are scattered across a gentle declivity in the upper *keshwa* and *puna* zones at an altitude of about 4,000 meters. There are no services of any kind. Access to the area is by footpath from the village of San Salvador, 8 kilometers distant and 1,000 meters below in the lower *keshwa* zone of the Vilcanota valley, the principal transport artery and agricultural belt of the Cuzco region. San Salvador serves as the capital of an administrative district which embraces several other hinterland communities and hamlets besides Ccamahuara and its neighbors. Quechua is spoken throughout the district, but Spanish is spoken by many people in the district capital, and by returned urban migrants and some army veterans in the communities. Ethnically, the hinterland communities are regarded as Indian, as opposed to the *mestizo* village of San Salvador.

Organizationally Ccamahuara resembles thousands of other so-called indigenous communities in the Peruvian highlands, as an aggregate of peasant families with a tradition of joint tenure of a territory, sanctioned by law in Ccamahuara's case since its official registration in 1966. Within this territory, community members enjoy heritable rights of cultivation, though the community retains reversionary rights to all plots and forbids their sale to outsiders. Grazing rights to both permanent pastures and to arable land lying fallow are held in common. In order to retain these rights to cultivation and pasturage a man has to fulfill certain formal and informal obligations of community membership, including participation in the prestige economy by sponsoring fiestas and occupying posts in the traditional civil hierarchy of political officials (the *varayoqkuna*) headed by the *alcalde* (mayor). In the past these officials had represented the community before the district authorities in San Salvador, but since legal registration they have been largely displaced by community representatives elected according to government statute.

Kinship terminology is of the Eskimo type. In theory both sons and daughters are entitled to inherit, but in practice sons are treated preferentially. Each farmstead consists of a nuclear, extended or stem family, with the farmsteads of a man and his sons showing a marked residential clustering. Close patrilateral kin rely heavily upon one another for mutual assistance, though the sphere of mutualism is frequently expanded to embrace other kin and neighbors as well. Beyond this sphere, cooperation assumes a transactional character, being represented either as "exchange labor" or "festive labor." A common pattern is for a set of kin and kin-of-kin who enjoy close, mutualistic relations to constitute the nucleus of a larger, socially more ramified team of contractual cooperators, which ploughs or weeds the fields of each team member in turn. Of relevance here is the fact that extensive forms of contractual collaboration of this kind are often gratuitous from a technoenvironmental viewpoint; rather, they utilize the pretext of cooperation for initiating and maintaining wider sets of social relations (cf. Bloch 1973).

In ecclesiastical terms, the district of San Salvador constitutes a parish, the larger dependent communities subordinate chapelries.[1] Each of these community chapelries has its own patron saint whose annual fiesta is celebrated by the members of that community. The parish as a whole also has its patron saint, for whose fiesta the patronal icons of the dependent chapelries converge on the parish church in San Salvador. The symbolism of this and other parish rituals establishes a pyramidal hierarchy of local patron saints, with the parish patron at the apex. Although there are no civil-religious *cargo* systems as in some Mesoamerican communities (see Carrasco 1961), community leaders in Ccamahuara—the *alcalde* and, latterly, the elected president—play an important part in the organization and execution of these local rituals. Each patronal image is regarded as the abode of a spirit whose tutelage is restricted to its community alone. As in all Catholic cultures, patron saints are generally drawn from the standard liturgical inventory of saints and divine guises of the Church[2]; patronal devotions are thus a means of syntagmatic differentiation between the communities of a locality (cf. Redfield & Villas Rojas 1934:108; Gudeman 1976:724). The patron of Ccamahuara is the Virgin of the Purification honored on February 2, while the fiesta of the eponymous patron of the parish, San Salvador or Christ Savior, is celebrated on August 6, the feast of the Transfiguration. The parish of San Salvador, with the diverse patronal devotions of its constituent chapelries and that of the parish as a whole, may thus be seen as a pyramidally structured microcosm of the universal Church, the communion of saints writ small.

Morphology of Regional Shrines

Pilgrimage centers in the Cuzco area are of a different order from the stereotypical patronal shrines of community and parish. Their catchments are regional rather than local, cross-cutting ecclesiastical and political boundaries. Iconologically, while all such regional shrines are either Christological or Marian guises, they draw their primary identities from particular local, mythological, or topographical associations, the name of a shrine's geographical site often featuring in its title. Thus, while many of these shrines are images of Christ crucified, they are generally known by the names of their locations.[3] Only a small selection of the regional shrines in the area feature in the pilgrimage itinerary and mythological complex of any given community or neighborhood. The locations of those pertinent to Ccamahuara are shown in Figure 9.1.

Each regional shrine is thought to be the locus of a separate spirit, known in the case of Christological shrines as a *taytacha* (little father). A key characteristic of regional shrines is their stressed miraculous quality. The term "miraculous" (*milagroso*) conveys two related meanings. In the first place it refers to the mystical theophany itself, that is to the sudden appearance or chance discovery of the shrine image and to the prodigious incidents which accompanied the event. Some myths specify precisely the date of this first divine manifesta-

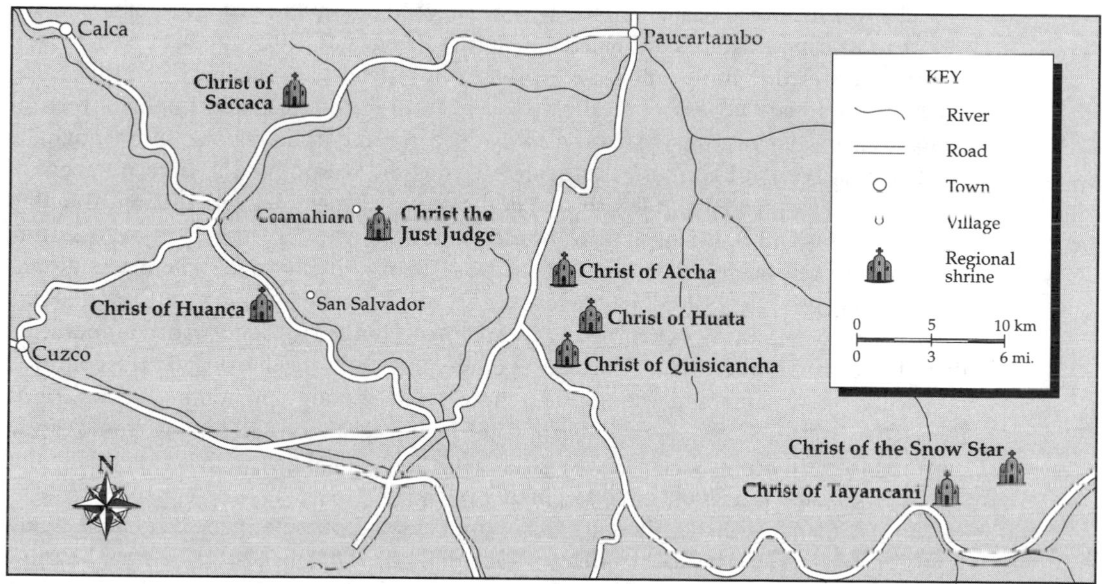

FIGURE 9.1 Regional shrines pertinent to Ccamahuara.

tion. Many of the shrines, and indeed the practice of Christian pilgrimage in general, date from the second half of the Spanish colonial period (Kubler 1946:361). However, in many instances there are obvious continuities with pre-Hispanic cults of the *wakas,* localized sources of sacredness. This was evident, for instance, in the case of the shrine known as Christ of the Snow Star (Señor de Ccoyllur Rit'i), situated at an altitude of 4,800 meters just below the permanent snows, which is explicitly linked by devotees to the mountain spirit (*apu*) of the nearby peak of Ausangate, for centuries revered as a powerful deity throughout this part of the Andes. Morote Best links the first miraculous appearances of Christian personages with the colonial religious movements which spread among the conquered Indians proclaiming the resurrection of the *wakas* (Morote Best 1953:103). But the divine impulse has continued to be felt since, and some shrines date from apparitions within living memory.

One continuity which many present-day regional shrines display with their pre-Hispanic counterparts lies in a close association with rocks. The hallowing of unusually shaped rocks and the petrification of mythical personages are pervasive themes in Andean religion and mythology, and have been comfortably assimilated to the Catholic cult. Certain shrines are stone statues, while others such as Christ of the Snow Star, are images of Christ painted on to large crags jutting from the mountainside, and are reputed to be mere painted overlays to the original divine manifestations. Often, chapels or sanctuaries have been built around the sacred rocks, sometimes faced with glass to protect them from the depredations of their worshipers. One shrine, that of Christ of Huanca, a mural of Christ undergoing scourging painted on a crag (*huanca* = rock or crag), is particularly interesting since it offers an example of the inverse of miraculous theophany—miraculous disappearance. The image of Christ and his torturers is said to be mysteriously fading, and when it disappears completely the Day of Judgement will have arrived (Barrionuevo 1909:211–212).

The word "miraculous" also refers to the supposed thaumaturgic powers of a religious image, to its capacity to bestow material or spiritual favors on its devotees, or alternatively to bring misfortune down upon the heads of those who have incurred its displeasure. Whereas the innate powers of local patronal icons are unstressed and implicit, those of regional shrines are overtly stressed and proclaimed. An important regional shrine might be described as "very miraculous," this being given as the reason for the large numbers of pilgrims who frequented it. A few shrines in the central Andes are international, attracting both Peruvians and Bolivians in their thousands, and sometimes pilgrims from Argentina and Chile as well. Such is the shrine of Christ of Huanca, situated a few kilometers distant from the village of San Salvador. Others, like that of Christ the Just Judge in Ccamahuara's neighboring community of Occoruro, have catchments limited to a handful of communities, though the staffs of these minor sanctuaries often nurse the hope that one day their shrines, too, will achieve fame and widespread renown. The waxing and waning of a shrine's popularity over time are read as indications of its increasing or declining powers. A local patronal shrine is not subject to such vagaries of fortune: its congregation is territorially and socially fixed, and its cult observed as a matter of course.[4]

In accordance with the criterion of active miraculous power, the people of Ccamahuara rank five shrines in a fraternal hierarchy as follows. 1. Christ of Huanca; 2. Christ of the Snow Star; 3. Christ of Tayancani; 4. Christ of Accha; 5. Christ the Just Judge. It is said that this group of five *taytachas* journeyed from place to place, each brother taking up residence at the spot where his shrine is located. Three shrines regularly visited by people from the community, those at Quisicancha, Huata, and Saccaca, do not figure in this hierarchy and are regarded as less important than the ranked shrines.[5]

Although the cosmologies of regional shrines are in principle universalistic, there is nevertheless a tendency towards the specialization of devotions according to socioeconomic criteria. Certain shrines are patronized chiefly by pilgrims from urban areas and by commercial farmers, smallholders, and artisans from rural areas, while others have clienteles consisting in the main of subsistence peasants and hacienda tenants. The distinction is perceived in ethnic terms, as one between *mestizo* and Indian devotions.[6] There is an ecological dimension to this devotional specialization, since broadly speaking the zonal location of a shrine reflects the provenance and livelihoods of its devotees. Those shrines patronized mainly by subsistence peasants and herders are situated in the mountains, in the upper *keshwa* or *puna* zones, while those frequented by people from the valleys and towns tend themselves to be located in the intermontane valleys, in the more temperate lower *keshwa* zone.[7] However, as one might expect in an area where environmental variation is so involute and where ethnic status is a matter of subtle relativities, the congregations of most regional shrines are amorphous. It is important to stress, therefore, that we are here speaking of a tendency only towards regional shrine specialization according to ecological, ethnic and class criteria.

Shrines also vary as to the organization of their staffs. The more important ones are each under the management of a religious community or lay brotherhood which organizes the annual fiesta and is expected to spend pilgrims' cash donations on chapel repairs, fees to clergy, and the provision of basic amenities. The sanctuary of Christ of Huanca, for example, is administered by a resident community of Mercedarian priests, while Christ of the Snow Star is run by a lay brotherhood. Though most of the devotees of this latter shrine are Indian, the brotherhood is a mainly *mestizo* organization, whose fund-raising activities are regularly reported in the society columns of the Cuzco press. At the other extreme, some of the minor shrines are effectively managed by one or two people. That of Christ of Huata, for example, which also has a predominantly Indian clientele, is administered by a local peasant who claims to have witnessed the original apparition forty years ago. It is noteworthy that even in such cases, where there appear to be no obvious grounds for an ethnic divide between shrine staff and devotees, the relation between them is nevertheless construed as one between *mestizos* and Indians. The shrine official at Huata dealt with pilgrims in a high-handed, imperious manner, insisted on speaking in Spanish to the mainly Quechua monolingual congregation, and was treated in turn much as an ethnic superior might be treated. Hierarchy between staff and pilgrims, then, expressed in the idiom of ethnicity, is at the heart of the regional devotions, complementing the ideology of equality which, as we shall see presently, manifests itself in a variety of ways—not all of them consistent with the notion of communitas—between the pilgrims themselves.

The principal fiesta of a regional shrine is the annual commemoration of the original apparition or divine manifestation. It generally consists of religious services and processions on the day of the fiesta itself and sometimes also during its novena and octave.[8] Fiestas are scattered throughout the year. Some are synchronized with appropriate universal feasts; thus, that of Christ of the Snow Star is celebrated during the novena of the movable feast of Corpus Christi, while both Christ of Huanca and Christ the Just Judge have their principal fiestas on September 14, the feast of the Exaltation of the Cross. Other regional fiestas bear no obvious relation to the Roman liturgical calendar, but fall randomly on various days. In these cases the shrine is sometimes referred to by the name of the saint on whose feast day the fiesta is held, but the saint's day serves solely as a temporal marker, and no cult attaches to the actual saint. Those shrines in Ccamahuara's ambit whose titular fiestas seem to be inserted arbitrarily into the calendar in this way are all unranked shrines according to traditional theogony, and do not figure in the fraternal hierarchy of *taytachas.* Those that do share the common characteristic of having some liturgical rationale for the timing of their fiestas.

Several regional fiestas occur during the dry-season months of June, July and August between harvesting and planting, when not only is agricultural activity at a minimum but travel is easier than in the rainy season. But apart from this loose, negative correlation—and there are many exceptions—there is no evident coordination between the timing of regional fiestas on the one hand and seasonal or production cycles on the other; the latter are so locally varied, close coordination is in any case precluded. Likewise their timing is independent of the various cycles of patronal fiestas of the communities and parishes which the regional devotions overarch. There is, however, a partial convergence between the regional fiesta cycle and the regional marketing system. During the fiesta of Christ of Huanca in September, for example, the nearby village of San Salvador plays host to a large regional fair. A similar fair is held in Urcos in February during the fiesta at the nearby pilgrimage center of the Virgin of Canincunca (Marzal 1971:114). Regional shrines associated with regional commerce in this way are patronized mainly by *mestizos,* and are situated in the lower *keshwa* zone close to the main transport routes.

The Organization of Pilgrimage

I turn now to the process of pilgrimage itself. Christian pilgrimage always contains an element of voluntariness, of a private contract entered into freely by a devotee with his chosen deity or saint, and in the Andes, as elsewhere in Christendom, is underpinned by a diversity of motivations. It is essentially a form of penance, but it might be undertaken in order to supplicate the sacred personage in question for some special favor, or in fulfillment of a vow to make the journey in return for some request already granted, as well as to atone for one's sins and to acquire spiritual merit or grace. Most regional shrines are visited all year round by a trickle of individual pilgrims, who come to deposit votive offerings before the shrine and to pray for its protection and intercession. The great gatherings of pilgrims occur during the principal annual fiestas, and on these occasions many devotees attend not as individuals but in groups based on their home communities, neighborhoods or parishes. Such groups are traditionally organized on a semivoluntary basis around a set of offices or *cargos,* which circulate among the members of a local community from year to year. The element of voluntariness for those who assume offices in the contingent is here alloyed with social obligation. The members of such a pilgrimage party refer to themselves as representing not a community (*comunidad*) or village (*pueblo* or *llahta*), nor an administrative dependency (*anexo* or *parcialidad*), but a *nación,* an archaic designation which translates roughly as "race" or "tribe." As far as could be ascertained, the term *nación* was never used where reference was being made to a community or village as a politicolegal or ecclesiastical entity.

There is a separate set of local pilgrimage offices for each pilgrimage undertaken by devotees from a particular community or village. In the early 1970s, five shrines were visited by contingents from Ccamahuara. The most important was the ranked shrine of Christ of the Snow Star some 70 kilometers away, whose fiesta took place during the novena of Corpus Christi. Formerly Christ of Tayancani had also featured in this itinerary, but had been dropped some years earlier. Separate contingents visited the ranked shrine of Accha, and the unranked shrines of Quisicancha, Huata, and Saccaca. The ranked shrine of Christ the Just Judge in Occoruro was also an object of veneration for the people of Ccamahuara, but being so close it did not for them constitute a place of pilgrimage, and their participation in its fiesta differed from their mode of participation in other regional devotions (cf. Christian 1972:122; Turner 1974:191). The major pilgrimage fiesta of the *mestizo* shrine of Christ of Huanca near San Salvador was celebrated simultaneously with, but entirely independently of, that of Christ the Just Judge. Although the mountain peasants of the vicinage availed themselves of the services offered by the accompanying regional fair in San Salvador, very few attended the religious activities at the Huanca sanctuary, despite its proximity and wide renown. Sponsored group pilgrimage was in fact prohibited at Huanca, and most mountain peasants in the area chose instead to patronize the more "traditional" fiesta of the Indian shrine of Christ the Just Judge in the mountains.

The ostensible purpose of a group pilgrimage was to transport a small portable miniature icon, the *lámina*, from the community to the shrine, where it reposed for a time—usually overnight—in the presence of the shrine image. A *lámina* was a painted image of Christ or the Virgin about 40 centimeters in height, set in a gabled wooden frame. There was a separate miniature icon for each pilgrimage, and when not elsewhere they were kept on the altar of the community chapel. Some people credited these pilgrimage icons, too, with the miraculous quality of divine manifestations, and they were afforded great reverence. Each was known by the name of the shrine to which it was attached, or more generally as a *taytacha* or *mamacha*.

The organization of a group pilgrimage centered on the office of sponsor (*patrón*), occupied by a different man each year for each pilgrimage. The sponsor had to shoulder most of the costs of the affair, and gained prestige in the eyes of other pilgrims and his fellow-villagers in general. He was obliged to satisfy the temporal needs of the pilgrims for the duration of the pilgrimage, providing potatoes, maize, roasted cavy (a small domestic rodent), rice, vermicelli, coca, coffee and rum. In addition he was expected to slaughter a sheep or a pig from his own herds for feasting the pilgrims on the eve of their departure and on their return to the community. He also had to hire a band of musicians. Because of its scale and duration, the sponsor of the five-day pilgrimage to Christ of the Snow Star incurred the heaviest cash outlay—somewhere in the region of 3,000 to 4,000 *soles* ($70–$90).[9] For some months before departure the sponsor was allowed to keep the pilgrimage icon in his house, where it was thought to exert a benign influence over the occupants, protecting them from thieves and supernatural dangers. During the pilgrimage the sponsor was expected to comport himself like the other pilgrims, and to defer like them to the decisions of the man who held the office of leader.

The leader of a pilgrimage was the most respected person in the entourage. He was the principal officiant in all the rituals; in particular he was the leader of the troupe of the dozen or so ritual dancers, and was expected to be completely familiar with the relevant choreography. He was in charge of the logistics of the journey, deciding when to stop and start, making food and load allocations, laying arrangements for transport and accommodation and so on. He was honored by the group in various ways. He was always served first at mealtimes, and was given the first dram of rum when the party stopped for refreshment. At the fiesta of Christ of the Snow Star in June, as the first rays of the morning sun struck the thousands of pilgrims camped out on the frozen ground around the sanctuary, the musicians of each contingent gathered around their leader to play a joyful *aubade* in his honor—a clear echo of the Inca solstitial ceremony of Inti Raymi. The leader was assisted in his duties by a lieutenant who acted as his ritual dance partner.

Without ritual dancers, the purpose of a pilgrimage could not be fulfilled. As well as providing entertainment for the pilgrims, they escorted the party's pilgrimage icon to and from its places of repose—the community chapel, the sponsor's house and the shrine itself. There are scores of different ritual dance styles in the Andes, each with its own costumes, instrumentation, music, choreography, and symbolism. Certain styles seem to have become ethnically diacritical. For example, of the various *ch'uncho* (savage) dance styles, that of *wayri ch'uncho* is regarded as typically Indian, while that of *ch'uncho extranjero* (foreign savage) is favored by people who consider themselves to be *mestizos.* The people of Ccamahuara were utilizing two main dance styles in the pilgrimages in the early 1970s. The most popular was that of the *wayri ch'unchos,* but occasionally *qolla* dancers were employed. The *wayri ch'unchos,* with their head-dresses of orange macaw feathers, red waistcoats, brightly colored scarves and wooden staves, represented the inhabitants of the tropical rain forests to the north of Cuzco.[10] Their leader was called the *arariwa,* a title also used in the context of agricultural cooperation where it referred to the man chosen by the sponsor of a contractual work party to allocate tasks to team members. The *qollas,* on the other hand, with their flat hats, white masks and the skins of alpaca lambs slung around their shoulders, represented the inhabitants of the *altiplano,* the herding region to the south of Cuzco.[11] In addition to the main dance troupe a pilgrimage contingent usually included at least one dancer in the burlesque style of *ukuku.* The *ukuku* was supposed to represent a bear; he wore a long smock of shaggy brown wool and a woollen mask and wig. He carried a small doll on whose behalf he would beg money from strangers, and a small rope whip. While in costume he spoke in a falsetto voice and was expected to keep up a constant patter of jokes, insults and sexual innuendo. As Gow (1978:208) has argued, the *ukuku* is the Andean trickster *par excellence.*

The dancers on a group pilgrimage would change into their costumes and go through their routines at specific junctures in the journey: the departure of the party from the sponsor's house, the depositing of the pilgrimage icon on the retable of the shrine sanctuary and its subsequent retrieval, the departure of the group from my lodgings where they had stayed *en route,* and the re-entry into the community. On the day following the return, the dancers were rewarded for their services to the sponsor by being decorated on his behalf by two nominated women in a ceremony called the *costumbre de cargo* (*cargo* custom). Each dancer in turn, starting with the leader, was given a ritual glass of maize-beer and was then festooned with a garland of maize-cobs, onions, carrots and other vegetables, and for *qollas,* a piece of pottery, all tied to a length of rope pinned to a shawl around the shoulders. All would show great pride at being so honored.

Apart from the sponsor, dancers and musicians, a group pilgrimage would include two female cross-bearers (*alfereces*) and up to fifty "lay" pilgrims, many sporting their best traditional or store-bought clothes for the occasion. Urban migrants would sometimes schedule their home visits so as to participate in pilgrimages from the community. Ideally the contingent marched single file along the mountain trails, the lieutenant at the head of the column and the leader bringing up the rear.[12]

Andean regional shrines are the nodal points in a highly variegated sacred topography, one with which people across a wide area are fully acquainted (cf. Turner 1974:210). Special prayers were recited and rituals performed on a Ccamahuaran pilgrimage at the *mons gaudii,* where the shrine or its environs first came into view, and at spots on the journey where other regional shrines became visible across the mountains. Routes were studded with sacred landmarks such as wayside crosses, chapels, and *apachitas,* heaps of stones left by passing pilgrims, and these landmarks became more frequent and charged with greater sanctity the closer one approached the shrine. But the significance of this topographical coding varied with directionality. The atmosphere on the outward journey was solemn, with the prayers and rituals associated with the various stages of the route being performed with a punctilious regard for detail. The pilgrims stayed in a compact group, the leader ensuring that when resting they sat together in an unbroken circle lest any evil spirits intrude. On the homeward journey, however, the group was often ragged and disorganized; there was much joking and fooling, and rituals were performed perfunctorily. Movement from the familiar to the unfamiliar was tightly controlled, but the return to the familiar was relaxed and informal (cf. Christian 1972:71).

Throughout a pilgrimage, the ethos within the contingent was fiercely egalitarian. The leader, despite his position and the respect accorded him, was simply *primus inter pares.* Constant reference was made to the notion that all pilgrims in the party were "brothers and sisters." Everyone slept in the same lodging houses and ate the same food. No one was supposed to carry food or drink of his own; all provisions were pooled, distributed among the pilgrims for transport and shared out equally under the leader's supervision. On the last stage of the journey, before the party re-entered the community, everyone was required to empty the contents of his bags on to the ground in order to ensure that no one stole any of the communal provisions. Inevitably, selfishness and personal animosities occasionally disrupted this communal atmosphere, but nevertheless a régime of complete equality was enjoined for the duration of the pilgrimage.

The internal solidarity of each of the contingents on a pilgrimage, however, was complemented by rigid boundaries between them, boundaries drawn both by ritual exchanges and by informal competition. Whenever one contingent passed another on the path, both groups had to line up facing each other, and the respective leaders exchanged pilgrimage icons. After intoning a short prayer, each leader held the other's icon while the members of his own party filed past one by one to kiss it. The whole company then twice over said the invocation, "God and Mary protect us." The episode was punctuated with appropriate pieces of music and terminated by the explosion of a skyrocket. At times this ritual proved irksome to the pilgrims, especially in the vicinity of a shrine where contingents were constantly passing one another, and they would occasionally make a diversion to another footpath in order to avoid the delay which the passing procedure entailed.

Latent opposition between contingents surfaced in a variety of ways. When encamped at a shrine each group kept itself apart from the others, marking out its territory with stones. Troupes of dancers vied with one another in the beauty of their costumes and the execution of their dances. Musicians competed with their virtuoso skills, a band taking up the tune of its neighbors but playing it louder, faster, and with more embellishments. The *ukuku* dancers of different contingents sometimes engaged in whipping contests, lashing out at each other's legs until one of them was forced to retire. On one occasion, during the fiesta of Christ of Huata, the *ch'uncho* dancers of Ccamahuara became embroiled in a violent fight with another *ch'uncho* troupe, who claimed that they were unfairly monopolizing the arena in front of the shrine sanctuary. Punches were thrown and the dancers' wooden staves clashed in earnest until the guardian of the shrine intervened and separated the two bands. At some regional fiestas special wardens patrolled the sanctuary and its precincts, armed with whips with which to subdue such outbreaks of conflict among the pilgrims. Opposition and conflict between contingents, in sum, were endemic in the pilgrimage process.

Friendship and Factionalism in Pilgrimage

A pilgrimage party, as already mentioned, referred to itself as the *nación* of a particular community, the community which was the provenance of the pilgrimage icon which it escorted. In practice, however, a contingent could have a span greater or less than a single community depending on the circumstances. Pilgrimage participation was grounded ultimately in networks of social relations rather than in mandated representation, and such networks could on the one hand transcend community boundaries and on the other display discontinuities within the same community arising from animosities and factionalism. An examination of the recruitment process of sponsored pilgrimage will show how competition and opposition between contingents could penetrate to the very heart of a community.

There were no formal election mechanisms for pilgrimage offices. The leader and sponsor together chose the officeholders for the following year from among their kin, friends, and acquaintances. A man would normally be sponsor for a particular pilgrimage only once, but there was no limit to the number of times he could occupy other offices. This meant that the posts tended to devolve through a network of kinsmen and friends, and it was possible for a group of families to monopolize positions for several years running. As far as lay pilgrims were concerned, continuity from one year to the next, though less pronounced than among the officeholders, was nevertheless evident, since many were the latter's kin, affines, and friends. Overall, then, the pilgrimage contingents traveling to a particular shrine in successive years displayed a degree of continuity in terms of personnel.

The most coveted sponsorship was that for the pilgrimage to Christ of the Snow Star, since after Huanca it was the most important ranked shrine in the community's shrine hierarchy. In 1973 there was a waiting list for the post, since it and the other offices for the pilgrimage were effectively monopolized by a small coterie of kinsmen md friends, as shown in Figure 9.2.

Competition for offices on other pilgrimages was less acute and consequently access to them was less exclusive. In these cases too, however, there was a tendency for recognizable sets of individuals to become associated with the principal offices. Some of the men belonging to the Snow Star coterie also featured prominently in the early 1970s in the organization of pilgrimages to the shrines of Accha, Quisicancha, and Saccaca. Meanwhile

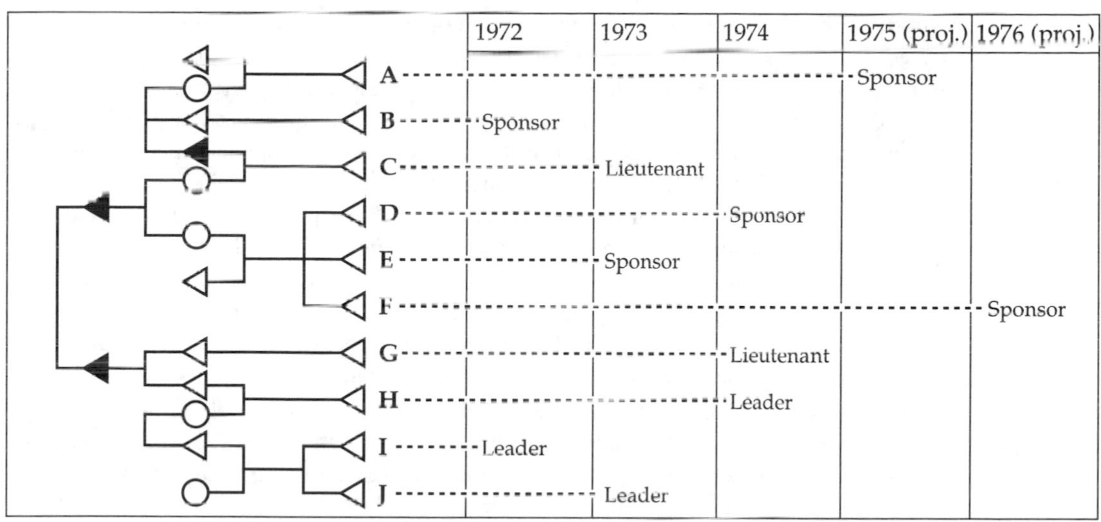

FIGURE 9.2 Genealogy of pilgrimage officers for Christ of the Snow Star, 1972–76.

the leading positions for the other major pilgrimage in the community calendar, that to the unranked shrine of Huata, were circulating through an identifiably separate set of individuals. Thus, while in principle there was open access to all pilgrimage contingents, in practice shrine allegiance reflected, or created, more or less well-defined discontinuities in terms of the social networks involved. Because of the overlap between them at the level of lay pilgrims, contingents for different shrines did not normally constitute factions. But differential participation in the higher echelons of the pilgrimage organizations provided potential nuclei around which mutually exclusive factions could crystallize in certain circumstances. Contingents would then stand opposed to one another depending *inter alia* on the allegiances of their members to the principal officers.

An example of this process is afforded by the imbroglio surrounding the Snow Star pilgrimage in 1974. The "official" sponsor for that year had been nominated by his brother, the sponsor for the previous year. However, resentment had been building up for some time against the nepotism which governed the occupancy of this prestigious post. Interestingly, it was the grouping associated with the Huata offices which chose to launch the offensive, and in 1974 they staged a rival pilgrimage to the shrine of Christ of the Snow Star, as a direct challenge to the official party. Their decision may well have been prompted by the fact that in that year, with the agreement of the official organizers, I had arranged for a film crew to record the pilgrimage for a British television company. This conferred still more prestige on the event and on the participants, and no doubt stiffened the resolve of the malcontents.

The rival pilgrimage was a small-scale affair, and though it poached a few people who might otherwise have joined the official party it was less than half the size of the latter, numbering about twenty individuals. The organizers had appropriated another pilgrimage icon from the community chapel, and had chosen the dance style of the *wayri ch'unchos* in contradistinction to the *qollas* of the official party. The two contingents kept themselves apart from each other, both on the journey and during their stay at the shrine itself. The rivals had selected as sponsor a man whose house overlooked that of the official sponsor, and the two homecoming fiestas were therefore held in full sight of each other. There was little visiting between them, each group maintaining a studied disregard of the other. The pilgrimage had on this occasion crystallized into two mutually exclusive contingents, and the divisions inherent in the pattern of distribution of offices were cast into sharp relief.

Since regional shrines could evidently serve as rallying points for polarized factional groupings within a community, we may enquire as to the nature of the social relationships caught up in pilgrimage participation and the degree to which they mirrored or fostered alliances in other spheres of activity. Shared secular interests were indeed embraced by joint pilgrimage. The division apparent in Ccamahuara in the early 1970s, for example, had a political dimension, for the Snow Star coterie numbered among its members several Spanish-speaking bilinguals who were active in the elective council system of the community. In particular it included the current administrative secretary (F in Figure 9.2), a young returned urban migrant, together with his political mentor (H), the man who as an army veteran had spearheaded the movement for the official registration of the community in 1966. Those men associated with the Huata offices, by contrast, were mainly Quechua monolinguals, and none carried much weight in community affairs. More generally, there was a degree of congruence in both cases between the respective pilgrimage networks and those deriving from contractual cooperation in agriculture, which I have argued was essentially a means of forging and maintaining social relations beyond the narrow, mutualistic groupings of kin and kin-of-kin. Pilgrimage participation nonetheless extended beyond these work partnerships to comprehend wider collectivities than they alone could generate. It was not merely a reflection of secular interests, whether political or economic, though it could well be used to further such interests. Rather, each regional devotion established within a community or neighborhood a field of relationships *sui generis*, a "partial network" to use Barnes's (1969:72–74) terminology, which was founded upon the shared, sacralized experience of a journey to a distant shrine, and which was renewed and reconstituted each year with each successive pilgrimage. The fervid experience of intense communalism on the journey and of voluntary, joint worship before a miraculous image created a special bond between fellow pilgrims which could perdure outside the context of the activity itself and which could independently modify relationships by inducing a greater degree of trust and confidence (*confiànza*) between the individuals concerned.

Communitas Reconsidered

From a sociological viewpoint, then, group pilgrimage in the Andes is a complex mosaic of egalitarianism, nepotism and factionalism, of brotherhood, competition and conflict. Having examined some of these diverse aspects, we are in a position to assess the relevance of Turner's ideas.

If communitas is the ultimate goal of pilgrimage, then for the pilgrims of the Andes a plethora of divisions and interferences contrived to frustrate its realization, sometimes in an apparently gratuitous fashion. The local ranking of shrines coupled with the practice of community-based sponsored pilgrimage could lead to factionalism even within a single community, as the case-study above has shown. On the journey the various parties of pilgrims from different communities maintained a ritualized distance from one another which accentuated, rather than attenuated, the boundaries between them. At the shrine itself they each maintained their separateness, and never coalesced into a single unified congregation. Furthermore the regional cult was differentiated into *mestizo* and Indian devotions, placing a sacralized construction on the fundamental ethnic opposition.

This is not to say that the notion of egalitarianism was not paramount in Andean pilgrimage. Egalitarianism, however, is not necessarily the same as communitas. Equality—no less a cultural invention than its converse—may manifest itself through competition, that is the attempt to generate differentials between opponents regarded as evenly matched, or through reciprocal exchange, either in a sacred or a secular context, as well as through the conjunction implied by communitas. All three manifestations—competition, reciprocity and conjunction—were evident in Andean pilgrimage. Intragroup collectivism was on the one hand offset by intergroup differentiation through ritual exchange and secular competition, and on the other was prone to factionalism within the group itself. It would seem unwarranted to represent the differentiation and opposition between pilgrimage contingents as features of normative communitas, since they did little to facilitate the attainment of the communitas ideal. Equally, it is difficult to argue that they were part of a structural residue carried over into an activity basically oriented towards existential communitas, for there was nothing to indicate that the pilgrims themselves aspired to a greater degree of interpersonal inclusiveness, or resented or strove to overcome the barriers imposed by *nación* allegiance. It would appear that the concept of communitas is of little value in explaining the essentially divisive quality of Andean pilgrimage.

Sponsored group pilgrimages are not, of course, peculiar to the central Andes. The material for the Mexican *municipio* of San Bernadino Contla, Tlaxcala state (Nutini 1968:63–75), which Turner utilizes, is strikingly similar in this regard. In Contla there were two kinds of organization concerned with religious fiestas: stewardships (*mayordomías*) tied to local patron saints and brotherhoods (*hermandades*) associated with pilgrimages. The brotherhoods were sponsored on a voluntary basis; each was associated with a particular shrine and possessed a portable religious image linked to it. Altogether, the forty brotherhoods in the *municipio* sponsored pilgrimages to seventeen different external shrines, which means that for some shrines at least there was more than one local brotherhood. Turner sees in the contrast between the stewardships and brotherhoods of Contla a dichotomy between exclusive and inclusive domains, between

> *. . . religious structures firmly attached to localized socio-cultural systems and those concerned with the maintenance of the highest common values of the widest accepted cultural community (1974:191).*

In both the Mexican and the Andean cases, this dichotomous contrast between exclusive and inclusive domains requires severe qualification. In neither instance do the majority of pilgrims shed their local identities to form a congeries of individual devotees. Rather, they carry these local identities outward into the wider, extralocal arena, participating in the regional devotions not *qua* individuals but as discrete groups based ostensibly on community membership, more or less formally constituted, which gather to pay homage simultaneously but separately to a common shrine. In the Andes these local, community identities were emblematized by pilgrimage icons hedged about with their own acolytes and ritual, which sacralized the boundaries and discontinuities between the different groups of devotees. Indeed, it would be more appropriate in such circumstances to see community, not communitas, as the hallmark of pilgrimage.[13]

Compared with the corporate religious identity of Ccamahuara as a dependent chapelry within the parish of San Salvador, however, the collective identity borne by pilgrims from Ccamahuara to a regional shrine was subtly nuanced. To begin with, first, it possessed a special lexical reference in the archaism *nación,* which seemed to be reserved for the context of pilgrimage. Second, it had as its emblem an icon distinct from those religious images in the community inventory—chief among them the patronal image—which were deployed in the local rituals of community and parish. Patronal images and pilgrimage icons were semiologically contrasted. The former were generally drawn from a standard liturgical series of saints and divine guises; within each parish they differentiated communities one from another, giving rise to mutually exclusive microcosmic enclaves. Pilgrimage icons, on the other hand, had no intrinsic iconological status, each being known only by the name of the shrine with which it was associated. Nominally, at least, the pilgrimage icons of a particular shrine were identical, and in theory were susceptible to infinite replication. In ritual terms, therefore, the catchment of a regional shrine was an unbounded field, a macrocosmic domain, which disaggregated the constituent elements of local microcosms and reassembled them in a wider, more extensive combination. In other words Ccamahuara's ritual identity was multifaceted, its patronal image epitomizing the facet directed inwards, towards the microcosm, the pilgrimage icons those directed outwards, towards the macrocosm.

Thirdly, this lexical and iconic mutation of community identity was matched sociologically as well. Local rituals were community concerns, being discharged by a collective mandate and overseen by the community's political representatives. But the latter did not play any official part in pilgrimage organization. Pilgrimage was voluntary, and its officers were not subject to community opprobrium in the event of default. This very autonomy from local political md ritual organization meant that the regional devotions could reflect, exacerbate, or provoke divisions within the community. In other words pilgrimage icons, the emblems of extralocal identity, could also serve as the markers of internal community differentiation. What is of interest here is that the immanent rivalry for the mantle, or mantles, of community identity was focused not on the patronal icon, which remained above division, but on the external shrines.[14]

In this regard the comparison between pilgrimage participation and contractual cooperation is instructive. Both gave rise to loosely structured groupings founded upon short-term convergence, or more accurately parallelism, of interest, but which were otherwise gratuitous. Both represented contexts in which fluid interpersonal relationships could be fixed and given meaning and cogency, free from the exigencies of any immediate, extrinsic, unilateral purpose. As we have seen, there was a continuity between the two sets of activities in terms of personnel, with joint pilgrimage participation building upon and amplifying the more restricted networks established in the sphere of production.

The fourth notable characteristic of community identity in the extralocal domain was the self-conscious affirmation of an egalitarian, collectivistic ethos within a pilgrimage contingent. These values were not, however, novel to pilgrimage. They were acknowledged in other contexts—as in the constitution of the community assembly and in the organization of certain community activities. They complemented the values of hierarchy and dependence which sustained the local structure of political control of which Ccamahuara was a subordinate element. Pilgrimage took the people beyond the territorial ambit of this control, allowing the fraternalistic ethos alone to hold sway. It was intensified and celebrated as signifying temporary release from local constraints and obligations. But its writ ran no further than the boundaries of the *nación,* and these boundaries became the more tightly drawn the further the party ventured from its homeland.

External opposition went hand in hand with internal levelling. Pilgrimage contingents at or *en route* to a shrine, whatever their provenance, stood opposed to one another as identical elements of the macrocosm: there was distinction without difference. Freed from the various local systems of politico-ecclesiastical administration, relations between contingents were decontrolled. Reciprocal exchange and veneration of pilgrimage icons provided a measure of ritual conciliation, but intergroup relations were essentially unstable, as the frequent competition and conflict clearly demonstrated. Egalitarianism reigned here, too, but it was the equality of opposition, rather than the equality of brotherhood. The two counterbalanced each other in classic Simmelian fashion.

Ultimately this inherent instability was contained by the organizational hierarchies of the regional devotions. At most shrines there were rudimentary structures of authority and control for keeping order among the assembled pilgrims, and the relationship between shrine staff and devotees was invariably cast in the idiom of ethnicity. But the manifestation of ethnic dualism in specific sets of cultic relations was a sociological feature of the regional devotions *per se,* for as we have seen it was sometimes invoked between people who would in other contexts regard themselves as ethnic equals. Both the egalitarim opposition between contingents and the hierarchical relations between pilgrims and staff were aspects of diverse social configurations which by virtue of their universalistic appeal the devotions themselves generated.

The study of pilgrimage, by the very nature of the phenomenon, demands that *a priori* assumptions concerning the relationship between religion and society be abandoned, however that relationship might be conceptualized. The link between ritual and secular processes should be regarded as analytically determinable in each case, rather than simply assumed. Thus I have sought to detach the Andean regional devotions from the "correspondence" view of ritual, by which it is seen always as symbolically and sociologically congruent with the social structure.[15] Turner's model goes beyond this by allowing for an inverse as well as a direct relation; but the simple dichotomy between structure and communitas cannot comprehend the complex interplay between the social relations of pilgrimage and those associated with secular activities. The social configurations manifested in Andean regional devotions are neither the sacralized correlates of structured social relations, whether political, jural or economic, nor their dialectical antitheses, secular revolts *manqués.* The devotions do indeed stand in a dialectical relation to the established religious order, their catchments confounding ecclesiastical boundaries and their shrines effecting transformations of the standard liturgical code. But the sociological components of the devotions are the self-same chapelries and parish seats which constitute the fixed local orders of ecclesiastical and political administration. Through the detachment of these collective identities from their local domains, hierarchy is temporarily annulled. Yet this creates not communitas, but simply a setting in which social interactions can take place *ex novo.* The regional devotions, in other words, while appropriating elements of the politico-ecclesiastical structure, at the same time abrogate the relations between them. They thus constitute a domain in which social relationships may be established, events may occur and processes unfold independently of activities outside the context of the cult. We have seen that they could stimulate neighborhood factionalism, foster intercommunity conflict, and generate new ethnically based hierarchies of control. Such processes occur not as perversions of a fraternalistic ideal but rather as the consequences of the very universalism which the shrines proclaim.

Notes

The fieldwork on which this article is based was made possible by a Foreign Area Fellowship from the U.S. Social Science Research Council, supplemented by a grant from the Radcliffe-Brown Fund of the Association of Social Anthropologists. I am grateful to both these bodies for their assistance. An earlier version of this article was presented to the anthropology seminar at the University of Manchester. Special thanks are due to Richard Werbner for many helpful comments and suggestions.

1. Although many parishes in the Peruvian Andes are, like San Salvador, coincident with administrative districts, it would be a mistake to regard the ecclesiastical system as merely reflecting secular political organization. Indeed, historically, the reverse was the case (van den Berghe & Primov 1977:84).

2. I use the term "guise" *faute de mieux* to refer to a representation of a saint or divine personage. Guises may be drawn from incidents in the subject's mythico-historical biography, or they may celebrate some facet of the subject's qualities, or they may commemorate a divine apparition at a certain spot, the dedication of a church or any other anniversary somehow associated with the personage in question. Each of the more widely recognized guises has come to be depicted by a specific iconographic type, recognizable by its mien, by certain symbolic appurtenances, or, in the case of Marian guises especially, by the color of its robes. Christian (1972:47–48 *et passim*) uses the archaism "advocation" for the same concept, though to the best of my knowledge the usage is without theological authority.

3. Viewed in the context of the Catholic liturgical system as a whole, there is a transformational relationship between the cults of such idiosyncratic shrines and the cults of universal divine guises. A discussion of this, however, lies beyond the scope of the present article.

4. A similar distinction between thaumaturgic and non-thaumaturgic shrines is made by the people of Santa Fé, New Mexico, who stressed to the ethnographer the nonmiraculous nature of their patronal Virgin (Grimes 1976). Mass pilgrimage following upon the proclamation of the miraculous healing powers of a hitherto "dormant" image can have catastrophic effects on the host community, as documented by Kagan (1973).

5. Foundation myths of miraculous shrines based on a fraternal relationship between them are common in the central Andes, though the particular shrines vary from place to place (see, for example, Núñez del Prado 1970:100). They are clearly transformations of the Incaic myths of the establishment of Cuzco and other settlements, which also featured a primal group of siblings, three brothers and three sisters, journeying from site to site (Cieza de León 1959:30 *sqq.*).

6. A well-known example of ethnic specialization of shrines is that of the two Virgins of Mexico, the Virgin of Guadalupe and the Virgin of Remedies. The first has traditionally appealed to the Indian sector of the population while the latter has been associated with Hispanic culture. Interestingly, however, these roles are gradually being reversed (Turner & Turner 1978).

7. A similar pattern of preferences according to the zonal location of shrines operates in respect of the regional devotions of the Nansa valley people of northern Spain (Christian 1972:51).

8. A novena is the nine-day period preceding a Catholic feast, an octave the eight-day period following it.

9. The average daily agricultural wage at the time was about 30 *soles*.
10. A comprehensive description of the costume, choreography, and music of the *wayri ch'unchos* is given in Roel Pineda (1950).
11. There is a clear complementarity between the roles of *wayri ch'uncho* and *qolla* dancers, expressed in both myth and ritual. Mock battles between them—with the *wayri ch'unchos* always emerging victorious—take place at the Corpus Christi fiesta in Ocongate (Ramirez 1969:80–81) and at the fiesta of the Virgin of Mount Carmel in Paucartambo (Barrionuevo 1969:186).
12. A detailed description of the journey appears in Sallnow (1974:110–117).
13. Compare also Gross's account (1971) of the pilgrimage to Bom Jesus de Lapa in north-eastern Brazil, in which a group of kin and neighbors from a single rural neighborhood share a truck to the shrine center hired by a self-selected leader, who frequently arranges accommodation as well. Gross writes that "contact with members of groups from other areas appears to be minimal" (1971:138), and that ". . . it is difficult to make a case for a sense of unity among pilgrims to Bom Jesus" (1971:145).
14. An analogous pattern of local differentiation with reference to distant shrines in Ghana is discussed in Werbner (1979).
15. The correspondence view of ritual, stemming largely from Robertson-Smith through Durkheim (see Werbner 1977), can assume many different forms. A recent Marxist version is that of Bloch (1977).

References

Barnes, J. A. (1969). Networks and political processes. In Clyde Mitchell (Ed.), *Social networks in urban situations.* Manchester: University Press.

Barrionuevo, A. (1969). *Cuzco, magic city.* Lima: Editorial Universo.

Bloch, M. (1973). The long-term and the short-term: The economic and political significance of the morality of kinship. In J. Goody (Ed.), *The character of kinship.* Cambridge: University Press.

Bloch, M. (1977). The past and the present in the present. *Man (NS), 12,* 278–292.

Carrasco, P. (1961). The civil-religious hierarchy in Mesoamerican communities: Pre-Spanish background and colonial development. American Anthropologist, 63, 484–497.

Christian, W. A. (1972). *Person and God in a Spanish valley.* New York: Seminar Press.

Cieza de León, Pedro de (1959). *The Incas of Pedro Cieza de León* (1553) (H. de Onis, Trans.). V. W. von Hagen (Ed.). Norman: University of Oklahoma Press.

Gow, D. D. (1978). Verticality and Andean cosmology: Quadripartition, opposition and mediation. *Actes du XLIIe Congrès International des Américanistes 1976, 4,* 199–212.

Grimes, R. L. (1976). *Symbol and conquest: Public ritual and drama in Santa Fe, New Mexico.* Ithaca, NY: Cornell University Press.

Gross, D. R. (1971). Ritual and conformity: A religious pilgrimage to northeastern Brazil. *Ethnology, 10,* 129–148.

Gudeman, S. (1976). Saints, symbols, and ceremonies. *American Ethnologist, 3,* 709–729.

Kagan, H. (1973). The Virgin of Bojacá: Miracles and change in a Colombian peasant community. Thesis, University of California (Riverside).

Kubler, G. (1946). The Quechua in the colonial world. In J. Steward (Ed.), *Handbook of South American Indians* (vol. 2). Washington, DC: Bureau of American Ethnology.

Marzal, M. (1971). *El mundo religioso de Urcos.* Cuzco: Instituto de Pastoral Andina.

Morote Best, E. (1953). Dios, la Virgen y los santos en los relatos popularies. *Tradición* (Cuzco), 5, 76–104.

Núñez del Prado, J. V. (1970). El mundo sobrenatural de los Quechuas del sur del Perú, a través de la comunidad de Qotobamba. *Allpanchis, 2,* 57–120.

Nutini, H. G. (1968). *San Bernadino Contla: Marriage and family structure in a Tlaxcalan municipio.* Pittsburgh: University Press.

Ramirez, J. A. (1969). La novena al Señor de Qoyllur Rit'i. *Allpanchis, 1,* 61–88.

Redfield, R., & Villas Rojas, A. (1934). *Chan Kom: A Maya village.* Washington, DC: Carnegie Institution.

Roel Pineda, J. (1950). La danza de los 'c'uncos' de Paucartambo. *Tradición* (Cuzco), 1, 59–70.

Sallnow, M. (1974). La peregrinación andina. *Allpanchis, 7,* 101–142.

Turner, V. W. (1969). *The ritual process: Structure and anti-structure.* London: Routledge & Kegan Paul.

Turner, V. W. (1974). *Dramas, fields and metaphors: Symbolic action in human society.* Ithaca, NY: Cornell University Press.

Turner, V. W., & Turner, E. (1978). *Image and pilgrimage in Christian culture: Anthropological perspectives.* Oxford: Basil Blackwell.

van den Berghe, P., & Primo, G. P. (1977). *Inequality in the Peruvian Andes: Class and ethnicity in Cuzco.* Columbia: University of Missouri Press.

Werbner, R. P. (1977). Introduction. In R. P. Werbner (Ed.), *Regional cults.* London: Academic Press.

Werbner, R. P. (1979). "Totemism" in history: The ritual passage of west African strangers. *Man (NS), 14,* 663–683.

Christianity and Colonialism in South Africa

JEAN COMAROFF
JOHN COMAROFF

Introduction

Although the literature on missions in Africa is very large, many have commented on the relative lack of systematic analyses of the evangelical encounter; analyses that go beyond detailed, if often sensitive, chronicles of events and actions (Heise 1967; Beidelman 1982:2ff.; Etherington 1983; Ranger n.d.; cf. Shapiro 1981:130). Indeed, the emerging picture is one of bewildering factual variation and a lack of theoretical convergence. Moreover, as Beidelman (1982:7) implies, the subject has lent itself to polemical debate rather than careful scrutiny. This is well exemplified in the South African literature, our present focus, where much of the discussion until quite recently cast those who stressed the philanthropic role of missionaries (Wilson 1969, 1976; Sillery 1971) against those who condemned them as agents of imperialism (for example, Majeke 1953; Dachs 1972). Much of that debate was addressed to the issue of "Whose side was the missionary really on?"—and, by extension, "Whose ends did he serve?"—thus translating a complex historical problem into a crude equation of cause and effect (cf. Bundy 1979:36ff.). Few would any longer debate the historical role of the missionary in these terms. Nonetheless, as Ranger notes in an extended review of the literature, another unfortunate tendency still remains:

> *An oddity of most recent historiography of early mission Christianity is that it has greatly overplayed the manifest political and economic factors in its expansion and greatly underplayed the cultural and the religious . . . [Even the formal church historians*

> *have] hardly discussed the impact of missionaries and their African catechists on the cultural imagination of Africa [n.d.:36].*

In this essay, we seek not only to examine the cultural implications of the mission, but also to inquire how they might be related to the sphere of manifest political processes. Rather than seek generalizations in the historical record, however, we analyze one instance of Protestant evangelism in Africa as a problem in the interplay of power and meaning. We stress the singularity of the case: the missionary project was everywhere made particular by variations in the structure of local communities, in the social and theological background of the evangelists, and in the wider politico-economic context and precise circumstances within which the encounter took place (Beidelman 1982:30).[1] If anything more general emerges from this study, then, it does not lie at the level of events and actions; instead, it concerns the generic nature of mission agency in the colonial process. This involves two interrelated dimensions. One is the capacity to act in the domain normally defined as "the political," the arena of concrete, institutionalized power relations. The other is the ability to exert power over the common-sense meanings and routine activities diffused in the everyday world. Both dimensions are simultaneously material and symbolic, and the relationship between "religion" and "politics" plays itself out in each.

The analysis has three steps. In the first, we show that it is impossible to arrive at any consistent conclusion about the purely "political" aspect of the role of the missionary among the Tswana, of his activities in the institutional arena of tangible power relations. For, from this standpoint, both the motivation and the consequences of his part in the imperial project remain variable and indeterminate—just as imperialism itself appears more inchoate, less crushingly methodical than is often allowed. But this poses an immediate question. If it is true that there is no consistency at this level, does it not follow that the labors of the evangelists are best treated in an idiographic manner? Can we do no more, at this stage, than seek their relevance in the uniqueness of each missionary encounter, as Beidelman (1982:29f.) seems to suggest?

In the second step of the analysis we begin to show that the role of missionary does in fact yield to systematic accounting in the Tswana case; that here, as elsewhere, it was both a vital and a consistent element in the colonial encounter. In order to do so, however, we reexamine the nature of their power to affect the course of history. For power, the capacity to impose the conditions of being on others, does not reside solely in palpable forces of influence. As Marx and Weber noted long ago, it has a second, less visible aspect. This involves the incorporation of human subjects into the "natural," taken-for-granted forms of economy and society. And these forms lie not just in the institutional domain of "politics," but also in such things as aesthetics and religion, built form and bodily presentation, medical knowledge and the mundane habits of everyday life (Bourdieu 1977:184f.). The construction of the subject in this mold, moreover, is rarely an act of overt persuasion. It requires the internalization of a set of values, an ineffable manner of seeing and being. As others have observed (Schapera 1958; Etherington 1978:116; Bundy 1979:41ff.), it is precisely here that the evangelist left his mark most deeply in southern Africa. For, while the colonial process often entailed material dispossession, even brute force, a critical part of the subjection of native peoples lay in the subtle colonization, by the missionary, of indigenous modes of perception and practice (cf. Shapiro 1981:130).

This, however, raises a final issue. On one hand, we show that the part of the missionary in the "political" domain was variable and indeterminate; on the other, we suggest that his efforts were decisive in the imposition of a new mode of being. Neither of these observations is novel, of course, although the exact contours of the present case are not a mere repetition of a universal process. What we seek to do here, however, is to explore *how* these two dimensions of historical agency relate to one another. As we shall indicate in the last section, the disjuncture between them underlines the double-sided role of the mission in the colonial process. For, ironically, the evangelist failed where he hoped most to succeed—in creating a unified black Protestant church in a South Africa built on Christian principles—yet succeeded where his actions were least tangible; in restructuring the native conceptual universe in important respects, he laid the ground for its integration into the industrial capitalist world (cf. Prins 1980:163 on the Lozi). Yet, while the signs and practices instilled by the mission came to underpin the new order, they also exposed its contradictions, and gave rise to more than one language of protest. In this way, orthodox Christianity was also to provide the instruments of its own negation.

Christianity and Colonialism: The Tswana Case

The Politics of Christianity

We begin, then, by examining the part played by missionaries in the 19th-century political life of a Tswana people, the Barolong boo Ratshidi (Tshidi).[2] The Tshidi, who lived along the Molopo River that today divides Botswana from South Africa, first met the Congregationalists of the London Missionary Society (LMS) in the 1820s (Moffat 1842:388; Molema 1966:13). The latter had set up a station in the nearby Batlhaping chiefdom; and, while they did not labor among the Tshidi, their presence in the region had much to do with the eventual founding of a Methodist mission to the Barolong.

It is impossible to know how the Tswana first perceived the Christian message; the evangelists suggest that they paid it little attention (Moffat 1842:284f.; Livingstone 1858:Chapter 1; Dachs 1972:648). But chiefs were quick to see temporal advantages in the presence of the mission, and made incessant requests for goods and military aid. The missionaries put this down to the unenlightened greed of the savage—his "carnal view of spiritual things" (Broadbent 1865:178)[3]—and yielded to many demands in the hope that it would prepare the way for their sacred task (Campbell 1822,1:74; Broadbent 1865:178).[4] As Robert Moffat (1842:284–285) explained in an unusually somber letter home:

> *Indifference and stupidity form the wreath on every brow—ignorance, the grossest ignorance of Divine things, forms the basis of every action; it is only things earthly, sensual, and devilish, which stimulate to activity and mirth. . . . Only satiate their mendicant spirits by perpetually giving, and we are all that is good, but refuse to meet their demands [and] their praises are turned to ridicule.*

The Europeans did not merely bear valued goods, however; they also gained repute for their technical skills—in irrigation and the sinking of wells, for example—and for the patent superiority of their guns in a theater of spears (Moffat 1842:247, 350ff.; Campbell 1822,1:85, 101; cf. Chirenje 1976:405).[5] As a result, they themselves became a prized resource (Schapera 1958:5) and, before long, chiefs were actively engaged in competing for them—and in preventing others from doing likewise, often by resort to malicious slander (Moffat 1842:298, 389f., 414ff.).[6]

The Tshidi had also tried to attract a missionary, but ironically their first sustained contact with the Methodists came almost by accident (Broadbent 1865; Molema 1966:11–32; 1951:9f.). The encounter occurred under conditions that were to enhance the role of the church in their subsequent history (cf. Eiselin 1934:68). In the early 19th century, the rise of the Zulu state had effects that were to be felt throughout the hinterland of southern Africa. Marauding "tribes," displaced by Shaka's military campaigns, fell upon their agrarian neighbors, razing their settlements and seizing their stock (Thompson 1969:391ff.; Lye 1969). This swelling wave of destruction, known indigenously as *defikane* (upheaval), overtook the Tshidi as well. Having been attacked by the fearsome Batlokwa, they were expelled from their home on the Molopo River and sought temporary refuge with another Barolong group, the Seleka (Stow 1905:490ff.; Molema 1966:4–10, 24f.; Matthews 1945:1ff.).

Amid this unrest, the Methodists had been looking for a settled place to work and, just before the arrival of the Tshidi, had thrown in their lot with the Seleka. They were to accompany the Barolong on a series of defensive migrations, and to help them secure land from the Sotho chief, Moshweshwe. This site, Thaba 'Nchu, became the refuge of the chiefdoms for almost a decade. In fact the Seleka were to remain there permanently. There, in 1837, the Barolong met the Boers, who had embarked on their own epic migration, the Great Trek, to escape the liberalism of the Cape Colonial government.[7] It was there, too, that the Wesleyan mission set up its area headquarters (Whiteside 1906:338ff.; Molema n.d.). Eventually, after a chain of events that need not detain us, the Tshidi departed this refuge to return to their former territory. Soon after they had resettled, Chief Montshiwa, who had recently succeeded to office, decided to recruit an evangelist (*moruti*, teacher). He duly sent his half-brother, Molema—the only royal among the small band of converts—to plead their case at Thaba 'Nchu, and the Rev. Joseph Ludorf arrived at his capital in January 1850. For the first time, the Tshidi had a missionary to themselves (Molema 1966:35).

It is not possible to detail the history of the Tshidi mission here. Hence, we offer three vignettes, each representative in its own way, that should serve to make the point. One tells of the intrusion of the Methodists into the internal political life of the chiefdom; the second recounts a dramatic instance of their participation in relations among southern Tswana and the settlers of the region; and the third concerns the intervention of an influential evangelist in transactions among the local population, the colonial state, and capitalist interests.

Samuel Broadbent and the "Native Dance"

The first vignette typifies a recurring conflict: Samuel Broadbent (1865:187) recalls that, when he heard the sounds of the "native dance" in the royal court, he went out "to oppose it, and preach to those . . . willing to hear." The "dance" refers to rainmaking rites, which the missionaries recognized to be important not only to the fabric of "heathen" belief, but also to the power of the chiefship (Moffat 1842:305f.; Livingstone 1858:22; Campbell 1822,1:197). Although aided by specialist rainmakers (*baroka*), often recruited from far afield, chiefs were themselves responsible for bringing rain; in fact, their authority was intimately connected to their ritual success, and some were famed practitioners of the art (Schapera 1971). *Pula,* which meant both "rain" and "well-being," appeared conspicuously in the symbolism of political ceremonial, and rulers always greeted the people "*ka* [with] *pula*" (Solomon 1855:47; Campbell 1822,2:157–158).

Broadbent was not the only one to see rainmaking as a critical impediment to the spread of the gospel; almost every missionary felt compelled to act against it (for example, Campbell 1822,2:4; Livingstone 1858:22; Moffat 1842:305). Among the Tshidi, such efforts were to have palpable results. Later, when a small Christian congregation took root under Molema,[8] its members refused to take part in these and other communal rituals, such as male initiation (Holub 1881,1:296; Mackenzie 1871:228f.). Montshiwa insisted that they do so, declaring that he would tolerate the church only if they complied. But the converts continued to resist, and the dispute led quickly to a deep cleavage between the "people of the word" and the ruler; an effect that, as Eiselin (1934:69) noted early on, occurred throughout southern Africa. Wittingly or not—the Methodists varied greatly in the degree to which they understood the implications of their actions (cf. Beidelman 1982:27)—the attempt to subvert "heathen ceremonies" sharpened a contradiction in their own project. It was a contradiction that was to have consequences far beyond their control.

On one hand, the Methodists had always worked under the aegis of the chiefs, soliciting their patronage and showing them deference.[9] This was not just a matter of political opportunism, although it was difficult to work where a ruler put obstacles in their path (Schapera 1958:5; Dachs 1972:648). It was also rationalized in terms of a stated commitment to the complementarity of church and state, of divine and worldly power (Moffat 1842:197f.).[10] Thus, while they argued for religious freedom for their converts, invoking the precept of individual self-determination, they avoided any hint of challenge to the "secular" legitimacy of the chiefship itself. Nor did they see why the temporal office could not coexist with a strong Christian presence; in their own society, after all, this was still positively valued. Indeed, *pace* the "missionary imperialist" thesis—which holds that the Protestants among the Tswana, finding local sovereigns an increasing thorn in their side, took steps to limit their power[11]—all evidence suggests that the Wesleyans desired a strong polity under a head, pagan or Christian, who could sustain order, and so provide a stable context for their efforts (Molema n.d.; Methodist Missionary Society n.d.).[12] Even if they had wished to dismantle the office, however, the events set in motion by their actions were to make any such intervention irrelevant.

For, on the other hand, by advancing the cause of Christianity as they did, the Wesleyans, like other missionaries in Africa (see, for example, Eiselin 1934:69; Ekechi 1972:36ff.; Beidelman 1982:25), eroded not only the spiritual aspect of the chiefship but its entire foundation. In seeking to restore religious authority to God, they drove a wedge between two dimensions of power and legitimacy which, for Tswana, were indissoluble. That is why, once they saw that the missions were there to stay, rulers worried about the long-term implications—notwithstanding the material benefits they might gain. As early as 1820, one chief told the Rev. John Campbell that he had been warned that the evangelists would make him "their servant" (Campbell 1822,1:77; cf. Chirenje 1976:403). The point, however, was not merely that the missions undermined royal sovereignty by opposing communal rites that were essential to the ruler's control over people and property. Nor was it that Christianity threatened the relations of inequality and servitude which made possible the extraction of labor and tribute (Mackenzie 1871:230; Livingstone 1858:123). It was rather that the unravelling of *puso* (government)—and its division into discrete domains of religion and politics, chapel and chiefship—engendered a new pluralism. For whatever the intentions of the mission, its converts remade the political sociology of the church in their own image. Around it they created another center, with its own leadership, power relations, and symbolic resources; and, in so doing, they expressed in Christian idiom long-standing tensions surrounding the chiefship. The intrusion of Christianity, in other words, attacked the real basis of the office: its *exclusive* dominion over the political process and, with it, every sphere of social life.

In sum, where before the chiefship was the epicenter of the social and symbolic world, it now became one of two foci of authority (cf. Chirenje 1976:401). Nor was the church any less "political" than the royal court. Indeed, its first native leader, Molema, later made a direct bid for chiefly office (J. L. Comaroff 1973:310), and for a century his descendants were to challenge the legitimacy of the ruling line. With the waning of the resources invested in the office itself, its holders were to find it ever more difficult to ward off such threats; and there were times that the Molema faction gained de facto control of the polity. But the final irony was that, once he had gained supremacy in the church and had built a firm power base, Molema rejected the missionaries, making it hard for them to work among Tshidi (Holub 1881,1:280; Mackenzie 1883:33). It was Montshiwa, the heathen chief, who fostered their presence, and who, when Molema died in 1882, declared "religious freedom" (Molema 1966:204); being continuously harassed by the Boers, he was more than ever in need of an agent and an adviser. On his initiative, too, Methodism finally became the "state" religion. Thus it was that a pagan ruler ended up in alliance with the evangelists that his Christian brother had cast aside. But the mission had acquired an ally weakened by its own actions. It had also created a force that it could no longer control.

The implication is clear: from the viewpoint of the missionaries, their involvement in the internal politics of the Tshidi was always indirect, almost incidental. The intention of opposing the "native dances," seen largely as an act against "heathenism," was to reclaim religion for God and to leave secular authority intact. But, given the indigenous political culture, this was impossible, and set in motion a process that had very mixed, contradictory consequences (see Linden 1977 for a strikingly similar analysis). By fracturing the chiefship and creating a practical distinction between the "political" and the "religious," it produced a dualistic order with competing foci of power relations. Moreover, it put the evangelists themselves in an equivocal political position, placed between a weakened ruler who courted them and a strong local congregation that was much less inclined to do so.

The equivocal political position of the evangelists becomes starkly evident when the Tshidi case is placed in regional perspective. In some Tswana chiefdoms, the same process resulted in rulers themselves converting and appropriating the church—leaving the "traditional" political domain to their opponents, and seeking to isolate and exclude the mission. For example, among the Ngwato, Kgama's domination of religious affairs led to a break with "his" evangelist, Hepburn (Chirenje 1976:412). Similarly, Sekgoma of the Tawana so antagonized the LMS that it pressed for his replacement, despite a policy of noninvolvement in such matters (Maylam 1980:145, 157). In many situations, too, control over the church became embroiled in succession disputes. Given similarities in Tswana social organization, the varying impact of Christianity on the fate of *particular* chiefs was largely a function of local exigency. The precise outcome of such historical encounters always depends on the interplay of local sociocultural forms and external forces, a process mediated by human action upon the world. In this instance, the process tore at the political fabric everywhere, but the way in which it worked itself out in terms of specific power relations varied widely. One thing is clear, however. The missionaries rarely escaped being caught in the fissure that they had created between church and chiefship. Neither the motivation nor the effect of their entry into internal politics, then, is reducible to the simple terms of colonial domination that some scholars have described (for example, Temu 1972:9,132; Dachs 1972); a view that, in any case, has been increasingly qualified of late (see, for example, Strayer 1978:101).

Joseph Ludorf and the "United Tswana Nation"

The second vignette begins with the discovery of diamonds in 1867 at Hopetown on the Orange River, some 200 miles south of the Molopo region. Later, major finds were also made along the not-too-distant Vaal and Harts Rivers. Almost immediately, six parties laid claim to the territory: the Boer Republics of the Orange Free State and Transvaal, which fought the dispute in alliance with one another, and four indigenous peoples. Of these, one, the Griqua, stole a march on the others when their chief, Nicholas Waterboer, petitioned the British High Commissioner to place his dominion—including the contested area—under Her Majesty's rule. The British had kept their distance from earlier conflicts in this region, but took an undisguised interest in the new turn of events. In the meantime, the Seleka asserted rights over half the disputed land on the ground that it had been theirs prior to their flight to Thaba 'Nchu. The Tshidi complemented this by maintaining that the other half was theirs by "ancestral inheritance."

The minutiae of the dispute are not of concern here. It is enough to know that it went to arbitration, at least after several ill-tempered meetings among the parties—and some farfetched strategies to establish prior ownership. Perhaps the most quixotic was a gambit by the Republics to claim the land by cession from the King of Portugal, whose "local" representative was Governor of Quelimane in northern Mocambique, and also acted as President of the Portuguese Diplomatic Commission to the Transvaal (Molema 1966:62–64). The Bloemhof hearing of 1871, under Lieutenant-Governor Keate of Natal, looms large in both South African history and the collective recollection of the Tshidi.[13] It ended predictably, with Waterboer winning the most valuable portions of the territory, which he duly ceded to Britain. After years of unconcern, the Crown now urged the Boers to respect the rights of "native tribes in friendly alliance with her Majesty's Government" (Molema 1966:57). The Seleka and Tshidi were also awarded territory—some of it land that the Transvaal considered its own—but, alas, no gemstones.

The Barolong case at Bloemhof was led with "skill and devotion" by the Reverend Ludorf (Matthews 1945:9), former missionary to the Tshidi, who was elated by the outcome. And here is the nub of the story. At the same time as the Boer Republics were angrily denouncing the Award, Ludorf was drafting a manifesto and constitution for a "United Barolong, Batlhaping and Bangwaketse Nation." Its capital was to be at Klipdrift, in the awarded territory, and he was to be its "commissioner . . . and diplomatic agent." In this spirit, he wrote to the chiefs, evoking Isaiah:

> *And now chiefs: rulers of the land, I appeal to you. Awake: arise and unite soon before your trophy is torn asunder by wolves; come ye together, make protective laws; stop all breaches and gaps and close your ranks. Safeguard the heritage of Tau your ancestor. Hear ye chiefs: Come together and unite. (Molema 1966:66–67)*

This must rank as one of the more remarkable documents of South African mission history.[14] Ludorf was convinced that the Republics would try to make it impossible for the chiefs to take possession of the land,[15] and he was correct; the next decade was a period of unremitting hostility. Most immediately, it is clear that he envisaged an independent confederation of southern Tswana states with a formal government (Molema 1951:136). This, in his view, was the only way to avoid Boer oppression. The "United Nation" was not to be absorbed into the empire either. Ludorf wanted it protected, not colonized, by Britain.[16] The plan came to nought, though; ignored by the Crown and derided by the Boers, the evangelist took ill and died a few weeks later.

Here, then, is the odd spectacle of a missionary defending Tswana from Boer subjugation by striving to found an *autonomous* state in the crevice between settler colonialism and British imperialism. By doing so, however, he denied himself the support and resources necessary to achieve his goals—even if he had lived longer. Ludorf's lead was not followed by other evangelists. Not only did his action openly violate the separation of church and state, and thus contravene official policy; it also highlighted the fact that the missions lacked the real power to engage in such pursuits with any hope of success. Still, his campaign was not dismissed as frivolous or misguided by his colleagues (see note 14). From their perspective, the protection of Tswana from Boer "enslavement," from "tribal" wars, and from unscrupulous freebooters was vital to their work. In this situation, it was difficult to avoid being drawn into "politics." And where it happened, it made as much sense, in principle at least, to promote an independent native state as it did to call for British overrule—which might later place constraints on the evangelists, who would themselves be subject to its authority. Both courses fell within the compass of mission ideology: it was a question on which reasonable men could, and did, disagree. The role of the missionary in concrete political process, in other words, was *intrinsically* indeterminate. Methodism did not, because it could not, mandate any one course of action. And even if it had, the Christians had little political capital, so that there was no guarantee that any position they adopted would ever be realized—whether or not it bore the visible imprimatur of imperialism.

John Mackenzie and the "Imperial Factor"

The final vignette narrates a different, yet complementary, story. It involves John Mackenzie of the LMS, who worked primarily among the Ngwato rather than the Tshidi, but who had great impact on the political destiny of all Tswana.[17] Indeed, if anyone might properly be termed a "missionary imperialist" it was he (Dachs 1972; Sillery 1971:183; see note 11). He would have regarded the description as both accurate and laudatory.

The bitter hostilities that followed the diamond field dispute gave the missionaries cause to fear for the lives and property of their congregants. Then, in 1878, amid the turmoil, there was an uprising on the part of some Tswana groupings to the south of the Tshidi. This uprising expressed dissatisfaction with the new province of Griqualand West, created after

Waterboer's cession (see above), and with the growing threat to the local chiefdoms posed by settlers and traders in the region. During the rising, the LMS station at Kuruman was attacked. Mackenzie, who was there at the time, blamed the nefarious intentions of the Boers and the lack of a strong British presence to control them. Thus, when the Boers persisted in occupying land given to the chiefdoms by Keate, Mackenzie decided that only firm political measures would stop them. He had long entertained hopes of imperial intervention. These now crystallized into a complex plan for implementing a form of indirect rule (Mackenzie 1887,1:passim; cf. Sillery 1971:Chapter 7; W. D. Mackenzie 1902). Like Ludorf, he believed that a political solution had become unavoidable; but his schemes involved the full weight of the Crown.

In contrast to most of his contemporaries, Mackenzie argued that blacks should eventually enjoy equal rights in a federated, nonracial South Africa, the goal being to ensure that "class would not be arrayed against class; the hatches would not be battened down over the heads of blacks, to be opened in bloodshed at some future period" (quoted in Sillery 1971:51). To this end, the Tswana ought not be governed by any colony, English or Dutch, but directly by imperial rule from London. Note the distinction between colonialism and imperialism here: it was crucial to the actors of the period, as it determined who would actually wield authority over the natives—and to what end. Mackenzie was an unyielding imperialist. He urged Britain to annex the borderland in order to stop freebooters and colonists from dispossessing the Tswana and reducing them to servitude. The plan specified arrangements for tenure, taxation, and "Territorial Government" in the dominion, which would later become part of a grand confederation of (British) Austral Africa. Mackenzie's preference for imperial rulers, rather than whites of settler or colonial origin, was phrased in language remarkable for the time. In his view, "one class of farmers" could not "legislate for another and unrepresented class." Because both the whites and the blacks were agriculturalists, the former could not oversee the latter without conflict of interest (see Sillery 1971:52).

Mackenzie pressed his plan on British authorities whenever possible, and found a sympathetic ear in Sir Bartle Frere, High Commissioner and Governor of the Cape, who conceded that the regulation of the frontier was beyond the scope of his colonial administration. The missionary persuaded him of the material and humanitarian advantages of an imperial presence, and this was conveyed to London. Although wary of the plan at first, the Colonial Office slowly warmed to it. Frere went as far as to invite Mackenzie to be Commissioner for Bechuanaland when a protectorate was created, and the LMS was asked for its approval. But the directors rejected "such a corporeal union of Church and State," referring[18]

> *to the sensitiveness of the natives . . . and their suspicion of, not to say hostility to, the British Government. Recently they appear to have regarded the Missionary as well as other white men, as linked in some way with the British Government, and this impression is likely to be deepened if one of the Missionary circle should become a government official* (Mackenzie 1887,1:115)

All this was premature, though: in 1880, Gladstone's liberal government came to power in England and quickly vetoed the proposal. In light of reverses elsewhere in the empire and with contemporary opinion opposed to further expansion, the annexation of Bechuanaland lost its appeal.

Mackenzie renewed his campaign with yet greater vigor. A complicated story, its next stage included a furlough in England in 1882–84, during which he canvassed widely and, with other humanitarian and economic interest groups, formed the South African Committee. Through a series of Conventions and parliamentary debates in the aftermath of the first Anglo-Boer War of 1880–81, the Committee tried to affect foreign policy, using the press, the public platform, and personal influence (Mackenzie 1887,1:131–178). Its efforts were finally rewarded, though it took an offer from the Cape Colony to shoulder part of the administrative cost before Gladstone's government would agree to establish a protectorate in Bechuanaland When it did, in 1884, Mackenzie was invited to become the resident Deputy Commissioner. He accepted, and duly left the LMS (Dachs, 1975:164ff.).

Two things should be noted about these events. The first is that Colonial Office personnel were unhappy with Mackenzie's appointment, expressly because it was not clear whether "the High Commissioner or H. M. Government would be able to control him" (quoted in Sillery 1971:82). But, they reassured themselves, they "could so easily get rid of him."[19] Second, their perception of Mackenzie's mandate was the inverse of his own. For the Colonial Office, his utility lay in his influence over the natives, and his ability to keep them from acts of aggression[20]; for him, it was a chance to husband the interests of the chiefdoms, to protect *them* from the whites (Mackenzie 1887,1:168–178, 181–199).

In South Africa itself,[21] the appointment was condemned by the Boers, for obvious reasons, and by many English-speaking Cape parliamentarians. Some of these politicians enjoyed the support of the local Afrikaner Bond (an association that embraced Dutch-speaking settlers across the country), and were particularly anxious that its members not be offended. Among them was Cecil Rhodes, already a magnate and a cabinet minister, whose own expansionist agenda at the time required amicable relations between the colonies and republics. For him, the "Imperial Factor" represented by Mackenzie was anathema: he envisaged an African dominion securely under the control of interests at the Cape. Bechuanaland, a vital link in its establishment, had thus to be absorbed by the Colony. The Governor and High Commissioner, Sir Hercules Robinson, concurred, leaving Mackenzie isolated and powerless. Under these unpromising conditions he left for Bechuanaland—not the large Protectorate that was to become Botswana, but the much smaller, ill-defined territory of British Bechuanaland, consisting mainly of southern Tswana land that had not yet been expropriated by whites.

Mackenzie's first goal was to settle outstanding disputes among the chiefdoms, the Transvaal, the white farmers, and the freebooters. The latter had formed two tiny republics, Stellaland and Goshen, from which they had repeatedly raided the Tlhaping and Tshidi. He proceeded to castigate the whites, to try and restore land they had taken from the Tswana, and to plead for armed help to quiet the troubled region. This further alienated the Boers, the Cape government, and the High Commissioner. As the situation degenerated, his requests met with increasingly irritable rejection from Robinson, who eventually recalled him for consultation and asked Rhodes to act in his stead. Mackenzie never did return to office. Opinion at the Cape was inclining toward the annexation of Bechuanaland, Rhodes himself taking a lead in bringing the case to the public eye; in so doing, he portrayed Mackenzie as an irrational protagonist of the blacks (Sillery 1971:105). In the face of growing hostility, the missionary resigned.

One final chapter in the career of John Mackenzie is salient here. It concerns a subsequent visit to Bechuanaland, in 1885, with the Warren Expedition, a force dispatched when the Colonial Office at last decided to put an end to the continuing attacks on native populations.[22] As a result of this foray, the Protectorate over the southern Tswana formally became the Crown Colony of British Bechuanaland,[23] and another Protectorate was established over the northern Tswana. The latter, however, was *not* a product of Mackenzie's effort; it was a preventive imperial response to rumors of German involvement in South West Africa (Maylam 1980:26; Halpern 1965:86). When the measure was explained to the chiefs, three of them made written offers of tracts of land for European settlement, this ostensibly being in "exchange" for the protection of the Crown. The missionary was instrumental in prompting these offers, albeit covertly, and is said to have "deliberately concealed his own handwriting of the [Ngwato] offer" (Dachs 1972:657; cf. Sillery 1971:130). While this chiefly gesture was curtly declined by the High Commissioner, the founding of the Colony and the Protectorate, under imperial rule, was a step in the direction of Mackenzie's original scheme.

It was thus only after he left government that Mackenzie saw his vision partially realized—and then due to a totally extraneous factor. It was also a short-term victory, as British Bechuanaland was to be annexed to the Cape a decade later, and the fate of the Protectorate was to hang in the balance for many years. But most ironic, perhaps, is the fact that Mackenzie's own part in the process was criticized by some missionaries as a violation of native interest. Rev. John Moffat described the "offers" elicited from the chiefs as "wholesale robbery of the Bechuana people under the guise of a philanthropic scheme for protecting them."[24] Moffat was himself to leave the LMS for government service. But his stance on policy was very different from that of Mackenzie. When Rhodes and the British South Africa Company sought control of Bechuanaland and the interior, he acted on its behalf (Sillery 1971:160f.; Maylam 1980:28). Mackenzie, by contrast, continued to fight against the "capitalists"—whom he expressly opposed to imperialists and philanthropists (see Dachs 1975:259)—and never missed an opportunity to rail against the mercenary goals of Rhodes. Where Moffat was happy to fuse mercantile and political agency in administering native territories, and was more sympathetic to rule from Cape Town than from London,[25] Mackenzie stuck to his imperialism. Indeed, he never abandoned his idyll of Bechuanaland as a settled agrarian society; a society in which white and black farmers might live together under an avuncular British authority, responsible only to the Colonial Office, which would "supercede" (if not remove) the chiefs and ensure the security of private property. But his ability to achieve this dream had always been limited by the lack of a power base, and by 1892 a Colonial Office minute described Mackenzie as an "extinct volcano."[26]

This fragment underlines the sheer complexity surrounding the political agency of missionaries in colonial southern Africa. It does so precisely because John Mackenzie was emphatic in presenting himself as a truly "humane" imperialist; although, of course, the imperialism for which he fought was barely recognizable in Cape Town, or even in London, where the cause of native rights was never a high priority, and where the evangelist was treated as anything from a mild irritation to a dangerous subversive. The primary relevance of his historical role to our analysis here is twofold.

One dimension concerns Mackenzie's encounter with the LMS position on the "corporeal union of Church and State." In order to influence policy, an evangelist had not just to defy official mission ideology; he had somehow to penetrate government circles. This, after all, was the bitter lesson of many unsuccessful entreaties to Whitehall and the Cape on the question of native rights. It is no coincidence that the most visible "missionary imperialists," like Mackenzie and John Moffat, were those who left the Society and took administrative positions. But, in so doing, they found themselves politically isolated. On one hand, they received no open support from their colleagues, who wished not to be tainted by association with government. Yet, on the other, they were not career politicians and had no autonomous power base. However charismatic an evangelist might have been, in other words, the nature of his relationship to formal political institutions limited his influence. It will be recalled that, for all Mackenzie's fervent campaigns, the creation of a Protectorate over Bechuanaland came as a result of Anglo-German diplomacy, and had little to do with him. Similarly, notwithstanding his efforts to oppose Rhodes and the "capitalists," the Cape colonialists and the Boers, theirs were the decisive voices in the debate over Bechuanaland. In yet another historical irony, it was an abortive attack on the Transvaal by troops of the British South Africa Company, the notorious Jameson Raid of 1895, that prevented the Protectorate from falling into mercantilist hands; and all this *after* Mackenzie had become an "extinct volcano." But perhaps the most poignant comment on his impotence was the dispatch with which he was relieved of office the moment he actually tried to play the role of imperialist.

In short, even the most politically active and imperialistically driven of missionaries were relatively ineffectual in the *realpolitik* of empire. The majority, of course, had no overt part in it anyway. And when they did, their intentions were often perverted in unexpected ways. Thus, for example, Mackenzie's appeal for armed support to protect Bechuanaland ended in his losing his post to a rival imperialist, Rhodes; yet this very intervention led to the founding of a Crown Colony soon after, and to Mackenzie being accused of "wholesale robbery."

All this, in turn, raises a second point, one which we first encountered in Ludorf's case. Even where missionaries wished to exert influence in the public domain, nothing in their Christianity per se prescribed one political doctrine above all others. Thus, both Mackenzie and Moffat saw themselves as champions of native rights, but one served the British South Africa Company and Cape Colonial interests while the other was a faithful advocate of the "Imperial Factor." This is hardly surprising, since the colonial history of southern Africa involved a long and sometimes acrid argument; an argument that, in the rhetoric of the time, cast metropolitan imperialist against settler colonialist, capitalist against philanthropist, and, on occasion, mercantilist against industrialist. Nor were the disagreements trivial, since they implied very different destinies for the victims. Yet there was nothing in nonconformist dogma that determined the stand to be adopted by the missionaries in the debate. They could—indeed, they had to—take sides. But the moment they did, they lost any *collective* identity in the political process. The "role of the missionary," in short, became indeterminate.

This is not to say that missionaries were never catalysts, or that they did not connive in the cause of the European domination of southern Africa (see, for example, Bundy 1979:36ff.). Nonetheless, as actors in the domain of formal politics, their generic role was necessarily equivocal. As the three vignettes suggest, they varied widely in their efforts to wield temporal influence. And for good structural reasons, they were rarely potent figures in the political arena, the consequences of their actions in that domain often being beyond their control. Moreover, far from speaking with a single voice, they expressed a variety of attitudes (cf. Beidelman 1982:30), ranging along the axes of argument present in the secular discourses of the era. This again was a function of their situation in the colonial world. As all this suggests, in summary, the position of the missionary in the realm of institutional political processes could not but be uncertain in its contemporary impact and ambiguous in its historical implications (cf. Crummey 1972:150f.). But this, as we have said, is only one part of a more complex story.

The Method in the Mission

We turn, then, to the second level of the missionary project distinguished above—that which lay implicit within the very nature of evangelical practice, and which, in its challenge to the Tswana world, laid down the terms of colonial subjection (cf. Bohannan 1964:22f.).

The Tswana system, c. 1830, was founded on a set of contradictory sociocultural principles. An agnatic ideology existed side by side with a form of endogamy that limited the emergence of descent corporations, and bred a field of ambiguous social relations. What is more, forces for political centralization and hierarchy were opposed by tendencies toward the dispersal and individuation of households. As we show elsewhere (for example, J. L. Comaroff 1982; J. Comaroff 1985), the conflicts generated by this structure had to be addressed in everyday practice—practice that, in turn, gave shape to communities on the ground. For example, the management of personal identity was made necessary by the contradictory implications of marriage arrangements; for, while agnation and matrilaterality involved contrasting values for the Tswana, father's brother's daughter unions confounded these categories, forging bonds simultaneously agnatic and matrilateral. Much of the stress on individual self-construction in Tshidi society, in fact, flowed from the attempt to reduce the ambiguities of relationship and rank created by these arrangements. Clearly, however, this mode of self-construction was very different from that envisaged in 19th-century Protestantism.

The reproduction of centralized chiefdoms, and the social order at large, involved politicoritual processes which imposed an authoritative imprint on the everyday world. Crucial here was the molding of the person and his or her experience in the context of mundane activity. Hence, built form and the organization of space marked out an asymmetrical opposition between the center of the polity (embodied in the chief and his court) and its productive periphery (the domestic unit whose material form invoked the female body). This spatial logic was reinforced by a division of labor in which women's labor and reproductive power subsidized the male construction of the social community.

Men represented themselves and communal values through the pliable medium of cattle, which served as both a currency and an icon of politico-economic relations. The husbandry and exchange of stock enabled the transaction of reproductive rights, the siphoning of ancestral power, and the creation of bonds of inequality and dependency. Thus the circulation of beasts complemented cultivation and nurture, and sustained the contrasts between center and periphery, politics and production, chief and commoner, male and female. And while the polity constantly threatened to fragment under the weight of its internal contradictions, the tendency was countered, for the most part, by the repeated symbolic restatement of established hierarchical arrangements. Further, this scheme implied a mode of being in which material objects were not definitively set apart from human subjects. Products embodied the social processes of their own construction (cf. Taussig 1980:36), and "time" and "work" were immanent features of such processes themselves (J. Comaroff 1985:127). Visible and invisible forces in the world existed in a reciprocal relationship, and material and moral being were interdependent. If chiefly potency waned, so did the productive capacity of the community. If polluting sexuality overflowed moral bounds, the land as a whole would be "spoiled."

It was into this world, this meaningful terrain that "comes without saying because it goes without saying" (Bourdieu 1977:167), that the nonconformist evangelists entered in the 19th century. While the literature on missions in colonial Africa affirms that their sway in matters specifically "religious" and "political" varied widely (see, for example, Crummey 1972:150f.; Strayer 1978:100ff.), many accounts speak similarly of their thoroughgoing influence on different aspects of the everyday world (see, for example, Schapera 1936:228f.; Bohannan 1964:22; Ekechi 1972:16f.; Etherington 1978:115f.; Beidelman 1982:11, 26f., 133f.; MacGaffey 1983:113f.). Their effect on Tswana social life was indeed pervasive. But it was in the *total* configuration of their imprint on seemingly disparate aspects of the mundane that their true impact lay (cf. Bundy 1979:37). The seeds sown in the humble soil of everyday Tshidi practice were to mature and to change local horizons irreversibly; "God's gardeners"—as they liked to call themselves—did more than just prepare the ground for colonial penetration.[27]

The implicit structures of the Methodist mission originated in late 18th-century British nonconformism, the product of the radical reorganization of productive relations set in motion by industrialization. Directed at the emerging working and middle-classes of the northern river valleys (Troeltsch 1949,2:721; Warner 1930:165), its message was of salvation attainable through arduous and methodical self-construction. Its rhetorical forms were cast in the factory and the foundry, and its model of orderly process was that of the self-regulating market. Wesley's creed celebrated an individualistic, free enterprise of the spirit. Money, "that precious talent which contains all the rest" (Warner 1930:155, quoting Wesley), featured prominently, being the sanctified currency of what had become a moral economy. This creed was a particular transformation of the Protestant ethic: it naturalized the essential categories and relations of industrial capitalism, centering its discourse upon the values of wage labor and private property, and discouraging any activity designed to subvert the divinely wrought inequality of the workplace (Warner 1930:125, 146f.). But its primary focus was the subject divided, charged with the duty of creating an immortal self, and submitting the body, now shameful and transient, to sober constraint.

We shall trace the impact of this ideology on the Tshidi by examining the introduction of a set of key practices which gave coherence to the mission project throughout the colonial epoch. For, while thwarted in their early effort to gain converts—apparently by the natives' "carnal view of spiritual things" (see p. 3)—the Christians proceeded to set up, piece by piece, the necessary techniques of "cultivation": the practical and social tools that would make the "wilderness . . . become a fruitful field" (Broadbent 1865:204). Trexler (1984:193) has asserted that, in 17th-century Mexico, Spanish Catholics measured spiritual conquest "not by the assimilation of ideas but by the native's physical and verbal comportment, which was called 'devotion.' " But where such Catholic evangelism relied heavily on collective ritual and dramatic spectacle, mission theater often incorporating local populations in a depiction of their own subjection, the nonconformist tradition was to use a less visible but more intrusive medium. It taught the unassuming "arts of civilization" (Mackenzie, in Dachs 1975:72), whose mundane logic worked upon the processes that most forcefully shaped the self and "natural" reality.

In fact, it was in the sphere of agricultural production that the nonconformists were to make their first tangible mark on the Tswana. Although their notion of labor had been shaped by the conditions of the urban workplace—they were themselves drawn from the ranks of artisans and the lower middle class (cf. Etherington 1978:29; Chadwick 1966,1:371)—the iconography of the now marginalized English peasantry provided their model of preindustrial peoples elsewhere. Biblical imagery came to their aid in injecting this vision with the values of industry and commerce. The Reverend Mackenzie again[28]:

> *In order to complete the work of elevating the people, we must teach them the arts of civilized life. . . . If they are no longer to start upon the marauding expedition, if they are not to depend upon the precarious results of the chase, then we must teach them to till their own land, sow and reap their own crops, build their own barns, as well as tend their own flocks. . . . [The missionary] longs to see . . . the African ship weighted with the produce of African soil and the results of African industry, mingling on the great ocean with ships of other lands, and returning home laden with the varied treasures of commerce. (Dachs 1975:721)*

No sooner had they built their first station among Barolong, than the evangelists laid out fields, demonstrated the utilities of the plow, and tackled the most acute limitation of local production—uncertain rainfall. With their implements they began to dig wells (Broadbent 1865:96), and their ability to draw water from beneath the ground made a deep impression on the Tshidi. But water, as we noted, was a symbolically charged resource in this drought-stricken land, the capacity to make rain being a crucial component of chiefly authority (see above). Already the missionary was picking at the seams of sovereign power. Nor did his well challenge just the ruler's control over fertility; it represented a novel resource to be freely obtained through the voluntary input of labor. Such were the values held out to potential converts, whose identification with the church would be marked by the trappings of propertied individualism.

In the Methodist model of peasant production, moreover, the plow was to be the major implement, its import being as much ideological as technical. It was adopted by many southern Tswana after 1830, and this, more than any formal act of "conversion," marked their entry into a world of commodity relations. For the plow not only permitted the yield of marketable surpluses, spurred on by missionary exhortations toward self-improvement and a novel structure of wants. It also had a thoroughgoing effect on the social division of labor (cf. Schapera 1936:242; Etherington 1978:119ff.; Ranger 1978:109). Because it required animals for draught, it breached the boundary between the formerly discrete arable and pastoral sectors; and, since females were precluded from handling cattle, the prime repository of male value, men assumed direct control over plow cultivation. Women, consequently, were relegated to the devalued tasks of tending and reaping, and lost their influence over the disposal of crops. The division of labor was based increasingly on the individuated household and agriculture became subject to the same competitive inequalities that surrounded the husbandry of stock. Only some units were able to mobilize draught teams, and prior patterns of stratification became more marked. Indeed, there grew up a small category of commercial farmers whose less affluent fellows soon became vulnerable to various forms of clientage and to the impending forces of proletarianization. It was in this manner that mission cultivation anticipated the reaping of a colonial harvest.

In terms of the categories of mission culture—the nuclear family, the private estate, and marriage as a sacred contract between individuals—the natives lived in sloth and moral chaos (cf. Vilakazi 1962:121). The point has been made repeatedly in accounts of missions in Africa. Protestant ideology presupposed the monogamous household as the elemental unit of production and consumption. Thus, at the same time as they introduced the plow, with all its social and material corollaries, the evangelists took pains to denounce such practices as polygyny and the "collective" ownership of resources (Broadbent 1865:85). If civilization was to flourish, the "holy family" of the Christian cosmos, and its conventional, gender-based division of labor, had to triumph over "communistic" interdependence. But a more implicit pursuit of this argument was to occur in respect of the shapes and connotations of built form and organized space. For the Christians saw the concentric arcs of Tswana circular settlements—their "heaps of . . . huts jostled together" (Broadbent 1865:189)—as material impediments to "healthy individualistic competition" (Mackenzie, quoted in Dachs 1972:652).

The imposition of the square on the circle seems to have epitomized the "orientation" of cultural evangelism (cf. Lévi-Strauss 1972:204). Mission buildings were placed at chiefly discretion within the arc of his centralized domain, and were square, free-standing structures on securely fenced lots. The distribution and external marking of buildings distinguished the sacred from the secular, the public from the private. The spatial organization of activities among church, schoolroom, printing press, and fields was governed by European divisions of time and labor. The early evangelists, like the South African regime that followed them, were to try to "rationalize" African communities by laying upon them the geometric grid of "civilization," arguably also a form conducive to the building up of hierarchical structures (Bundy 1979:37). Would-be converts were encouraged to build "neat" square houses on discretely enclosed sites—models of moral and material propriety, cut loose from the ramifying connections of indigenous production and exchange. Of course, "civilized" homes were made of "proper" materials, "fitted up," as one contemporary observer put it, "in European style" (Holub 1881, vol. 2:13), and implying a new order of "needs" that hitched these communities irrevocably to the commodity market. Such standards of Christian decency also applied to dress, and converts had to ensure that their distinction from their fellows was shown in their attire (cf. Beidelman 1982:20). "Traditional" body coverings were tantamount to nakedness in missionary eyes, and expressed a flagrant lack of physical containment:

> *for if a man becomes a Christian he cannot continue to live in the habits of a heathen. The African who believes that Jesus is preparing for him a glorious mansion in Heaven, will endeavor to build for himself a decent house on earth; and he who anticipates being hereafter attired in the pure white robe of the Redeemer's righteousness, will now throw aside the filthy garments of the heathen. (Mackenzie, in Dachs 1975:72)*

To this end, the evangelists ensured that local communities were well served by colonial merchants (Moffat 1842:605). A moral discourse about bodily shame and physical modesty, rather than any material coercion (Foucault 1980), ensured a continuing demand for such "necessities" of civilization. As Etherington has noted in the Nguni context,

> *The clothing which zealous missionaries thrust upon their converts for the sake of modesty . . . was for a time the most distinct emblem of black Christianity. Whether the convert earned his shirt by working for wages or fabricated it with European looms and needles, he was entering into new kinds of economic relationships. (1978:116)*

The practical reforms initiated by the missionaries also entailed a particular conception of time (cf. Wilson 1971:73). Thus, Moffat (1842:339) tells how, "when the place of worship was built, a wooden Dutch clock had been fixed upon the wall, for the purpose of regulating the hours of worship." The weekly schedule and annual calendar of the church ordered everyday routine in both its secular and sacred dimensions, demarcating what in the Tshidi world had been a continuous cycle of events and seasons. In the mission itself, the neophyte was set on the path to redemption when his career was objectified in time—time here being seen as a resource to be put to work in the interests of moral and material accumulation. And in its schools, as Oliver (1952:52) has said of East Africa, "life was regulated almost as severely by the mission bell as it was in England by the factory hooter." Thompson (1967) has argued that the impersonal clock is the fundamental instrument for inculcating the organizational forms of capitalist production. It enables labor to be prized free from its embeddedness in a field of generalized social relations, rendering it measurable in terms that permit its transfer from worker to employer. This was to be the fate of the Tswana as colonial subjects, but they were first introduced to time as commodity by the evangelists, whose model of "industry" dictated that every mortal put his temporal resources to work on his own account, and whose church bells punctuated local community rhythms, announcing to one and all the worth of timeliness. This had special significance here since, as we have noted (see note 1), the missionaries did not set up residential stations, but lived among the people, seeing themselves as a leaven in the midst of the uncivilized.

The objectification of time into a commodity, then, abstracted what had formerly been an intrinsic aspect of social practice. A parallel process occurred with the introduction of literacy, an essential component of the nonconformist mission. For Protestantism was the faith of the book, in that it required the convert to make a self-conscious commitment to "the word," that is, to a textualized truth (Beidelman 1982:14). Chapel and school stood side by side, for learning was universally regarded by evangelists "as the door to the church" (Etherington 1978:54); and, as has been widely acknowledged, the missionaries were perhaps the most significant agents of Western education in colonial Africa. The Methodists among the Tswana devoted considerable energy to translating, printing, and teaching the bible—by 1830, 200 pupils were being instructed on a regular basis (Broadbent 1865:175)—and gradually created an "elite" that was to step forward when the colonial government needed to staff the lower reaches of its bureaucracy. Even those not drawn by the Christian message sent their children to the mission schools (Chirenje 1976:411).

But the effect of this literacy campaign was not merely to train personnel to minister colonial rule. The written word also has the capacity to transform the consciousness of those who come into contact with it, taking language out of its immediate context of use and reference.[29] Like time and money, it circulates in disembodied form—in this case, as tracts available for consumption. The act of reading, of course, involves a silent, private transaction, an apparent exchange of reason between reader and message. It is an exchange which cannot but impinge on experience, as is indicated by the reflections of early Tshidi writers on their own history, culture, and political predicament (for example, Plaatje n.d.; Molema 1920; Matthews 1945).

As this suggests, literacy, along with time and money, may engender a novel perception of the world and the place of the actor within it. In the case of the Methodist mission, it served to open up a discourse about the self as both subject and object, and encouraged the transcendence of a purely sensual existence. The effort to instill a sense of rational self-consciousness, so central to nonconformist evangelism, helped to create a subject divided—just as the introduction of "money" and the abstraction of "time" encouraged that divided self to seek its spiritual destiny by alienating its labor in return for wages. These processes tended to resituate the person within the material and meaningful relations of the industrial world. Not surprisingly, later generations of illiterate Tshidi were to try to regain a sense of lost mastery over their universe through the symbolic manipulation of money and the printed word (J. Comaroff 1985:226, 235f., 250).

Thus, the seemingly disparate facets of the practical mission—agricultural reform, the reconstruction of personhood and social space, and the abstraction of time and the word—all reinforced each other, regrouping on native soil to form an analogue of their European parent culture. This unity was compelling, drawing the Tswana into its orbit however tangentially they took part in the "religious" activities of the church. Christianity first took root in the fissures of the local polity, initially attracting the marginal and the powerless; yet the mission, by its very presence, engaged all Tshidi in an inescapable dialogue on its own terms, even if they rejected its message. This dialogue had two consequences. First, it marked out a contrast between *sekgoa* (European ways) and *setswana* (Tswana ways), the latter being objectified, as never before, into a system of signs and conventions. And, second, it set in motion a confrontation between these two "systems," a confrontation that had a palpable effect on both. For Christianity was received through the grid of local cultural forms and became the subject of an extended process of accommodation and struggle. In its course, Tshidi were transformed by Methodism even while they resisted or remolded its more explicit doctrines and practices. It is true that the direct appeal of the church varied within the community: as in many other African contexts, senior royals remained aloof until after overrule; junior royals, the poor, and women of all ranks found identification more immediately congenial. But when all was said and done, conversation with the mission engendered conversion—not as an all-or-none commitment to Protestant ideology, but as a subtle internalization of its categories and values. Only this can explain why many Tswana (and others like them in South Africa; Bundy 1979) sought to participate in commodity and labor markets *before* the formation of the colonial state, when the taxation and other coercive measures forced them to do so.

Revelation and Resistance

We have demonstrated that the manifest "political" role of the missionaries to the Tshidi was inherently ambiguous. Yet, we have argued, they had a decisive impact on this chiefdom, instilling in its population the signs and practices of a powerful new order. In this respect, they played a vital part in the more general process of colonization; for while the incorporation of a subject people always involved some degree of material coercion, it was the subtle inculcation of European values that was especially crucial (Schapera 1936:225; Bohannan 1964:22). Indeed, precisely because this mode of penetration was ostensibly apolitical—and rarely seen to be objectionable because it was rarely seen at all (Bourdieu 1977:167)—it had enormous historical force. But the story does not end there. We also suggested, at the outset, that it was in the relationship between the two dimensions of the historical role of the missionary that the contradictions of the colonial process are revealed.

In patiently nurturing the Protestant subject in South Africa, the missionary made it possible for him to become a colonial object. Once they had been enticed, often unwittingly, into the conversation with Christianity, Tshidi were drawn into a dialogue whose terms they could not but internalize—a dialogue that cast them as citizens in a world of rational individualism. In this world, they were told, they could fashion their own lives by exercising free choice; personal achievement would be rewarded by the accumulation of goods and moral worth. Practically speaking, this meant cultivating for the market or selling their labor. After all, they had been taught to put time to work, and to want what money could buy. In other words, they were not merely prepared for wage labor and for cash cropping, the two sides of the role of peasant proletarian that was to become the lot of most black South Africans. They were also made familiar with all the positive values said to go with the marketplace, including a series of sociocultural forms. Most notably among these was the monogamous (nuclear) family, the unit of production and consumption basic to the division of labor in industrial capitalist society. As we have noted, many Tshidi did not respond to the message exactly as the Methodists might have liked. Apart from all else, they read it through the filter of their own culture. And in any case, as Williams (1977:113) has noted, no hegemony is ever complete. Still, its impact on Tshidi consciousness ran very deep.

This, however, is where the paradox lay. The Methodist mission might have proclaimed the right of self-determination for all, and taught the Tshidi the language that colonialism compelled them to speak (see Molema 1966). But they were not in a position to deliver the liberal democracy promised by their ideology and implied by their practices. That they could not do so was due to the very indeterminacy of their role in "political" processes. Because, at the level of explicit power relations, they could be neither imperialists nor liberators—if anything, they were more likely to be hostages to the vagaries of local circumstance—they lacked the ability to carve out the universe of which a Ludorf or a Mackenzie might have dreamed (cf. Crummey 1972:4).

In short, the evangelists, by virtue of their politics of the spirit, introduced the Tshidi to an altogether novel world view. Yet, lacking the manifest power to consummate their project, they could not produce the world to go with it. As a result, they succeeded only in exposing native communities to more coercive forces. Thus, as the first generation of colonial subjects entered the workplace in an ostensibly Christian state, they were quickly made aware of the discrepancy between the values learned from the mission and the harsh realities of life in a racially coded society. The literate began to interrogate the biblical text, and to question how accurately it captured their own experience. It was they who were to express the first open resistance to the colonial order by pointing to its inconsistency with biblical injunction, and by freeing from the holy text itself a charter for liberation: the message of the chosen suffering in exile, whose historical destiny was to regain their promised land.

At first, this interrogation, among the Tshidi as elsewhere, occurred primarily among the small black bourgeoisie in the context of the church itself. But it did not remain long within those confines. When the South African Native National Congress (forerunner of the African National Congress) was founded in 1912, many of its leaders were alumni of the mission schools and active members of their congregations (cf. Rotberg 1965:146–147 on Zambia). Others, however, contested the legitimacy of the orthodox denominations, and so there emerged an independent Black Christian movement (Sundkler 1961). But for adherents of this movement, no less than for their counterparts in the missions, the language of protest remained within terms that had been introduced by the evangelists (Gerhart 1978:39ff.). Hence, the struggle was framed in the rhetoric of liberal democracy, individual equality, and the separation of church and state. In fact, the early leaders spent much time and energy claiming human rights by virtue of having proven themselves sufficiently "civilized" to act as responsible citizens. Even in its ostensible rejection, the culture of the mission, now heavily reinforced by the ideology of the South African state, had triumphed.

There was another, and eventually more widespread, statement of resistance to the hegemony of the new order. It was the response, largely if not exclusively, of the illiterate peasant proletarian underclass and found its expression in popular cult movements such as Zionist Christianity. Here there emerged a different form of protest, one that remained largely implicit in the practices of the small churches. These churches were often more radical in their rejection of the colonial and postcolonial worlds than were other black denominations, for they set about reclaiming the everyday domains that had been transformed by the mission and the social order it heralded (Sundkler 1961; Kiernan 1976). Within such sects as the Zion Christian Church, the definition of personhood, community, work, space, and time—as well as the ostensible division of "religion" and "politics" inherent in mission culture—are all vigorously contested. But here, too, the categories of that culture provide the signs, the points of departure, for the acts of reversal and inversion that have served to mark an opposition to Protestant orthodoxy and all it represents. Indeed, this provides final evidence for the thoroughgoing efficacy of missionary colonization.

Conclusion

We began by distinguishing two forms of power, each associated with one dimension of the role of the missions among the Tswana. With respect to the first, power exercised in the domain of institutionalized politics, we showed that the historical agency of the evangelists was necessarily indeterminate. This was not because they were an aggregate of random individuals, each behaving according to his own lights; nor was it due to systematic variation in factors social and theological. It stemmed, rather, from the fact that nonconformist Protestant ideology and the society from which it first came, were founded on a particular kind of distinction between church and state, religion and politics, spiritual and worldly authority. In the area of local politics, the enactment of this distinction unravelled the social fabric in such a way that missionaries were likely to be caught between Christian and non-Christian; they were also sometimes opposed by powerful Protestant chiefs and, ironically, were often in the end rejected by the very congregations they had spawned (cf. Rigby 1981). In the sphere of political relations among indigenous communities, the white settlers, and the imperial government, the same distinction of church and state created yet further ambivalence for the evangelists, as it rationalized a *range* of policy positions and courses of action. The fact that Ludorf and Mackenzie represented two quite different responses to the same environment—one an embryonic separatist nationalism, the other a "humanitarian" imperialism (Sillery 1971)—captures the ambiguity in a dramatic form.

But, if the balance sheet of intention and effect in this first domain is irreducibly ambiguous, the second presents a very different picture. For it is here, as we have said, that the seeds of colonial domination were most deeply planted, providing the South African state, at its birth, with a "theodicy of its own privilege" (Weber, see Bourdieu 1977:188). This process, of course, was not a mechanical one. It was the product of an encounter between experiencing actors in which the signs and practices of Christianity became the subject of a *conversation*, refracted through the lens of native categories. Still, while the message was mediated, the signs themselves were deeply instilled—which is why the key to the historical role of the missionary lies here.

Nonetheless, this is not the end of the matter, for there was a contradiction between the two dimensions of the missionary project. This, in turn, gave rise to a discourse of resistance—or, more accurately, discourses of resistance, as there is never just one way of debating a new orthodoxy. Indeed, if there is any general inference to be drawn from this case it lies here. It is not merely that the position of the evangelist in the colonial process was always two dimensional, but that the precise relationship between the two dimensions—the manifest exercise of power and the diffuse control over everyday meaning—gave form to the missionary role in different times and places. In the South African case, the discovery by the colonized that the church had prepared them for a New Jerusalem but could only deliver them into a New Babylon (van Onselin 1982; cf. Sundkler 1980:46–47) elicited a range of reactions and forms of protest. For a long time, those reactions made use of the terms of orthodox Protestantism, if only to invert or parody them. The ultimate power of Christianity in South Africa is enshrined in the fact that it took many decades for blacks to cast aside the language and ideology of the mission (Gerhart 1978); to move, that is, from revelation to revolution.

Notes

Acknowledgments. We are grateful to Professor Isaac Schapera, among the earliest and most distinguished students of missionaries in southern Africa, for his constructive comments on the first draft of this essay.

1. Among the more significant features that distinguished the Tswana missions from many others in Africa was the fact that they did not establish discrete "residential" stations set apart from native communities. Due to the nucleated character of Tswana chiefdoms, evangelists found it necessary to locate themselves within local settlements and the orbit of chiefly authority. As has been pointed out, the difference between such nonresidential stations and those that established separate "organic" communities is crucial to the sociology of the missionary encounter (Hutchinson 1957; Oliver 1952:60ff.).

2. The documentation of missionary involvement in Tshidi history is extensive. The primary sources on which we rely here are Campbell (1822), Moffat (1842), Broadbent (1865), Mackenzie (1871, 1883, 1887), and Ludorf (Methodist Missionary Society, Bechuanaland Correspondence 1838–57, Box XVII). Secondary materials include the writings of indigenous scholars, for example, Molema (1920, 1951, 1966) and Matthews (1945).

3. See Beidelman (1982:118) and Prins (1980:198) for similar reactions on the part of missionaries to the Kaguru and Barotse.

4. Rotberg (1965:43) and Ekechi (1972:11), for example, note much the same behavior among Protestant missionaries in East and West Africa, respectively.

5. Hellberg (1965:48f.), Crummey (1972:30), Temu (1972:38), and Beidelman (1982:25), among others, record comparable reactions of Africans elsewhere.

6. Cf. Oliver (1952:67) on East Africa.

7. For accounts from contrasting perspectives, see Agar-Hamilton (1928:10f., 1937:15); Voigt (1899,1:1f.); Theal (1926:294); Schoon (1972:7); and Thompson (1969).

8. Ludorf had left in 1852, when Montshiwa fled from the Boers (Molema 1966:38f.). Later the ruler created a ring of hamlets to guard the vacated territory and assigned one to Molema. Thus, Mafikeng became a Christian village; in the 1880s, however, the chief made his capital among its easily defended rocks.

9. This is clear not only from Ludorf's letters (Methodist Missionary Society n.d.) but also from Moffat (1842), Broadbent (1865), and Livingstone (1858). The one missionary ambivalent on the matter was Macken-

zie, who sometimes spoke approvingly of the reduced power of chiefs (for example, 1871:81; cf. Dachs 1972), but took pains not to subvert the Ngwato ruler when the opportunity arose (Mackenzie 1883:Chapter 19).

10. Prins (1980:210) on the Paris Mission to the Barotse. The separation of church and state, however, was not sustained by Protestants everywhere; for one contrasting case, see Rotberg (1965:55ff.).

11. See Dachs (1972). In our view, the "missionary-imperialist" thesis is ill-conceived. Not only is it based largely on the biography of one man, John Mackenzie, whose views and career were notably singular (see note 9; also below); it also depends on a questionable reading of his actions. Etherington (1978:25f.) applies the same thesis to missions in Natal, where it seems to account better for a situation in which Zulus were more openly resistant to "conversion."

12. Cf. Ayandele (1966:31) on Nigeria.

13. See the *Cambridge History of the British Empire* (Newton & Benians 1936:428ff.) for an account of the relevant events. Matthews (1945:19) and Molema (1966:65f.) tell of their place in Tshidi historical consciousness.

14. Ludorf has been ridiculed by apologists for the Boers (Theal 1900:368ff.) and celebrated in mission histories (Whiteside 1906:340f.).

15. This is clear from Ludorf's letter to Arnot on November 8, 1871 (see Molema 1966:67).

16. This, again, was expressed in a letter (to Barkly on November 15, 1871; see Molema 1966:67).

17. The LMS and the Wesleyans had similar policies in respect of political involvement, at least in this part of southern Africa. Hence, denominational contrasts among nonconformists did not play a significant role here in determining the overt political activities of the different missionaries.

18. This is stated in a letter from J. O. Whitehouse, Acting Foreign Secretary of the LMS, to Mackenzie on November 27, 1879 (Dachs 1975:134).

19. These were the words of Anthony Evelyn Ashley, Under-Secretary of State for the Colonies on February 12, 1884; quoted in Dachs (1975:163) and Sillery (1971:82).

20. This is on the public record in Hansard (Third Series), Vol. CCLXXXV:79, February 28, 1884; quoted in Sillery (1971:82).

21. Since this period of Mackenzie's life is detailed in Sillery (1971:86ff.), we do not annotate it here.

22. For an account from the Tshidi perspective, see Molema (1966:155).

23. The constitutional history of British Bechuanaland and the Protectorate is summarized by, among others, Sillery (1952:Pt. l) and Stevens (1967:Pt. II).

24. This was said in a letter to Bower on July 17, 1885 (Dachs 1975:153).

25. See his letter to Shippard on July 10, 1889 (Dachs 1975:242).

26. The minute was written by Edward Fairfield on November 24, 1892, C.O 417/90:259; quoted in Maylam (1980:28).

27. Hence the title of a biography of Robert Moffat by Edwin Smith (1925), himself a missionary: *Robert Moffat: One of God's Gardeners.*

28. Cf. Ajayi (1965:10–11) on Nigeria.

29. See Goody (1980:131). In stressing that these effects occur in specific historical circumstances, however, we differ from Goody, who attributes to literacy a more determinist and generalizing role.

References

Agar-Hamilton, John A. I. (1928). *The native policy of the Voortrekkers.* Cape Town: Maskew Miller.

Agar-Hamilton, John A. I. (1937). *Road to the north: South Africa, 1852–1886.* London: Longmans, Green.

Ajayi, J. F. Ade (1965). *Christian missions in Nigeria 1841–1891: The making of a new elite.* London: Longmans.

Ayandele, Emmanuel A. (1966). *The missionary impact on modern Nigeria 1842–1914.* London: Longmans, Green.

Beidelman, Thomas O. (1982). *Colonial evangelism: A socio-historical study of an East African mission at the grassroots.* Bloomington: Indiana University Press.

Bohannan, Paul (1964). *Africa and Africans.* Garden City, NY: The Natural History Press.

Bourdieu, Pierre (1977). *Outline of a theory of practice.* (Richard Nice, Trans.). New York: Cambridge University Press.

Broadbent, Samuel (1865). *A narrative of the first introduction of Christianity amongst the Barolong Tribe of*

Bechuanas, South Africa. London: Wesleyan Mission House.

Bundy, Colin (1979). *The rise and fall of the South African peasantry.* London: Heinemann.

Campbell, John (1822). *Travels in South Africa . . . being a narrative of a second journey.* 2 volumes. London: Westley.

Chadwick, Owen (1966). *The Victorian church.* Part I. New York: Oxford University Press.

Chirenje, J. Mutero (1976). Church, state, and education in Bechuanaland in the nineteenth century. *International Journal of African Historical Studies, 9,* 401–418.

Comaroff, Jean (1985). *Body of power, spirit of resistance: The culture and history of a South African people.* Chicago: The University of Chicago Press.

Comaroff, John L. (1973). *Competition for office and political processes among the Barolong boo Ratshidi.* Ph.D. dissertation. University of London.

Comaroff, John L. (1982). Dialectical systems, history and anthropology. *Journal of Southern African Studies, 8,* 143–172.

Crummey, Donald (1972). *Priests and politicians: Protestant and Catholic missions in orthodox Ethiopia 1830–1868.* Oxford: Clarendon Press.

Dachs, Anthony J. (1972). Missionary imperialism: The case of Bechuanaland. *Journal of African History, 13,* 647–658.

Dachs, Anthony J. (Ed.) (1975). *Papers of John Mackenzie.* Johannesburg: Witwatersrand University Press.

Eiselin, Werner M. (1934). Christianity and the religious life of the Bantu. In Isaac Schapera (Ed.), *Western civilization and the natives of South Africa* (pp. 65–82). London: Routledge & Kegan Paul.

Ekechi, F. K. (1972). *Missionary enterprise and rivalry in Igboland 1857–1914.* London: Frank Cass.

Etherington, Norman (1978). *Preachers, peasants and politics in Southeast Africa, 1835–1880: African Christian communities in Natal, Pondoland and Zululand.* London: Royal Historical Society.

Etherington, Normal (1983). Missionaries and the intellectual history of Africa. A historical survey. *Itinerario, 2,* 27–45.

Foucault, Michel (1980). *The history of sexuality* (Robert Hurley, Trans.). New York: Vintage Books.

Gerhart, Gail M. (1978). *Black power in South Africa.* Berkeley: University of California Press.

Goody, Jack (1980). Thought and writing. In Ernest Gellner (Ed.), *Soviet and Western anthropology* (pp. 119–134). New York: Columbia University Press.

Halpern, Jack (1965). *South Africa's hostages.* Harmondsworth: Penguin.

Heise, D. R. (1967). Prefatory findings in the sociology of missions. *Journal for the Scientific Study of Religions, 6,* 39–63.

Hellberg, Carl-J. (1965). *Missions on a colonial frontier west of Lake Victoria.* Upsala: Gleerups.

Holub, Emil (1881). *Seven years in South Africa* (2 vols.). (Ellen E. Frewer, Trans.). Boston: Houghton Mifflin.

Hutchinson, Bertram (1957). Some social consequences of nineteenth century missionary activity among the South African Bantu. *Africa, 27,* 160–177.

Kiernan, James P. (1976). The work of Zion: An analysis of an African Zionist ritual. *Africa, 46,* 340–355.

Lévi-Strauss, Claude (1972). *Tristes tropiques* (John Russell, Trans.). New York: Atheneum.

Linden, Ian (1977). *Church and revolution in Rwanda.* Manchester: Manchester University Press.

Livingstone, David (1858). *Missionary travels and researches in South Africa.* New York: Harper & Brothers.

Lye, William F. (1969). The distribution of the Sotho peoples after the Difaqane. In Leonard Thompson (Ed.), *African societies in southern Africa* (pp. 191–229). London: Heinemann.

MacGaffey, Wyatt (1983). *Modern Kongo prophets: Religion in a plural society.* Bloomington: Indiana University Press.

Mackenzie, John (1871). *Ten years north of the Orange River.* Edinburgh: Edmonston and Douglas.

Mackenzie, John (1883). *Day dawn in dark places.* London: Cassell.

Mackenzie, John (1887). *Austral Africa: Losing it or ruling it.* 2 volumes. London: Sampson Low.

Mackenzie, William D. (1902). *John Mackenzie, South African missionary and statesman.* London: Hodder and Stoughton.

Majeke, Nositho (1953). *The role of the missionaries in conquest.* Johannesburg: Society of Young Africa.

Matthews, Z. K. (1945). A short history of the Tshidi Barolong. *Fort Hare Papers, 1,* 9–28.

Maylam, Paul R. (1980). *Rhodes, the Tswana, and the British: Colonialism, collaboration, and conflict in the Bechuanaland Protectorate, 1885–99.* London: Greenwood Press.

Methodist Missionary Society (n.d.). *Bechuanaland Correspondence 1838–57, Box XVII.* University of London: Methodist Missionary Archives.

Moffat, Robert (1842). *Missionary labours and scenes in Southern Africa.* London: Snow.

Molema, Silas Modiri (1920). *The Bantu, past and present.* Edinburgh: Green.

Molema, Silas Modiri (1951). *Chief Moroka.* Cape Town: Methodist Publishing House.

Molema, Silas Modiri (1966). *Montshiwa, Barolong Chief and Patriot, 1815–96.* Cape Town: Struik.

Molema, Silas Modiri (n.d.). *A history of Methodism among the Tshidi Barolong.* Pamphlet.

Newton, A. P., & Benians, E. A. (Eds.) (1936). *The Cambridge history of the British Empire, Vol. 8, South Africa, Rhodesia and the protectorates.* Cambridge: Cambridge University Press.

Oliver, Roland (1952). *The missionary factor in East Africa.* London: Longmans, Green.

Plaatje, Solomon T. (n.d.). *Native life in South Africa.* New York: The Crisis.

Prins, Gwyn (1980). *The hidden hippopotamus.* Cambridge: Cambridge University Press.

Ranger, Terence O. (1978). Growing from the roots: Reflections on peasant research in central and southern Africa. *Journal of Southern African Studies, 5,* 99–133.

Ranger, Terence O. (n.d.). *Religious movements and politics in Sub Saharan Africa.* ms.

Rigby, Peter (1981). Pastors and pastoralists: The differential penetration of Christianity among East African cattle herders. *Comparative Studies in Society and History, 23,* 96–129.

Rotberg, Robert I. (1965). *Christian missionaries and the creation of Northern Rhodesia 1880–1924.* Princeton, NJ: Princeton University Press.

Schapera, Isaac (1936). The contributions of Western civilisation to modern Kxatla culture. *Transactions of the Royal Society of South Africa, 24,* 221–252.

Schapera, Isaac (1958). Christianity and the Tswana. *Journal of the Royal Anthropological Institute, 88,* 1–9.

Schapera, Isaac (1971). *Rainmaking rites of Tswana Tribes.* Leiden: Afrika-Studiecentrum.

Schoon, H. F. (Ed.) (1972). *The diary of Erasmus Smit* (W. G. A. Mears, Trans.). Cape Town: Struik.

Shapiro, Judith (1981). Ideologies of Catholic missionary practice in a postcolonial era. *Comparative Studies in Society and History 23,* 130–149.

Sillery, Anthony (1952). *The Bechuanaland protectorate.* Cape Town: Oxford University Press.

Sillery, Anthony (1971). *John Mackenzie of Bechuanaland 1835–1899 A study in humanitarian imperialism.* Cape Town: Balkema.

Smith, Edwin G. (1925). *Robert Moffat: One of God's gardeners.* Edinburgh: Turnbull and Spears.

Solomon, Edward S. (1855). *Two lectures on the native tribes of the Interior.* Cape Town: Saul Solomon.

Stevens, Richard P. (1967). *Lesotho, Botswana, and Swaziland.* London: Pall Mall Press.

Stow, George W. (1905). *The native races of South Africa.* London: Swan Sonnenschein.

Strayer, Robert W. (1978). *The making of mission communities in East Africa.* London: Heinemann.

Sundkler, Bengt (1961). *Bantu prophets in South Africa.* London: Oxford University Press for the International African Institute.

Sundkler, Bengt (1980). *Bara Bukoba.* London: Hurst.

Taussig, Michael (1980). *The devil and commodity fetishism in South America.* Chapel Hill: University of North Carolina. Press.

Temu, A. J. (1972). *British Protestant missions.* London: Longman.

Theal, George M. (1900). *History of South Africa: The republics and native territories from 1854 to 1872.* London: Swan Sonnenschein.

Theal, George M. (1926). *History of South Africa from 1795–1872* (vol. 2). London: George Allen & Unwin.

Thompson, Edward P. (1967). Time, work-discipline and industrial capitalism. *Past and Present, 38,* 56–97.

Thompson, Leonard (1969). Co-operation and conflict: The high veld. In Monica Wilson & Leonard Thompson (Eds.), *The Oxford history of South Africa* (vol. 1) (pp. 391–446). Oxford: Oxford University Press.

Trexler, Richard C. (1984). We think, they act: Clerical readings of missionary theatre in 16th century Spain. In Steven Kaplan (Ed.), *Understanding popular culture.* Berlin: Mouton.

Troeltsch, Ernst (1949). *The social teaching of the Christian churches* (vol. 2). (Olive Wyon, Trans.). London: George Allen and Unwin.

van Onselin, Charles (1982). *Studies in the social and economic history of the Witwatersrand, 1886–1914* (vol. 1). New York: Longman.

Vilakazi, Absolom (1962). *Zulu transformations.* Pietermaritzburg: University of Natal Press.

Voigt, Johan C. (1899). *Fifty years of the history of the Republic of South Africa (1795–1845)* (2 vol.). London: T. Fisher Unwin.

Warner, Wellman J. (1930). *The Wesleyan movement in the Industrial Revolution.* London: Longmans, Green.

Whiteside, J. (1906). *History of the Wesleyan Methodist Church of South Africa.* London: Elliot Stock.

Williams, Raymond (1977). *Marxism and literature.* Oxford: Oxford University Press.

Wilson, Monica (1969). Co-operation and conflict: The eastern cape frontier. In Monica Wilson & Leonard Thompson (Eds.), *The Oxford history of South Africa* (vol. 1) (pp. 233–271). Oxford: Oxford University Press.

Wilson, Monica (1971). The growth of peasant communities. In Monica Wilson & Leonard Thompson (Eds.), *The Oxford history of South Africa* (vol. 2) (pp. 49–103). Oxford: Oxford University Press.

Wilson, Monica (1976). *Missionaries: Conquerors or servants of God?* Address given at the opening of the South African Missionary Museum. Lovedale: South African Missionary Museum.

Hindu Culture for an Indian Nation: Gender, Politics, and Elite Identity in Urban South India

MARY HANCOCK

Sri Jayendra Saraswati, Śaṅkarācharya of Kanchi, after a three-day worship of Lord Venkateswara at Tirumala, has come out with a solution to "redeem the nation from (he present turmoils and restore peace and tranquility among its various citizens."... In the course of the dhyanam *[meditation], three things occurred to him as the factors responsible for the present disquiet. These were a steep fall in the spirit of nationalism and the quality of polity and the existence of constitutional lacunae. The Acharya said despite the handicaps the people's spiritual fervour had not died out completely. He felt that a "movement for spiritual, national and economic development" was the only answer to stem the rot. (*The Hindu, *July 6, 1987)*

Prologue: Hindu Culture for an Indian Nation

During the 1980s, right-wing Hindu nationalist organizations grew in size and strength in India and among Hindu Indian populations abroad (Basu et al. 1993). Most of the groups are part of a nexus, composed of the Rashtriya Swayamsevak Sangh (RSS) and its "family" of affiliated groups: a religious association, the Vishwa Hindu Parishad (VHP); a trade union, the Bharatiya Mazdoor Sangh (BMS); a student association, Akhil Bharatiya Vidyarthi Parishad (ABVP); and a political party, the Bharatiya Janata Party (BJP). Hindu nationalism, known as Hindutva, is promoted in a variety of English and vernacular publications put out by these organizations.

At the time of this writing, the most recent major offensive by Hindu nationalists had been the orchestration, in December 1992, of the destruction of a mosque at Ayodhya in the northern state of Uttar Pradesh that allegedly had been constructed on the birth site of the Hindu deity Ram. Thousands of volunteers, organized by the RSS and VHP, descended on the mosque and were met by Muslim opponents; several days of violence ensued, with death tolls reaching into the thousands (Basu et al. 1993). In the weeks that followed, riots occurred in other major Indian cities. Moreover, for several months prior to the destruction of the mosque, the RSS and its affiliates had fueled communal antagonisms, systematically inciting smaller-scale confrontations throughout India and promoting, through the mass media, the idea that Hindus were a majority at risk. The gains of Hindu nationalism have also been evident in the growth of the BJP's electoral base in the northern states comprising the Hindi belt.

Because much of the current wave of Hindu nationalism has emanated from centers in the Hindi belt, peninsular India sometimes has been thought to be immune to its spread. Its northern, "Aryan" associations supposedly ensured that it would not play in the south. This view carried special weight with regard to Tamil Nadu, because a cultural nationalism framed in terms of the Dravidian linguistic and ethnic identity of the southern populations has been a dominant element of political and social life since the early 20th century (see Barnett 1976; Hardgrave 1969; Irschick 1969; Washbrook 1989). Proponents of Dravidianism defined their identity in opposition to that of northern Indo-Aryan populations and to that of Tamil Brahmans, who were regarded as descendants of the early Aryan conquerors of the southern populations.

The confrontational tactics of nationalists in Kerala and the related successes of the BJP in Andhra Pradesh and Karnataka, however, indicate that Hindu nationalism does have bases in the south (Andersen & Damle 1987:209–246).[1] In Tamil Nadu, while the BJP has yet to claim either legislative assembly or parliamentary seats, the VHP and affiliated organizations have found receptive audiences for ritually mediated forms of Hindu nationalism, such as the *Ramshila pūjas* in which bricks for the construction of a Ram temple at Ayodhya were blessed. The movement heralded in the epigraph also exemplifies the receptivity to Hindutva that has developed in the south in recent years.

This growth owes much to the work of Hindu nationalists who, in the attempt to stoke anti-Muslim sentiment, have framed a series of large-scale conversions to Islam by Untouchables as part of a Muslim conspiracy to dominate the sociopolitical and economic life of India (Seshadri n.d.). This commenced in 1981 following one such conversion in Meenakshipuram, a village in southern Tamil Nadu, and gained momentum with the publicization of subsequent conversions and reconversions and through communal violence thought by many to have been orchestrated by the RSS and its affiliates (e.g., Geetha & Rajudurai 1990; Narayan 1982). The nationalist campaign included articles in the mainstream and RSS-controlled press purporting to document this conspiracy. Both the Arya Samaj[2] and the VHP called for government inquiries into mass conversions, claiming that they were prompted by an influx of "foreign money" (i.e., funds from Muslims in other countries). The same groups also sponsored public rituals and other performances as part of an effort to proselytize among those low-caste and Untouchable populations considered susceptible to Islamic influence.[3]

Among the religious leaders who contributed to these projects was Jayendra Saraswati, the Śaṅkarācharya of Kanchipuram, to whom the epigraph refers. In 1981 he requested a government inquiry into the Arya Samaj's allegations about the use of foreign funds to encourage conversions and called for the formation of a pan-Hindu association to combat the problem (*Data India* 1981:407). He subsequently made shows of public support for the RSS[4] and, in 1983, convened a three-day Hindu Arts Festival in Madras, intended to "revive [the] nationalist spirit" (*The Hindu,* March 31, 1983).

The coalition of religious leaders and nationalist groups, brokered by the VHP, was also successful in securing the patronage of Tamil Nadu politicians. Shortly after the Meenakshipuram incident, R. Veerappan, the State Hindu Religious and Charitable Endowments Minister,[5] indicated that the government was considering legislation to ban mass conversions and announced that a special campaign to "reassure Harijans of equality" would be inaugurated (*The Hindu,* August 11, 1981). Following Saraswati's Hindu Arts Festival, which had been attended by elected officials, including the state's chief minister, M. G. Ramachandran, Veerappan asserted that the government "respected Hindus" and that the festival had strengthened Hinduism by showing the "scientific basis of [its] customs" (*The Hindu,* April 5, 1983). As the 1980s progressed, the conversion issue was incorporated into the accelerating right-wing Hindu discourse focusing on the Ayodhya mosque as the most potent symbol of the Muslim "threat" to Hindu India (Seshadri n.d.).

These combined efforts demonstrated that Hindutva, when filtered through religious practice, could be made attractive and even familiar to Tamils in ways that the Aryan imagery of the RSS could not. In 1987, my middle-class Brahman acquaintances in Madras seemed mostly uninterested and not particularly well informed about the formal programs of Hindu nationalist organizations as reported in the national press.[6] They did, however, disparage the politicization and "corruption" of religious practices and institutions that they encountered on a day-to-day basis, something they associated with the current state government's administration of temples. They were also deeply disturbed by the "preferential" treatment accorded by the government to religious minorities and to members of "Scheduled" and "Backward" groups.[7] Accordingly, many among the urban bourgeoisie were eager "consumers" (in de Certeau's [1984] sense) of proposals such as Jayendra Saraswati's, and were active in voluntary associations that were geared to the rather ambiguous, but nonetheless nationalist, ends identified by the Śaṅkarācharya. Women, in particular, seemed receptive to such programs, an attitude that can be attributed both to the government's solicitation of female voluntarism in the delivery of social services (this was consistent with bourgeois nationalisms of the colonial and postcolonial eras) and to the spaces for autonomous action that such practices offered women. In the present article I explore this willingness to "consume" Hindutva by considering Jayendra Saraswati's mediation of Hindu nationalism through the Jan̲ Kalyāṇ movement.

Consenting to What?

While living in Madras I had seen press releases about the Śaṅkarācharya's movement for several months before I encountered it directly. It was dubbed Jan̲ Kalyāṇ (a Sanskritized expression ordinarily translated as "People's Welfare"), and its founder was and is a Hindu preceptor who heads an important *matam* (monastery and teaching center), reputed to have been founded by the Hindu reformer Śaṅkara in the eighth century C.E. The monastery, located in Kanchipuram, just outside Madras City, is currently estimated to be the wealthiest of the matams that trace their genealogy to Śaṅkara. Saraswati is the 69th in the line of preceptors initiated by Śaṅkara (Cenkner 1983; Mines & Gourishankar 1990). As head of the matam, Saraswati controlled several voluntary associations, of which Jan̲ Kalyāṇ was one. It was through these organizations and others (including RSS affiliates) that he staged the public events described above and pursued what he called "social activism" via the brokerage of cross-caste alliances. With this agenda he has distinguished his style of leadership from that of previous Śaṅkarācharyas.

My personal introduction to Jan̲ Kalyāṇ occurred in December 1987, when I attended a public performance of devotional songs that had been sponsored by one of the voluntary associations affiliated with the monastery. Its president, Uma Radhakrishnan (a pseudonym), a Smarta Brahman in her late sixties, had organized the event, which it took place in what people referred to in English as a "private temple."[8] The performance was introduced by a short dedication to the goddess Kamakshi. Following that, Radhakrishnan delivered a short speech about Jan̲ Kalyāṇ and distributed copies of its slogan and members' pledge to the audience. She then asked the audience to join her in a prayer consisting of 16 repetitions of the Sanskrit phrase that served as the movement's slogan. *Bhajans* (devotional songs) in honor of Kamakshi were then performed by the musicians hired by Radhakrishnan for the evening. The audience of nearly one hundred men and women consisted largely of Smartas and other Brahmans who resided in Mylapore and adjacent sections of the city.

Though Jan̲ Kalyāṇ was represented by its founder as a "grassroots" movement of national scope, its operations and effectiveness suggested otherwise. In the first place, it remained locally centered in Tamil Nadu's municipalities, and in Madras especially. Second, the bulk of its membership was drawn from the urban Smārta Brahman bourgeoisie, part of the matam's original core constituency.[9] Despite its ostensible commitment to social welfare, Jan̲ Kalyāṇ functioned both as node for brokering cross-caste alliances among middle- and upper-class populations, and as a vehicle for Smārtas to assert a group identity derived from their efforts to create ties with and speak for other caste and class groups.

As is the case with other urban bourgeoisie, Smārtas' internal organization is mediated by diverse voluntary associations, from neighborhood ladies' clubs to groups of international societies like the Lions (Caplan 1985; Khare 1970; Sharma 1986; Singh 1976; Vatuk 1972). While some associations mediate cross-caste networks among middle- and upper-class urbanites, there are also caste-specific networks, in particular the statewide caste association, the Tamil Brahman Association (TAMBRAS), which operates through a series of local units. TAMBRAS was established in 1981; in addition to representing collective grievances of Tamil Brahmans to the government, its local units sponsor public ritual events advertised as carrying the Śaṅkarācharyas's blessings and similar in form and content to those put on by Jan̲ Kalyāṇ Saraswati depended on voluntary associations like these to publicize Jan̲ Kalyāṇ and to recruit members.

One of the most prominent features of Jan̲ Kalyāṇ was its attention to what Saraswati defined as "cultural" phenomena. In Jan̲ Kalyāṇ's promotional literature the term *kalaccāram* is used to gloss "culture." This is a Tamilized Sanskrit word that refers to textually mediated artistic an scientific knowledge. Culture was also circumscribed in the forms of belief and practice promoted through Jan̲ Kalyāṇ that derive from the theological principles of *advaitavedānta*, a school of Hindu thought associated with the teachings of Śaṅkara and currently promulgated through the matams he founded. Smārtas, though not a sect in themselves, derive collective identity through their adherence to and teaching of these precepts and the heads of the Kanchipuram matam, past and present, have been members of the Smārta community.

The discourse of culture provided opportunities for its Smārta membership to assert an identity that had continuities with their previous roles as cultural mediators.[10] Jaṉ Kalyāṇ was a vehicle by which members (Smārtas) articulated a group identity through the deployment of key symbols embodying what Saraswati defined as Indian culture. It thereby created opportunities for Smārtas to identify their particular, caste-based community with the more extensive community of the nation. This amounted to a rhetorical claim that, by virtue of their ownership of the key elements of the cultural traditions that allegedly defined India, Smārtas as a community were brokers for, and legitimate representatives of, the Indian nation.[11] Smārta claims of culture brokerage were lodged performatively through Jaṉ Kalyāṇ, with ritual and devotional music conducted by and for a mostly Smārta membership. In addition they were reiterated in Jaṉ Kalyāṇ's members' pledge, which stipulated that members apply moral discipline to the poor.

Although not a women's movement, Jaṉ Kalyāṇ resembled many other modern discourses of national culture in its public deployment of women (see Ryan 1990:3–18) as metaphors representing the "traditions" that supposedly generated the "Hindu nation" and as actors engaged in the cultural production of that imagined community (after Anderson 1991). In so doing it adopted the rhetoric of "womanhood" found in colonial and postcolonial constructs of the nation—for example, the metonymic connection between oppressive institutions like *sati*[12] with India's civilizational deficits (Mani 1990); the early nationalist feminization of Indian tradition (Chatterjee 1993:117–134); the Dravidianist gendering of language as Mother Tamil (Lakshmi 1990; Ramaswamy 1993); and M. K. Gandhi's feminization of the nation (Kishwar 1985; Nandy 1983:48–55; Patel 1988) These varied representations come together in one aspect of the Gandhian construct of the nation that continues to be celebrated in bourgeois nationalism: the "separate spheres" ideology (see Chatterjee 1993; Minault & Papanek 1982; Patel 1988). In that ideology the nation is thought to encompass a "private sphere" of naturalized, feminine virtue (e.g., *ahimsa*, or nonviolence) that is different from, but strategically connected to, a "public sphere" of political action.

Despite the appropriation of femininity as a sign under which the Indian nation might be written, there have been ambiguities with regard to the spaces for female action accommodated by various nationalisms. Women, marked as spiritual and tradition-bound, have been cast as both reformers and as beings in need of the reforms promised by modernity. In Gandhian nationalism this tension was partially resolved by conceiving of woman's nature as essentially domestic and—if freed from the strictures of child marriage, sati, and dowry—as a resource for the nation. Viewed as patient, pure, courageous, and self-sacrificing, women were models for nonviolent civil disobedience; similarly, the home was envisioned as the site of feminine action for the nation—for example, spinning thread for *khadi* (cotton cloth that is unbleached and otherwise unrefined).[13] The focus on woman as mother also cohered with the urban, upper-caste, middle-class Hindu male's perception of what a woman should be (Patel 1988:378). This image stood in counterpoint, however, to the equally important figure of woman as renouncer of family life—working selflessly for the nation—and was represented in the paradigmatic form of the ascetic Brahman widow.

The tension between these two images—both caught within the terrain of separate spheres ideology—was never dissolved (Patel 1988) even though Gandhi's fashioning of ideal womanhood shifted from an early focus on the mother to a later concentration on the widow. In both cases, however, women were defined in and through a patriarchally ordered domestic life and conceptualized as both source and homology of the nation. In practice, this gave way to further contradictions, for women who wished to participate in the mass disobedience actions orchestrated by Gandhi had to renegotiate the boundaries between the home and the world, thereby risking the damage to their own and their families' reputations that followed from transgressions of patriarchal norms (see Visweswaran 1994:57–59).

This conflation of femininity and domesticity is frequently invoked as part of the common sense of urban elites in India. As I will detail below, Jayendra Saraswati's solicitation of women and his usage of feminine ritual idioms reiterates this conflation, while connecting it to the feminized idioms of the monistic and tantric-influenced teachings of his matam. One of the ritual genres associated with femininity and domesticity throughout Hindu South Asia, *tiruvilakku pūja* (literally, "worship of the holy flame," that is the goddess as embodied in the oil lamp), was annexed by the Śaṅkarācharya to publicize Jan̲ Kalyāṇ and to recruit members. This usage of women and femininity (following the Gandhian wife/mother paradigm) was a critical feature in Jan̲ Kalyaṇ's claim to represent the "cultural" domain that grounded the "Hindu nation" and in its conscription of "culture" as symbolic capital to contest the legitimacy of a realm it defined as "political" (the secular state). Moreover, by entwining its nationalist message with everyday domestic practice, it inserted nationalism into the home, whence men, urged on by their wives, mothers, and sisters, might be persuaded to take up the cause of Hindu nationalism in other public venues.

On the basis of both its short life (the movement was defunct for all practical purposes by 1990[14]) and its use of "social service" for Smārta Brahman self-representation, it could be argued that Jan̲ Kalyaṇ was merely a reactionary social twitch—a "public transcript" of underclass acquiescence (to paraphrase Scott 1990:85–90) and unworthy of further scrutiny. Critics have in fact described it as a Brahmanical version of Hindutva camouflaged by a thin veil of social reform, an aspect that probably accounts for its failure in Tamil Nadu (Pandian 1990).

It is precisely this aspect of Jan̲ Kalyāṇ, however, that invites attention. Clearly, Saraswati was making claims through Jan̲ Kalyāṇ about the continuities between Smārta interests and the interests of the nation. It is evident also that these types of elite appropriations of nationalist discourse have not actually abated, for they continue to be articulated by the Śaṅkarācharya and upper-caste associations such as TAMBRAS in prosaic and ostensibly benign terms. And the need to specify local appropriations of Hindutva only increases as Hindu nationalism makes inroads within India's diverse population. To whom were Saraswati's claims addressed, and in what ways did they make sense to audiences? In what cultural debates were these discourses of identity situated? What continuities and discontinuities existed between Jan̲ Kalyāṇ's discursive construction and its enactment, especially with regard to its deployment of feminine idioms and its solicitation of women workers?

Feminine idioms and women's bodies were among the modalities with which Jan̲ Kalyāṇ sought to both penetrate and reshape what Gramsci described as "common sense":

a sedimentation of "conceptions of life and of man," "popular knowledge" that is "not something rigid or immobile, but is continually transforming itself, enriching itself with scientific ideas and with philosophical opinions which have entered ordinary life" (Gramsci 1971:326). With Jan̲ Kalyāṇ's imagery of a gendered, Hindu national culture, Saraswati sought a "hegemonic principle" consistent with caste and class privilege but at the same time capable of articulating different (and antagonistic) interests and idioms associated with different classes and castes (Gramsci 1971:349–350).

In practice, however, Jan̲ Kalyāṇ was less salient as a form of class domination than it was as an ensemble of hegemonic practices designed to secure the compliance of elites in the constitution of their own nationalized identities. My analysis focuses on Saraswati's efforts to solicit Brahman consent to Hindutva. I use this case to examine the production of hegemonic power through the "hailing" or interpellation of subjects, and the ways that hegemony is implicated in the very constitution of subjects. Such processes are implied by Gramsci in his discussion of the educational relationships of hegemony (Gramsci 1971:5–14, 343–377) and developed by poststructural theorists (Althusser 1971; Butler 1993:121–124; de Lauretis 1987:6–11; Foucault 1972:78–108). Jan̲ Kalyāṇ, moreover, reveals a distinction between hegemonic practices and effects. For while Jan̲ Kalyāṇ's ritual program implicated it in the constitution of Brahman identity, it failed as a mass movement. This, as I have suggested, was due to the political marginality of Brahmans in southern India and is a reminder that hegemony is always a contested matter, and that its effects may be uneven and limited. I further maintain that the limits of hegemony are also recognizable in its subject-constituting dimensions. This failure—more aptly, this lack of closure or resolution—lies at the heart of its hegemonic project, in the education of consent.

The education of consent is understood here as a complex, ideological process by which persons are constituted as subjects of gender, caste, and nation. Women were doubly caught in Jan̲ Kalyāṇ's solicitation of consent. They were positioned as agents whose function was to seek the consent of others—Brahmans as well as poor and low-caste persons—in implementing Saraswati's project. They were also asked to assume the sedimented identity of Brahman-Hinduwoman, and thus to embody the nation. The horizon of desire and imagination signaled by that intersection of positions, however, was not wholly contained by Saraswati's project. Even the most loyal acted on understandings and wishes that ran counter to or were unanticipated by Jan̲ Kalyāṇ's tenets. These observations suggest neither a resisting nor a complying subject but, rather, a complex—and to some extent underdetermined—subjectivity, one in which both consent and resistance are concatenated in indirect and "negative" forms of agency as well as in voluntary, conscious anion.[15] This in turn undermines the closure or totalization ascribed to interpellation by Althusser (1971) but retains his attention to subject-constitution as a mode of domination. Furthermore, it removes the necessity that the effects of hegemony be consistent with its practice.

In order to understand Jan̲ Kalyāṇ as hegemonic practice, I will examine Jan̲ Kalyāṇ's charter and operations as conveyed by its author and interpreted by one of its members, the Smārta woman mentioned above who headed the devotional society. Analytically, Jan̲ Kalyāṇ offers a window on the gendered politics of culture in Tamil Nadu, particularly as these discourses are emergent in debates surrounding "Brahmanism" and Hindutva. It also offers an opportunity for addressing broader issues related to women's consent and agency within the entwined structural inequalities of caste and class.

Jan̲ Kalyāṇ as a Discourse of Hindu Nationalism

In remarks accompanying the formal inauguration of Jan̲ Kalyāṇ in October 1987, Saraswati stressed the *national* scope of the program—it was not just for Hindus but for all Indians (*The Hindu*, October 3, 1987). At the same time, however, he asserted that Indianness was ultimately derived from the worldview and practices of Hinduism that contained the essence of the "country's traditions." In terms even more starkly substantive, he has located Hinduism in the blood of India's people (Sunil 1987) and in the land. "Bharat being a karma, jnana and dharma' bhumi, the term Dharmo Rakshati Rakshitaha should be expressly declared side by side with . . . the country's motto . . . [and] India should be called Hindustan" (*The Hindu*, October 3, 1987).[16]

If the nation is, as Anderson has suggested, an "imagined community" (1991), how did Jan̲ Kalyāṇ propose to fashion persons capable of such imaginings? How were Hindu "citizens" to be created? Prior to launching the movement, Jayendra Saraswati had already established English-medium schools and had produced audiocassettes and pamphlets detailing the lives of the Śaṅkarācharyas, the history of the maṭam, and the formats of important rituals. Jan̲ Kalyāṇ's members' pledge continued in this vein, specifying the creation of "book banks" and "exhibits," assistance at private schools and hospitals, the conduct of public ritual, dress and commensal codes, and the performance of certain domestic and neighborhood duties as obligations of membership.

The official tenets and practices described in the pledge suggested on the one hand that India already *was* culturally a Hindu nation, and on the other, that its cultural identity was incomplete and had to be brought to fruition by Jan̲ Kalyāṇ's work. The same themes resound in the styles of public ritual that were the authorized modes of self-presentation and recruitment. Saraswati mapped the social distinctions between cultural leaders and followers in an interview in which he discussed his plans for Jan̲ Kalyāṇ, differentiating "intelligent" and "unintelligent" citizens, and specifying the latter—rural, "common people"— as his "true parish" (Sunil 1987:11). Glossing these people in the same interview with lower castes, he observed it was they who were enticed by the monetary inducements of "other religions." The caste system, however, was not in itself a problem: "it should exist just the way it has . . . [because] they are all equal . . . [b]ut they have specialist functions" (Sunil 1987:11–12). The practices advocated in Jan̲ Kalyāṇ were therefore meant to circumscribe moral self-improvement and social service, including attention to public space and activity, with the values of Hindu "culture," the subjects of which define themselves and others in light of caste and class distinctions.

In stipulating the practices of cultural citizenship, the members' pledge provided a blueprint for the ways in which class and caste distinctions were consolidated and represented as integrative rather than conflictual categories. Membership duties implied the existence of both autonomy and moral agency among Jan̲ Kalyāṇ's volunteers. Members were capable of self-discipline; they were to be abstemious in consumption, and capable of material sacrifice. Those who were served by Jan̲ Kalyāṇ, on the other hand, were inferior in their passivity (they *received* assistance) and in their propensity to succumb to violence and to moral depravity. It was the poor—especially "Backward" and Untouchable groups—who engaged in communal violence, who suffered familial disputes, and who were unable either to redress these problems or recognize their causes, thus necessitating the intervention of Jan̲ Kalyāṇ.

The contrasting levels of members' affluence were acknowledged in the references to their employment, to the yearly dues calculated on the basis of salary, and to the private homes and cars that they were expected to decorate with the movement's logos. This material affluence accompanied their superior cultural capital; one article suggested that those who sought membership must already be capable of imagining India as a Hindu nation. They also had to be willing to teach those who were culturally impoverished. Finally, in order to have transformative effects, these cultural endowments had to be used to refashion public life: to clean public spaces, to initiate new types of Hindu public ceremony, and to expand the Hindu colonization of public space with new temples, maṭams, and "cow protection homes." The members' pledge thus yielded a vision of the Hindu nation by enumerating the criteria for good citizenship, indicating what categories of persons were and were not predisposed to it, and prescribing correctives for the latter.

The Ritual Remaking of Society

The outline of Hindu society offered in the members' pledge privileged the role of ritual practice, although it told very few specific details of those activities apart from the references to daily water offerings and mantra recitations. I encountered Jan̲ Kalyāṇ in December 1987, after having been invited to attend one of the public ritual performances staged by members to recruit volunteers. The analysis of Jan̲ Kalyāṇ's ritual infrastructure offered here is based on my discussions with Uma Radhakrishnan about her efforts in the movement. With this material I explore Jan̲ Kalyāṇ's annexation of "womanhood," and the possible ways that middle-class Brahman women might read these processes.

A few days after the Kamakshi bhajans, my research assistant and I visited Uma at her home in an affluent neighborhood on the city's south side. Her life was one of marked material privilege. She lived with her husband in a spacious, well-furnished house; her husband, then retired, had been highly placed in the Indian civil service, and her father had been similarly employed when she was growing up. In our subsequent conversations (which were conducted in English), she detailed the history of her involvement in Jan̲ Kalyāṇ but presented it within a life history narrative that focused on her religious interests. She began by describing the founding of the Samājam (the group that sponsored the bhajans) in April 1985. She had sought an audience with Saraswati, and on that occasion he had told her:

> *"There is a supreme* Śakti,[17] *above all* mahās *[saints], and by praying to that, one is worshiping all. . . ." He then advised me to sponsor a śakti pūja*[18] *on every full moon day in some public place, so that people would come to understand the principle of the supreme śakti power. I told him, though, that to do that on such a big scale would be difficult, and I asked that he assign me some other activity. He then said that I should sponsor bhajans on the full moon day [of each month]. I agreed to this, and began immediately on the next full moon day, May 4, 1985. . . . I organize everything having to do with these performances—I place advertisements, engage performers, reserve the*

hall and equipment, and send invitations to special guests. . . . I try to get everything by donation though I pay some of the costs myself.[19]

In September 1987 Saraswati asked her to assist him with his new campaign, Jan̠ Kalyāṇ; on that occasion he had given her a copy of the movement's flag and asked her to teach people a Sanskrit prayer that they were to repeat three times each day.[20] She explained, "In the morning, it should be said for the sake of ancestors, at noon for the gods, and in the evening for the family. The meaning of the prayer is 'surrender to the one who saves you from all danger.' "

I asked her about her willingness to take on the sorts of responsibilities that the Śaṅkarācharya had stipulated. She replied that her inclination had stemmed from her own background in music—she had studied singing with several Carnatic musicians and in 1972 had founded the Madras Music Circle. She quickly pointed out, however, that the Śaṅkarācharya had not known of that when he asked her to sponsor bhajans; she attributed that to his special insight into peoples' characters. She went on:

In 1979, I had to abandon it [the Music Circle] because I had other obligations. Many were connected to my husband's job, he was in the civil service, and was a Chief Secretary at that time. . . . However, most of my time now is free for doing the work connected with the bhajans. My husband is a noninterfering type—he doesn't help out a great deal, but neither does he hinder me. He does assist by taking phone messages and keeping a diary for me, he also types letters when I need that done.

She also pointed out that the Śaṅkarācharya's request and her acquiescence were both ascribable to the goddess's intention. It was her conviction that she had been drawn by the goddess Kamakshi to receive the Śaṅkarācharya's instructions about her participation in both the Samājam and Jan̠ Kalyāṇ. Her notion of the goddess's intervention was paired, however, with the displacement of her own intentionality. She said that despite growing up in a wealthy and devout Brahman household she had not been particularly religious before receiving the Śaṅkarācharya's directives: "When I got married, my husband was the district collector. I was very busy with our household, and I did not have a great deal of religious interest. After my daughter got married, my interest started to build." Since founding the Samājam, however, she explained, "my mind has no longer been on the family. . . . Now, I think mostly about organizing the bhajans, and my work for Jan̠ Kalyāṇ."

She said that the purpose of the Jan̠ Kalyāṇ movement was to establish uniform standards for Hindu practice and that there were to be no caste barriers. The Śaṅkarācharya, she pointed out, was going to put out books and cassettes with the correct formats for daily devotions and for festivals. One of the activities prescribed was the public performance of tiruviḷakku pūja, an act ordinarily performed by women in their homes. Uma described her observance of this ceremony:

I am organizing a tiruvilakku pūja myself to take place in . . . February. This will be the first I have done. In Kanyakumari, 1,008 ladies gathered to do this pūja in accordance with the Acharya's directions. . . . To do this pūja, the lamp should be decorated with vermilion powder and flowers, and a water pot placed in front of it. For

> *the food offering, puffed rice, beaten rice, and crystal sugar should be given. It's not a complicated pūja—one lights the lamp and tells the 108 names of Lakshmi [goddess of prosperity and domesticity]. One then circles the lamp.*

Uma had already begun to plan the tiruviḷakku pūja that she had scheduled for February. A hall had been engaged and she was having invitations printed.

Although she had said that Jan̲ Kalyāṇ was caste-blind and suggested that women's friendships and shared concerns could cut across caste boundaries, other comments that she made undermined those apparently egalitarian sentiments. When I asked her about the other domestic rituals that she performed, she spoke about a pūja honoring the goddess Santoshima that had recently become popular in Madras. She said that she had completed that pūja cycle four times, each for some specific aim, and that all had been successful. Two of the cycles, she noted, had been for her grandson's benefit—once for his exams, the second time for a related reason:

> *He had been denied a seat in engineering college because he was a Brahman, a member of a forward community. Merit carries no weight because of the anti-Brahman sentiment—those with lower marks gained admission, yet he was rejected for no good reason. We tried to use influence to gain his admission, but nothing came of that either. Then, I did Santoshima pūja, and one Friday—just when I was completing it—I got a call from my daughter to say that the boy had gotten a seal in another engineering college. Santoshima had gotten him a seat in the best college, and in the best course—electrical engineering.*

She, like many other Brahmans, ascribed the caste inequalities that required the goddess's intervention to governmental policies of discrimination in favor of low-caste groups. It thus seemed that what she sought in everyday ritual and in her work for Jan̲ Kalyāṇ was a form of personal autonomy, albeit one located in a naturalized system of privilege that stemmed from "merit" and, in Saraswati's words, "intelligence."[21]

Women, Womanhood, and the Politics of Inclusion in Jan̲ Kalyāṇ

Uma's experiences and perceptions, while not necessarily shared by others in the movement, are illuminating insofar as they reiterate what other Brahman women found appealing in Jan̲ Kalyāṇ. They are also valuable in the ways they evoke more generalized categories of caste, class, and nation—categories emergent in her narratives. They are described in neither objective nor disinterested terms but are positionally appropriated. What this enables us to read in her words is the complexity of her consent to Hindutva—she incorporated little of the obvious rhetoric of Hindu nationalism, focusing instead on the engendering rituals of being *cumankali,* the personal autonomy that she derived from her work for Jan̲ Kalyāṇ, and the reverse discrimination toward Brahmans that she associated with governmental policies on education.

Let me consider her articulation of Brahman identity first. In southern India, and especially in Tamil Nadu, there is a political distinction between Brahmans and non-Brahmans that derives from the ways the colonial administration recognized and officialized caste as a politically salient category. Historians have commented on how, in the latter half of the 19th century, the census, famine reports, and other administrative reports were used to work out an exhaustive taxonomy of Indian society based on caste and religion.[22] This enumerative grid proved useful in local articulations of populist forms of cultural nationalism, particularly the Non-Brahman movement, as it emerged in the early 20th century (see Barnett 1976:15–31).[23]

The Non-Brahman movement was encouraged by the colonial administration, for it was perceived as a way of diminishing the strength of the (then) Brahman-dominated nationalist organizations (Washbrook 1976). A revisionist history provided a charter for the movement's populist agenda by identifying non-Brahmans as the descendants of the original Dravidian inhabitants of the southern peninsular. Brahmans, by contrast, were described as the descendants of the Aryan populations who had moved into the south and subjugated local populations by forcing them to adopt Hinduism and the caste system. The growth of the Non-Brahman movement was also aided by the colonial state's initiation of positive discrimination policies in education, civil service, and political representation. The populist philosophy and revisionist history articulated by the Non-Brahman movement's leaders and publicists provided platforms for a series of political parties, such as the Justice Party, the Dravida Kazhagam (DK), the Dravida Munnetra Kazhagam (DMK), and the All India Annadurai-DMK (AIA-DMK). Since independence their political power in the state's government has grown. The association of the Congress party with "Brahmanism" contributed to the DMK victory in Tamil Nadu's legislative assembly in 1967. Since then, with the exception of three periods when the central government controlled Tamil Nadu, the DMK (or its rival offshoot, the AIA-DMK) has remained in power.

Under these parties Tamil Nadu has retained and expanded the positive discrimination authored under colonialism and, in an atmosphere of interclass and intercaste conflict, has enlarged the state list of "Backward Classes," which complements the central "Schedule" of groups that have historically suffered discrimination. Tamil Brahmans, like Uma, are designated as "Forward" and see this as a mark of reverse discrimination. Adding fuel to Brahman discontent was the DMK government's increasing intervention in Hindu religious institutions during the 1970s. What Saraswati derided as "political" uses of religion resonated with what I heard from Smārtas and other middle- and upper-class people in Madras, who similarly disparaged what they saw as the state's intrusion into religious life and the waste of temple resources. They criticized the policies and institutions developed and implemented under the rubric of the government's protection of religious institutions. They considered the Hindu Religious and Charitable Endowments (HRCE) department, the scope of which was broadened after the DMK took control of the Tamil Nadu state government in 1967, to be one of the main culprits.

Such dissatisfactions contributed to Brahman receptivity to Hindutva in that its critique of secularism resonated with their own sense of relative deprivation. In promoting Hindu culture as a corrective for secularism Hindutva invited Brahmans (and others having a historical stake in the brokerage of culture) to assume authority in that arena. Similar usages of culture in contesting the state have been made by Saraswati and his predecessor in the past. They have sought to weaken the authority of the HRCE through associations formed to mediate between the state and Hindu religious institutions, such as the Dharma Peeta Samudaya Sangha (1961) and the Devika Peravai (1966).[24] The tiruviḷakku pūja that Jayendra Saraswati recommended to Uma typified the modes of goddess devotion that he and his predecessor have appropriated and publicized over the past few decades.

Saraswati's interest in women's ritual was hardly surprising in light of the fact that feminine idioms are foregrounded in the teachings of the Kanchipuram maṭam. The maṭam controls a large goddess temple through which he has sought to attract non-Brahman groups into their following; he and his predecessor have also authored songs and prayers honoring the goddess. They have urged their followers to incorporate these elements into their own practice and to participate in collective, public ritual.[25] Consequently, the familiarity that many urban women have with such styles of public ritual has grown over the past three to four decades. At the same time the relocation of domestic practice into public venues results in more diverse audiences and beneficiaries and offers opportunities for framing these practices as nationalistic.

Several Smārta women told me about their organization of group performances of tiruvilakku pūja to commemorate the birthdays of the Śaṅkarācharyas (started in 1957); recent organizers had sought TAMBRAS's assistance with publicity and fund-raising. For these pūjas, the women brought their own sets of accoutrements (oil lamps, cups and spoons, and incense burners), and they prayed and made offerings in synchrony, led by a priest seated in front of the group. The organizer prepared food and flower offerings and provided participants with souvenirs such as pamphlets or pictures.

Underscoring this feminization of public worship were Saraswati's endorsements of the values associated with being cumankali, as embodied in the paradigmatic wife/mother who is devoted to her husband, docile, and modest. It is the matrix of meanings embedded in this construction of "womanhood" to which Uma herself consented and to which she sought other women's consent. Both the desexualized mother and the sexually available wife are encompassed in the cumaṅkali, something explicable by reference to the complex of meanings ascribed to the Hindu notion of śakti. Often personified as the goddess, śakti may be conceptualized as an energy or capacity for action that can be either creative or destructive in its effects. Sexual desire, sensations, and fluids are among its manifestations in both men and women, although women's sexuality is often conceptualized as being more intense and volatile than that of men (see Daniel 1984; Wadley 1975). This underpins ritually mediated ideas about the importance of "controlling" women's śakti, that is, channeling it toward the productive ends of fertility, prosperity, and health via (hetero)sexual relations, female subordination to male authority, and adherence to the behavioral code of the cumaṅkali with its emphasis on patience, chastity, and self-sacrifice (Wadley 1982). The patriarchal landscape of the Śaṅkarācharya's interest in the cumaṅkali is further clarified when viewed in conjunction with other positions he espoused: he condemned family planning and birth control, and he spoke out against women's property rights and in favor of ritual restrictions on widows.

Although a woman becomes cumaṅkali at marriage, the ritual reiteration of this status is found in a body of heterogeneous ritual forms known collectively as *nōṉpus*, cycles completed by women to fulfill vows made to deities. They incorporate forms of bodily discipline, such as fasting, as well as forms of ritual deference found in pūja (see Logan 1980; Reynolds 1982). Tiruviḷakku pūja is often performed as a component of a nonpu cycle, and it draws from the same pool of meanings, making it a signifying practice (after Comaroff 1985) of being cumaṅkali. As such, it is one of the "controls" of śakti that ratifies patriarchal ideology.[26] Ordinarily, women perform this puja at home in order to acquire husbands and/or to seek a long life for the husbands they already have.

The "womanhood" that is invoked is modeled on Lakshmi, regarded as embodiment of beauty, auspiciousness, and wifely propriety. Female appreciation for this model was never far from the surface of daily life. One friend, a married Brahman woman, commented on the pleasure she experienced when she saw elderly cumaṅkalis—she referred specifically to the beauty of their faces, the clarity of their eyes, and luminescence of their skin, as well as to their dress, jewelry, and comportment. Her own style of grooming, like that of most married Brahman women, incorporated a similar set of aesthetic diacritics—oiled, plaited hair, diamond earrings, gold bangles, a carefully tended marriage necklace, toe rings, a modestly tied sari. Such an appearance earned the compliment that a woman was "Lakshmi-like," embodying a feminized and distinction-producing ideal of beauty (Bourdieu 1984).

Through the ritual practices of being cumankali, patriarchal relations of force and gendered dependency are internalized, meaning that the maintenance of a socially valued feminine identity is contingent on women's acquiescence to these multiple relations of force. While the docility attributed to the "Lakshmī-like" woman belies the intensity and effectiveness of this force, it is nonetheless its diagnostic indicator (Abu-Lughod 1990). These relations of force have concrete expression in everyday acts of physical and emotional violence and in the threat of such action. Equally diagnostic of the force that sustains the cumaṅkali condition are restrictions on women's movements and everyday activities, and the demand that they be responsive to the needs and desires of their husbands.

Tiruviḷakku pūja incorporates the material accoutrements of cumaṅkali identity. In it, an oil lamp is worshipped as the embodiment of Lakshmī.[27] The goddess is praised in this pūja by the woman's circumambulation of the lamp, accompanied by prayer and offerings of vermilion,[28] flower petals, or copper coins. Offerings such as milk and fruit are prepared and offered. It is common for women to fast on the days that they perform this pūja.

One factor facilitating the relocation of these observances to public arenas is that they are not class- or caste-specific. Tiruviḷakku pūja and similar rituals are predicated on a universalized and patriarchally encompassed "womanhood," characterized by patience, auspiciousness, and chastity and defined within the domestic sphere. Paradoxically, such rituals also offered certain kinds of autonomy to women—particular performers were often recognized for their skills in decorating pūja spaces or in singing or for their devotionalism; many women noted that the rituals offered a respite from other household duties. Uma's comments about the centrality of devotionalism in her daily life exemplify this

The popularity of the pūja was also related to its limited demands on time and material resources. Written instructions for this pūja could be found in cheap pamphlets, although women also shared information orally. There was flexibility with regard to offerings and it could be done on a weekly or daily basis, for an indefinite period, or for a specified duration (e.g., 42 days). There were, however, details of form and usage that varied among caste, regional, sectarian, linguistic, and socioeconomic groups. Among elite families like Uma's, such rituals often fall within the realm of family status production: they are among the unremunerated forms of women's labor (such as entertainment, social service, and coaching children with schoolwork) that contribute to the household's status and reputation, reckoned in terms of material wealth, cultural capital, and moral value.[29]

The breadth in the social distribution of the ritual and its related universalization of "womanhood" are points that must be taken into account in considering its deployment in Jan̲ Kalyāṇ. These qualities suggest why upper-caste efforts to exert hegemonic power have sometimes been characterized by the appropriation of women's ritual and by the annexation of women as brokers of alliances among caste/class clusters. Because of their popularity and universalizing rhetoric, these practices can be translated across caste and class lines and used to coopt the interests of subordinated groups. In connection with Jan̲ Kalyāṇ Saraswati reiterated an earlier directive: that Brahman women locate and patronize "neglected" goddess shrines, especially those found in slums. The canonical rites of passage, known as *samskaras* are by contrast so firmly associated with upper castes that they are of little use in attracting the participation of the lower castes.

Viewed in this light, the Śaṅkarācharya's exhibition of the cumankali as the nation's metaphor and metonym and the annexation of women as missionaries in his program of cultural proselytization and social service are explicable. Many who were directly involved in Jan̲ Kalyāṇ or at least sympathetic to its aims saw their involvement in it as consistent with their involvement in activities they glossed collectively as *bhakti* (devotion) or *karmayoga* (worship through service), both of which are among the patterns of modern Hindu religiosity that can be linked to class privilege (Subramanian 1988).[30]

As I indicated in an earlier section of this article, the history of Indian nationalism has seen similar deployments of "womanhood," and this has not abated; indeed, the common sense that Saraswati tapped has been inflected by this.[31] Tamil Nadu's former chief minister, M. G. Ramachandran (1977–87), sought mass support by popularizing mother-goddess devotion (Lakshmi 1990) and contributed (ironically, along with the Śaṅkarācharyas) to the publicization of goddess shrines and ritual. Nor has the Hindu right been idle in this area. Its rhetoric incites male Hindu citizens to protect their women and their "motherland" against "foreigners" (Basu et al. 1993:84). The right has also targeted women as an electoral bloc and as workers by appealing both to the idioms of motherhood and to desires for female empowerment using a language close to that of bourgeois feminism (Basu et al.1993:79–87; Sarkar 1991).

Through women workers, feminine idioms, and moral discipline, Jan̲ Kalyāṇ sought to incorporate the poor as clients and beneficiaries of its moral and material largess. With this, Jayendra Saraswati continued efforts, begun earlier, to establish alliances among his core constituency of urban Smārtas, wealthy non-Brahmans, and poor and Untouchable populations. Uma's consent to the Śaṅkarācharya's directives and his vision of a Hindu nation was, for her, consent to the engendering practices of cumankali identity, consent to the entwined ideologies of class and gender perpetuated through status production work, and consent to the conceptualization of caste identity implied in her assumption of the role of culture broker. Saraswati's version of Hindutva kept class, caste, and gender distinctions intact by naturalizing them through Hindu practice. Religious idioms thus helped frame a nationalism that cohered with bourgeois class ideology at the same time as they provided an ideological cement for dependency relations that perpetuated social inequalities.

Bringing the Nation Home

Uma Radhakrishnan's role in Jan̲ Kalyāṇ illustrates the institutional structures in which the movement originated. Of greater significance, however, is its revelation of how Jan̲ Kalyāṇ linked the education of consent to the constitution of identity. Examining this role brings the politics of Hindu nationalism home; alternatively, it reveals the degree to which this politics of identity revolves around questions of "home" and of "self."

In juxtaposing the interior world of the home and the exterior world of the street and public buildings, the lamp pūja offers a compelling image of some ways in which public culture is currently imagined and contested in urban India. Do such places and performances "domesticate" the exterior world for participants and observers? Do they "publicize" the domestic interior? What happens when everyday ritual is extricated from its domestic trappings? Does it make the world (the nation) a "home"? The bridge between the domestic interior and an exterior public world in Jan̲ Kalyāṇ's appropriation of the lamp pūja was femininity. In creating that bridge, Jan̲ Kalyāṇ constituted femininity in ways consistent with what Chakravarti (1986) has described as "purdah culture," with its normative ideal of the good wife. In conscripting "womanhood" for the nation, it linked the "home" and the "world," metaphorically and metonymically, through women's bodies. The mechanism for this was the displacement of ritual practice from its domestic site to public venues and the enlargement of its pool of beneficiaries and spectators from husband/family to the nation's citizenry.

The pūja's valorization of bourgeois domesticity was central to Jan̲ Kalyāṇ's representation of the Hindu nation. It construed the Hindu nation as a domestic interior—a protected space flooded by the auspiciousness of the cumankali, centered by the authentic self, and offering a stable ground of identity. It suggested to audiences that just as the cumankali warded off widowhood with the lamp pūja, the aesthetic instruments of the pūja defined the nation against an oppositional exterior—the state, the street, or "foreign invaders."[32]

As enacted by Jan̲ Kalyāṇ's members, the ritual syntax and imagery of the pūja represent an interiority comprising "womanhood," the nation, and Hindu tradition. This appeal to Brahmanical common sense was glossed by Saraswati as "culture" and placed in opposition to "politics." The nation, naturalized with the idioms of femininity and Hinduism, could thus be pitted against the state. In Saraswati's script, culture was a substantialized phenomenon that could be read through women's bodies. It was a system that generated and naturalized identity, difference, and inequality among persons. It was defined against and in light of the "disembodied" world of the political. With this discourse of culture Jan̲ Kalyaṇ sought to claim the nation rhetorically, by setting the terms by which its community might be imagined and by etching its spaces and bodies with the stylus of Hinduism. Its claims, however, were belied by its failure as a mass movement. My analysis of Ja<u>n</u> Kalyāṇ, focusing on the indeterminacies of consent, points to the distinctions between hegemonic practices and their effects. Ja<u>n</u> Kalyāṇ's failure reveals the political limits of hegemonic discourses and, more broadly, the political boundaries of culture.

Notes

Acknowledgments. Fieldwork on which this article is based was conducted in India in 1985 and 1987–88. The Government of India granted permission for the research and the American Institute for Indian Studies funded my work. I am indebted to those organizations and to my friends in Madras. Different versions of this article have been presented at the Conference on Modern Hinduism, and to audiences at the Universities of Chicago, Wisconsin (Madison), and California (Santa Barbara). This article was completed during my tenure (1993–94) as an NEH Residential Scholar at the School of American Research in Santa Fe, NM. Diane Mines prepared the English translation of the Ja<u>n</u> Kalyāṇ member's pledge. In the course of writing I have benefited from discussions with colleagues, and I wish to thank Arjun Appadurai, Barney Bate, Eytan Bercovitch, Carol Breckenridge, Mala DeAlwis, Sandria Freitag, C. S. Lakshmi, Toby Lazarowitz, Philip Lutgendorf, McKim Marriott, Mattison Mines, Diane Mines, Kirin Narayan, and Paula Richman. I am grateful as well to Don Brenneis, Michael Herzfeld, and four anonymous *AE* reviewers for their close readings of the manuscript and Jane Huber for her editorial assistance; their suggestions and criticisms were enormously helpful. Responsibility for the content of this article is my own.

1. *Aside* magazine estimated RSS strength (full- and part-time volunteers) in Tamil Nadu to be between 120,000 and 350,000 (Jagadheesan 1993).

2. The Arya Samaj is an association formed by Dayananda Saraswati in 1875 to promote a nationalistic version of Vedic Hinduism.

3. In April 1982, the Arya Samaj sponsored a public reconversion ceremony for Christians in several southern districts (*Data India* 1982:226). In June 1982, the VHP organized a *Gnana Ratham* (Chariot of Knowledge) that toured rural areas to campaign against "social evils" and bore VHP promotional material, films, a public address system, and deity images (*Data India* 1982:419–420; *The Organiser,* June 27, 1982). The *Organiser* reported that the ratham was launched by Jayendra Saraswati who anticipated that it would teach rural masses "disciplined devotion." As a sequel the VHP launched a *Śakti Ratham* (Chariot of the Goddess) in 1984, a bus outfitted as a Mariyamman temple, the aim of which was to promote bhakti and aid in the state's "Hindu Renaissance" (*The Organiser,* August 16, 1984). Local protests of these events were unreported in *The Organiser* (*Data India* 1982:419–420).

4. In addition to launching the Gnana Ratham (see previous note), Saraswati blessed an RSS youth camp meeting in Salem, a city in western Tamil Nadu (*The Organiser,* June 27, 1982).

5. The HRCE began in 1926 as a provincial board appointed to administer Hindu temples; in 1951 it became a department under the authority of the executive branch of the state government. Currently, the HRCE appoints executive officers and managing committees of temples and extracts what it deems as "surplus" funds from temples. These are used to cover its own administrative costs, as well as to subvene some temples' operating budgets and to support state-authored social welfare programs (see Presler 1987).

6. I expect that by 1992 the organized Hindu right had entered its immediate concerns because of the conflict surrounding Ayodhya, which was linked to local caste and sectarian violence incited by the RSS and affiliated groups. *Aside* magazine, reporting on local responses to the carnage at Ayodhya, noted:

> *Publicly, most Hindus expressed their horror over "this act of brutality," but this was frequently qualified by an off the record aside that usually began, "But if you were to ask for my personal opinion . . ." and went on, "I am glad it's been pulled down. It's been simmering too long. The minorities need to be shown their place." (J. V. 1992)*

7. Caste and tribal groups are designated as "Scheduled" or "Backward" by the central and state govern-

ments, respectively, in recognition of past social and economic discrimination. Those so designated are entitled to receive the benefit of affirmative action in education, employment, and political representation.

8. They are described as "private" because they are not administered by the Hindu Religious and Charitable Endowments Board, but are managed by self-appointed individuals or committees.

9. During the colonial period, Smārtas were prominent among south India's Western-educated elite. At the turn of the 20th century, they dominated those sections of the provincial civil services and professions open to Indians, making them part of that "large stratum of urban professionals steeped . . . in the values of bourgeois liberalism" (Vanaik 1985:62; 1990). Since that time, the organization and political power of the non-Brahman movement in the south have effectively diminished the political presence of Brahmans at the state level of government. By and large, however, Smārtas have been able to maintain a relatively privileged status (through employment in industry, central government services and the white-collar professions), in part because of the socioeconomic advantages offered by property and education. Though census enumerations do not include caste, Brahmans in Tamil Nadu are not estimated at more than 3 percent of the state's population (Singer 1972).

10. Saraswati's representation of Smārtas as culture brokers depended on prior authorization by colonial administrators and judges (Cohn 1987; Dirks 1992; Rudolph & Rudolph 1967) *and* by anthropologists, notably Milton Singer, whose collaboration with the Indologist V. Raghavan produced the contours of an Indic "Great Tradition" in which Smārtas were both protagonists and authors (see Singer 1972:78–80, 225–227; Raghavan 1956).

11. The idea of an Indian culture is part of the discourse of nationhood, although this discourse is unstable because the boundaries of "culture" are ambiguous. The point of departure for current debates is the constitutional recognition of distinct religious and cultural groups, and the constitution's assertion of the obligations of state and central governments to protect the interests and autonomy of these groups (see the Constitution of India, Part 3, Articles 25–30). At the same time, however, because the nation is also identified as a community, and imagined as a mosaic of constituent but nonetheless bounded communities, "culture" is also brought into play at another level—as an ideological glue whose key idioms are pluralism, tolerance, and integration (see, for example, Committee on Emotional Integration 1962).

The efforts by Ja<u>n</u> Kalyāṇ and other cultural nationalist movements to contest the government's reading of secularism are grounded in the ambiguity, and hence the instability, of these deployments of culture. Rhetorically, Ja<u>n</u> Kalyāṇ used culture against politics (i.e., central and state-level institutions); but it relied on the political ideology of "cultural" autonomy articulated in the Constitution to do so. With this argument, Saraswati emphasized the gulf between the authenticity of (Hindu) "culture" and the expediency of (secular) "politics." This nationalist rhetoric was linked, as well, to a critique of the anti-Brahmanism associated with the policies of the current government in Tamil Nadu. Ja<u>n</u> Kalyāṇ recoded Brahmanism as Hindu tradition, arguing that Hindu tradition, as interpreted by Saraswati, was the most effective regulator of social life and political action. For further exploration of the link between bourgeois appropriations of culture and the discourse of "modernity," see Niranjana (1993).

12. Satī refers to a woman has been burned on her husband's funeral pyre.

13. In Gandhian polices of noncooperation, it acted as both symbol and practical enactment of moral and economic self-sufficiency and political self-rule.

14. In 1989, shortly before the parliamentary elections in November, the Śaṅkarācharya signaled his intention to reorganize Ja<u>n</u> Kalyāṇ as a political party, Bharat Ja<u>n</u> Kalyāṇ, although that aim remains unrealized.

15. This has been a useful direction in conceptualizing subaltern resistance; it is also appropriate for dealing with issues of women's agency in the context of patriarchy (Comaroff 1985; de Lauretis 1987; Sangari 1993; Spivak 1988).

16. Bharat is one of the names for India preferred among Hindu nationalists. Karma refers to a Hindu theological concept, referring to the moral weight of action; jnana is an esoteric, theological knowledge; dharma is the Hindu moral/legal notion of action that is appropriate on the basis of caste, gender, life stage, and occupation; bhumi is the earth or land. "Dharmo Rakshati Rakshitaha" means "Dharma protects those who protect dharma."

17. Śakti is feminized cosmological energy; it is also a name for the goddess.

18. Pūja refers to a paradigmatic form of Hindu worship. It is directed to a deity and consists of onomastic

praise, offerings of food, and the redistribution of that food.

19. All quotations attributed to Uma Radhakrishnan are based on verbatim notes I look during our conversations.

20. This practice appeared to be modeled on one of the ritual obligations prescribed for upper-caste male householders: the prayers known as *cantiyavāntaṉam.* Its gender-neutral reworking is worth noting as a gesture of inclusiveness consistent with the other enlargements of women's ritual roles that the movement conceded. This appeal to women, however, should be read in tandem with the other, implicit exclusions of caste and class that the movement enacted.

21. Similar observations about elite representations of caste and class differences are found in Caplan (1985) and Dickey (1993).

22. See reviews in Cohn (1987), Dirks (1992), Irschick (1969), and Washbrook (1976).

23. Although Non-Brahman ideology often incorporated an explicit anti-Brahmanism, Non-Brahman parties have been politically allied at times with parties and groups that they identified as having "Brahman" interests, such as the Home Rule League, the Indian National Congress, and, after independence, the Congress and Congress (I) parties—a complex situation reflecting both class alliances and political expediency (Washbrook 1976, 1989). Furthermore, although "Non-Brahman" was adopted as a label because it conveyed opposition to Brahman identity, the parties and interest groups that identified themselves as Non-Brahman did not include *all* persons who were not Brahman. Untouchables, most notably, have contested the Non-Brahman movement on these grounds (Washbrook 1989).

24. Described, respectively, in Hindu Religious Endowments Commission (1960–62:499–510) and in Presler (1987:110–133).

25. An older Smārta woman recalled that the previous Śaṅkarācharya had toured the South in the late 1930s and urged women to conduct public, collective devotions to the goddess, using praise songs that he had authored. She herself had belonged to one such group, organized by a friend, that had gathered regularly to recit *Lalitha Sahasranāmam* (1,000 names of the goddess). Although she was in her seventies when I met her, she had recently found a similar type of group at the behest of the elder Śaṅkarācharya. Women, dressed in identical blue and red saris, gathered each week at one of the goddess shrines in a local temple and sang devotional songs.

26. Though widely observed among women of different castes and classes, tiruviḷakku pūja is not among the canonical practices prescribed for upper-caste Hindus. The latter, collectively known as samskāras (rituals of refinement or purification), mark transitions in the life cycle as it is conceived from the standpoint of the upper-caste male. Women, though they may participate in these rituals, are "muted" (Madan 1987); that is, they are among the beneficiaries of the acts, and symbolically they, specifically as wives of the performer, serve as cogs in the ritual process. For example, many samskāras are opened with a series of gestures in which the wife of the performer transfers the cosmic energy of śakti to her husband through a blade of darbha grass that she holds in her hand.

27. Such lamps (made of bronze, silver, brass, or a five-metal alloy), along with jewelry, saris, and household utensils, are requisite parts of the trousseau with which a woman's family is expected to outfit her at marriage. There are dense symbolic associations between these objects and "womanhood," and in principle (though not always in practice) they are her personal property.

28. Vermilion, or *kunkumam,* is the red powder that women smear in the part of their hair, marking their married status.

29. The concept of status production work is developed in Caplan (1985) and Papanek (1979). See also Madan (1987) and Marriott (1976) on the conflation of moral and material value.

30. Jaṉ Kalyāṇ's efforts to engage elite women as recruiters and volunteers is consistent with the model of elite voluntarism that has been encouraged by the state since independence. It enables the state to reduce its own expenditures in these areas (Caplan 1985; Committee on the Status of Women in India 1974). By conferring honor and recognition on service providers, the state also offers routes to prestige for these women and their families.

31. The constitution of "womanhood" in ritual intersects with other mass cultural representations of femininity in India. See Ghadially (1988), Krishnan and Dighe (1990), Lakshmi (1984), Mankekar (1993), Tharu and Lalita (1993), Uberoi (1990), and Vasudevan (1989).

32. In southern India, the feminine imagery of the nation derives salience from a set of local distinctions, coded lexically in Tamil as *akam* and *puṟam,* that is, the relational interior of home, self, and mind/heart versus the relational exterior of the yard outside the house, the public (Ramanujan 1985).

References

Abu-Lughod, Lila (1990). The romance of resistance: Tracing transformations of power through Bedouin women. *American Ethnologist, 17,* 41–55.

Althusser, Louis (1971). Ideology and ideological state apparatuses (notes toward an investigation). In *Lenin, philosophy and other essays.* (Ben Brewster, Trans.) (pp. 127–186). New York: Monthly Review Press.

Andersen, Walter, & Damle, S. (1987). *Brotherhood in saffron.* Boulder, CO: Westview.

Anderson, Benedict (1991). *Imagined Communities* (rev. ed.). London: Verso.

Barnett, Marguerite (1976). *The politics of cultural nationalism in South India.* Princeton, NJ: Princeton University Press.

Basu, Tapan, Pradip Datta, Sumit Sarkar, Tanika Sarkar, & Sambuddha Sen (1993). *Khaki shorts and saffron flags: A critique of the Hindu right.* New Delhi: Orient Longman.

Bourdieu, Pierre (1984). *Distinction: A social critique of the judgement of taste* (Richard Nice, Trans.). Cambridge, MA: Harvard University Press.

Butler, Judith (1993). *Bodies that matter: On the discursive limits of "sex."* New York: Routledge.

Caplan, Patricia (1985). *Class and gender in India.* London: Tavistock.

Cenkner, William (1983). *A tradition of teachers: Śaṅkara and the Jagadgurus today.* Delhi: Motilal Banarsidas.

Chakravarti, Uma (1986). Pati-vrata. *Seminar, 31,* 17–21.

Chatterjee, Partha (1993). *The nation and its fragments: Colonial and postcolonial histories.* Princeton, NJ: Princeton University Press.

Cohn, Bernard (1987). *An anthropologist among the historians and other essays.* Delhi: Oxford University Press.

Comaroff, Jean (1985). *Body of power, spirit of resistance.* Chicago: University of Chicago Press

Committee on Emotional Integration (1962). *Report of the Committee on Emotional Integration.* New Delhi: Ministry of Education.

Committee on the Status of Women in India (1974) *Towards equality.* New Delhi: Department of Social Welfare, Ministry of Education and Social Welfare.

Daniel, E. Valentine (1984). *Fluid signs: Being a person the Tamil Way.* Berkeley: University of California Press.

Data India (1981–90). *Data India.* New Delhi: Press Institute of India.

de Certeau, Michel (1984). *The practice of everyday life.* Berkeley: University of California Press.

de Lauretis, Teresa (1987). *Technologies of gender: Essays on theory, film and fiction.* Bloomington: Indiana University Press.

Dickey, Sara (1993). *Cinema and the urban poor in south India.* Cambridge: Cambridge University Press.

Dirks, Nicholas (1992). Castes of mind. *Representations, 37,* 56 78.

Fabricius, Johann (1972). Tamil and English dictionary. 4th ed. Travancore, India: Evangelical Lutheran Mission Publishing House. (Original work published 1779)

Foucault, Michel (1972). *Power/knowledge.* New York: Pantheon.

Geetha, V., & Rajadurai, S. V. (1990). Communal violence in Madras: A portent? *Economic and Political Weekly, 25,* 2122–2123.

Ghadially, Rehanna (Ed.) (1988). *Women in Indian society.* New Delhi: Sage.

Gramsci, Antonio (1971). *Selections from the prison notebooks* (Quinton Hoare & Geoffrey Nowell-Smith, Trans. and Eds.). London: Lawrence and Wishart. (Original work published 1925–1935)

Hardgrave, Robert (1969). *The Nadars of Tamilnad: The political culture of a community in change.* Berkeley: University of California Press.

Hindu Religious Endowments Commission (1960–62). *Report of the Hindu Religious Endowments Commission.* New Delhi: Ministry of Law.

Irschick, Eugene (1969). *Politics and social conflict in south India.* Berkeley: University of California Press.

Jagadheesan, L. R. (1993). After the ban. *Aside Magazine,* January 15:10–13.

J. V. (1992). The Ayodhya outrage. *Aside Magazine,* December 31:17–20.

Khare, Ravindra (1970). *The changing Brahmans.* Chicago: University of Chicago Press.

Kishwar, Madhu (1985). Women in Gandhi. *Economic and Political Weekly, 20,* October 5 and 19:1691–1702, 1753–1758.

Krishnan, Prabha, & Dighe, Anita (1990). *Affirmation and denial: The construction of femininity on Indian television.* New Delhi: Sage.

Kriyāvin̲ Tārkalat Tamil̤ Akarāti (1992). *Kriyāvin̲ Tārkalat Tamil̤ Akarāti. (A dictionary of contemporary Tamil.)* Madras: Cre-A.

Lakshmi, C. S. (1984). *The face behind the mask.* New Delhi: Vikas.

Lakshmi, C. S. (1990). Mother, mother-community and mother-politics in Tamil Nadu. *Economic and Political Weekly, 25,* WS72–WS83.

Logan, Penelope (1980). *Domestic worship and the festival cycle in the south Indian city of Madurai.* Ph.D. dissertation, University of Manchester.

Madan, Triloki N. (1987). *Non-renunciation: Themes and interpretations of Hindu culture.* Delhi: Oxford University Press.

Mani, Lata (1990). Contentious traditions: The debate on *Satī* in colonial India. In Kumkum Sangari & Sudesh Vaid (Eds.), *Recasting women* (pp. 88–126). New Brunswick, NJ: Rutgers University Press.

Mankekar, Purnima (1993). National texts and gendered lives: Ethnography of television viewers in a north Indian city. *American Ethnologist, 20,* 543–563.

Marriott, McKim (1976). Hindu transactions: Diversity without dualism. In Bruce Kapferer (Ed.), *Transaction and meaning* (pp. 109–142). Philadelphia: Institute for the Study of Human Issues.

Minault, Gail, & Papanek, Hanna (Eds.) (1982). *Separate worlds: Studies of purdah in South Asia.* Delhi: Chanakya Publications.

Mines, Mattison, & Gourishankar, Vijayalakshmi (1990). Leadership and individuality in South Asia: The case of the South Indian big-man. *Journal of Asian Studies, 49,* 761–786.

Nandy, Ashis (1983). *The intimate enemy.* Delhi: Oxford University Press.

Narayan, Gita (1982). Communal riots go south. *The Illustrated Weekly of India, 103,* April 18:20–21.

Niranjana, Tejaswini (1993). Whose culture is it? Contesting the modern. *Journal of Arts and Ideas, 25–26,* 139–151.

Pandian, M. S. S. (1990). From exclusion to inclusion: Brahmanism's new face in Tamil Nadu. *Economic and Political Weekly, 25,* 1938–1939.

Papanek, Hanna (1979). Family status production work. *Signs, 4,* 775–781.

Patel, Sujata (1988). Construction and reconstruction of woman in Gandhi. *Economic and Political Weekly, 23,* 377–387.

Presler, Franklin (1987). *Religion under bureaucracy.* Cambridge: Cambridge University Press.

Raghavan, V. (1956). Variety and integration in the pattern of Indian culture. *Far Eastern Quarterly, 15,* 497–505.

Ramanujan, A. K. (1985). Afterword. In A. K. Ramanujan (Ed. and Trans.). *Poems of love and war* (pp. 229–297). New Delhi: Oxford University Press.

Ramaswamy, Sumathi (1993). En/gendering language: The poetics of Tamil identity. *Comparative Studies in Society and History, 35,* 683–725.

Reynolds, Holly (1982). The auspicious married woman. In Susan Wadley (Ed.), *The powers of Tamil women* (pp. 35–60). Syracuse, NY: Maxwell School of Public Citizenship and Public Affairs.

Rudolph, Lloyd, & Rudolph, Suzanne (1967). *The modernity of tradition.* Chicago: University of Chicago Press.

Ryan, Mary (1990). *Women in public: Between banners and ballots, 1825–1880.* Baltimore: Johns Hopkins University Press.

Sangari, Kumkum (1993). Consent, agency and rhetorics of incitement. *Economic and Political Weekly, 28,* 867–882.

Sarkar, Tanika (1991). The woman as communal subject. *Economic and Political Weekly, 26,* 2057–2062.

Scott, James (1990). *Domination and the arts of resistance.* New Haven, CT: Yale University Press.

Seshadri, H. V. (n.d.). *Hindu renaissance under way.* Bangalore, India: Jagarana Prakashana.

Sharma, Ursula (1986). *Women's work, class and the urban household.* London: Tavistock.

Singer, Milton (1972). *When a great tradition modernizes.* Chicago: University of Chicago Press, Midway Reprint.

Singh, Andrea (1976). *Neighborhood and networks in urban India.* Delhi: Marwah.

Spivak, Gayatri (1988). Subaltern studies: Deconstructing historiography. In Ranajit Guha & Gayatri Spivak (Eds.), *Selected subaltern studies* (pp. 3–32). New York: Oxford University Press.

Subramanian, V. (1988). Karmayoga and the rise of the Indian middle class. *Journal of Arts and Ideas, 14–15,* 133–142.

Sunil, K. (1987). The curious case of the missing monk. *The Illustrated Weekly of India, 108,* September 13:9–17.

Tharu, Susie, & Lalita, K. (Eds.) (1993). *Women writing in India. Volume 2: The twentieth century.* New York: The Feminist Press.

Uberoi, Patricia (1990). Identity and national ethos in Indian calendar art. *Economic and Political Weekly, 25*, WS41–WS47.

Vanaik, Achin (1985). The Rajiv congress in search of stability. *New Left Review, 151*, 55–83.

Vanaik, Achin (1990). *The painful transition*. London: Verso.

Vasudevan, Ravi (1989). *The melodramatic mode and the commercial Hindi cinema screen, 30*, 29–50.

Vatuk, Sylvia (1972). *Kinship and urbanization*. Berkeley: University of California Press.

Visweswaran, Kamala (1994). *Fictions of feminist ethnography*. Minneapolis: University of Minnesota Press.

Wadley, Susan (1975). *Shakti: Power in the conceptual structure of Karimpur religion*. Chicago: University of Chicago Press.

Wadley, Susan (Ed.) (1982). *The powers of Tamil women*. Syracuse, NY: Maxwell School of Citizenship and Public Affairs.

Washbrook, David (1976). *The emergence of provincial politics: The Madras presidency, 1870–1920*. Cambridge: Cambridge University Press.

Washbrook, David (1989). Caste, class and dominance in modern Tamil Nadu. In Francine Frankel & M. S. A. Rao (Eds.), *Dominance and state power in modern India, 1* (pp. 204–264). Delhi: Oxford University Press.

Acknowledgments

"Ritual Hierarchy and Secular Equality in a Sepik River Village" by Simon J. Harrison, reproduced by permission of the American Anthropological Association from *American Ethnologist* 12:3, August 1985, pp. 413–426. Not for further reproduction. Copyright © 1985 by the American Anthropological Association.

"Dancing with Corpses Reconsidered: An Interpretation of *Famadihana* (in Arivonimamo, Madagascar)" by David Graeber, reproduced by permission of the American Anthropological Association from *American Ethnologist* 22:2, May 1995, pp. 258–278. Not for further reproduction. Copyright © 1995 by the American Anthropological Association.

"Blood, Oil, Honey, and Water: Symbolism in Spirit Possession Sects in Northeastern Brazil" by Dolores J. Shapiro, reproduced by permission of the American Anthropological Association from *American Ethnologist* 22:4, November 1995, pp. 828–847. Not for further reproduction. Copyright © 1995 by the American Anthropological Association.

"Taboo as Cultural Practice among Malagasy Speakers" by Michael Lambek, reproduced with permission of the Royal Anthropological Institute of Great Britain and Ireland from *Man* 27:2, June 1992, pp. 245–266.

"From Saints for Shibboleths: Image, Structure, and Identity in Maya Religious Syncretism" by John M. Watanabe, reproduced by permission of the American Anthropological Association from *American Ethnologist* 17:1, February 1990, pp. 131–150. Not for further reproduction.

"Salāt in Indonesia: The Social Meanings of an Islamic Ritual" by John R. Bowen, reproduced with permission of the Royal Anthropological Institute of Great Britain and Ireland from *Man* 24:4, December 1989, pp. 600–619.

"Communitas Reconsidered: The Sociology of Andean Pilgrimage" by M. J. Sallnow, reproduced with permission of the Royal Anthropological Institute of Great Britain and Ireland from *Man* 16:2, June 1981, pp. 163–182.

"Christianity and Colonialism in South Africa" by Jean Comaroff and John Comaroff, reproduced by permission of the American Anthropological Association from *American Ethnologist* 13:1, February 1986, pp. 1–22. Not for further reproduction.

"Hindu Culture for an Indian Nation: Gender, Politics, and Elite Identity in Urban South India" by Mary Hancock, reproduced by permission of the American Anthropological Association from *American Ethnologist* 22:4, November 1995, pp. 907–925. Not for further reproduction. Copyright © 1995 by the American Anthropological Association.